HISTORY OF THE FRENCH REVOLUTION FROM 1789 TO 1814

HISTORY OF THE FRENCH REVOLUTION FROM 1789 TO 1814

FRANÇOIS-AUGUSTE-MARIE-ALEXIS MIGUET,
L. CECIL JANE

ISBN: 978-93-5344-907-0

Published: -

LECTOR HOUSE LLP
E-MAIL: lectorpublishing@gmail.com

HISTORY OF THE FRENCH REVOLUTION FROM 1789 TO 1814

BY

F.A.M. MIGNET

WITH AN INTRODUCTION BY
L. CECIL JANE

INTRODUCTION BY L. CECIL JANE

Of the great incidents of History, none has attracted more attention or proved more difficult of interpretation than the French Revolution. The ultimate significance of other striking events and their place in the development of mankind can be readily estimated. It is clear enough that the barbarian invasions marked the death of the classical world, already mortally wounded by the rise of Christianity. It is clear enough that the Renaissance emancipated the human intellect from the trammels of a bastard mediaevalism, that the Reformation consolidated the victory of the "new learning" by including theology among the subjects of human debate. But the French Revolution seems to defy complete analysis. Its complexity was great, its contradictions numerous and astounding. A movement ostensibly directed against despotism culminated in the establishment of a despotism far more complete than that which had been overthrown. The apostles of liberty proscribed whole classes of their fellow-citizens, drenching in innocent blood the land which they claimed to deliver from oppression. The apostles of equality established a tyranny of horror, labouring to extirpate all who had committed the sin of being fortunate. The apostles of fraternity carried fire and sword to the farthest confines of Europe, demanding that a continent should submit to the arbitrary dictation of a single people. And of the Revolution were born the most rigid of modern codes of law, that spirit of militarism which to-day has caused a world to mourn, that intolerance of intolerance which has armed anti-clerical persecutions in all lands. Nor were the actors in the drama less varied than the scenes enacted. The Revolution produced Mirabeau and Talleyrand, Robespierre and Napoleon, Sieyès and Hébert. The marshals of the First Empire, the doctrinaires of the Restoration, the journalists of the Orleanist monarchy, all were alike the children of this generation of storm and stress, of high idealism and gross brutality, of changing fortunes and glory mingled with disaster.

To describe the whole character of a movement so complex, so diverse in its promises and fulfilment, so crowded with incident, so rich in action, may well be declared impossible. No sooner has some proposition been apparently established, than a new aspect of the period is suddenly revealed, and all judgments have forthwith to be revised. That the Revolution was a great event is certain; all else seems to be uncertain. For some it is, as it was for Charles Fox, much the greatest of all events and much the best. For some it is, as it was for Burke, the accursed thing, the abomination of desolation. If its dark side alone be regarded, it oppresses the very soul of man. A king, guilty of little more than amiable weakness and legitimate or pious affection; a queen whose gravest fault was but the frivolity of youth and beauty, was done to death. For loyalty to her friends, Madame Roland died; for loving her husband, Lucille Desmoulins perished. The agents of the Terror spared neither age nor sex; neither the eminence of high attainment nor the insignificance of dull mediocrity won mercy at their hands. The miserable Du Barri was dragged from her obscure retreat to share the fate of a Malesherbes, a Bailly, a Lavoisier. Robespierre was no more protected by his cold incorruptibility, than was Barnave by his eloquence, Hébert by his sensuality, Danton by his practical good sense. Nothing availed to save from the all-devouring guillotine. Those who did survive seem almost to have survived by chance, delivered by some caprice of fortune or by the criminal levity of "les tricoteuses," vile women who degraded the very dregs of their sex.

For such atrocities no apology need be attempted, but their cause may be explained, the factors which produced such popular fury may be understood. As he stands on the terrace of Versailles or wanders through the vast apartments of the château, the traveller sees in imagination the dramatic panorama of the long-dead past. The courtyard is filled with half-demented women, clamouring that the Father of his People should feed his starving children. The Well-Beloved jests cynically as, amid torrents of rain, Pompadour is borne to her grave. Maintenon, gloomily pious, urges with sinister whispers the commission of a great crime, bidding the king save his vice-laden soul. Montespan laughs happily in her brief days of triumph. And dominating the scene is the imposing figure of the Grand Monarque. Louis haunts his great creation; Louis in his prime, the admired and feared of Europe, the incarnation of kingship; Louis surrounded by his gay and brilliant court, all eager to echo his historic boast, to sink in their master the last traces of their identity.

Then a veil falls. But some can lift it, to behold a far different, a far more stirring vision, and to such the deeper causes of the Terror are revealed. For they behold a vast multitude, stained with care, haggard, forlorn, striving, dying, toiling even to their death, that the passing whim of a tyrant may be gratified. Louis commanded; Versailles arose, a palace of rare delight for princes and nobles, for wits and courtly prelates, for grave philosophers and ladies frail as fair. A palace and a hell, a grim monument to regal egoism, created to minister to the inflated vanity of a despot, an eternal warning to mankind that the abuse of absolute power is an accursed thing. Every flower, in those wide gardens has been watered with the tears of stricken souls; every stone in that vast pile of buildings was cemented with human blood. None can estimate the toll of anguish exacted that Versailles might be; none can tell all its cost, since for human suffering there is no price. The weary toilers went to their doom, unnoticed, unhonoured, their misery unregarded, their pain ignored, And the king rejoiced in his glory, while his poets sang paeans in his praise.

But the day of reckoning came, and that day was the Terror. The heirs of those who toiled made their account with the heirs of those who played. The players died bravely, like the gallant gentlemen they were; their courage is applauded, a world laments their fate. The misery, thus avenged, is forgotten; all the long agony of centuries, all the sunless hours, all the darkness of a land's despair. For that sadness was hidden; it was but the exceeding bitter lot of the poor, devoid of that dramatic interest which illumines one immortal hour of pain. Yet he who would estimate aright the Terror, who would fully understand the Revolution, must reflect not only upon the suffering of those who fell victims to an outburst of insensate frenzy, but also upon the suffering by which that frenzy was aroused. In a few months the French people took what recompense they might for many decades of oppression. They exacted retribution for the building of Versailles, of all the châteaux of Touraine; for all the burdens laid upon them since that day when liberty was enchained and France became the bond-slave of her monarchs. Louis XVI. paid for the selfish glory of Louis XIV.; the nobles paid for the pleasures which their forefathers had so carelessly enjoyed; the privileged classes for the privileges which they had usurped and had so grievously misused.

The payment fell heavily upon individuals; the innocent often suffered for the guilty; a Liancourt died while a Polignac escaped. Many who wished well to France, many who had laboured for her salvation, perished; virtue received the just punishment of vice. But the Revolution has another side; it was no mere nightmare of horrors piled on horrors. It is part of the pathos of History that no good has been unattended by evil, that by suffering alone is mankind redeemed, that through the valley of shadow lies the path by which the race toils slowly towards the fulfilment of its high destiny. And if the victims of the guillotine could have foreseen the future, many might have died gladly. For by their death they brought the new France to birth. The Revolution rises superior to the crimes and follies of its authors; it has atoned to posterity for all the sorrow that it caused, for all the wrong that was done in its name. If it killed laughter, it also dried many tears. By it privilege was slain in France, tyranny rendered more improbable, almost impossible. The canker of a debased feudalism was swept away. Men were made equal before the law. Those barriers by which the flow of economic life in France was checked were broken down. All careers were thrown open to talent. The right of the producer to a voice in the distribution of the product was recognised. Above all, a new gospel of political liberty was expounded. The world, and the princes of the world, learned that peoples do not exist for the pleasure of some despot and the profit of his cringing satellites. In the order of nature, nothing can be born save through suffering; in the order of politics, this is no less true. From the sorrow of brief months has grown the joy of long years; the Revolution slew that it might also make alive.

Herein, perhaps, may be found the secret of its complexity, of its seeming contradictions. The authors of the Revolution pursued an ideal, an ideal expressed in three words, Liberty, Equality, Fraternity. That they might win their quest, they had both to destroy and to construct. They had to sweep away the past, and from the resultant chaos to construct a new order. Alike in destruction and construction, they committed errors; they fell far below their high ideals. The altruistic enthusiasts of the National Assembly gave place to the practical politicians of the Convention, the diplomatists of the Directory, the generals of the Consulate. The Empire was far from realising that bright vision of a regenerate nation which had dazzled the eyes of Frenchmen in the first hours of the States-General. Liberty was sacrificed to efficiency; equality to man's love for titles of honour; fraternity to desire of glory. So it has been with all human effort. Man is imperfect, and his imperfection mars his fairest achievements. Whatever great movement may be considered, its ultimate attainment has fallen far short of its initial promise. The authors of the Revolution were but men; they were no more able than their fellows to discover and to hold fast to the true way of happiness. They wavered between the two extremes of despotism and anarchy; they declined from the path of grace. And their task remained unfulfilled. Many of their dreams were far from attaining realisation; they inaugurated no era of perfect bliss; they produced no Utopia. But their labour was not in vain. Despite its disappointments, despite all its crimes and blunders, the French Revolution was a great, a wonderful event. It did contribute to the uplifting of humanity, and the world is the better for its occurrence.

That he might indicate this truth, that he might do something to counteract the distortion of the past, Mignet wrote his *Histoire de la Révolution Française*. At the moment when he came from Aix to Paris, the tide of reaction was rising steadily in France. Decazes had fallen; Louis XVIII. was surrendering to the ultra-royalist cabal. Aided by such fortuitous events as the murder of the Duc de Berri, and supported by an artificial majority in the Chamber, Villèle was endeavouring to bring back the *ancien régime*. Compensation for the *émigrés* was already mooted; ecclesiastical control of education suggested. Direct criticism of the ministry was rendered difficult, and even dangerous, by the censorship of the press. Above all, the champions of reaction relied upon a certain misrepresentation of the recent history of their country. The memory of the Terror was still vivid; it was sedulously kept alive. The people were encouraged to dread revolutionary violence, to forget the abuses by which that violence had been evoked and which it had swept away. To all complaints of executive tyranny, to all demands for greater political liberty, the reactionaries made one answer. They declared that through willingness to hear such complaints Louis XVI. had lost his throne and life; that through the granting of such demands, the way had been prepared for the bloody despotism of Robespierre. And they pointed the apparent moral, that concessions to superficially mild and legitimate requests would speedily reanimate the forces of anarchy. They insisted that by strong government and by the sternest repression of the disaffected alone could France be protected from a renewal of that nightmare of horror, at the thought of which she still shuddered. And hence those who would prevent the further progress of reaction had first of all to induce their fellow-countrymen to realise that the Revolution was no mere orgy of murder. They had to deliver liberty from those calumnies by which its curtailment was rendered possible and even popular.

Understanding this, Mignet wrote. It would have been idle for him to have denied that atrocities had been committed, nor had the day for a panegyric on Danton, for a defence of Robespierre, yet dawned. Mignet did not attempt the impossible. Rather by granting the case for his opponents he sought to controvert them the more effectively. He laid down as his fundamental thesis that the Revolution was inevitable. It was the outcome of the past history of France; it pursued the course which it was bound to pursue. Individuals and episodes in the drama are thus relatively insignificant and unimportant. The crimes committed may be regretted; their memory should not produce any condemnation of the movement as a whole. To judge the Revolution by the Terror, or by the Consulate, would be wrong and foolish; to declare it evil, because it did not proceed in a gentle and orderly manner would be to outrage the historical sense. It is wiser and more profitable to look below the surface, to search out those deep lessons which may be learned. And Mignet closes his work by stating one of these lessons, that which to him was, perhaps, the most vital: "On ne peut régir désormais la France d'une manière durable, qu'en satisfaisant le double besoin qui lui a fait entreprendre la révolution. Il lui faut, dans le gouvernement, une liberté politique réelle, et dans la société, le bien-être matériel que produit le développement sans cesse perfectionné de la civilisation."

It was not Mignet's object to present a complete account of the Revolution, and while he records the more important events of the period, he does not attempt to deal exhaustively with all its many sides. It is accordingly possible to point out various omissions. He does not explain the organisation of the "deputies on mission," he only glances at that of the commune or of the Committee of Public Safety. His account of the Consulate and of the Empire appears to be disproportionately brief. But the complexity of the period, and the wealth of materials for its history, render it impossible for any one man to discuss it in detail, and Mignet's work gains rather than loses by its limitations. Those facts which illustrate his fundamental thesis are duly recorded; the causes and results of events are clearly indicated; the actions of individuals are described in so far as they subserve the author's purpose. The whole book is marked by a notable impartiality; it is only on rare occasions, as in the case of Lafayette, that the circumstances in which it was written have been permitted to colour the judgments passed. Nor is the value of the work seriously reduced by the fact that modern research compels its revision in certain particulars, since it is so clearly not intended to be a final and detailed history of the period. It is a philosophical study of a great epoch, and as such, however its point of view may be criticised, it is illuminating and well worthy of preservation. It supplies a thoughtful and inspiring commentary upon the French Revolution.

L. CECIL JANE.

1915.

BIOGRAPHICAL NOTE.—François Auguste Marie Mignet was born at Aix in Provence in 1796. He was educated at Avignon and in his native town, at first studying law. But, having gained some literary successes, he removed to Paris in 1821 and devoted himself to writing. He became professor of history at the *Athenée*, and after the Revolution of 1830 was made director of the archives in the Foreign Office, a post which he held until 1848. He was then removed by Lamartine and died in retirement in 1854. His *Histoire de la Révolution Française* was first published in 1824; a translation into English appeared in Bogue's European library in 1846 and is here re-edited. Among Mignet's other works may be mentioned *Antoine Perez et Philippe II.* and *Histoire de Marie Stuart*. As a journalist, he wrote mainly on foreign policy for the *Courrier Français*.

BIBLIOGRAPHY

Éloge de Charles VII., 1820; Les Institutions de Saint Louis, 1821; De la féodalité, des institutions de Saint Louis et de l'influence de la législation de ce prince, 1822; Histoire de la révolution française, 1824 (trans. 2 vols., London, 1826, Bonn's Libraries, 1846); La Germanie au VIIIe et au IXe siècle, sa conversion au christianisme, et son introduction dans la société civilisée de l'Europe occidentale, 1834; Essai sur la formation territoriale et politique de la France depuis la fin de XIe siècle jusqu'a la fin du XVe, 1836; Notices et Mémoires historiques, 1843; Charles Quint, son abdication, son séjour, et sa mort au monastère de Yuste, 1845; Antonio Perez et Philippe II., 1845 (translated by C. Cocks, London, 1846; translated from second French edition by W. F. Ainsworth, London, 1846); Histoire de Marie Stuart, 2 vols., 1851 (translated by A. R. Scoble, 1851); Portraits et Notices, historiques et littéraires, 2 vols., 1852; Éloges historiques, 1864; Histoire de la rivalité de François I. et de Charles Quint, 1875; Nouveaux éloges historiques, 1877.

CONTENTS

CHAPTER II

FROM THE NIGHT OF THE 4TH OF AUGUST TO THE 5TH AND 6TH OF OCTOBER, 1789

CHAPTER III

FROM THE 6TH OF OCTOBER, 1789, TO THE DEATH OF MIRABEAU, APRIL, 1791

CHAPTER IV

FROM APRIL, 1791, TO THE 30TH SEPTEMBER. THE END OF THE CONSTITUENT ASSEMBLY

THE NATIONAL LEGISLATIVE ASSEMBLY

CHAPTER V

FROM THE 1ST OF OCTOBER, 1791, TO THE 21ST OF SEPTEMBER, 1792

THE NATIONAL CONVENTION

CHAPTER VI

FROM THE 20TH OF SEPTEMBER, 1792, TO THE 21ST OF JANUARY, 1793

CHAPTER VII

FROM THE 21ST OF JANUARY, 1793, TO THE 2ND OF JUNE

CHAPTER VIII

FROM THE 2ND OF JUNE, 1793, TO APRIL, 1794

CHAPTER IX

FROM THE DEATH OF DANTON, APRIL, 1794, TO THE 9TH THERMIDOR, (27TH JULY, 1794)

CHAPTER X

FROM THE 9TH THERMIDOR TO THE 1ST PRAIRIAL, YEAR III. (20TH MAY, 1795). EPOCH OF THE RISE AND FALL OF THE DEMOCRATIC PARTY

CHAPTER XI

FROM THE 1ST PRAIRIAL (20TH OF MAY, 1795) TO THE 4TH BRUMAIRE (26TH OF OCTOBER), YEAR IV., THE CLOSE OF

THE CONVENTION

THE EXECUTIVE DIRECTORY

CHAPTER XII

FROM THE INSTALLATION OF THE DIRECTORY, ON THE 27TH OCTOBER, 1795, TO THE COUP-D'ÉTAT OF THE 18TH FRUCTIDOR, YEAR V. (3RD AUGUST, 1797)

CHAPTER XIII

FROM THE 18TH FRUCTIDOR, IN THE YEAR V. (4TH OF SEPTEMBER, 1797), TO THE 18TH BRUMAIRE, IN THE YEAR VIII. (9TH OF NOVEMBER, 1799)

THE CONSULATE

CHAPTER XIV

FROM THE 18TH BRUMAIRE (9TH OF NOVEMBER, 1799) TO THE 2ND OF DECEMBER, 1804

THE EMPIRE

CHAPTER XV

FROM THE ESTABLISHMENT OF THE EMPIRE, 1804-1814

INTRODUCTION

I am about to take a rapid review of the history of the French revolution, which began the era of new societies in Europe, as the English revolution had begun the era of new governments. This revolution not only modified the political power, but it entirely changed the internal existence of the nation. The forms of the society of the middle ages still remained. The land was divided into hostile provinces, the population into rival classes. The nobility had lost all their powers, but still retained all their distinctions: the people had no rights, royalty no limits; France was in an utter confusion of arbitrary administration, of class legislation and special privileges to special bodies. For these abuses the revolution substituted a system more conformable with justice, and better suited to our times. It substituted law in the place of arbitrary will, equality in that of privilege; delivered men from the distinctions of classes, the land from the barriers of provinces, trade from the shackles of corporations and fellowships, agriculture from feudal subjection and the oppression of tithes, property from the impediment of entails, and brought everything to the condition of one state, one system of law, one people.

In order to effect such mighty reformation as this, the revolution had many obstacles to overcome, involving transient excesses with durable benefits. The privileged sought to prevent it; Europe to subject it; and thus forced into a struggle, it could not set bounds to its efforts, or moderate its victory. Resistance from within brought about the sovereignty of the multitude, and aggression from without, military domination. Yet the end was attained, in spite of anarchy and in spite of despotism: the old society was destroyed during the revolution, and the new one became established under the empire.

When a reform has become necessary, and the moment for accomplishing it has arrived, nothing can prevent it, everything furthers it. Happy were it for men, could they then come to an understanding; would the rich resign their superfluity, and the poor content themselves with achieving what they really needed, revolutions would then be quietly effected, and the historian would have no excesses, no calamities to record; he would merely have to display the transition of humanity to a wiser, freer, and happier condition. But the annals of nations have not as yet presented any instance of such prudent sacrifices; those who should have made them have refused to do so; those who required them have forcibly compelled them; and good has been brought about, like evil, by the medium and with all the violence of usurpation. As yet there has been no sovereign but force.

In reviewing the history of the important period extending from the opening of the states-general to 1814, I propose to explain the various crises of the revolution, while I describe their progress. It will thus be seen through whose fault, after commencing under such happy auspices, it so fearfully degenerated; in what way it changed France into a republic, and how upon the ruins of the republic it raise the empire. These various phases were almost inevitable, so irresistible was the power of the events which produced them. It would perhaps be rash to affirm that by no possibility could the face of things have been otherwise; but it is certain that the revolution, taking its rise from such causes, and employing and arousing such passions, naturally took that course, and ended in that result. Before we enter upon its history, let us see what led to the convocation of the states-general, which themselves brought on all that followed. In retracing the preliminary causes of the revolution, I hope to show that it was as impossible to avoid as to guide it.

From its establishment the French monarchy had had no settled form, no fixed and recognised public right. Under the first races the crown was elective, the nation sovereign, and the king a mere military chief, depending on the common voice for all decisions to be made, and all the enterprises to be undertaken. The nation elected its chief, exercised the legislative power in the Champs de Mars under the presidentship of the king, and the judicial power in the courts under the direction of one of his officers. Under the feudal regime, this royal democracy gave way to a royal aristocracy. Absolute power ascended higher, the nobles stripped the people of it, as the prince afterwards despoiled the nobles. At this period the monarch had become hereditary; not as king, but as individually possessor of a fief; the legislative authority belonged to the seigneurs, in their vast territories or in the barons' parliaments; and the judicial authority to the vassals in the manorial courts. In a word, power had become more and more concentrated, and as it had passed from the many to the few, it came at last from the few to be invested in one alone. During centuries of continuous efforts, the kings of France were battering down the feudal edifice, and at length they established themselves on its ruins, having step by step usurped the fiefs, subdued the vassals, suppressed the parliaments of barons, annulled or subjected the manorial courts, assumed the legislative power, and effected that judicial authority should be exercised in their name and on their behalf, in parliaments of legists.

The states-general, which they convoked on pressing occasions, for the purpose of obtaining subsidies, and which were composed of the three orders of the nation, the clergy, the nobility, and the third estate or commons, had no regular existence. Originated while the royal prerogative was in progress, they were at first controlled, and finally suppressed by it. The strongest and most determined opposition the kings had to encounter in their projects of aggrandizement, proceeded much less from these assemblies, which they authorized or annulled at pleasure, than from the nobles vindicating against them, first their sovereignty, and then their political importance. From Philip Augustus to Louis XI. the object of all their efforts was to preserve their own power; from Louis XI. to Louis XIV. to become the ministers of that of royalty. The Fronde was the last campaign of the aristocracy. Under Louis XIV. absolute monarchy definitively established itself, and dominated without dispute.

The government of France, from Louis XIV. to the revolution, was still more arbitrary than despotic; for the monarchs had much more power than they exercised. The barriers that opposed the encroachments of this immense authority were exceedingly feeble. The crown disposed of persons by *lettres de cachet*, of property by confiscation, of the public revenue by imposts. Certain bodies, it is true, possessed means of defence, which were termed privileges, but these privileges were rarely respected. The parliament had that of ratifying or of refusing an impost, but the king could compel its assent, by a *lit de justice*, and punish its members by exile. The nobility were exempt from taxation; the clergy were entitled to the privilege of taxing themselves, in the form of free gifts; some provinces enjoyed the right of compounding the taxes, and others made the assessment themselves. Such were the trifling liberties of France, and even these all turned to the benefit of the privileged classes, and to the detriment of the people.

And this France, so enslaved, was moreover miserably organized; the excesses of power were still less endurable than their unjust distribution. The nation, divided into three orders, themselves subdivided into several classes, was a prey to all the attacks of despotism, and all the evils of inequality. The nobility were subdivided: into courtiers, living on the favours of the prince, that is to say, on the labour of the people, and whose aim was governorships of provinces, or elevated ranks in the army; ennobled parvenus, who conducted the interior administration, and whose object was to obtain comptrollerships, and to make the most of their place while they held it, by jobbing of every description; legists who administered justice, and were alone competent to perform its functions; and landed proprietors who oppressed the country by the exercise of those feudal rights which still survived. The clergy were divided into two classes: the one destined for the bishoprics and abbeys, and their rich revenues; the other for the apostolic function and its poverty. The third estate, ground down by the court, humiliated by the nobility, was itself divided into corporations, which, in their turn, exercised upon each other the evil and the contempt they received from the higher classes. It possessed scarcely a third part of the land, and this was burdened with the feudal rents due to the lords of the manor, tithes to the clergy, and taxes to the king. In compensation for all these sacrifices it enjoyed no political right, had no share in the administration, and was admitted to no public employment.

Louis XIV. wore out the main-spring of absolute monarchy by too protracted tension and too violent use. Fond of sway, rendered irritable by the vexations of his youth, he quelled all resistance, forbad every kind of opposition,—that of the aristocracy which manifested itself in revolt,— that of the parliaments displayed by remonstrance,—that of the protestants, whose form was a liberty of conscience which the church deemed heretical, and royalty factious. Louis XIV. subdued the nobles by summoning them to his court, where favours and pleasures were the compensation for their dependence. Parliament, till then the instrument of the crown, attempted to become its counterbalance, and the prince haughtily imposed upon it a silence and submission of sixty years' duration. At length, the revocation of the edict of Nantes completed this work of despotism. An arbitrary government not only will not endure resistance, but it demands that its subjects shall approve and imitate it. After having subjected the actions of men, it persecutes conscience; needing to be ever in motion, it seeks victims when they do not fall in its way. The immense power of Louis XIV. was exercised, internally, against the heretics; externally, against all Europe. Oppression found ambitious men to counsel it, dragoons to serve, and success to encourage it; the wounds of France were hidden by laurels, her groans were drowned in songs of victory. But at last the men of genius died, the victories ceased, industry emigrated, money disappeared; and the fact became evident, that the very successes of despotism exhaust its resources, and consume its future ere that future has arrived.

The death of Louis XIV. was the signal for a reaction; there was a sudden transition from intolerance to incredulity, from the spirit of obedience to that of discussion. Under the regency, the third estate acquired in importance, by their increasing wealth and intelligence, all that the nobility lost in consideration, and the clergy in influence. Under Louis XV., the court prosecuted ruinous wars attended with little glory, and engaged in a silent struggle with opinion, in an open one with the parliament. Anarchy crept into its bosom, the government fell into the hands of royal mistresses, power was completely on the decline, and the opposition daily made fresh progress.

The parliaments had undergone a change of position and of system. Royalty had invested them with a power which they now turned against it. No sooner had the ruin of the aristocracy been accomplished by the combined efforts of the parliament and of royalty, than the conquerors quarrelled, according to the common practice of allies after a victory. Royalty sought to destroy an instrument that became dangerous when it ceased to be useful, and the parliament sought to govern royalty. This struggle, favourable to the monarch under Louis XIV., of mixed reverses and success under Louis XV., only ceased with the revolution. The parliament, from its very nature, was only called upon to serve as an instrument. The exercise of its prerogative, and its ambition as a body, leading it to oppose itself to the strong and support the weak, it served by turns the crown against the aristocracy and the nation against the crown. It was this that made it so popular under Louis XV. and Louis XVI., although it only attacked the court from a spirit of rivalry. Opinion, without inquiring into its motives, applauded not its ambition but its resistance, and supported it because defended by it. Rendered daring by such encouragement, it became formidable to authority. After annulling the will of the most imperious and best-obeyed of monarchs; after protesting against the Seven Years' War; after obtaining the control of financial operations and the destruction of the Jesuits, its resistance became so constant and energetic, that the court, meeting with it in every direction, saw the necessity of either submitting to or subjecting it. It accordingly carried into execution the plan of disorganization proposed by the chancellor Maupeou. This daring man, who, to employ his own expression, had offered *retirer la couronne du greffe*, replaced this hostile parliament by one devoted to power, and subjected to a similar operation the entire magistracy of France, who were following the example of that of Paris.

But the time had passed for coups d'état. The current had set in against arbitrary rule so decidedly that the king resorted to it with doubt and hesitation, and even encountered the disapprobation of his court. A new power had arisen—that of opinion; which, though not recognised, was not the less influential, and whose decrees were beginning to assume sovereign authority. The nation, hitherto a non-entity, gradually asserted its rights, and without sharing power influenced it. Such is the course of all rising powers; they watch over it from without, before they are admitted into the government; then, from the right of control they pass to that of co-operation. The epoch at which the third estate was to share the sway had at last arrived. It had at former periods attempted to effect this, but in vain, because its efforts were premature. It was then but just emancipated, and possessed not that which establishes superiority, and leads to the acquisition of power; for right is only obtained by might. Accordingly, in insurrections as in the states-general, it had held but the third rank; everything was done with its aid, but nothing for it. In times of feudal tyranny, it had served the kings against the nobles; when ministerial and fiscal despotism prevailed, it assisted the nobles against the kings; but, in the first instance, it was nothing more than the servant of the crown; in the second, than that of the aristocracy. The struggle took place in a sphere, and on the part of interests, with which it was reputed to have no connexion. When the nobles were definitively beaten in the time of the Fronde, it laid down its arms; a clear proof how secondary was the part it had played.

At length, after a century of absolute submission, it reappeared in the arena, but on its own account. The past cannot be recalled; and it was not more possible for the nobles to rise from their defeat than it would now be for absolute monarchy to regain its position. The court was to have another antagonist, for it must always have one, power never being without a candidate. The third estate, which increased daily in strength, wealth, intelligence, and union, was destined to combat and to displace it. The parliament did not constitute a class, but a body; and in this new contest, while able to aid in the displacement of authority, it could not secure it for itself.

The court had favoured the progress of the third estate, and had contributed to the development of one of its chief means of advancement, its intelligence. The most absolute of monarchs aided the movement of mind, and, without intending it, created public opinion. By encouraging praise, he prepared the way for blame; for we cannot invite an examination in our favour, without undergoing one afterwards to our prejudice. When the songs of triumph, and gratulation, and adulation were exhausted, accusation began, and the philosophers of the eighteenth century succeeded to the litterateurs of the seventeenth. Everything became the object of their researches and reflections; governments, religion, abuses, laws. They proclaimed rights, laid bare men's wants, denounced injustice. A strong and enlightened public opinion was formed, whose attacks the government underwent without venturing to attempt its suppression. It even converted those whom it attacked; courtiers submitted to its decisions from fashion's sake, power from necessity, and the age of reform was ushered in by the age of philosophy, as the latter had been by the age of the fine arts.

Such was the condition of France, when Louis XVI. ascended the throne on the 11th of May, 1774. Finances, whose deficiencies neither the restorative ministry of cardinal de Fleury, nor the bankrupt ministry of the abbé Terray had been able to make good, authority disregarded, intractable parliaments, an imperious public opinion; such were the difficulties which the new reign inherited from its predecessors. Of all princes, Louis XVI., by his tendencies and his virtues, was best suited to his epoch. The people were weary of arbitrary rule, and he was disposed to renounce its exercise; they were exasperated with the burdensome dissoluteness of the court of Louis XV.; the morals of the new king were pure and his wants few; they demanded reforms that had become indispensable, and he appreciated the public want, and made it his glory to satisfy it. But it was as difficult to effect good as to continue evil; for it was necessary to have sufficient strength either to make the privileged classes submit to reform, or the nation to abuses; and Louis XVI. was neither a regenerator nor a despot. He was deficient in that sovereign will which alone accomplishes great changes in states, and which is as essential to monarchs who wish to limit their power as to those who seek to aggrandize it. Louis XVI. possessed a sound mind, a good and upright heart, but he was without energy of character and perseverance in action. His projects of amelioration met with obstacles which he had not foreseen, and which he knew not how to overcome. He accordingly fell beneath his efforts to favour reform, as another would have fallen in his attempt to prevent it. Up to the meeting of the states-general, his reign was one long and fruitless endeavour at amelioration.

In choosing, on his accession to the throne, Maurepas as prime minister, Louis XVI. eminently contributed to the irresolute character of his reign. Young, deeply sensible of his duties and of his own insufficiency, he had recourse to the experience of an old man of seventy-three, who had lost the favour of Louis XV. by his opposition to the mistresses of that monarch. In him the king found not a statesman, but a mere courtier, whose fatal influence extended over the whole course of his reign. Maurepas had little heed to the welfare of France, or the glory of his master; his sole care was to remain in favour. Residing in the palace at Versailles, in an apartment communicating with that of the king, and presiding over the council, he rendered the mind of Louis XVI. uncertain, his character irresolute; he accustomed him to half-measures, to changes of system, to all the inconsistencies of power, and especially to the necessity of doing everything by others, and nothing of himself.

Maurepas had the choice of the ministers, and these cultivated his good graces as assiduously as he the king's. Fearful of endangering his position, he kept out of the ministry men of powerful connections, and appointed rising men, who required his support for their own protection, and to effect their reforms. He successively called Turgot, Malesherbes, and Necker to the direction of affairs, each of whom undertook to effect ameliorations in that department of the government which had been the immediate object of his studies.

Malesherbes, descended from a family in the law, inherited parliamentary virtues, and not parliamentary prejudices. To an independent mind, he united a noble heart. He wished to give to every man his rights; to the accused, the power of being defended; to protestants, liberty of conscience; to authors, the liberty of the press; to every Frenchman, personal freedom; and he proposed the abolition of the torture, the re- establishment of the edict of Nantes, and the suppression of *lettres de cachet* and of the censure. Turgot, of a vigorous and comprehensive mind, and an extraordinary firmness and strength of character, attempted to realize still more extensive projects. He joined Malesherbes, in order, with his assistance, to complete the establishment of a system which was to bring back unity to the government and equality to the country. This virtuous citizen constantly occupied himself with the amelioration of the condition of the people; he undertook, alone, what the revolution accomplished at a later period, — the suppression of servitude and privilege. He proposed to enfranchise the rural districts from statute labour, provinces from their barriers, commerce from internal duties, trade from its shackles, and lastly, to make the nobility and clergy contribute to the taxes in the same proportion as the third estate. This great minister, of whom Malesherbes said, "he has the head of Bacon and the heart of l'Hôpital," wished by means of provincial assemblies to accustom the nation to public life, and prepare it for the restoration of the states-general. He would have effected the revolution by ordinances, had he been able to stand. But under the system of special privileges and general servitude, all projects for the public good were impraticable. Turgot dissatisfied the courtiers by his ameliorations, displeased the parliament by the abolition of statute labour, wardenships, and internal duties, and alarmed the old minister by the ascendancy which his virtue gave him over Louis XVI. The prince forsook him, though at the same time observing that Turgot and himself were the only persons who desired the welfare of the people: so lamentable is the condition of kings!

Turgot was succeeded in 1776 in the general control of the finances by Clugny, formerly comptroller of Saint Domingo, who, six months after, was himself succeeded by Necker. Necker was a foreigner, a protestant, a banker, and greater as an administrator than as a statesman; he accordingly conceived a plan for reforming France, less extensive than that of Turgot, but which he executed with more moderation, and aided by the times. Appointed minister in order to find money for the court, he made use of the wants of the court to procure liberties for the people. He re-established the finances by means of order, and made the provinces contribute moderately to their administration. His views were wise and just; they consisted in bringing the revenue to a level with the expenditure, by reducing the latter; by employing taxation in ordinary times, and loans when imperious circumstances rendered it necessary to tax the future as well as the present; by causing the taxes to be assessed by the provincial assemblies, and by instituting the publication of accounts, in order to facilitate loans. This system was founded on the nature of loans, which, needing credit, require publicity of administration; and on that of taxation, which needing assent, requires also a share in the administration. Whenever there is a deficit and the government makes applications to meet it, if it address itself to lenders, it must produce its balance-sheet; if it address itself to the tax-payers, it must give them a share in its power. Thus loans led to the production of accounts, and taxes to the states-general; the first placing authority under the jurisdiction of opinion, and the second placing it under that of the people. But Necker, though less impatient for reform than Turgot, although he desired to redeem abuses which his predecessor wished to destroy, was not more fortunate than he. His economy displeased the courtiers; the measures of the provincial assemblies incurred the disapprobation of the parliaments, which wished to monopolize opposition; and the prime minister could not forgive him an appearance of credit. He was obliged to quit power in 1781, a few months after the publication of the famous *Comptes rendus* of the finances, which suddenly initiated France in a knowledge of state matters, and rendered absolute government for ever impossible.

The death of Maurepas followed close upon the retirement of Necker. The queen took his place with Louis XVI., and inherited all his influence over him. This good but weak prince required to be directed. His wife, young, beautiful, active, and ambitious, gained great ascendancy over him. Yet it may be said that the daughter of Marie Thérèse resembled her mother too much or too little. She combined frivolity with domination, and disposed of power only to invest with it men who caused her own ruin and that of the state. Maurepas, mistrusting court ministers, had always chosen popular ministers; it is true he did not support them; but if good was not brought about, at least evil did not increase. After his death, court ministers succeeded the popular ministers, and by their faults rendered the crisis inevitable, which others had endeavoured to prevent by their reforms. This difference of choice is very remarkable; this it was which, by the change of men, brought on the change in the system of administration. The revolution dates from this epoch; the abandonment of reforms and the return of disorders hastened its approach and augmented its fury.

Calonne was called from an intendancy to the general control of the finances. Two successors had already been given to Necker, when application was made to Calonne in 1783. Calonne was daring, brilliant and eloquent; he had much readiness and a fertile mind. Either from error or design he adopted a system of administration directly opposed to that of his predecessor. Necker recommended economy, Calonne boasted of his lavish expenditure. Necker fell through courtiers, Calonne sought to be upheld by them. His sophisms were backed by his liberality; he convinced the queen by *fêtes*, the nobles by pensions; he gave a great circulation to the finances, in order that the extent and facility of his operations might excite confidence in the justness of his views; he even deceived the capitalists, by first showing himself punctual in his payments. He continued to raise loans after the peace, and he exhausted the credit which Necker's wise conduct had procured to the government. Having come to this point, having deprived himself of a resource, the very employment of which he was unable to manage, in order to prolong his continuance in power he was obliged to have recourse to taxation. But to whom could he apply? The people could pay no longer, and the privileged classes would not offer anything. Yet it was necessary to decide, and Calonne, hoping more from something new, convoked an assembly of notables, which began its sittings at Versailles on the 22nd of February, 1787. But a recourse to others must prove the end of a system founded on prodigality. A minister who had risen by giving, could not maintain himself by asking.

The notables, chosen by the government from the higher classes, formed a ministerial assembly, which had neither a proper existence nor a commission. It was, indeed, to avoid parliaments and states-general, that Calonne addressed himself to a more subordinate assembly, hoping to find it more docile. But, composed of privileged persons, it was little disposed to make sacrifices. It became still less so, when it saw the abyss which a devouring administration had excavated. It learned with terror, that the loans of a few years amounted to one thousand six hundred and forty-six millions, and that there was an annual deficit in the revenue of a hundred and forty millions. This disclosure was the signal for Calonne's fall. He fell, and was succeeded by Brienne, archbishop of Sens, his opponent in the assembly. Brienne thought the majority of the notables was devoted to him, because it had united with him against Calonne. But the privileged classes were not more disposed to make sacrifices to Brienne than to his predecessor; they had seconded his attacks, which were to their interest, and not his ambition, to which they were indifferent.

The archbishop of Sens, who is censured for a want of plan, was in no position to form one. He was not allowed to continue the prodigality of Calonne; and it was too late to return to the retrenchments of Necker. Economy, which had been a means of safety at a former period, was no longer so in this. Recourse must be had either to taxation, and that parliament opposed; or loans, and credit was exhausted; or sacrifices on the part of the privileged classes, who were unwilling to make them. Brienne, to whom office had been the chief object of life, who with, the difficulties of his position combined slenderness of means attempted everything, and succeeded in nothing. His mind was active, but it wanted strength; and his character rash without firmness. Daring, previous to action, but weak afterwards, he ruined himself by his irresolution, want of foresight, and constant variation of means. There remained only bad measures to adopt, but he could not decide upon one, and follow that one; this was his real error.

The assembly of notables was but little submissive and very parsimonious. After having sanctioned the establishment of provincial assemblies, a regulation of the corn trade, the abolition of corvées, and a new stamp tax, it broke up on the 25th of May, 1787. It spread throughout France what it had discovered respecting the necessities of the throne, the errors of the ministers, the dilapidation of the court, and the irremediable miseries of the people.

Brienne, deprived of this assistance, had recourse to taxation, as a resource, the use of which had for some time been abandoned. He demanded the enrolment of two edicts—that of the stamps and that of the territorial subsidies. But parliament, which was then in the full vigour of its existence and in all the ardour of its ambition, and to which the financial embarrassment of the ministry offered a means of augmenting its power, refused the enrolment. Banished to Troyes, it grew weary of exile, and the minister recalled it on condition that the two edicts should be accepted. But this was only a suspension of hostilities; the necessities of the crown soon rendered the struggle more obstinate and violent. The minister had to make fresh applications for money; his existence depended on the issue of several successive loans to the amount of four hundred and forty millions. It was necessary to obtain the enrolment of them.

Brienne, expecting opposition from the parliament, procured the enrolment of this edict by a *lit de justice*, and to conciliate the magistracy and public opinion, the protestants were restored to their rights in the same sitting, and Louis XVI. promised an annual publication of the state of finances, and the convocation, of the states-general before the end of five years. But these concessions were no longer sufficient: parliament refused the enrolment, and rose against the ministerial tyranny. Some of its members, among others the duke of Orleans, were banished. Parliament protested, by a decree, against *lettres de cachet*, and required the recall of its members. This decree was annulled by the king, and confirmed by parliament. The warfare increased.

The magistracy of Paris was supported by all the magistracy of France, and encouraged by public opinion. It proclaimed the rights of the nation, and its own incompetence in matters of taxation; and, become liberal from interest, and rendered generous by oppression, it exclaimed against arbitrary imprisonment, and demanded regularly convoked states-general. After this act of courage, it decreed the irremovability of its members, and the incompetence of any who might usurp their functions. This bold manifesto was followed by the arrest of two members, d'Eprémenil and Goislard, by the reform of the body, and the establishment of a plenary court.

Brienne understood that the opposition of the parliament was systematic, that it would be renewed on every fresh demand for subsidies, or on the authorization of every loan. Exile was but a momentary remedy, which suspended opposition, without destroying it. He then projected the reduction of this body to judicial functions, and associated with himself Lamoignon, keeper of the seals, for the execution of this project. Lamoignon was skilled in coups d'état. He had audacity, and combined with Maupeou's energetic determination a greater degree of consideration and probity. But he made a mistake as to the force of power, and what it was possible to effect in his times. Maupeou had re-established parliament, changing its members; Lamoignon wished to disorganize it. The first of these means, if it had succeeded, would only have produced temporary repose; the second must have produced a definitive one, since it aimed at destroying the power, which the other only tried to displace; but Maupeou's reform did not last, and that of Lamoignon could not be effected. The execution of the latter was, however, tolerably well framed. All the magistracy of France was exiled on the same day, in order that the new judicial organization might take place. The keeper of the seals deprived the parliament of Paris of its political attributes, to invest with them a plenary court, ministerially composed, and reduced its judicial competence in favour of bailiwicks, the jurisdiction of which he extended. Public opinion was indignant; the Châtelet protested, the provinces rose, and the plenary court could neither be formed nor act. Disturbances broke out in Dauphiné, Brittany, Provence, Flanders, Languedoc, and Béarn; the ministry, instead of the regular opposition of parliament, had to encounter one much more animated and factious. The nobility, the third estate, the provincial states, and even the clergy, took part in it. Brienne, pressed for money, had called together an extraordinary assembly of the clergy, who immediately made an address to the king, demanding the abolition of his plenary court, and the recall of the states-general: they alone could thenceforth repair the disordered state of the finances, secure the national debt, and terminate such conflicts of authority.

The archbishop of Sens, by his contest with the parliament, had postponed the financial, by creating a political difficulty. The moment the latter ceased, the former re-appeared, and made his retreat inevitable. Obtaining neither taxes nor loans, unable to make use of the plenary court, and not wishing to recall the parliaments, Brienne, as a last resource, promised the convocation of the states-general. By this means he hastened his ruin. He had been called to the financial department in order to remedy embarrassments which he had augmented, and to procure money which he had been unable to obtain. So far from it, he had exasperated the nation, raised a rebellion in the various bodies of the state, compromised the authority of the government, and rendered inevitable the states-general, which, in the opinion of the court, was the worst means of raising money. He succumbed on the 25th of August, 1788. The cause of his fall was a suspension of the payment of the interest on the debt, which was the commencement of bankruptcy. This minister has been the most blamed because he came last. Inheriting the faults, the embarrassments of past times, he had to struggle with the difficulties of his position with insufficient means. He tried intrigue and oppression; he banished, suspended, disorganized parliament; everything was an obstacle to him, nothing aided him. After a long struggle, he sank under lassitude and weakness; I dare not say from incapacity, for had he been far stronger and more skilful, had he been a Richelieu or a Sully, he would still have fallen. It no longer appertained to any one arbitrarily to raise money or to oppress the people. It must be said in his excuse, that he had not created that position from which he was not able to extricate himself; his only mistake was his presumption in accepting it. He fell through the fault of Calonne, as Calonne had availed himself of the confidence inspired by Necker for the purposes of his lavish expenditure. The one had destroyed credit, and the other, thinking to re-establish it by force, had destroyed authority.

The states-general had become the only means of government, and the last resource of the throne. They had been eagerly demanded by parliament and the peers of the kingdom, on the 13th of July, 1787; by the states of Dauphiné in the assembly of Vizille; by the clergy in its assembly at Paris. The provincial states had prepared the public mind for them; and the notables were their precursors. The king after having, on the 18th of December, 1787, promised their convocation in five years, on the 8th of August, 1788, fixed the opening for the 1st of May, 1789. Necker was recalled, parliament re-established, the plenary court abolished, the bailiwicks destroyed, and the provinces satisfied; and the new minister prepared everything for the election of deputies and the holding of the states.

At this epoch a great change took place in the opposition, which till then had been unanimous. Under Brienne, the ministry had encountered opposition from all the various bodies of the state, because it had sought to oppress them. Under Necker, it met with resistance from the same bodies, which desired power for themselves and oppression for the people. From being despotic, it had become national, and it still had them all equally against it. Parliament had maintained a struggle for authority, and not for the public welfare; and the nobility had united with the third estate, rather against the government than in favour of the people. Each of these bodies had demanded the states-general: the parliament, in the hope of ruling them as it had done in 1614; and the nobility, in the hope of regaining its lost influence. Accordingly, the magistracy proposed as a model for the states-general of 1789, the form of that of 1614, and public opinion abandoned it; the nobility refused its consent to the double representation of the third estate, and a division broke out between these two orders.

This double representation was required by the intellect of the age, the necessity of reform, and by the importance which the third estate had acquired. It had already been admitted in the provincial assemblies. Brienne, before leaving the ministry, had made an appeal to the writers of the day, in order to know what would be the most suitable method of composing and holding the states-general. Among the works favourable to the people, there appeared the celebrated pamphlet of Sieyès on the Third Estate, and that of d'Entraigues on the States-general.

Opinion became daily more decided, and Necker wishing, yet fearing, to satisfy it, and desirous of conciliating all orders, of obtaining general approbation, convoked a second assembly of notables on the 6th of November, 1788, to deliberate on the composition of the states-general, and the election of its members. He thought to induce it to accept the double representation of the third estate, but it refused, and he was obliged to decide, in spite of the notables, that which he ought to have decided without them. Necker was not the man to avoid disputes by removing all difficulties beforehand. He did not take the initiative as to the representation of the third estate, any more than at a later period he took it with regard to the question of voting by orders or by poll. When the states-general were assembled, the solution of this second question, on which depended the state of power and that of the people, was abandoned to force.

Be this as it may, Necker, having been unable to make the notables adopt the double representation of the third estate, caused it to be adopted by the council. The royal declaration of the 27th of November decreed that the deputies in the states-general should amount to at least a thousand, and that the deputies of the third estate should be equal in number to the deputies of the nobility and clergy together. Necker moreover obtained the admission of the curés into the order of the clergy, and of protestants into that of the third estate. The district assemblies were convoked for the elections; every one exerted himself to secure the nomination of members of his own party, and to draw up manifestoes setting forth his views. Parliament had but little influence in the elections, and the court none at all. The nobility selected a few popular deputies, but mainly such as were devoted to the interests of their order, and as much opposed to the third estate as to the oligarchy of the great families of the court. The clergy nominated bishops and abbés attached to privilege, and curés favourable to the popular cause, which was their own; lastly, the third estate selected men enlightened, firm, and unanimous in their wishes. The deputation of the nobility was comprised of two hundred and forty-two gentlemen, and twenty-eight members of the parliament; that of the clergy, of forty-eight archbishops or bishops, thirty-five abbés or deans, and two hundred and eight curés; and that of the communes, of two ecclesiastics, twelve noblemen, eighteen magistrates of towns, two hundred county members, two hundred and twelve barristers, sixteen physicians, and two hundred and sixteen merchants and agriculturists. The opening of the states-general was then fixed for the 5th of May, 1789.

Thus was the revolution brought about. The court in vain tried to prevent, as it afterwards endeavoured to annul it. Under the direction of Maurepas, the king nominated popular ministers, and made attempts at reform; under the influence of the queen, he nominated court ministers, and made attempts at authority. Oppression met with as little success as reform. After applying in vain to courtiers for retrenchments, to parliament for levies, to capitalists for loans, he sought for new tax-payers, and made an appeal to the privileged orders. He demanded of the notables, consisting of the nobles and the clergy, a participation in the charges of the state, which they refused. He then for the first time applied to all France, and convoked the states-general. He treated with the various bodies of the nation before treating with the nation itself; and it was only on the refusal of the first, that he appealed from it to a power whose intervention and support he dreaded. He preferred private assemblies, which, being isolated, necessarily remained secondary, to a general assembly, which representing all interests, must combine all powers. Up to this great epoch every year saw the wants of the government increasing, and resistance becoming more extensive. Opposition passed from parliaments to the nobility, from the nobility to the clergy, and from them all to the people. In proportion as each participated in power it began its opposition, until all these private oppositions were fused in or gave way before the national opposition. The states-general only decreed a revolution which was already formed.

CHAPTER I

FROM THE 5TH OF MAY, 1789, TO THE NIGHT OF THE 4TH OF AUGUST

Opening of the states-general—Opinion of the court, of the ministry, and of the various bodies of the kingdom respecting the states—Verification of powers—Question of vote by order or by poll—The order of the commons forms itself into a national assembly—The court causes the Hall of the states to be closed—Oath of the Tennis-court—The majority of the order of the clergy unites itself with the commons—Royal sitting of the 23rd of June—Its inutility—Project of the court—Events of the 12th, 13th, and 14th of July—Dismissal of Necker—Insurrection of Paris—Formation of the national guard—Siege and taking of the Bastille—Consequences of the 14th of July—Decrees of the night of the 4th of August—Character of the revolution which had just been brought about.

The 5th of May, 1789, was fixed for the opening of the states-general. A religious ceremony on the previous day prefaced their installation. The king, his family, his ministers, the deputies of the three orders, went in procession from the church of Notre-Dame to that of Saint Louis, to hear the opening mass. Men did not without enthusiasm see the return of a national ceremony of which France had for so long a period been deprived. It had all the appearance of a festival. An enormous multitude flocked from all parts to Versailles; the weather was splendid; they had been lavish of the pomp of decoration. The excitement of the music, the kind and satisfied expression of the king, the beauty and demeanour of the queen, and, as much as anything, the general hope, exalted every one. But the etiquette, costumes, and order of the ranks of the states in 1614, were seen with regret. The clergy, in cassocks, large cloaks, and square caps, or in violet robes and lawn sleeves, occupied the first place. Then came the nobles, attired in black coats with waistcoats and facings of cloth of gold, lace cravats, and hats with white plumes, turned up in the fashion of Henry IV. The modest third estate came last, clothed in black, with short cloaks, muslin cravats, and hats without feathers or loops. In the church, the same distinction as to places existed between the three orders.

The royal session took place the following day in the Salle des Menus. Galleries, arranged in the form of an amphitheatre, were filled with spectators. The deputies were summoned and introduced according to the order established in 1614.

The clergy were conducted to the right, the nobility to the left, and the commons in front of the throne at the end of the hall. The deputations from Dauphiné, from Crépi in Valois, to which the duke of Orleans belonged, and from Provence, were received with loud applause. Necker was also received on his entrance with general enthusiasm. Public favour was testified towards all who had contributed to the convocation of the states-general. When the deputies and ministers had taken their places, the king appeared, followed by the queen, the princes, and a brilliant suite. The hall resounded with applause on his arrival. When he came in, Louis XVI. took his seat on the throne, and when he had put on his hat, the three orders covered themselves at the same time. The commons, contrary to the custom of the ancient states, imitated the nobility and clergy, without hesitation: the time when the third order should remain uncovered and speak kneeling was gone by. The king's speech was then expected in profound silence. Men were eager to know the true feeling of the government with regard to the states. Did it purpose assimilating the new assembly to the ancient, or to grant it the part which the necessities of the state and the importance of the occasion assigned to it?

"Gentlemen," said the king, with emotion, "the day I have so anxiously expected has at length arrived, and I see around me the representatives of the nation which I glory in governing. A long interval had elapsed since the last session of the states-general, and although the convocation of these assemblies seemed to have fallen into disuse, I did not hesitate to restore a custom from which the kingdom might derive new force, and which might open to the nation a new source of happiness."

These words which promised much, were only followed by explanations as to the debt and announcements of retrenchment in the expenditure. The king, instead of wisely tracing out to the states the course they ought to follow, urged the orders to union, expressed his want of money, his dread of innovations, and complained of the uneasiness of the public mind, without suggesting any means of satisfying it. He was nevertheless very much applauded when he delivered at the close of his discourse the following words, which fully described his intentions: "All that can be expected from the dearest interest in the public welfare, all that can be required of a sovereign, the first friend of his people; you may and ought to hope from my sentiments. That a happy spirit of union may pervade this assembly, gentlemen, and that this may be an ever memorable epoch for the happiness and prosperity of the kingdom, is the wish of my heart, the most ardent of my desires; it is, in a word, the reward which I expect for the uprightness of my intentions, and my love of my subjects."

Barentin, keeper of the seals, spoke next. His speech was an amplification respecting the states-general, and the favours of the king. After a long preamble, he at last touched upon the topics of the occasion. "His Majesty," he said, "has not changed the ancient method of deliberation, by granting a double representation in favour of the most numerous of the three orders, that on which the burden of taxation chiefly falls. Although the vote by poll, by producing but one result, seems to have the advantage of best representing the general desire, the king wishes this new form should be adopted only with the free consent of the states, and the approval of his majesty. But whatever may be the opinion on this question, whatever distinctions may be drawn between the different matters that will become subjects of deliberation, there can be no doubt but that the most entire harmony will unite the three orders on the subject of taxation." The government was not opposed to the vote by poll in pecuniary matters, it being more expeditious; but in political questions it declared itself in favour of voting by order, as a more effectual check on innovations. In this way it sought to arrive at its own end,—namely, subsidies, and not to allow the nation to obtain its object, which was reform. The manner in which the keeper of the seals determined the province of the states- general, discovered more plainly the intentions of the court. He reduced them, in a measure, to the inquiry into taxation, in order to vote it, and to the discussion of a law respecting the press, for the purpose of fixing its limits, and to the reform of civil and criminal legislation. He proscribed all other changes, and concluded by saying: "All just demands have been granted; the king has not noticed indiscreet murmurs; he has condescended to overlook them with indulgence; he has even forgiven the expression of those false and extravagant maxims, under favour of which attempts have been made to substitute pernicious chimeras for the unalterable principles of monarchy. You will with indignation, gentlemen, repel the dangerous innovations which the enemies of the public good seek to confound with the necessary and happy changes which this regeneration ought to produce, and which form the first wish of his majesty."

This speech displayed little knowledge of the wishes of the nation, or it sought openly to combat them. The dissatisfied assembly looked to M. Necker, from whom it expected different language. He was the popular minister, had obtained the double representation, and it was hoped he would approve of the vote by poll, the only way of enabling the third estate to turn its numbers to account. But he spoke as comptroller-general and as a man of caution. His speech, which lasted three hours, was a lengthened budget; and when, after tiring the assembly, he touched on the topic of interest, he spoke undecidedly, in order to avoid committing himself either with the court or the people.

The government ought to have better understood the importance of the states-general. The restoration of this assembly alone announced a great revolution. Looked for with hope by the nation, it reappeared at an epoch when the ancient monarchy was sinking, and when it alone was capable of reforming the state and providing for the necessities of royalty. The difficulties of the time, the nature of their mission, the choice of their members, everything announced that the states were not assembled as tax- payers, but as legislators. The right of regenerating France had been granted them by opinion, was devolved on them by public resolutions, and they found in the enormity of the abuses and the public encouragement, strength to undertake and accomplish this great task.

It behoved the king to associate himself with their labours. In this way he would have been able to restore his power, and ensure himself from the excesses of a revolution, by himself assisting in bringing it about. If, taking the lead in these changes, he had fixed the new order of things with firmness, but with justice; if, realizing the wishes of France, he had determined the rights of her citizens, the province of the states- general and the limits of royalty; if, on his own part, he had renounced arbitrary power, inequality on the part of the nobility, and privileges on the part of the different bodies; in a word, if he had accomplished all the reforms which were demanded by public opinion, and executed by the constituent assembly, he would have prevented the fatal dissensions which subsequently arose. It is rare to find a prince willing to share his power, or sufficiently enlightened to yield what he will be reduced to lose. Yet Louis XVI. would have done this, if he had been less influenced by those around him, and had he followed the dictates of his own mind. But the greatest anarchy pervaded the councils of the king. When the states- general assembled, no measures had been taken, nothing had been decided on, which might prevent dispute. Louis XVI. wavered between his ministry, directed by Necker, and his court, directed by the queen and a few princes of his family.

Necker, satisfied with obtaining the representation of the third estate, dreaded the indecision of the king and the discontent of the court. Not appreciating sufficiently the importance of a crisis which he considered more as a financial than a social one, he waited for the course of events in order to act, and flattered himself with the hope of being able to guide these events, without attempting to prepare the way for them. He felt that the ancient organization of the states could no longer be maintained; that the existence of three orders, each possessing the right of refusal, was opposed to the execution of reform and the progress of administration. He hoped, after a trial of this triple opposition, to reduce the number of the orders, and bring about the adoption of the English form of government, by uniting the clergy and nobility in one chamber, and the third estate in another. He did not foresee that the struggle once begun, his interposition would be in vain: that half measures would suit neither party; that the weak through obstinacy, and the strong through passion, would oppose this system of moderation. Concessions satisfy only before a victory.

The court, so far from wishing to organize the states-general, sought to annul them. It preferred the casual resistance of the great bodies of the nation, to sharing authority with a permanent assembly. The separation of the orders favoured its views; it reckoned on fomenting their differences, and thus preventing them from acting. The states-general had never achieved any result, owing to the defect of their organization; the court hoped that it would still be the same, since the two first orders were less disposed to yield to the reforms solicited by the last. The clergy wished to preserve its privileges and its opulence, and clearly foresaw that the sacrifices to be made by it were more numerous than the advantages to be acquired. The nobility, on its side, while it resumed a political independence long since lost, was aware that it would have to yield more to the people than it could obtain from royalty. It was almost entirely in favour of the third estate, that the new revolution was about to operate, and the first two orders were induced to unite with the court against the third estate, as but lately they had coalesced with the third estate against the court. Interest alone led to this change of party, and they united with the monarch without affection, as they had defended the people without regard to public good.

No efforts were spared to keep the nobility and clergy in this disposition. The deputies of these two orders were the objects of favours and allurements. A committee, to which the most illustrious persons belonged, was held at the countess de Polignac's; the principal deputies were admitted to it. It was here that were gained De Eprémenil and De Entraigues, two of the warmest advocates of liberty in parliament, or before the states-general, and who afterwards became its most decided opponents. Here also the costume of the deputies of the different orders was determined on, and attempts made to separate them, first by etiquette, then by intrigue, and lastly, by force. The recollection of the ancient states-general prevailed in the court; it thought it could regulate the present by the past, restrain Paris by the army, the deputies of the third estate by those of the nobility, rule the states by separating the orders, and separate the orders by reviving ancient customs which exalted the nobles and lowered the commons. Thus, after the first sitting, it was supposed that all had been prevented by granting nothing.

On the 6th of May, the day after the opening of the states, the nobility and clergy repaired to their respective chambers, and constituted themselves. The third estate being, on account of its double representation, the most numerous order, had the Salle des États allotted to it, and there awaited the two other orders; it considered its situation as provisional, its members as presumptive deputies, and adopted a system of inactivity till the other orders should unite with it. Then a memorable struggle commenced, the issue of which was to decide whether the revolution should be effected or stopped. The future fate of France depended on the separation or reunion of the orders. This important question arose on the subject of the verification of powers. The popular deputies asserted very justly, that it ought to be made in common, since, even if the union of the orders were refused, it was impossible to deny the interest which each of them had in the examination of the powers of the others; the privileged deputies argued, on the contrary, that since the orders had a distinct existence, the verification ought to be made respectively. They felt that one single co-operation would, for the future, render all separation impossible.

The commons acted with much circumspection, deliberation, and steadiness. It was by a succession of efforts, not unattended with peril, by slow and undecided success, and by struggles constantly renewed, that they attained their object. The systematic inactivity they adopted from the commencement was the surest and wisest course; there are occasions when the way to victory is to know how to wait for it. The commons were unanimous, and alone formed the numerical half of the states-general; the nobility had in its bosom some popular dissentients; the majority of the clergy, composed of several bishops, friends of peace, and of the numerous class of the curés, the third estate of the church, entertained sentiments favourable to the commons. Weariness was therefore to bring about a union; this was what the third estate hoped, what the bishops feared, and what induced them on the 13th of May to offer themselves as mediators. But this mediation was of necessity without any result, as the nobility would not admit voting by poll, nor the commons voting by order. Accordingly, the conciliatory conferences, after being prolonged in vain till the 27th of May, were broken up by the nobility, who declared in favour of separate verification.

The day after this hostile decision, the commons determined to declare themselves the assembly of the nation, and invited the clergy to join them *in the name of the God of peace and the common weal*. The court taking alarm at this measure, interfered for the purpose of having the conferences resumed. The first commissioners appointed for purposes of reconciliation were charged with regulating the differences of the orders; the ministry undertook to regulate the differences of the commissioners. In this way, the states depended on a commission, and the commission had the council of the prince for arbiter. But these new conferences had not a more fortunate issue than the first. They lingered on without either of the orders being willing to yield anything to the others, and the nobility finally broke them up by confirming all its resolutions.

Five weeks had already elapsed in useless parleys. The third estate, perceiving the moment had arrived for it to constitute itself, and that longer delay would indispose the nation towards it, and destroy the confidence it had acquired by the refusal of the privileged classes to co- operate with it, decided on acting, and displayed herein the same moderation and firmness it had shown during its inactivity. Mirabeau announced that a deputy of Paris had a motion to propose; and Sieyès, physically of timid character, but of an enterprising mind, who had great authority by his ideas, and was better suited than any one to propose a measure, proved the impossibility of union, the urgency of verification, the justice of demanding it in common, and caused it to be decreed by the assembly that the nobility and clergy should be *invited* to the Salle des États in order to take part in the verification, which would take place, *whether they were absent or present*.

The measure for general verification was followed by another still more energetic. The commons, after having terminated the verification on the 17th of June, on the motion of Sieyès, constituted themselves *the National Assembly*. This bold step, by which the most numerous order and the only one whose powers were legalized, declared itself the representation of France and refused to recognise the other two till they submitted to the verification, determined questions hitherto undecided, and changed the assembly of the states into an assembly of the people. The system of orders disappeared in political powers, and this was the first step towards the abolition of classes in the private system. This memorable decree of the 17th of June contained the germ of the night of the 4th of August; but it was necessary to defend what they had dared to decide, and there was reason to fear such a determination could not be maintained.

The first decree of *the National Assembly* was an act of sovereignty. It placed the privileged classes under its dependence, by proclaiming the indivisibility of the legislative power. The court remained to be restrained by means of taxation. The assembly declared the illegality of previous imposts, voted them provisionally, as long as it continued to sit, and their cessation on its dissolution; it restored the confidence of capitalists by consolidating the public debt, and provided for the necessities of the people, by appointing a committee of subsistence.

Such firmness and foresight excited the enthusiasm of the nation. But those who directed the court saw that the divisions thus excited between the orders had failed in their object; and that it was necessary to resort to other means to obtain it. They considered the royal authority alone adequate to prescribe the continuance of the orders, which the opposition of the nobles could no longer preserve. They took advantage of a journey to Marly to remove Louis XVI. from the influences of the prudent and pacific counsels of Necker, and to induce him to adopt hostile measures. This prince, alike accessible to good and bad counsels, surrounded by a court given up to party spirit, and entreated for the interests of his crown and in the name of religion to stop the pernicious progress of the commons, yielded at last, and promised everything. It was decided that he should go in state to the assembly, annul its decrees, command the separation of the orders as constitutive of the monarchy, and himself fix the reforms to be effected by the states-general. From that moment the privy council held the government, acting no longer secretly, but in the most open manner. Barentin, the keeper of the seals, the count d'Artois, the prince de Condé, and the prince de Conti conducted alone the projects they had concerted. Necker lost all his influence; he had proposed to the king a conciliatory plan, which might have succeeded before the struggle attained this degree of animosity, but could do so no longer. He had advised another royal sitting, in which the vote by poll in matters of taxation was to be granted, and the vote by order to remain in matters of private interest and privilege. This measure, which was unfavourable to the commons, since it tended to maintain abuses by investing the nobility and clergy with the right of opposing their abolition, would have been followed by the establishment of two chambers for the next states-general. Necker was fond of half measures, and wished to effect, by successive concessions, a political change which should have been accomplished at once. The moment was arrived to grant the nation all its rights, or to leave it to take them. His project of a royal sitting, already insufficient, was changed into a stroke of state policy by the new council. The latter thought that the injunctions of the throne would intimidate the assembly, and that France would be satisfied with promises of reform. It seemed to be ignorant that the worst risk royalty can be exposed to is that of disobedience.

Strokes of state policy generally come unexpectedly, and surprise those they are intended to influence. It was not so with this; its preparations tended to prevent success. It was feared that the majority of the clergy would recognise the assembly by uniting with it; and to prevent so decided a step, instead of hastening the royal sitting, they closed the Salle des États, in order to suspend the assembly till the day of the sitting. The preparations rendered necessary by the presence of the king was the pretext for this unskilful and improper measure. At that time Bailly presided over the assembly. This virtuous citizen had obtained, without seeking them, all the honours of dawning liberty. He was the first president of the assembly, as he had been the first deputy of Paris, and was to become its first mayor. Beloved by his own party, respected by his adversaries, he combined with the mildest and most enlightened virtues, the most courageous sense of duty. Apprised on the night of the 20th of June, by the keeper of the seals, of the suspension of the sitting, he remained faithful to the wishes of the assembly, and did not fear disobeying the court. At an appointed hour on the following day, he repaired to the Salle des États, and finding an armed force in possession, he protested against this act of despotism. In the meantime the deputies arrived, dissatisfaction increased, all seemed disposed to brave the perils of a sitting. The most indignant proposed going to Marly, and holding the assembly under the windows of the king; one named the Tennis- court; this proposition was well received, and the deputies repaired thither in procession. Bailly was at their head; the people followed them with enthusiasm; even soldiers volunteered to escort them, and there, in a bare hall, the deputies of the commons standing with upraised hands, and hearts full of their sacred mission, swore, with only one exception, not to separate till they had given France a constitution.

This solemn oath, taken on the 20th of June, in the presence of the nation, was followed on the 22nd by an important triumph. The assembly, still deprived of their usual place of meeting, unable to make use of the Tennis-court, the princes having hired it purposely that it might be refused them, met in the church of Saint Louis. In this sitting, the majority of the clergy joined them in the midst of patriotic transports. Thus, the measures taken to intimidate the assembly, increased its courage, and accelerated the union they were intended to prevent. By these two failures the court prefaced the famous sitting of the 23rd of June.

At length it took place. A numerous guard surrounded the hall of the states-general, the door of which was opened to the deputies, but closed to the public. The king came surrounded with the pomp of power; he was received, contrary to the usual custom, in profound silence. His speech completed the measure of discontent by the tone of authority with which he dictated measures rejected by public opinion and by the assembly. The king complained of a want of union, excited by the court itself; he censured the conduct of the assembly, regarding it only as the order of the third estate; he annulled its decrees, enjoined the continuance of the orders, imposed reforms, and determined their limits; enjoined the states-general to adopt them, and threatened to dissolve them and to provide alone for the welfare of the kingdom, if he met with more opposition on their part. After this scene of authority, so ill-suited to the occasion, and at variance with his heart, Louis XVI. withdrew, having commanded the deputies to disperse. The clergy and nobility obeyed. The deputies of the people, motionless, silent, and indignant, remained seated. They continued in that attitude some time, when Mirabeau suddenly breaking silence, said: "Gentlemen, I admit that what you have just heard might be for the welfare of the country, were it not that the presents of despotism are always dangerous. What is this insulting dictatorship? The pomp of arms, the violation of the national temple, are resorted to—to command you to be happy! Who gives this command? Your mandatary. Who makes these imperious laws for you? Your mandatary; he who should rather receive them from you, gentlemen—from us, who are invested with a political and inviolable priesthood; from us, in a word, to whom alone twenty-five millions of men are looking for certain happiness, because it is to be consented to, and given and received by all. But the liberty of your discussions is enchained; a military force surrounds the assembly! Where are the enemies of the nation? Is Catiline at our gates? I demand, investing yourselves with your dignity, with your legislative power, you inclose yourselves within the religion of your oath. It does not permit you to separate till you have formed a constitution."

The grand master of the ceremonies, finding the assembly did not break up, came and reminded them of the king's order.

"Go and tell your master," cried Mirabeau, "that we are here at the command of the people, and nothing but the bayonet shall drive us hence."

"You are to-day," added Sieyès, calmly, "what you were yesterday. Let us deliberate."

The assembly, full of resolution and dignity, began the debate accordingly. On the motion of Camus, it was determined to persist in the decrees already made; and upon that of Mirabeau the inviolability of the members of the assembly was decreed.

On that day the royal authority was lost. The initiative in law and moral power passed from the monarch to the assembly. Those who, by their counsels, had provoked this resistance, did not dare to punish it. Necker, whose dismissal had been decided on that morning, was, in the evening, entreated by the queen and Louis XVI. to remain in office. This minister had disapproved of the royal sitting, and, by refusing to be present at it, he again won the confidence of the assembly, which he had lost through his hesitation. The season of disgrace was for him the season of popularity. By this refusal he became the ally of the assembly, which determined to support him. Every crisis requires a leader, whose name becomes the standard of his party; while the assembly contended with the court, that leader was Necker.

At the first sitting, that part of the clergy which had united with the assembly in the church of Saint Louis, again sat with it; a few days after, forty-seven members of the nobility, among whom was the duke of Orleans, joined them; and the court was itself compelled to invite the nobility, and a minority of the clergy, to discontinue a dissent that would henceforth be useless. On the 27th of June the deliberation became general. The orders ceased to exist legally, and soon disappeared. The distinct seats they had hitherto occupied in the common hall soon became confounded; the futile pre-eminences of rank vanished before national authority.

The court, after having vainly endeavoured to prevent the formation of the assembly, could now only unite with it, to direct its operations. With prudence and candour it might still have repaired its errors and caused its attacks to be forgotten. At certain moments, the initiative may be taken in making sacrifices; at others, all that can be done is to make a merit of accepting them. At the opening of the states-general, the king might himself have made the constitution, now he was obliged to receive it from the assembly; had he submitted to that position, he would infallibly have improved it. But the advisers of Louis XVI., when they recovered from the first surprise of defeat, resolved to have recourse to the use of the bayonet, after they had failed in that of authority. They led the king to suppose that the contempt of his orders, the safety of his throne, the maintenance of the laws of the kingdom, and even the well-being of his people depended on his reducing the assembly to submission; that the latter, sitting at Versailles, close to Paris, two cities decidedly in its favour, ought to be subdued by force, and removed to some other place or dissolved; that it was urgent that this resolution should be adopted in order to stop the progress of the assembly, and that in order to execute it, it was necessary speedily to call together troops who might intimidate the assembly and maintain order at Paris and Versailles.

While these plots were hatching, the deputies of the nation began their legislative labours, and prepared the anxiously expected constitution, which they considered they ought no longer to delay. Addresses poured in from Paris and the principal towns of the kingdom, congratulating them on their wisdom, and encouraging them to continue their task of regenerating France. The troops, meantime, arrived in great numbers; Versailles assumed the aspect of a camp; the Salle des États was surrounded by guards, and the citizens refused admission. Paris was also encompassed by various bodies of the army, ready to besiege or blockade it, as the occasion might require. These vast military preparations, trains of artillery arriving from the frontiers, and the presence of foreign regiments, whose obedience was unlimited, announced sinister projects. The populace were restless and agitated; and the assembly desired to enlighten the throne with respect to its projects, and solicit the removal of the troops. At Mirabeau's suggestion, it presented on the 9th of July a firm but respectful address to the king, which proved useless. Louis XVI. declared that he alone had to judge the necessity of assembling or dismissing troops, and assured them, that those assembled formed only a precautionary army to prevent disturbances and protect the assembly. He moreover offered the assembly to remove it to Noyon or Soissons, that is to say, to place it between two armies and deprive it of the support of the people.

Paris was in the greatest excitement; this vast city was unanimous in its devotion to the assembly. The perils that threatened the representatives of the nation, and itself, and the scarcity of food disposed it to insurrection. Capitalists, from interest and the fear of bankruptcy; men of enlightenment and all the middle classes, from patriotism; the people, impelled by want, ascribing their sufferings to the privileged classes and the court, desirous of agitation and change, all had warmly espoused the cause of the revolution. It is difficult to conceive the movement which disturbed the capital of France. It was arising from the repose and silence of servitude; it was, as it were, astonished at the novelty of its situation, and intoxicated with liberty and enthusiasm. The press excited the public mind, the newspapers published the debates of the assembly, and enabled the public to be present, as it were, at its deliberations, and the questions mooted in its bosom were discussed in the open air, in the public squares. It was at the Palais Royal, more especially, that the assembly of the capital was held. The garden was always filled by a crowd that seemed permanent, though continually renewed. A table answered the purpose of the *tribune*, the first citizen at hand became the orator; there men expatiated on the dangers that threatened the country, and excited each other to resistance. Already, on a motion made at the Palais Royal, the prisons of the Abbaye had been broken open, and some grenadiers of the French guards, who had been imprisoned for refusing to fire on the people, released in triumph. This outbreak was attended by no consequences; a deputation had already solicited, in behalf of the delivered prisoners, the interest of the assembly, who had recommended them to the clemency of the king. They had returned to prison, and had received pardon. But this regiment, one of the most complete and bravest, had become favourable to the popular cause.

Such was the disposition of Paris when the court, having established troops at Versailles, Sèvres, the Champ de Mars, and Saint Denis, thought itself able to execute its project. It commenced, on the 11th of July, by the banishment of Necker, and the complete reconstruction of the ministry. The marshal de Broglie, la Galissonnière, the duke de la Vauguyon, the Baron de Breteuil, and the intendant Foulon, were appointed to replace Puységur, Montmorin, La Luzerne, Saint Priest, and Necker. The latter received, while at dinner on the 11th of July, a note from the king enjoining him to leave the country immediately. He finished dining very calmly, without communicating the purport of the order he had received, and then got into his carriage with Madame Necker, as if intending to drive to Saint Omer, and took the road to Brussels.

On the following day, Sunday, the 12th of July, about four in the afternoon, Necker's disgrace and departure became known at Paris. This measure was regarded as the execution of the plot, the preparations for which had so long been observed. In a short time the city was in the greatest confusion; crowds gathered together on every side; more than ten thousand persons flocked to the Palais Royal all affected by this news, ready for anything, but not knowing what measure to adopt. Camille Desmoulins, a young man, more daring than the rest, one of the usual orators of the crowd, mounted on a table, pistol in hand, exclaiming: "Citizens, there is no time to lose; the dismissal of Necker is the knell of a Saint Bartholomew for patriots! This very night all the Swiss and German battalions will leave the Champ de Mars to massacre us all; one resource is left; to take arms!" These words were received with violent acclamations. He proposed that cockades should be worn for mutual recognition and protection. "Shall they be green," he cried, "the colour of hope; or red, the colour of the free order of Cincinnatus?" "Green! green!" shouted the multitude. The speaker descended from the table, and fastened the sprig of a tree in his hat. Every one imitated him. The chestnut-trees of the palace were almost stripped of their leaves, and the crowd went in tumult to the house of the sculptor Curtius.

They take busts of Necker and the duke of Orleans, a report having also gone abroad that the latter would be exiled, and covering them with crape, carry them in triumph. This procession passes through the Rues Saint Martin, Saint Denis, and Saint Honoré, augmenting at every step. The crowd obliges all they meet to take off their hats. Meeting the horse-patrol, they take them as their escort. The procession advances in this way to the Place Vendôme, and there they carry the two busts twice round the statue of Louis XIV. A detachment of the Royal-allemand comes up and attempts to disperse the mob, but are put to flight by a shower of stones; and the multitude, continuing its course, reaches the Place Louis XV. Here they are assailed by the dragoons of the prince de Lambesc; after resisting a few moments they are thrown into confusion; the bearer of one of the busts and a soldier of one of the French guards are killed. The mob disperses, part towards the quays, part fall back on the Boulevards, the rest hurry to the Tuileries by the Pont Tournant. The prince de Lambesc, at the head of his horsemen, with drawn sabre pursues them into the gardens, and charges an unarmed multitude who were peaceably promenading and had nothing to do with the procession. In this attack an old man is wounded by a sabre cut; the mob defend themselves with the seats, and rush to the terraces; indignation becomes general; the cry *To arms!* soon resounds on every side, at the Palais Royal and the Tuileries, in the city and in the faubourgs.

We have already said that the regiment of the French guard was favourably disposed towards the people: it had accordingly been ordered to keep in barracks. The prince de Lambesc, fearing that it might nevertheless take an active part, ordered sixty dragoons to station themselves before its dépôt, situated in the Chaussée-d'Antin. The soldiers of the guards, already dissatisfied at being kept as prisoners, were greatly provoked at the sight of these strangers, with whom they had had a skirmish a few days before. They wished to fly to arms, and their officers using alternately threats and entreaties, had much difficulty in restraining them. But they would hear no more, when some of their men brought them intelligence of the attack at the Tuileries, and the death of one of their comrades: they seized their arms, broke open the gates, and drew up in battle array at the entrance of the barracks, and cried out, "*Qui vive?*"—"Royal- allemand."—"Are you for the third estate?" "We are for those who command us." Then the French guards fired on them, killed two of their men, wounded three, and put the rest to flight. They then advanced at quick time and with fixed bayonets to the Place Louis XV. and took their stand between the Tuileries and the Champs Élysées, the people and the troops, and kept that post during the night. The soldiers of the Champ de Mars were immediately ordered to advance. When they reached the Champs Élysées, the French guards received them with discharges of musketry. They wished to make them fight, but they refused: the Petits-Suisses were the first to give this example, which the other regiments followed. The officers, in despair, ordered a retreat; the troops retired as far as the Grille de Chaillot, whence they soon withdrew into the Champ de Mars. The defection of the French guard, and the manifest refusal even of the foreign troops to march on the capital, caused the failure of the projects of the court.

During the evening the people had repaired to the Hôtel de Ville, and requested that the tocsin might be sounded, the districts assembled, and the citizens armed. Some electors assembled at the Hôtel de Ville, and took the authority into their own hands. They rendered great service to their fellow-citizens and the cause of liberty by their courage, prudence, and activity, during these days of insurrection; but in the first confusion of the rising it was with difficulty they succeeded in making themselves heard. The tumult was at its height; each only answered the dictates of his own passions. Side by side with well-disposed citizens were men of suspicious character, who only sought in insurrection opportunities for pillage and disorder. Bands of labourers employed by government in the public works, for the most part without home or substance, burnt the barriers, infested the streets, plundered houses, and obtained the name of brigands. The night of the 12th and 13th was spent in tumult and alarm.

The departure of Necker, which threw the capital into this state of excitement, had no less effect at Versailles and in the assembly. It caused the same astonishment and discontent. The deputies repaired early in the morning to the Salle des États; they were gloomy, but their silence arose from indignation rather than dejection. "At the opening of the session," said a deputy, "several addresses of adherence to the decrees were listened to in mournful silence by the assembly, more attentive to their own thoughts than to the addresses read." Mounier began; he exclaimed against the dismissal of ministers beloved by the nation, and the choice of their successors. He proposed an address to the king demanding their recall, showing him the dangers attendant on violent measures, the misfortunes that would follow the employment of troops, and telling him that the assembly solemnly opposed itself to an infamous national bankruptcy. At these words, the feelings of the assembly, hitherto restrained, broke out in clapping of hands, and cries of approbation. Lally-Tollendal, a friend of Necker, then came forward with a sorrowful air, and delivered a long and eloquent eulogium on the banished minister. He was listened to with the greatest interest; his grief responded to that of the public; the cause of Necker was now that of the country. The nobility itself sided with the members of the third estate, either considering the danger common, or dreading to incur the same blame as the court if it did not disapprove its conduct, or perhaps it obeyed the general impulse.

A noble deputy, the count de Virieu, set the example, and said: "Assembled for the constitution, let us make the constitution; let us tighten our mutual bonds; let us renew, confirm, and consecrate the glorious decrees of the 17th of June; let us join in the celebrated resolution made on the 20th of the same month. Let us all, yes, all, all the united orders, swear to be faithful to those illustrious decrees which now can alone save the kingdom." "*The constitution shall be made, or we will cease to be,*" added the duc de la Rochefoucauld. But this unanimity became still more confirmed when the rising of Paris, the excesses which ensued the burning of the barriers, the assembling of the electors at the Hôtel de Ville, the confusion of the capital, and the fact that citizens were ready to be attacked by the soldiers or to slaughter each other, became known to the assembly. Then one cry resounded through the hall: "Let the recollection of our momentary divisions be effaced! Let us unite our efforts for the salvation of the country!" A deputation was immediately sent to the king, composed of eighty members, among whom were all the deputies of Paris. The archbishop of Vienne, president of the assembly, was at its head. It was to represent to the king the dangers that threatened the capital, the necessity of sending away the troops, and entrusting the care of the city to a militia of citizens; and if it obtained these demands from the king, a deputation was to be sent to Paris with the consolatory intelligence. But the members soon returned with an unsatisfactory answer.

The assembly now saw that it must depend on itself, and that the projects of the court were irrevocably fixed. Far from being discouraged, it only became more firm, and immediately voted unanimously a decree proclaiming the responsibility of the present ministers of the king, and of all his counsellors, *of whatever rank they might be;* it further passed a vote of regret for Necker and the other disgraced ministers; it resolved that it would not cease to insist upon the dismissal of the troops and the establishment of a militia of citizens; it placed the public debt under the safeguard of French honour, and adhered to all its previous decrees. After these measures, it adopted a last one, not less necessary; apprehending that the Salle des États might, during the night, be occupied by a military force for the purpose of dispersing the assembly, it resolved to sit permanently till further orders. It decided that a portion of the members should sit during the night, and another relieve them early in the morning. To spare the venerable archbishop of Vienne the fatigue of a permanent presidency, a vice-president was appointed to supply his place on these extraordinary occasions. Lafayette was elected to preside over the night sittings. It passed off without a debate; the deputies remaining in their seats, observing silence, but apparently calm and serene. It was by these measures, this expression of public regret, by these decrees, this unanimous enthusiasm, this sustained good sense, this inflexible conduct, that the assembly rose gradually to a level with its dangers and its mission.

On the 13th the insurrection took at Paris a more regular character. Early in the morning the populace flocked to the Hôtel de Ville; the tocsin was sounded there and in all the churches; and drums were beat in the streets to call the citizens together. The public places soon became thronged. Troops were formed under the titles of volunteers of the Palais Royal, volunteers of the Tuileries, of the Basoche, and of the Arquebuse. The districts assembled, and each of them voted two hundred men for its defence. Arms alone were wanting; and these were eagerly sought wherever there was any hope of finding them. All that could be found at the gun-smiths and sword-cutlers were taken, receipts being sent to the owners. They applied for arms at the Hôtel de Ville. The electors who were still assembled, replied in vain that they had none; they insisted on having them. The electors then sent the head of the city, M. de Flesselles, the Prévôt des marchands, who alone knew the military state of the capital, and whose popular authority promised to be of great assistance in this difficult conjuncture. He was received with loud applause by the multitude: *"My friends,"* said he, *"I am your father; you shall be satisfied."* A permanent committee was formed at the Hôtel de Ville, to take measures for the general safety.

About the same time it was announced that the Maison des Lazaristes, which contained a large quantity of grain, had been despoiled; that the Garde- Meuble had been forced open to obtain old arms, and that the gun-smiths' shops had been plundered. The greatest excesses were apprehended from the crowd; it was let loose, and it seemed difficult to master its fury. But this was a moment of enthusiasm and disinterestedness. The mob itself disarmed suspected characters; the corn found at the Lazaristes was taken to the Halle; not a single house was plundered, and carriages and vehicles filled with provisions, furniture and utensils, stopped at the gates of the city, were taken to the Place de Grève, which became a vast depôt. Here the crowd increased every moment, shouting *Arms!* It was now about one o'clock. The provost of the merchants then announced the immediate arrival of twelve thousand guns from the manufactory of Charleville, which would soon be followed by thirty thousand more.

This appeased the people for some time, and the committee was enabled to pursue quietly its task of organizing a militia of citizens. In less than four hours the plan was drawn up, discussed, adopted, printed, and proclaimed. It was resolved that the Parisian guard should, till further orders, be increased to forty-eight thousand men. All citizens were invited to enrol their names; every district had its battalion; every battalion its leaders; the command of this army of citizens was offered to the duc d'Aumont, who required twenty-four hours to decide. In the meantime the marquis de la Salle was appointed second in command. The green cockade was then exchanged for a blue and red one, which were the colours of the city. All this was the work of a few hours. The districts gave their assent to the measures adopted by the permanent committee. The clerks of the Châtelet, those of the Palais, medical students, soldiers of the watch, and what was of still greater value, the French guards offered their services to the assembly. Patrols began to be formed, and to perambulate the streets.

The people waited with impatience the realisation of the promise of the provost of the merchants, but no guns arrived; evening approached, and they feared during the night another attack from the troops. They thought they were betrayed when they heard of an attempt to convey secretly from Paris nearly fifty cwt. of powder, which had been intercepted by the people at the barriers. But soon after some cases arrived, labelled *Artillery*. At this sight, the commotion subsided; the cases were escorted to the Hôtel de Ville, it being supposed that they contained the guns expected from Charleville. On opening them, they were found to contain old linen and pieces of wood. A cry of treachery arose on every side, mingled with murmurs and threats against the committee and the provost of the merchants. The latter apologized, declaring he had been deceived; and to gain time, or to get rid of the crowd, sent them to the Chartreux, to seek for arms. Finding none there, the mob returned, enraged and mistrustful. The committee then felt satisfied there was no other way of arming Paris, and curing the suspicions of the people, than by forging pikes; and accordingly gave orders that fifty thousand should be made immediately. To avoid the excesses of the preceding night, the town was illuminated, and patrols marched through it in every direction.

The next day, the people that had been unable to obtain arms on the preceding day, came early in the morning to solicit some from the committee, blaming its refusal and failures of the day before. The committee had sent for some in vain; none had arrived from Charleville, none were to be found at the Chartreux, and the arsenal itself was empty.

The mob, no longer satisfied with excuses, and more convinced than ever that they were betrayed, hurried in a mass to the Hôtel des Invalides, which contained a considerable depot of arms. It displayed no fear of the troops established in the Champ de Mars, broke into the Hôtel, in spite of the entreaties of the governor, M. de Sombreuil, found twenty-eight thousand guns concealed in the cellars, seized them, took all the sabres, swords, and cannon, and carried them off in triumph. The cannon were placed at the entrance of the Faubourgs, at the palace of the Tuileries, on the quays and on the bridges, for the defence of the capital against the invasion of troops, which was expected every moment.

Even during the same morning an alarm was given that the regiments stationed at Saint Denis were on the march, and that the cannon of the Bastille were pointed on the Rue Saint Antoine. The committee immediately sent to ascertain the truth; appointed bands of citizens to defend that side of the town, and sent a deputation to the governor of the Bastille, soliciting him to withdraw his cannon and engage in no act of hostility. This alarm, together with the dread which that fortress inspired, the hatred felt for the abuses it shielded, the importance of possessing so prominent a point, and of not leaving it in the power of the enemy in a moment of insurrection, drew the attention of the populace in that direction. From nine in the morning till two, the only rallying word throughout Paris was "à la Bastille! à la Bastille!" The citizens hastened thither in bands from all quarters, armed with guns, pikes, and sabres. The crowd which already surrounded it was considerable; the sentinels of the fortress were at their posts, and the drawbridges raised as in war.

A deputy of the district of Saint Louis de la Culture, named Thuriot de la Rosière, then requested a parley with De Launay, the governor. When admitted to his presence he summoned him to change the direction of the cannon. The governor replied, that the cannon had always been placed on the towers, and it was not in his power to remove them; yet, at the same time, having heard of the alarm prevalent among the Parisians, he had had them withdrawn a few paces, and taken out of the port-holes. With some difficulty Thuriot obtained permission to enter the fortress further, and examine if its condition was really as satisfactory for the town as the governor represented it to be. As he advanced, he observed three pieces of cannon pointed on the avenues leading to the open space before the fortress, and ready to sweep those who might attempt to attack it. About forty Swiss, and eighty Invalides, were under arms. Thuriot urged them, as well as the staff of the place, in the name of honour and of their country, not to act as the enemies of the people. Both officers and soldiers swore they would not make use of their arms unless attacked. Thuriot then ascended the towers, and perceived a crowd gathering in all directions, and the inhabitants of the Faubourg Saint Antoine, who were rising in a mass. The multitude without, not seeing him return, were already demanding him with great clamour. To satisfy the people, he appeared on the parapet of the fortress, and was received with loud applause from the gardens of the arsenal. He then rejoined his party, and having informed them of the result of his mission, proceeded to the committee.

But the impatient crowd now clamoured for the surrender of the Bastille. From time to time the cry arose, "The Bastille! we will have the Bastille!" At length, two men, more determined than the rest, darting from the crowd, sprang on a guardhouse, and struck at the chains of the drawbridge with heavy hatchets. The soldiers shouted to them to retire, and threatened to fire; but they continued to strike, succeeded in breaking the chains and lowering the bridge, and then rushed over it, followed by the crowd. In this way they advanced to cut the chains of the second bridge. The garrison now dispersed them with a discharge of musketry. They returned, however, to the attack, and for several hours their efforts were confined to the second bridge, the approach to which was defended by a ceaseless fire from the fortress. The mob infuriated by this obstinate resistance, tried to break in the gates with hatchets, and to set fire to the guard-house. A murderous discharge of grapeshot proceeded from the garrison, and many of the besiegers were killed and wounded. They only became the more determined, and seconded by the daring and determination of the two brave men, Elie and Hulin, who were at their head, they continued the attack with fury.

The committee of the Hôtel de Ville were in a state of great anxiety. The siege of the Bastille seemed to them a very rash enterprise. They ever and anon received intelligence of the disasters that had taken place before the fortress. They wavered between fear of the troops should they prove victorious, and that of the multitude who clamoured for ammunition to continue the siege. As they could not give what they did not possess, the mob cried treachery. Two deputations had been sent by the committee for the purpose of discontinuing hostilities, and inviting the governor to confide the keeping of the place to the citizens; but in the midst of the tumult, the cries, and the firing, they could not make themselves heard. A third was sent, carrying a drum and banner, that it might be more easily distinguished, but it experienced no better fortune: neither side would listen to anything. The assembly at the Hôtel de Ville, notwithstanding it efforts and activity, still incurred the suspicions of the populace. The provost of the merchants, especially, excited the greatest mistrust. "He has already deceived us several times during the day," said one. "He talks," said another, "of opening a trench; he only wants to gain time, to make us lose ours." Then an old man cried: "Comrades, why do you listen to traitors? Forward, follow me! In less than two hours the Bastille will be taken!"

The siege had lasted more than four hours when the French guards arrived with cannon. Their arrival changed the appearance of the combat. The garrison itself begged the governor to yield. The unfortunate De Launay, dreading the fate that awaited him, wished to blow up the fortress, and bury himself under its ruins and those of the faubourg. He went in despair towards the powder magazine, with a lighted match. The garrison stopped him, raised a white standard on the platform, and reversed the guns, in token of peace. But the assailants still continued to fight and advance, shouting, "Lower the bridges!" Through the battlements a Swiss officer proposed to capitulate, with permission to retire from the building with the honours of war. "No! no!" clamoured the crowd. The same officer proposed to lay down arms, on the promise that their lives should be spared. "Lower the bridge," rejoined the foremost of the assailants, "you shall not be injured." The gates were opened and the bridge lowered, on this assurance, and the crowd rushed into the Bastille. Those who led the multitude wished to save from its vengeance the governor, Swiss soldiers, and Invalides; but cries of "Give them up! give them up! they fired on their fellow-citizens, they deserve to be hanged!" rose on every side. The governor, a few Swiss soldiers and Invalides were torn from the protection of those who sought to defend them, and put to death by the implacable crowd.

The permanent committee knew nothing of the issue of the combat. The hall of the sittings was invaded by a furious multitude, who threatened the provost of the merchants and electors. Flesselles began to be alarmed at his position; he was pale and agitated. The object of the most violent reproaches and threats, they obliged him to go from the hall of the committee to the hall of the general assembly, where a great crowd of citizens was assembled. "Let him come; let him follow us," resounded from all sides. "This is too much!" rejoined Flesselles. "Let us go, since they request it; let us go where I am expected." They had scarcely reached the great hall, when the attention of the multitude was drawn off by shouts on the Place de Grève. They heard the cries of "Victory! victory! liberty!" It was the arrival of the conquerors of the Bastille which this announced. They themselves soon entered the hall with the most noisy and the most fearful pomp. The persons who had most distinguished themselves were carried in triumph, crowned with laurels. They were escorted by more than fifteen hundred men, with glaring eyes and dishevelled hair, with all kinds of arms, pressing one upon another, and making the flooring yield beneath their feet. One carried the keys and standard of the Bastille; another, its regulations suspended to his bayonet; a third, with horrible barbarity, raised in his bleeding hand the buckle of the governor's stock. With this parade, the procession of the conquerors of the Bastille, followed by an immense crowd that thronged the quays, entered the hall of the Hôtel de Ville to inform the committee of their triumph, and decide the fate of the prisoners who survived. A few wished to leave it to the committee, but others shouted: "No quarter for the prisoners! No quarter for the men who fired on their fellow-citizens!" La Salle, the commandant, the elector Moreau de Saint-Méry, and the brave Elie, succeeded in appeasing the multitude, and obtained a general amnesty.

It was now the turn of the unfortunate Flesselles. It is said that a letter found on De Launay proved the treachery of which he was suspected. "I am amusing the Parisians," he wrote, "with cockades and promises. Hold out till the evening, and you shall be reinforced." The mob hurried to his office. The more moderate demanded that he should be arrested and confined in the Châtelet; but others opposed this, saying that he should be conveyed to the Palais-Royal, and there tried. This decision gave general satisfaction. "To the Palais-Royal! To the Palais-Royal!" resounded from every side. "Well—be it so, gentlemen," replied Flesselles, with composure, "let us go to the Palais-Royal." So saying, he descended the steps, passed through the crowd, which opened to make way for him, and which followed without offering him any violence. But at the corner of the Quay Pelletier a stranger rushed forward, and killed him with a pistol- shot.

After these scenes of war, tumult, dispute, and vengeance, the Parisians, fearing, from some intercepted letters, that an attack would be made during the night, prepared to receive the enemy. The whole population joined in the labour of fortifying the town; they formed barricades, opened intrenchments, unpaved streets, forged pikes, and cast bullets. Women carried stones to the tops of the houses to crush the soldiers as they passed. The national guard were distributed in posts; Paris seemed changed into an immense foundry and a vast camp, and the whole night was spent under arms, expecting the conflict.

While the insurrection assumed this violent, permanent, and serious character at Paris, what was doing at Versailles? The court was preparing to realize its designs against the capital and assembly. The night of the 14th was fixed upon for their execution. The baron de Breteuil, who was at the head of the ministry, had promised to restore the royal authority in three days. Marshal de Broglie, commander of the army collected around Paris, had received unlimited powers of all kinds. On the 15th the declaration of the 23rd of June was to be renewed, and the king, after forcing the assembly to adopt it, was to dissolve it. Forty thousand copies of this declaration were in readiness to be circulated throughout the kingdom; and to meet the pressing necessities of the treasury more than a hundred millions of paper money was created. The movement in Paris, so far from thwarting the court, favoured its views. To the last moment it looked upon it as a passing tumult that might easily be suppressed; it believed neither in its perseverance nor in its success, and it did not seem possible to it that a town of citizens could resist an army.

The assembly was apprised of these projects. For two days it had sat without interruption, in a state of great anxiety and alarm. It was ignorant of the greater portion of what was passing in Paris. At one time it was announced that the insurrection was general, and that all Paris was marching on Versailles; then that the troops were advancing on the capital. They fancied they heard cannon, and they placed their ears to the ground to assure themselves. On the evening of the 14th it was announced that the king intended to depart during the night, and that the assembly would be left to the mercy of the foreign regiments. This last alarm was not without foundation. A carriage and horses were kept in readiness, and the body-guard remained booted for several days. Besides, at the Orangery, incidents truly alarming took place; the troops were prepared and stimulated for their expedition by distributions of wine and by encouragements. Everything announced that a decisive moment had arrived.

Despite the approaching and increasing danger, the assembly was unshaken, and persisted in its first resolutions. Mirabeau, who had first required the dismissal of the troops, now arranged another deputation. It was on the point of setting out, when the viscount de Noailles, a deputy, just arrived from Paris, informed the assembly of the progress of the insurrection, the pillage of the Invalides, the arming of the people, and the siege of the Bastille. Wimpfen, another deputy, to this account added that of the personal dangers he had incurred, and assured them that the fury of the populace was increasing with its peril. The assembly proposed the establishment of couriers to bring them intelligence every half hour.

M. M. Ganilh and Bancal-des-Issarts, despatched by the committee at the Hôtel de Ville as a deputation to the assembly, confirmed all they had just heard. They informed them of the measures taken by the electors to secure order and the defence of the capital; the disasters that had happened before the Bastille; the inutility of the deputations sent to the governor, and told them that the fire of the garrison had surrounded the fortress with the slain. A cry of indignation arose in the assembly at this intelligence, and a second deputation was instantly despatched to communicate these distressing tidings to the king. The first returned with an unsatisfactory answer; it was now ten at night. The king, on learning these disastrous events, which seemed to presage others still greater, appeared affected. Struggling against the part he had been induced to adopt, he said to the deputies, —"You rend my heart more and more by the dreadful news you bring of the misfortunes of Paris. It is impossible to suppose that the orders given to the troops are the cause of these disasters. You are acquainted with the answer I returned to the first deputation; I have nothing to add to it." This answer consisted of a promise that the troops of the Champ de Mars should be sent away from Paris, and of an order given to general officers to assume the command of the guard of citizens. Such measures were not sufficient to remedy the dangerous situation in which men were placed; and it neither satisfied nor gave confidence to the assembly.

Shortly after this, the deputies d'Ormesson and Duport announced to the assembly the taking of the Bastille, and the deaths of De Launay and Flesselles. It was proposed to send a third deputation to the king, imploring the removal of the troops. "No," said Clermont Tonnerre, "leave them the night to consult in; kings must buy experience as well as other men." In this way the assembly spent the night. On the following morning, another deputation was appointed to represent to the king the misfortunes that would follow a longer refusal. When on the point of starting, Mirabeau stopped it: "Tell him," he exclaimed, "that the hordes of strangers who invest us, received yesterday, visits, caresses, exhortations, and presents from the princes, princesses, and favourites; tell him that, during the night, these foreign satellites, gorged with gold and wine, predicted in their impious songs the subjection of France, and invoked the destruction of the national assembly; tell him, that in his own palace, courtiers danced to the sound of that barbarous music, and that such was the prelude to the massacre of Saint Bartholomew! Tell him that the Henry of his ancestors, whom he wished to take as his model, whose memory is honoured by all nations, sent provisions into a Paris in revolt when besieging the city himself, while the savage advisers of Louis send away the corn which trade brings into Paris loyal and starving."

But at that moment the king entered the assembly. The duke de Liancourt, taking advantage of the access his quality of master of the robes gave him, had informed the king, during the night, of the desertion of the French guard, and of the attack and taking of the Bastille. At this news, of which his councillors had kept him in ignorance, the monarch exclaimed, with surprise, "this is a revolt!" "No sire! it is a revolution." This excellent citizen had represented to him the danger to which the projects of the court exposed him; the fears and exasperations of the people, the disaffection of the troops, and he determined upon presenting himself before the assembly, to satisfy them as to his intentions. The news at first excited transports of joy. Mirabeau represented to his colleagues, that it was not fit to indulge in premature applause. "Let us wait," said he, "till his majesty makes known the good intentions we are led to expect from him. The blood of our brethren flows in Paris. Let a sad respect be the first reception given to the king by the representatives of an unfortunate people: the silence of the people is the lesson of kings."

The assembly resumed the sombre demeanour which had never left it during the three preceding days. The king entered without guards, and only attended by his brothers. He was received, at first, in profound silence; but when he told them he was *one with the nation*, and that, relying on the love and fidelity of his subjects, he had ordered the troops to leave Paris and Versailles; when he uttered the affecting words—*Eh bien, c'est moi qui me fie à vous*, general applause ensued. The assembly arose spontaneously, and conducted him back to the château.

This intelligence diffused gladness in Versailles and Paris, where the reassured people passed, by sudden transition, from animosity to gratitude. Louis XVI. thus restored to himself, felt the importance of appeasing the capital in person, of regaining the affection of the people, and of thus conciliating the popular power. He announced to the assembly that he would recall Necker, and repair to Paris the following day. The assembly had already nominated a deputation of a hundred members, which preceded the king to the capital. It was received with enthusiasm. Bailly and Lafayette, who formed part of it, were appointed, the former mayor of Paris, the latter commander-in-chief of the citizen guard. Bailly owed this recompense to his long and difficult presidency of the assembly, and Lafayette to his glorious and patriotic conduct. A friend of Washington, and one of the principal authors of American independence, he had, on his return to his country, first pronounced the name of the states-general, had joined the assembly, with the minority of the nobility, and had since proved himself one of the most zealous partisans of the revolution.

On the 27th, the new magistrates went to receive the king at the head of the municipality and the Parisian guard. "Sire," said Bailly, "I bring your majesty the keys of your good town of Paris; they are the same which were presented to Henry IV.; he had regained his people; now the people have regained their king." From the Place Louis XV. to the Hôtel de Ville, the king passed through a double line of the national guard, placed in ranks three or four deep, and armed with guns, pikes, lances, scythes, and staves. Their countenances were still gloomy; and no cry was heard but the oft-repeated shout of "Vive la Nation!" But when Louis XVI. had left his carriage and received from Bailly's hands the tri-coloured cockade, and, surrounded by the crowd without guards, had confidently entered the Hôtel de Ville, cries of "Vive le Roi!" burst forth on every side. The reconciliation was complete; Louis XVI. received the strongest marks of affection. After approving the choice of the people with respect to the new magistrates, he returned to Versailles, where some anxiety was entertained as to the success of his journey, on account of the preceding troubles. The national assembly met him in the Avenue de Paris; it accompanied him as far as the château, where the queen and her children ran to his arms.

The ministers opposed to the revolution, and all the authors of the unsuccessful projects, retired from court. The count d'Artois and his two sons, the prince de Condé, the prince de Conti, and the Polignac family, accompanied by a numerous train, left France. They settled at Turin, where the count d'Artois and the prince de Condé were soon joined by Calonne, who became their agent. Thus began the first emigration. The emigrant princes were not long in exciting civil war in the kingdom, and forming an European coalition against France.

Necker returned in triumph. This was the finest moment of his life; few men have had such. The minister of the nation, disgraced for it, and recalled for it, he was welcomed along the road from Bâle to Paris, with every expression of public gratitude and joy. His entry into Paris was a day of festivity. But the day that raised his popularity to its height put a term to it. The multitude, still enraged against all who had participated in the project of the 14th of July, had put to death, with relentless cruelty, Foulon, the intended minister, and his nephew, Berthier. Indignant at these executions, fearing that others might fall victims, and especially desirous of saving the baron de Besenval, commander of the army of Paris, under marshal de Broglie, and detained prisoner, Necker demanded a general amnesty and obtained it from the assembly of electors. This step was very imprudent, in a moment of enthusiasm and mistrust. Necker did not know the people; he was not aware how easily they suspect their chiefs and destroy their idols. They thought he wished to protect their enemies from the punishment they had incurred; the districts assembled, the legality of an amnesty pronounced by an unauthorised assembly was violently attacked, and the electors themselves revoked it. No doubt, it was advisable to calm the rage of the people, and recommend them to be merciful; but instead of demanding the liberation of the accused, the application should have been for a tribunal which would have removed them from the murderous jurisdiction of the multitude. In certain cases that which appears most humane is not really so. Necker, without gaining anything, excited the people against himself, and the districts against the electors; from that time he began to contend against the revolution, of which, because he had been for a moment its hero, he hoped to become the master. But an individual is of slight importance during a revolution which raises the masses; that vast movement either drags him on with it, or tramples him under foot; he must either precede or succumb. At no time is the subordination of men to circumstances more clearly manifested: revolutions employ many leaders, and when they submit, it is to one alone.

The consequences of the 14th of July were immense. The movement of Paris communicated itself to the provinces; the country population, imitating that of the capital, organized itself in all directions into municipalities for purposes of self-government; and into bodies of national guards for self-defence. Authority and force became wholly displaced; royalty had lost them by its defeat, the nation had acquired them. The new magistrates were alone powerful, alone obeyed; their predecessors were altogether mistrusted. In towns, the people rose against them and against the privileged classes, whom they naturally supposed enemies to the change that had been effected. In the country, the châteaux were fired and the peasantry burned the title-deeds of their lords. In a moment of victory it is difficult not to make an abuse of power. But to appease the people it was necessary to destroy abuses, in order that, they might not, while seeking to get rid of them, confound privilege with property. Classes had disappeared, arbitrary power was destroyed; with these, their old accessory, inequality, too, must be suppressed. Thus must proceed the establishment of the new order of things, and these preliminaries were the work of a single night.

The assembly had addressed to the people proclamations calculated to restore tranquillity. The Châtelet was constituted a court for trying the conspirators of the 14th of July, and this also contributed to the restoration of order by satisfying the multitude. An important measure remained to be executed, the abolition of privileges. On the night of the 4th of August, the viscount de Noailles gave the signal for this. He proposed the redemption of feudal rights, and the suppression of personal servitude. With this motion began the sacrifice of all the privileged classes; a rivalry of patriotism and public offerings arose among them. The enthusiasm became general; in a few hours the cessation of all abuses was decreed. The duke du Châtelet proposed the redemption of tithes and their conversion into a pecuniary tax; the bishop of Chartres, the abolition of the game-laws; the count de Virieu, that of the law protecting doves and pigeons. The abolition of seigneurial courts, of the purchase and sale of posts in the magistracy, of pecuniary immunities, of favouritism in taxation, of surplice money, first-fruits, pluralities, and unmerited pensions, were successively proposed and carried. After sacrifices made by individuals, came those of bodies, of towns and provinces. Companies and civic freedoms were abolished. The marquis des Blacons, a deputy of Dauphiné, in the name of his province, pronounced a solemn renunciation of its privileges. The other provinces followed the example of Dauphiné, and the towns that of the provinces. A medal was struck to commemorate the day; and the assembly decreed to Louis XVI. the title of *Restorer of French Liberty*.

That night, which an enemy of the revolution designated at the time, the Saint Bartholomew of property, was only the Saint Bartholomew of abuses. It swept away the rubbish of feudalism; it delivered persons from the remains of servitude, properties from seigneurial liabilities; from the ravages of game, and the exaction of tithes. By destroying the seigneurial courts, that remnant of private power, it led to the principle of public power; in putting an end to the purchasing posts in the magistracy, it threw open the prospect of unbought justice. It was the transition from an order of things in which everything belonged to individuals, to another in which everything was to belong to the nation. That night changed the face of the kingdom; it made all Frenchmen equal; all might now obtain public employments; aspire to the idea of property of their own, of exercising industry for their own benefit. That night was a revolution as important as the insurrection of the 14th of July, of which it was the consequence. It made the people masters of society, as the other had made them masters of the government, and it enabled them to prepare the new, while destroying the old constitution.

The revolution had progressed rapidly, had obtained great results in a very short time; it would have been less prompt, less complete, had it not been attacked. Every refusal became for it the cause of a new success; it foiled intrigue, resisted authority, triumphed over force; and at the point of time we have reached, the whole edifice of absolute monarchy had fallen to the ground, through the errors of its chiefs. The 17th of June had witnessed the disappearance of the three orders, and the states- general changed into the national assembly; with the 23rd of June terminated the moral influence of royalty; with the 14th of July its physical power; the assembly inherited the one, the people the other; finally, the 4th of August completed this first revolution. The period we have just gone over stands prominently out from the rest; in its brief course force was displaced, and all the preliminary changes were accomplished. The following period is that in which the new system is discussed, becomes established, and in which the assembly, after having been destructive, becomes constructive.

CHAPTER II

FROM THE NIGHT OF THE 4TH OF AUGUST TO THE 5TH AND 6TH OF OCTOBER, 1789

State of the constituent assembly—Party of the high clergy and nobility— Maury and Cazales—Party of the ministry and of the two chambers: Mounier, Lally-Tollendal—Popular party: triumvirate of Barnave, Duport, and Lameth—Its position—Influence of Sieyès—Mirabeau chief of the assembly at that period—Opinion to be formed of the Orleans party—Constitutional labours—Declaration of rights—Permanency and unity of the legislative body—Royal sanction—External agitation caused by it—Project of the court—Banquet of the gardes-du-corps—Insurrection of the 5th and 6th October—The king comes to reside at Paris.

The national assembly, composed of the élite of the nation, was full of intelligence, pure intentions, and projects for the public good. It was not, indeed, free from parties, or wholly unanimous; but the mass was not dominated by any man or idea; and it was the mass which, upon a conviction ever untrammelled and often entirely spontaneous, decided the deliberations and bestowed popularity. The following were the divisions of views and interests it contained within itself:—

The court had a party in the assembly, the privileged classes, who remained for a long time silent, and took but a tardy share in the debates. This party consisted of those who during the dispute as to the orders had declared against union. The aristocratic classes, notwithstanding their momentary agreement with the commons, had interests altogether contrary to those of the national party; and, accordingly, the nobility and higher clergy, who formed the Right of the assembly, were in constant opposition to it, except on days of peculiar excitement. These foes of the revolution, unable to prevent it by their sacrifices, or to stop it by their adhesion, systematically contended against all its reforms. Their leaders were two men who were not the first among them in birth or rank, but who were superior to the rest in talents. Maury and Cazalès represented, as it were, the one the clergy, and the other the nobility.

These two orators of the privileged classes, according to the intentions of their party, who put little faith in the duration of these changes, rather protested than stood on the defensive; and in all their discussions their aim was not to instruct the assembly, but to bring it into disrepute. Each introduced into his part the particular turn of his mind and character: Maury made long speeches, Cazalès lively sallies. The first preserved at the tribune his habits as a preacher and academician; he spoke on legislative subjects without understanding them, never seizing the right view of the subject, nor even that most advantageous to his party; he gave proofs of audacity, erudition, skill, a brilliant and well- sustained facility, but never displayed solidity of judgment, firm conviction, or real eloquence. The abbé Maury spoke as soldiers fight. No one could contradict oftener or more pertinaciously than he, or more flippantly substitute quotations and sophisms for reasoning, or rhetorical phrases for real bursts of feeling. He possessed much talent, but wanted the faculty which gives it life and truth. Cazalès was the opposite of Maury: he had a just and ready mind; his eloquence was equally facile, but more animated; there was candour in his outbursts, and he always gave the best reasons. No rhetorician, he always took the true side of a question that concerned his party, and left declamation to Maury. With the clearness of his views, his ardent character, and the good use he made of his talents, his only fault was that of his position; Maury, on the other hand, added the errors of his mind to those which were inseparable from the cause he espoused.

Necker and the ministry had also a party; but it was less numerous than the other, on account of its moderation. France was then divided into the privileged classes opposed to the revolution, and the people who strenuously desired it. As yet there was no place for a mediating party between them. Necker had declared himself in favour of the English constitution, and those who from ambition or conviction were of his views, rallied round him. Among these was Mounier, a man of strong mind and inflexible spirit, who considered that system as the type of representative governments; Lally-Tollendal, as decided in his views as the former, and more persuasive; Clermont-Tonnerre, the friend and ally of Mounier and Lally; in a word, the minority of the nobility, and some of the bishops, who hoped to become members of the upper chamber, should Necker's views be adopted.

The leaders of this party, afterwards called the monarchical party, wished to affect a revolution by compromise, and to introduce into France a representative government, ready formed, namely, that of England. At every point, they besought the powerful to make a compromise with the weak. Before the 14th of July they asked the court and privileged classes to satisfy the commons; afterwards, they asked the commons to agree to an arrangement with the court and the privileged classes. They thought that each ought to preserve his influence in the state; that deposed parties are discontented parties, and that a legal existence must be made for them, or interminable struggles be expected on their part. But they did not see how little their ideas were appropriate to a moment of exclusive passions. The struggle was begun, the struggle destined to result in the triumph of a system, and not in a compromise. It was a victory which had made the three orders give place to a single assembly, and it was difficult to break the unity of this assembly in order to arrive at a government of two Chambers. The moderate party had not been able to obtain this government from the court, nor were they to obtain it from the nation: to the one it had appeared too popular; for the other, it was too aristocratic.

The rest of the assembly consisted of the national party. As yet there were not observed in it men who, like Robespierre, Pétion, Buzot, etc., wished to begin a second revolution when the first was accomplished. At this period the most extreme of this party were Duport, Barnave, and Lameth, who formed a triumvirate, whose opinions were prepared by Duport, sustained by Barnave, and managed by Alexander Lameth. There was something remarkable and announcing the spirit of equality of the times, in this intimate union of an advocate belonging to the middle classes, of a counsellor belonging to the parliamentary class, and a colonel belonging to the court, renouncing the interests of their order to unite in views of the public good and popular happiness. This party at first took a more advanced position than that which the revolution had attained. The 14th of July had been the triumph of the middle class; the constituent assembly was its legislature, the national guard its armed force, the mayoralty its popular power. Mirabeau, Lafayette, Bailly, relied on this class; one was its tribune, the other its general, and the third its magistrate. Duport, Barnave, and Lameth's party were of the principles and sustained the interests of that period of the revolution; but this party, composed of young men of ardent patriotism, who entered on public affairs with superior qualities, fine talents, and elevated positions, and who joined to the love of liberty the ambition of playing a leading part, placed itself from the first rather in advance of the revolution of July the 14th. Its fulcrum within the assembly was the members of the extreme left without, in the clubs, in the nation, in the party of the people, who had co-operated on the 14th of July, and who were unwilling that the bourgeoisie alone should derive advantage from the victory. By putting itself at the head of those who had no leaders, and who being a little out of the government aspired to enter it, it did not cease to belong to this first period of the revolution; only it formed a kind of democratic opposition, even in the middle class itself, only differing from its leaders on a few unimportant points, and voting with them on most questions. It was, among these popular men, rather a patriotic emulation than a party dissension.

Duport, who was strong-minded, and who had acquired premature experience of the management of political passions, in the struggles which parliament had sustained against the ministry, and which he had chiefly directed, knew well that a people reposes the moment it has gained its rights, and that it begins to grow weak as soon as it reposes. To keep in vigour those who governed in the assembly, in the mayoralty, in the militia; to prevent public activity from slackening, and not to disband the people, whose aid he might one day require, he conceived and executed the famous confederation of the clubs. This institution, like everything that gives a great impulse to a nation, caused a great deal of good, and a great deal of harm. It impeded legal authority, when this of itself was sufficient; but it also gave an immense energy to the revolution, when, attacked on all sides, it could only save itself by the most violent efforts. For the rest, the founders of this association had not calculated all its consequences. They regarded it simply as a wheel destined to keep or put in movement the public machine, without danger, when it tended to abate or to cease its activity; they did not think they were working for the advantage of the multitude. After the flight of Varennes, this party had become too exacting and too formidable; they forsook it, and supported themselves against it with the mass of the assembly and the middle class, whose direction was left vacant by the death of Mirabeau. At this period, it was important to them speedily to fix the constitutional revolution; for to protract it would have been to bring on the republican revolution.

The mass of the assembly, we have just mentioned, abounded in just, experienced, and even superior minds. Its leaders were two men, strangers to the third estate, and adopted by it. Without the abbé Sieyès, the constituent assembly would probably have had less unity in its operation, and without Mirabeau, less energy in its conduct.

Sieyès was one of those men who create sects in an age of enthusiasm, and who exercise the ascendancy of a powerful reason in an enlightened era. Solitude and philosophical studies had matured him at an early age. His views were new, strong, and extensive, but somewhat too systematic. Society had especially been the subject of his examination; he had watched its progress, investigated its springs. The nature of government appeared to him less a question of right than a question of epoch. His vast intellect ranged the society of our days in its divisions, relations, powers, and movement. Sieyès, though of cold temperament, had the ardour which the pursuit of truth inspires, and the passion which its discovery gives; he was accordingly absolute in his views, disdaining those of others, because he considered them incomplete, and because, in his opinion, half truth was error. Contradiction irritated him; he was not communicative. Desirous of making himself thoroughly known, he could not do so with every one. His disciples imparted his systems to others, which surrounded him with a sort of mystery, and rendered him the object of a species of reverence. He had the authority which complete political science procures, and the constitution might have emerged from his head completely armed, like the Minerva of Jupiter, or the legislation of the ancients, were it not that in our days every one sought to be engaged in the task, or to criticise it. Yet, with the exception of some modifications, his plans were generally adopted, and he had in the committees more disciples than colleagues.

Mirabeau obtained in the tribune the same ascendancy as Sieyès in the committees. He was a man who only waited the occasion to become great. At Rome, in the best days of the republic, he would have been a Gracchus; in its decline, a Catiline; under the Fronde, a cardinal de Retz; and in the decrepitude of a monarchy, when such a being could only find scope for his immense faculties in agitation, he became remarkable for the vehemence of his passions, and for their punishment, a life passed in committing excesses, and suffering for them. This prodigious activity required employment; the revolution provided it. Accustomed to the struggle against despotism, irritated by the contempt of a nobility who were inferior to him, and who excluded him from their body; clever, daring, eloquent, Mirabeau felt that the revolution would be his work, and his life. He exactly corresponded to the chief wants of his time. His thought, his voice, his action, were those of a tribune. In perilous circumstances, his was the earnestness which carries away an assembly; in difficult discussions, the unanswerable sally which at once puts an end to them; with a word he prostrated ambition, silenced enmities, disconcerted rivalries. This powerful being, perfectly at his ease in the midst of agitation, now giving himself up to the impetuosity, now to the familiarities of conscious strength, exercised a sort of sovereignty in the assembly. He soon obtained immense popularity, which he retained to the last; and he whom, at his first entrance into the legislature, every eye shunned, was, at his death, received into the Pantheon, amidst the tears of the assembly; and of all France. Had it not been for the revolution, Mirabeau would have failed in realizing his destiny, for it is not enough to be great: one must live at the fitting period.

The duke of Orleans, to whom a party has been given, had but little influence in the assembly; he voted with the majority, not the majority with him. The personal attachment of some of its members, his name, the fears of the court, the popularity his opinions enjoyed, hopes rather than conspiracies had increased his reputation as a factious character. He had neither the qualities nor the defects of a conspirator; he may have aided with his money and his name popular movements, which would have taken place just the same without him, and which had another object than his elevation. It is still a common error to attribute the greatest of revolutions to some petty private manoeuvring, as if at such an epoch a whole people could be used as the instrument of one man.

The assembly had acquired the entire power; the corporations depended on it; the national guards obeyed it. It was divided into committees to facilitate its operations, and execute them. The royal power, though existing of right, was in a measure suspended, since it was not obeyed, and the assembly had to supply its action by its own. Thus, independently of committees entrusted with the preparation of its measures, it had appointed others to exercise a useful superintendence without. A committee of supply occupied itself with provisions, an important object in a year of scarcity; a committee of inquiry corresponded with the corporations and provinces; a committee of researches received informations against the conspirators of the 14th of July. But finance and the constitution, which the past crises had adjourned, were the special subjects of attention.

After having momentarily provided for the necessities of the treasury, the assembly, although now become sovereign, consulted, by examining the *cahiers*, the wishes of its constituents. It then proceeded to form its institutions with a method, a liberal and extensive spirit of discussion, which was to procure for France a constitution conformable with justice and suited to its necessities. The United States of America, at the time of its independence, had set forth in a declaration the rights of man, and those of the citizen. This will ever be the first step. A people rising from slavery feels the necessity of proclaiming its rights, even before it forms its government. Those Frenchmen who had assisted at the American revolution, and who co-operated in ours, proposed a similar declaration as a preamble to our laws. This was agreeable to an assembly of legislators and philosophers, restricted by no limits, since no institutions existed, and directed by primitive and fundamental ideas of society, since it was the pupil of the eighteenth century. Though this declaration only contained general principles, and confined itself to setting forth in maxims what the constitution was to put into laws, it was calculated to elevate the mind, and impart to the citizens a consciousness of their dignity and importance. At Lafayette's suggestion, the assembly had before commenced this discussion; but the events at Paris, and the decrees of the 4th of August, had interrupted its labours; they were now resumed, and concluded, by determining the principles which were to form the table of the new law, and which were the assumption of right in the name of humanity.

These generalities being adopted, the assembly turned its attention to the organization of the legislative power. This was one of its most important objects; it was to fix the nature of its functions, and establish its relations with the king. In this discussion the assembly had only to decide the future condition of the legislative power. Invested as it was with constituent authority, it was raised above its own decisions, and no intermediate power could suspend or prevent its mission. But what should be the form of the deliberative body in future sessions? Should it remain indivisible, or be divided into two chambers? If the latter form should be adopted, what should be the nature of the second chamber? Should it be made an aristocratic assembly, or a moderative senate? And, whatever the deliberative body might be, was it to be permanent or periodical, and should the king share the legislative power with it? Such were the difficulties that agitated the assembly and Paris during the month of September.

If we consider the position of the assembly and its ideas of sovereignty, we shall easily understand the manner in which these questions were decided. It regarded the king merely as the hereditary agent of the nation, having neither the right to assemble its representatives nor that of directing or suspending them. Accordingly, it refused to grant him the initiative in making laws and dissolving the assembly. It considered that the legislative body ought not to be dependent on the king. It moreover feared that by granting the government too strong an influence over the assembly, or by not keeping the latter always together, the prince might profit by the intervals in which he would be left alone, to encroach on the other powers, and perhaps even to destroy the new system. Therefore to an authority in constant activity, they wished to oppose an always existing assembly, and the permanence of the assembly was accordingly declared. The debate respecting its indivisibility, or its division, was very animated. Necker, Mounier, and Lally-Tollendal desired, in addition to a representative chamber, a senate, to be composed of members to be appointed by the king on the nomination of the people. They considered this as the only means of moderating the power, and even of preventing the tyranny of a single assembly. They had as partisans such members as participated in their ideas, or who hoped to form part of the upper chamber. The majority of the nobility did not wish for a house of peers, but for an aristocratic assembly, whose members it should elect. They could not agree; Mounier's party refusing to fall in with a project calculated to revive the orders, and the aristocracy refusing to accept a senate, which would confirm the ruin of the nobility. The greater portion of the deputies of the clergy and of the commons were in favour of the unity of the assembly. The popular party considered it illegal to appoint legislators for life; it thought that the upper chamber would become the instrument of the court and aristocracy, and would then be dangerous, or become useless by uniting with the commons. Thus the nobility, from dissatisfaction, and the national party, from a spirit of absolute justice, alike rejected the upper chamber.

This determination of the assembly has been the object of many reproaches. The partisans of the peerage have attributed all the evils of the revolution to the absence of that order; as if it had been possible for anybody whatsoever to arrest its progress. It was not the constitution which gave it the character it has had, but events arising from party struggles. What would the upper chamber have done between the court and the nation? If in favour of the first, it would have been unable to guide or save it; if in favour of the second, it would not have strengthened it; in either case, its suppression would have infallibly ensued. In such times, progress is rapid, and all that seeks to check it is superfluous. In England, the house of lords, although docile, was suspended during the crisis. These various systems have each their epoch; revolutions are achieved by one chamber, and end with two.

The royal sanction gave rise to great debates in the assembly, and violent clamours without. The question was as to the part of the king in the making of laws; the deputies were nearly all agreed on one point. They were determined, in admitting his right to sanction or refuse laws; but some desired that this right should be unlimited, others that it should be temporary. This, in reality, amounted to the same thing, for it was not possible for the king to prolong his refusal indefinitely, and the veto, though absolute, would only have been suspensive. But this faculty, bestowed on a single man, of checking the will of the people, appeared exorbitant, especially out of the assembly, where it was less understood.

Paris had not yet recovered from the agitation of the 14th of July; the popular government was but beginning, and the city experienced all its liberty and disorder. The assembly of electors, who in difficult circumstances had taken the place of a provisional corporation, had just been replaced. A hundred and eighty members nominated by the districts, constituted themselves legislators and representatives of the city. While they were engaged on a plan of municipal organization, each desired to command; for in France the love of liberty is almost the love of power. The committees acted apart from the mayor; the assembly of representatives arose against the committees, and the districts against the assembly of representatives. Each of the sixty districts attributed to itself the legislative power, and gave the executive power to its committees; they all considered the members of the general assembly as their subordinates, and themselves as invested with the right of annulling their decrees. This idea of the sovereignty of the principal over the delegate made rapid progress. Those who had no share in authority, formed assemblies, and then gave themselves up to discussion; soldiers debated at the Oratoire, journeymen tailors at the Colonnade, hairdressers in the Champs Élysées, servants at the Louvre; but the most animated debates took place in the Palais Royal. There were inquired into the questions that occupied the national assembly, and its discussions criticised. The dearth of provisions also brought crowds together, and these mobs were not the least dangerous.

Such was the state of Paris when the debate concerning the veto was begun. The alarm which this right conferred on the king excited, was extreme. It seemed as though the fate of liberty depended on the decision of this question, and that the veto alone would bring back the ancient system. The multitude, ignorant of the nature and limits of power, wished the assembly, on which it relied, to do all, and the king, whom it mistrusted, to do nothing. Every instrument left at the disposal of the court appeared the means of a counter-revolution. The crowds at the Palais Royal grew turbulent; threatening letters were sent to those members of the assembly, who, like Mounier, had declared in favour of the absolute veto. They spoke of dismissing them as faithless representatives, and of marching upon Versailles. The Palais Royal sent a deputation to the assembly, and required the commune to declare that the deputies were revocable, and to make them at all times dependent on the electors. The commune remained firm, rejected the demands of the Palais Royal, and took measures to prevent the riotous assemblies. The national guard supported it; this body was well disposed; Lafayette had acquired its confidence; it was becoming organised, it wore a uniform, submitted to discipline after the example of the French guard, and learned from its chief the love of order and respect for the law. But the middle class that composed it had not yet taken exclusive possession of the popular government. The multitude which was enrolled on the 14th of July, was not as yet entirely disbanded. This agitation from without rendered the debates upon the veto stormy; in this way a very simple question acquired great importance, and the ministry, perceiving how fatal the influence of an absolute decision might prove, and seeing, also, that the *unlimited veto* and the *suspensive veto* were one and the same thing, induced the king to be satisfied with the latter, and give up the former. The assembly declared that the refusal of his sanction could not be prolonged by the prince beyond two sessions; and this decision satisfied every one.

The court took advantage of the agitation in Paris to realise other projects. For some time it had influenced the king's mind. At first, he had refused to sanction the decrees of the 4th of August, although they were constitutive, and consequently he could not avoid promulgating them. After accepting them, on the remonstrances of the assembly, he renewed the same difficulties relative to the declaration of rights. The object of the court was to represent Louis XVI. as oppressed by the assembly, and constrained to submit to measures which he was unwilling to accept; it endured its situation with impatience and strove to regain its former authority. Flight was the only means, and it was requisite to legitimate it; nothing could be done in the presence of the assembly, and in the neighbourhood of Paris. Royal authority had fallen on the 23rd of June, military power on the 14th of July; there was no alternative but civil war. As it was difficult to persuade the king to this course, they waited till the last moment to induce him to flee; his hesitation caused the failure of the plan. It was proposed to retire to Metz, to Bouillé, in the midst of his army; to call around the monarch the nobility, the troops who continued faithful, the parliaments; to declare the assembly and Paris in a state of rebellion; to invite them to obedience or to force them to it; and if the ancient system could not be entirely re-established, at least to confine themselves to the declaration of the 20th of June. On the other hand, if the court had an interest in removing the king from Versailles, that it might effect something, it was the interest of the partisans of the revolution to bring him to Paris; the Orleans faction, if one existed, had an interest in driving the king to flight, by intimidating him, in the hope that the assembly would appoint its leader *lieutenant-general of the kingdom*; and, lastly, the people, who were in want of bread, wished for the king to reside at Paris, in the hope that his presence would diminish, or put a stop to the dearth of provisions. All these causes existing, an occasion was only wanting to bring about an insurrection; the court furnished this occasion. On the pretext of protecting itself against the movements in Paris, it summoned troops to Versailles, doubled the household guards, and sent for the dragoons and the Flanders regiment. All this preparation of troops gave rise to the liveliest fears; a report spread of an anti-revolutionary measure, and the flight of the king, and the dissolution of the assembly, were announced as at hand. Strange uniforms, and yellow and black cockades, were to be seen at the Luxembourg, the Palais Royal, and at the Champs Élysées; the foes of the revolution displayed a degree of joy they had not manifested for some time. The behaviour of the court confirmed these suspicions, and disclosed the object of all these preparations.

The officers of the Flanders regiment, received with anxiety in the town of Versailles, were fêted at the château, and even admitted to the queen's card tables. Endeavours were made to secure their devotion, and a banquet was given to them by the king's guards. The officers of the dragoons and the chasseurs, who were at Versailles, those of the Swiss guards, of the hundred Swiss, of the prevoté, and the staff of the national guard were invited. The theatre in the château, which was reserved for the most solemn fêtes of the court, and which, since the marriage of the second brother of the king, had only been used for the emperor Joseph II., was selected for the scene of the festival. The king's musicians were ordered to attend this, the first fête which the guards had given. During the banquet, toasts to the king and royal family were drunk with enthusiasm, while the nation was omitted or rejected. At the second course, the grenadiers of Flanders, the two bodies of Swiss, and the dragoons were admitted to witness the spectacle, and share the sentiments which animated the guests. The enthusiasm increased every moment. Suddenly the king was announced; he entered attired in a hunting dress, the queen leaning on his arm, and carrying the dauphin. Shouts of affection and devotion arose on every side. The health of the royal family was drunk, with swords drawn; and when Louis XVI. withdrew, the music played, "*O Richard! O mon roi! l'univers t'abandonne.*" The scene now assumed a very significant character; the march of the Hullans, and the profusion of wine, deprived the guests of all reserve. The charge was sounded; tottering guests climbed the boxes, as if mounting to an assault; while cockades were distributed; the tri-coloured cockade, it is said, was trampled on, and the guests then spread through the galleries of the château, where the ladies of the court loaded them with congratulations, and decorated them with ribbons and cockades.

Such was this famous banquet of the 1st of October, which the court was imprudent enough to repeat on the third. One cannot help lamenting its fatal want of foresight; it could neither submit to nor change its destiny. This assembling of the troops, so far from preventing aggression in Paris, provoked it; the banquet did not make the devotion of the soldiers any more sure, while it augmented the ill disposition of the people. To protect itself there was no necessity for so much ardour, nor for flight was there needful so much preparation; but the court never took the measure calculated to make its designs succeed, or else it only half took it, and, in order to decide, it always waited until there was no longer any time.

The news of this banquet, and the appearance of black cockades, produced the greatest sensation in Paris. From the 4th, suppressed rumours, counter-revolutionary provocations, the dread of conspiracies, indignation against the court, and increasing alarm at the dearth of provisions, all announced an insurrection; the multitude already looked towards Versailles. On the 5th, the insurrection broke out in a violent and invincible manner; the entire want of flour was the signal. A young girl, entering a guardhouse, seized a drum, and rushed through the streets beating it, and crying, "Bread! Bread!" She was soon surrounded by a crowd of women. This mob advanced towards the Hôtel de Ville, increasing as it went. It forced the guard that stood at the door, and penetrated into the interior, clamouring for bread and arms; it broke open doors, seized weapons, sounded the tocsin, and marched towards Versailles. The people soon rose *en masse*, uttering the same demand, till the cry, "To Versailles!" rose on every side. The women started first, headed by Maillard, one of the volunteers of the Bastille. The populace, the national guard, and the French guards requested to follow them. The commander, Lafayette, opposed their departure a long time, but in vain; neither his efforts nor his popularity could overcome the obstinacy of the people. For seven hours he harangued and retained them. At length, impatient at this delay, rejecting his advice, they prepared to set forward without him; when, feeling that it was now his duty to conduct as it had previously been to restrain them, he obtained his authorization from the corporation, and gave the word for departure about seven in the evening.

The excitement at Versailles was less impetuous, but quite as real; the national guard and the assembly were anxious and irritated. The double banquet of the household troops, the approbation the queen had expressed, *J'ai été enchantée de la journée de Jeudi*—the king's refusal to accept simply the Rights of Man, his concerted temporizings, and the want of provisions, excited the alarm of the representatives of the people and filled them with suspicion. Pétion, having denounced the banquets of the guards, was summoned by a royalist deputy to explain his denunciation, and make known the guilty parties. "Let it be expressly declared," exclaimed Mirabeau, "that whosoever is not king is a subject and responsible, and I will speedily furnish proofs." These words, which pointed to the queen, compelled the Right to be silent. This hostile discussion was preceded and succeeded by debates equally animated, concerning the refusal of the sanction, and the scarcity of provisions in Paris. At length, just as a deputation was despatched to the king, to require his pure and simple acceptance of the Rights of Man, and to adjure him to facilitate with all his power the supplying Paris with provisions, the arrival of the women, headed by Maillard, was announced.

Their unexpected appearance, for they had intercepted all the couriers who might have announced it, excited the terrors of the court. The troops of Versailles flew to arms and surrounded the château, but the intentions of the women were not hostile. Maillard, their leader, had recommended them to appear as suppliants, and in that attitude they presented their complaints successively to the assembly and to the king. Accordingly, the first hours of this turbulent evening were sufficiently calm. Yet it was impossible but that causes of hostility should arise between an excited mob and the household troops, the objects of so much irritation. The latter were stationed in the court of the château opposite the national guard and the Flanders regiment. The space between was filled by women and volunteers of the Bastille. In the midst of the confusion, necessarily arising from such a juxtaposition, a scuffle arose; this was the signal for disorder and conflict. An officer of the guards struck a Parisian soldier with his sabre, and was in turn shot in the arm. The national guards sided against the household troops; the conflict became warm, and would have been sanguinary, but for the darkness, the bad weather, and the orders given to the household troops first to cease firing and then to retire. But as these were accused of being the aggressors, the fury of the multitude continued for some time; their quarters were broken into, two of them were wounded, and another saved with difficulty.

During this tumult, the court was in consternation; the flight of the king was suggested, and carriages prepared; a picket of the national guard saw them at the gate of the Orangery, and, after closing the gate, compelled them to go back; moreover, the king, either ignorant of the designs of the court, or conceiving them impracticable, refused to escape. Fears were mingled with his pacific intentions, when he hesitated to repel the aggression or to take flight. Conquered, he apprehended the fate of Charles I. of England; absent, he feared that the duke of Orleans would obtain the lieutenancy of the kingdom. But, in the meantime, the rain, fatigue, and the inaction of the household troops, lessened the fury of the multitude, and Lafayette arrived at the head of the Parisian army.

His presence restored security to the court, and the replies of the king to the deputation from Paris, satisfied the multitude and the army. In a short time, Lafayette's activity, the good sense and discipline of the Parisian guard, restored order everywhere. Tranquillity returned. The crowd of women and volunteers, overcome by fatigue, gradually dispersed, and some of the national guard were entrusted with the defence of the château, while others were lodged with their companions in arms at Versailles. The royal family, reassured after the anxiety and fear of this painful night, retired to rest about two o'clock in the morning. Towards five, Lafayette, having visited the outposts which had been confided to his care, and finding the watch well kept, the town calm, and the crowds dispersed or sleeping, also took a few moments repose.

About six, however, some men of the lower class, more enthusiastic than the rest, and awake sooner than they, prowled round the château. Finding a gate open, they informed their companions, and entered. Unfortunately, the interior posts had been entrusted to the household guards, and refused to the Parisian army. This fatal refusal caused all the misfortunes of the night. The interior guard had not even been increased; the gates scarcely visited, and the watch kept as negligently as on ordinary occasions. These men, excited by all the passions that had brought them to Versailles, perceiving one of the household troops at a window, began to insult him. He fired, and wounded one of them. They then rushed on the household troops who defended the château breast to breast, and sacrificed themselves heroically. One of them had time to warn the queen, whom the assailants particularly threatened; and half dressed, she ran for refuge to the king. The tumult and danger were extreme in the château.

Lafayette, apprised of the invasion of the royal residence, mounted his horse, and rode hastily to the scene of danger. On the square he met some of the household troops surrounded by an infuriated mob, who were on the point of killing them. He threw himself among them, called some French guards who were near, and having rescued the household troops, and dispersed their assailants, he hurried to the château. He found it already secured by the grenadiers of the French guard, who, at the first noise of the tumult, had hastened and protected the household troops from the fury of the Parisians. But the scene was not over; the crowd assembled again in the marble court under the king's balcony, loudly called for him, and he appeared. They required his departure for Paris; he promised to repair thither with his family, and this promise was received with general applause. The queen was resolved to accompany him; but the prejudice against her was so strong that the journey was not without danger; it was necessary to reconcile her with the multitude. Lafayette proposed to her to accompany him to the balcony; after some hesitation, she consented. They appeared on it together, and to communicate by a sign with the tumultuous crowd, to conquer its animosity, and awaken its enthusiasm, Lafayette respectfully kissed the queen's hand; the crowd responded with acclamations. It now remained to make peace between them and the household troops. Lafayette advanced with one of these, placed his own tricoloured cockade on his hat, and embraced him before the people, who shouted *"Vivent les gardes-du-corps!"* Thus terminated this scene; the royal family set out for Paris, escorted by the army, and its guards mixed with it.

The insurrection of the 5th and 6th of October was an entirely popular movement. We must not try to explain it by secret motives, nor attribute it to concealed ambition; it was provoked by the imprudence of the court. The banquet of the household troops, the reports of flight, the dread of civil war, and the scarcity of provisions alone brought Paris upon Versailles. If special instigators, which the most careful inquiries have still left doubtful, contributed to produce this movement, they did not change either its direction or its object. The result of this event was the destruction of the ancient régime of the court; it deprived it of its guard, it removed it from the royal residence at Versailles to the capital of the revolution, and placed it under the surveillance of the people.

CHAPTER III

FROM THE 6TH OF OCTOBER, 1789, TO THE DEATH OF MIRABEAU, APRIL, 1791

Results of the events of October—Alteration of the provinces into departments—Organization of the administrative and municipal authorities according to the system of popular sovereignty and election—Finances; all the means employed are insufficient—Property of the clergy declared national—The sale of the property of the clergy leads to assignats—Civil constitution of the clergy—Religious opposition of the bishops— Anniversary of the 14th of July—Abolition of titles—Confederation of the Champ de Mars—New organization of the army—Opposition of the officers— Schism respecting the civil constitution of the clergy—Clubs—Death of Mirabeau—During the whole of this period the separation of parties becomes more decided.

The period which forms the subject of this chapter was less remarkable for events than for the gradually decided separation of parties. In proportion as changes were introduced into the state and the laws, those whose interests or opinions they injured declared themselves against them. The revolution had had as enemies, from the beginning of the states-general, the court; from the union of orders and the abolition of privileges, the nobility; from the establishment of a single assembly and the rejection of the two chambers, the ministry and the partisans of the English form of government. It had, moreover, against it since the departmental organization, the provinces; since the decree respecting the property and civil constitution of the clergy, the whole ecclesiastical body; since the introduction of the new military laws, all the officers of the army. It might seem that the assembly ought not to have effected so many changes at once, so as to have avoided making so many enemies; but its general plans, its necessities, and the very plots of its adversaries, required all these innovations.

After the 5th and 6th of October, the assembly emigrated as the court had done after the 14th of July. Mounier and Lally-Tollendal deserted it, despairing of liberty from the moment their views ceased to be followed. Too absolute in their plans, they wanted the people, after having delivered the assembly on the 14th of July, suddenly to cease acting, which was displaying an entire ignorance of the impetus of revolutions. When the people have once been made use of, it is difficult to disband them, and the most prudent course is not to contest, but to regulate intervention. Lally-Tollendal renounced his title of Frenchman, and returned to England, the land of his ancestors. Mounier repaired to Dauphiné, his native province, which he endeavoured to excite to a revolt against the assembly. It was inconsistent to complain of an insurrection, and yet to provoke one, especially when it was to the profit of another party, for his was too weak to maintain itself against the ancient régime and the revolution. Notwithstanding his influence in Dauphiné, whose former movements he had directed, Mounier was unable to establish there a centre of permanent resistance, but the assembly was thereby warned to destroy the ancient provincial organisation, which might become the frame- work of a civil war.

After the 5th and 6th of October, the national representatives followed the king to the capital, which their common presence had contributed greatly to tranquillise. The people were satisfied with possessing the king, the causes which had excited their ebullition had ceased. The duke of Orleans, who, rightly or wrongly, was considered the contriver of the insurrection, had just been sent away; he had accepted a mission to England; Lafayette was resolved to maintain order; the national guard, animated by a better spirit, acquired every day habits of discipline and obedience; the corporation, getting over the confusion of its first establishment, began to have authority. There remained but one cause of disturbance—the scarcity of provisions. Notwithstanding the zeal and foresight of the committee entrusted with the task of providing supplies, daily assemblages of the people threatened the public tranquillity. The people, so easily deceived when suffering, killed a baker called François, who was unjustly accused as a monopolist. On the 21st of October a martial law was proclaimed, authorizing the corporation to employ force to disperse the mob, after having summoned the citizens to retire. Power was vested in a class interested in maintaining order; the districts and the national guard were obedient to the assembly. Submission to the law was the prevailing passion of that epoch. The deputies on their side only aspired at completing the constitution and effecting the re-organisation of the state. They had the more reason for hastening their task, as the enemies of the assembly made use of what remained of the ancient régime, to occasion it embarrassment. Accordingly, it replied to each of their endeavours by a decree, which, changing the ancient order of things, deprived them of one of their means of attack.

It began by dividing the kingdom more equally and regularly. The provinces, which had witnessed with regret the loss of their privileges, formed small states, the extent of which was too vast, and the administration too independent. It was essential to reduce their size, change their names, and subject them to the same government. On the 22nd of December, the assembly adopted in this respect the project conceived by Sieyès, and presented by Thouret in the name of the committee, which occupied itself constantly on this subject for two months.

France was divided into eighty-three departments, nearly equal in extent and population; the departments were subdivided into districts and cantons. Their administration received a uniform and hierarchical form. The department had an administrative council composed of thirty-six members, and an executive directory composed of five members: as the names indicate, the functions of the one were to decide, and of the other to act. The district was organised in the same way; although on a smaller scale, it had a council and a directory, fewer in number, and subordinate to the superior directory and council. The canton composed of five or six parishes, was an electoral not an administrative division; the active citizens, and to be considered such it was necessary to pay taxes amounting to three days' earnings, united in the canton to nominate their deputies and magistrates. Everything in the new plan was subject to election, but this had several degrees. It appeared imprudent to confide to the multitude the choice of its delegates, and illegal to exclude them from it; this difficult question was avoided by the double election. The active citizens of the canton named electors intrusted with nominating the members of the national assembly, the administrators of the department, those of the district, and the judges of tribunals; a criminal court was established in each department, a civil court in each district, and a police-court in each canton.

Such was the institution of the department. It remained to regulate that of the corporation: the administration of this was confided to a general council and a municipality, composed of members whose numbers were proportioned to the population of the towns. The municipal officers were named immediately by the people, and could alone authorize the employment of the armed force. The corporation formed the first step of the association, the kingdom formed the last; the department was intermediate between the corporation and the state, between universal interests and purely local interests.

The execution of this plan, which organized the sovereignty of the people, which enabled all citizens to concur in the election of their magistrates, and entrusted them with their own administration, and distributed them into a machinery which, by permitting the whole state to move, preserved a correspondence between its parts, and prevented their isolation, excited the discontent of some provinces. The states of Languedoc and Brittany protested against the new division of the kingdom, and on their side the parliaments of Metz, Rouen, Bordeaux, and Toulouse rose against the operations of the assembly which suppressed the Chambres de Vacations, abolished the orders, and declared the commissions of the states incompetent. The partisans of the ancient régime employed every means to disturb its progress; the nobility excited the provinces, the parliaments took resolutions, the clergy issued mandates, and writers took advantage of the liberty of the press to attack the revolution. Its two principal enemies were the nobles and the bishops. Parliament, having no root in the nation, only formed a magistracy, whose attacks were prevented by destroying the magistracy itself, whereas the nobility and the clergy had means of action which survived the influence of the body. The misfortunes of these two classes were caused by themselves. After harassing the revolution in the assembly, they afterwards attacked it with open force— the clergy, by internal insurrections—the nobility, by arming Europe against it. They had great expectations from anarchy, which, it is true, caused France many evils, but which was far from rendering their own position better. Let us now see how the hostilities of the clergy were brought on; for this purpose we must go back a little.

The revolution had commenced with the finances, and had not yet been able to put an end to the embarrassments by which it was caused. More important objects had occupied the attention of the assembly. Summoned, no longer to defray the expenses of administration, but to constitute the state, it had suspended its legislative discussions, from time to time, in order to satisfy the more pressing necessities of the treasury. Necker had proposed provisional means, which had been adopted in confidence, and almost without discussion. Despite this zeal, he did not without displeasure see the finances considered as subordinate to the constitution, and the ministry to the assembly. A first loan of thirty millions (1,200,000l.), voted the 9th of August, had not succeeded; a subsequent loan of eighty millions (3,200,000l.), voted the 27th of the same month, had been insufficient. Duties were reduced or abolished, and they yielded scarcely anything, owing to the difficulty of collecting them. It became useless to have recourse to public confidence, which refused its aid; and in September, Necker had proposed, as the only means, an extraordinary contribution of a fourth of the revenue, to be paid at once. Each citizen was to fix his proportion himself, making use of that simple form of oath, which well expressed these first days of honour and patriotism:—"*I declare with truth.*"

Mirabeau now caused Necker to be invested with a complete financial dictatorship. He spoke of the urgent wants of the state, of the labours of the assembly which did not permit it to discuss the plan of the minister, and which at the same time prevented its examining any other; of Necker's skill, which ensured the success of his own measure; and urged the assembly to leave with him the responsibility of its success, by confidently adopting it. As some did not approve of the views of the minister, and others suspected the intentions of Mirabeau with respect to him, he closed his speech, one of the most eloquent he ever delivered, by displaying bankruptcy impending, and exclaiming, "Vote this extraordinary subsidy, and may it prove sufficient! Vote it; for if you have doubts respecting the means, you have none respecting the want, and our inability to supply it. Vote it, for the public circumstances will not bear delay, and we shall be accountable for all postponement. Beware of asking for time; misfortune never grants it. Gentlemen, on the occasion of a ridiculous motion at the Palais Royal, an absurd incursion, which had never had any importance, save in feeble imaginations, or the minds of men of ill designs and bad faith, you once heard these words, '*Catiline is at the gates of Rome, and yet they deliberate!*' And yet there were around us neither Catiline, nor perils, nor factions, nor Rome. But now bankruptcy, hideous bankruptcy, is there; it threatens to consume you, your properties, your honour, and yet you deliberate!" Mirabeau had carried away the assembly by his oratory; and the patriotic contribution was voted with unanimous applause.

But this resource had only afforded momentary relief. The finances of the revolution depended on a more daring and more vast measure. It was necessary not only to support the revolution, but to repair the immense deficit which stopped its progress, and threatened its future destiny. One way alone remained—to declare ecclesiastical property national, and to sell it for the rescue of the state. Public interest prescribed this course; and it could be done with justice, the clergy not being the proprietors, but the simple administrators of this property, devoted to religion, and not to the priests. The nation, therefore, by taking on itself the expenses of the altar, and the support of its ministers might procure and appropriate an important financial resource, and obtain a great political result.

It was important not to leave an independent body, and especially an ancient body, any longer in the state; for in a time of revolution everything ancient is hostile. The clergy, by its formidable hierarchy and its opulence, a stranger to the new changes, would have remained as a republic in the kingdom. Its form belonged to another system: when there was no state, but only bodies, each order had provided for its own regulation and existence. The clergy had its decretals, the nobility its law of fiefs, the people its corporations; everything was independent, because everything was private. But now that functions were becoming public, it was necessary to make a magistracy of the priesthood as they had made one of royalty; and, in order to make them dependent on the state, it was essential they should be paid by it, and to resume from the monarch his domains, from the clergy its property, by bestowing on each of them suitable endowments. This great operation, which destroyed the ancient ecclesiastical régime, was effected in the following manner:

One of the most pressing necessities was the abolition of tithes. As these were a tax paid by the rural population to the clergy, the sacrifice would be for the advantage of those who were oppressed by them. Accordingly, after declaring they were redeemable, on the night of the 4th of August, they were suppressed on the 11th, without providing any equivalent. The clergy opposed the measure at first, but afterwards had the good sense to consent. The archbishop of Paris gave up tithes in the name of all his brethren, and by this act of prudence he showed himself faithful to the line of conduct adopted by the privileged classes on the night of the 4th of August; but this was the extent of his sacrifices.

A short time after, the debate respecting the possession of ecclesiastical property began. Talleyrand, bishop of Autun, proposed to the clergy that they should renounce it in favour of the nation, which would employ it in defraying the expenses of worship, and liquidating its debt. He proved the justice and propriety of this measure; and he showed the great advantages which would accrue to the state. The property of the clergy amounted to several thousand millions of francs. After paying its debts, providing for the ecclesiastical services and that of hospitals, and the endowment of its ministers, sufficient would still remain to extinguish the public debt, whether permanent or annuities, and to reimburse the money paid for judicial offices. The clergy rose against this proposition. The discussion became very animated; and it was decided, in spite of their resistance, that they were not proprietors, but simple depositaries of the wealth that the piety of kings and of the faithful had devoted to religion, and that the nation, on providing for the service of public worship, had a right to recall such property. The decree which placed it at its disposal was passed on the 2nd of December, 1789.

From that moment the hatred of the clergy to the revolution broke out. At the commencement of the states-general it had been less intractable than the nobility, in order to preserve its riches; it now showed itself as opposed as they to the new régime, of which it became the most tenacious and furious foe. Yet, as the decree placed ecclesiastical property at the disposal of the nation, without, as yet, displacing it, it did not break out into opposition at once. The administration was still confided to it, and it hoped that the possessions of the church might serve as a mortgage for the debt, but would not be sold.

It was, indeed, difficult to effect the sale, which, however, could not be delayed, the treasury only subsisting on anticipations, and the exchequer, which supplied it with bills, beginning to lose all credit on account of the number it had issued.

They obtained their end, and proceeded with the new financial organisation in the following manner: The necessities of this and the following year required a sale of this property to the amount of four hundred millions of francs; to facilitate it, the corporation of Paris made considerable subscriptions, and the municipalities of the kingdom followed the example of Paris. They were to return to the treasury the equivalent of the property they received from the state to sell to private individuals; but they wanted money, and they could not deliver the amount since they had not yet met with purchasers. What was to be done? They supplied municipal notes intended to reimburse the public creditors, until they should acquire the funds necessary for withdrawing the notes. Once arrived thus far, they saw that, instead of municipal notes, it would be better to create exchequer bills, which would have a compulsory circulation, and answer the purpose of specie: this was simplifying the operation by generalising it. In this way the assignats had their origin.

This invention was of great utility to the revolution, and alone secured the sale of ecclesiastical property. The assignats, which were a means of payment for the state, became a pledge to the creditors. The latter by receiving them were not obliged to accept payment in land for what they had furnished in money. But sooner or later the assignats would fall into the hands of men disposed to realise them, and then they were to be destroyed at the same time that they ceased to be a pledge. In order that they might fulfil their design, their forced circulation was required; to render them safe, the quantity was limited to the value of the property proposed for sale; and that they might not fall by too sudden a change, they were made to bear interest. The assembly, from the moment of their issue, wished to give them all the consistency of money. It was hoped that specie concealed by distrust would immediately re-appear, and that the assignats would enter into competition with it. Mortgage made them quite as sure, and interest made them more profitable; but this interest, which was attended with much inconvenience, disappeared after the first issue. Such was the origin of the paper money issued under so much necessity, and with so much prudence, which enabled the revolution to accomplish such great things, and which was brought into discredit by causes that belonged less to its nature than to the subsequent use made of it.

When the clergy saw by a decree of the 29th of December the administration of church property transferred to the municipalities, the sale they were about to make of it to the value of four hundred millions of francs, and the creation of a paper money calculated to facilitate this spoliation, and render it definitive, it left nothing undone to secure the intervention of God in the cause of its wealth. It made a last attempt: it offered to realize in its own name the loan of four hundred millions of francs, which was rejected, because otherwise, after having decided that it was not the proprietor of church property, it would thus have again been admitted to be so. It then sought every means of impeding the operations of the municipalities. In the south, it raised catholics against protestants; in the pulpit, it alarmed consciences; in the confessional, it treated sales as sacrilegious, and in the tribune it strove to render the sentiments of the assembly suspected. It excited as much as possible religious questions for the purpose of compromising the assembly, and confounding the cause of its own interest with that of religion. The abuses and inutility of monastic vows were at this period admitted by every one, even by the clergy. At their abolition on the 13th of February, 1790, the bishop of Nancy proposed incidentally and perfidiously that the catholic religion alone should have a public worship. The assembly were indignant at the motives that suggested such a proposition, and it was abandoned. But the same motion was again brought forward in another sitting, and after stormy debates the assembly declared that from respect to the Supreme Being and the catholic religion, the only one supported at the expense of the state, it conceived it ought not to decide upon the question submitted to it.

Such was the disposition of the clergy, when, in the months of June and July, 1790, the assembly turned its attention to its internal organization. The clergy waited with impatience for this opportunity of exciting a schism. This project, the adoption of which caused so much evil, went to re-establish the church on its ancient basis, and to restore the purity of its doctrine; it was not the work of philosophers, but of austere Christians, who wished to support religion by the state, and to make them concur mutually in promoting its happiness. The reduction of bishoprics to the same number as the departments, the conformity of the ecclesiastical circumscription with the civil circumscription, the nomination of bishops by electors, who also chose deputies and administrators, the suppression of chapters, and the substitution of vicars for canons, were the chief features of this plan; there was nothing in it that attacked the dogmas or worship of the church. For a long time the bishops and other ecclesiastics had been nominated by the people; as for diocesan limits, the operation was purely material, and in no respect religious. It moreover generously provided for the support of the members of the church, and if the high dignitaries saw their revenues reduced, the curés, who formed the most numerous portion, had theirs augmented.

But a pretext was wanting, and the civil constitution of the clergy was eagerly seized upon. From the outset of the discussion, the archbishop of Aix protested against the principles of the ecclesiastical committee. In his opinion, the appointment or suspension of bishops by civil authority was opposed to discipline; and when the decree was put to the vote, the bishop of Clermont recapitulated the principles advanced by the archbishop of Aix, and left the hall at the head of all the dissentient members. The decree passed, but the clergy declared war against the revolution. From that moment it leagued more closely with the dissentient nobility. Equally reduced to the common condition, the two privileged classes employed all their means to stop the progress of reform.

The departments were scarcely formed when agents were sent by them to assemble the electors, and try new nominations. They did not hope to obtain a favourable choice, but aimed at fomenting divisions between the assembly and the departments. This project was denounced from the tribune, and failed as soon as it was made known. Its authors then went to work in another way. The period allotted to the deputies of the states-general had expired, their power having been limited to one year, according to the desire of the districts. The aristocrats availed themselves of this circumstance to require a fresh election of the assembly. Had they gained this point, they would have acquired a great advantage, and with this view they themselves appealed to the sovereignty of the people. "Without doubt," replied Chapelier, "all sovereignty rests with the people; but this principle has no application to the present case; it would be destroying the constitution and liberty to renew the assembly before the constitution is completed. This is, indeed, the hope of those who wish to see liberty and the constitution perish, and to witness the return of the distinction of orders, of prodigality in the public expenditure, and of the abuses that spring from despotism." At this moment all eyes were turned to the Right, and rested on the abbé Maury. "*Send those people to the Châtelet,*" cried the latter, sharply; "*or if you do not know them, do not speak of them.*" "The constitution," continued Chapelier, "can only be made by one assembly. Besides, the former electors no longer exist; the bailiwicks are absorbed in the departments, the orders are no longer separate. The clause respecting the limitation of power is consequently without value; it will therefore be contrary to the constitution, if the deputies do not retain their seats in this assembly; their oath commands them to continue there, and public interest requires it."

"You entangle us in sophisms," replied the abbé Maury; "how long have we been a national convention? You talk of the oath we took on the 20th of June, without considering that it cannot weaken that which we made to our constituents. Besides, gentlemen, the constitution is completed; you have, only now to declare that the king enjoys the plenitude of the executive power. We are here for the sole purpose of securing to the French nation the right of influencing its legislation, of establishing the principle that taxation shall be consented to by the people, and of securing our liberty. Yes, the constitution is made; and I will oppose every decree calculated to limit the rights of the people over their representatives. The founders of liberty ought to respect the liberty of the nation; the nation is above us all, and we destroy our authority by limiting the national authority."

The abbé Maury's speech was received with loud applause from the Right. Mirabeau immediately ascended the tribune. "It is asked," said he, "how long the deputies of the people have been a national convention? I answer, from the day when, finding the door of their session-house surrounded by soldiers, they went and assembled where they could, and swore to perish rather than betray or abandon the rights of the nation. Whatever our powers were, that day their nature was changed; and whatever powers we may have exercised, our efforts and labours have rendered them legitimate, and the adhesion of the nation has sanctified them. You all remember the saying of the great man of antiquity, who had neglected legal forms to save his country. Summoned by a factious tribune to declare whether he had observed the laws, he replied, 'I swear I have saved my country!' Gentlemen," he exclaimed, turning to the deputies of the commons, "I swear that you have saved France!"

The assembly then rose by a spontaneous movement, and declared that the session should not close till their task was accomplished.

Anti-revolutionary efforts were increasing, at the same time, without the assembly. Attempts were made to seduce or disorganize the army, but the assembly took prudent measures in this respect. It gained the affections of the troops by rendering promotion independent of the court, and of titles of nobility. The count d'Artois and the prince de Condé, who had retired to Turin after the 14th of July, corresponded with Lyons and the south; but the emigrants not having yet the external influence they afterwards acquired at Coblentz, and failing to meet with internal support, all their efforts were vain. The attempts at insurrection, originating with the clergy in Languedoc, had as little effect. They brought on some transient disturbances, but did not effect a religious war. Time is necessary to form a party; still more is required to induce it to decide on serious hostilities. A more practicable design was that of carrying off the king and conveying him to Peronne. The marquis de Favras, with the support of *Monsieur*, the king's brother, was preparing to execute it, when it was discovered. The Châtelet condemned to death this intrepid adventurer, who had failed in his enterprise, through undertaking it with too much display. The king's flight, after the events of October, could only be effected furtively, as it subsequently happened at Varennes.

The position of the court was equivocal and embarrassing. It encouraged every anti-revolutionary enterprise and avowed none; it felt more than ever its weakness and dependence on the assembly; and while desirous of throwing off the yoke, feared to make the attempt because success appeared difficult. Accordingly, it excited opposition without openly co-operating in it; with some it dreamed of the restoration of the ancient régìme, with others it only aimed at modifying the revolution. Mirabeau had been recently in treaty with it. After having been one of the chief authors of reform, he sought to give it stability by enchaining faction. His object was to convert the court to the revolution, not to give up the revolution to the court. The support he offered was constitutional; he could not offer any other; for his power depended on his popularity, and his popularity on his principles. But he was wrong in suffering it to be bought. Had not his immense necessities obliged him to accept money and sell his counsels, he would not have been more blameable than the unalterable Lafayette, the Lameths and the Girondins, who successively negotiated with it. But none of them gained the confidence of the court; it only had recourse to them in extremity. By their means it endeavoured to suspend the revolution, while by the means of the aristocracy it tried to destroy it. Of all the popular leaders, Mirabeau had perhaps the greatest ascendancy over the court, because he was the most winning, and had the strongest mind.

The assembly worked unceasingly at the constitution, in the midst of these intrigues and plots. It decreed the new judicial organization of France. All the new magistracies were temporary. Under the absolute monarchy, all powers emanated from the throne, and all functionaries were appointed by the king; under the constitutional monarchy, all powers emanating from the people, the functionaries were to be appointed by it. The throne alone was transmissible; the other powers being the property neither of a man nor of a family, were neither of life-tenure, nor hereditary. The legislation of that period depended on one sole principle, the sovereignty of the nation. The judicial functions had themselves that changeable character. Trial by jury, a democratic institution formerly common to nearly all the continent, but which in England alone had survived the encroachments of feudalism and the throne, was introduced into criminal causes. For civil causes special judges were nominated. Fixed courts were established, two courts of appeal to prevent error, and a *cour de cassation* intended to secure the preservation of the protecting forms of the law. This formidable power, when it proceeds from the throne, can only be independent by being fixed; but it must be temporary when it proceeds from the people; because, while depending on all, it depends upon no one.

In another matter, quite as important, the right of making peace or war, the assembly decided a new and delicate question, and this in a sure, just, and prompt manner, after one of the most luminous and eloquent discussions that ever distinguished its sittings. As peace and war belonged more to action than to will, it confided, contrary to the usual rule, the initiative to the king. He who was best able to judge of its fitness was to propose the question, but it was left to the legislative body to decide it.

The popular torrent, after having burst forth against the ancient regime, gradually subsided into its bed; new dykes restrained it on all sides. The government of the revolution was rapidly becoming established. The assembly had given to the new régime its monarch, its national representation, its territorial division, its armed force, its municipal and administrative power, its popular tribunals, its currency, its clergy; it had made an arrangement with respect to its debt, and it had found means to reconstruct property without injustice.

The 14th of July approached: that day was regarded by the nation as the anniversary of its deliverance, and preparations were made to celebrate it with a solemnity calculated to elevate the souls of the citizens, and to strengthen the common bonds of union. A confederation of the whole kingdom was appointed to take place in the Champ de Mars; and there, in the open air, the deputies sent by the eighty-three departments, the national representatives, the Parisian guard, and the monarch, were to take the oath to the constitution. By way of prelude to this patriotic fête, the popular members of the nobility proposed the abolition of titles; and the assembly witnessed another sitting similar to that of the 4th of August. Titles, armorial bearings, liveries, and orders of knighthood, were abolished on the 20th of June, and vanity, as power had previously done, lost its privileges.

This sitting established equality everywhere, and made things agree with words, by destroying all the pompous paraphernalia of other times. Formerly titles had designated functions; armorial bearings had distinguished powerful families; liveries had been worn by whole armies of vassals; orders of knighthood had defended the state against foreign foes, Europe against Islamism; but now, nothing of this remained. Titles had lost their truth and their fitness; nobility, after ceasing to be a magistracy, had even ceased to be an ornament; and power, like glory, was henceforth to spring from plebeian ranks. But whether the aristocracy set more value on their titles than on their privileges, or whether they only awaited a pretext for openly declaring themselves, this last measure, more than any other, decided the emigration and its attacks. It was for the nobility what the civil constitution had been for the clergy, an occasion, rather than a cause of hostility.

The 14th of July arrived, and the revolution witnessed few such glorious days—the weather only did not correspond with this magnificent fête. The deputies of all the departments were presented to the king, who received them with much affability; and he, on his part, met also with the most touching testimonies of love, but as a constitutional king. "Sire," said the leader of the Breton deputation, kneeling on one knee, and presenting his sword, "I place in your hands the faithful sword of the brave Bretons: it shall only be reddened by the blood of your foes." Louis XVI. raised and embraced him, and returned the sword. "It cannot be in better hands than in those of my brave Bretons," he replied; "I have never doubted their loyalty and affection; assure them that I am the father and brother, the friend of all Frenchmen." "Sire," returned the deputy, "every Frenchman loves, and will continue to love you, because you are a citizen- king."

The confederation was to take place in the Champ de Mars. The immense preparations were scarcely completed in time; all Paris had been engaged for several weeks in getting the arrangements ready by the 14th. At seven in the morning, the procession of electors, of the representatives of the corporation, of the presidents of districts, of the national assembly, of the Parisian guard, of the deputies of the army, and of the federates of the departments, set out in complete order from the site of the Bastille. The presence of all these national corps, the floating banners, the patriotic inscriptions, the varied costumes, the sounds of music, the joy of the crowd, rendered the procession a most imposing one. It traversed the city, and crossed the Seine, amidst a volley of artillery, over a bridge of boats, which had been thrown across it the preceding day. It entered the Champ de Mars under a triumphal arch, adorned with patriotic inscriptions. Each body took the station assigned it in excellent order, and amidst shouts of applause.

The vast space of the Champ de Mars was inclosed by raised seats of turf, occupied by four hundred thousand spectators. An antique altar was erected in the middle; and around it, on a vast amphitheatre, were the king, his family, the assembly, and the corporation. The federates of the departments were ranged in order under their banners; the deputies of the army and the national guards were in their ranks, and under their ensigns. The bishop of Autun ascended the altar in pontifical robes; four hundred priests in white copes, and decorated with flowing tricoloured sashes, were posted at the four corners of the altar. Mass was celebrated amid the sounds of military music; and then the bishop of Autun blessed the oriflamme, and the eighty-three banners.

A profound silence now reigned in the vast inclosure, and Lafayette, appointed that day to the command in chief of all the national guards of the kingdom, advanced first to take the civic oath. Borne on the arms of grenadiers to the altar of the country, amidst the acclamations of the people, he exclaimed with a loud voice, in his own name, and that of the federates and troops: "We swear eternal fidelity to the nation, the law, and the king; to maintain to the utmost of our power the constitution decreed by the national assembly, and accepted by the king; and to remain united with every Frenchman by the indissoluble ties of fraternity."

Forthwith the firing of cannon, prolonged cries of "Vive la nation!" "Vive le roi!" and sounds of music, mingled in the air. The president of the national assembly took the same oath, and all the deputies repeated it with one voice. Then Louis XVI. rose and said: "I, king of the French, swear to employ all the power delegated to me by the constitutional act of the state, in maintaining the constitution decreed by the national assembly and accepted by me." The queen, carried away by the enthusiasm of the moment, rose, lifted up the dauphin in her arms, and showing him to the people, exclaimed: "Behold my son, he unites with me in the same sentiments." At that moment the banners were lowered, the acclamations of the people were heard, and the subjects believed in the sincerity of the monarch, the monarch in the affection of the subjects, and this happy day closed with a hymn of thanksgiving.

The fêtes of the confederation were protracted for some days. Illuminations, balls, and sports were given by the city of Paris to the deputies of the departments. A ball took place on the spot where had stood, a year before, the Bastille; gratings, fetters, ruins, were observed here and there, and on the door was the inscription, *"Ici on danse,"* a striking contrast with the ancient destination of the spot. A contemporary observes: "They danced indeed with joy and security on the ground where so many tears had been shed; where courage, genius, and innocence had so often groaned; where so often the cries of despair had been stifled." A medal was struck to commemorate the confederation; and at the termination of the fêtes the deputies returned to their departments.

The confederation only suspended the hostility of parties. Petty intrigues were resumed in the assembly as well as out of doors. The duke of Orleans had returned from his mission, or, more strictly speaking, from his exile. The inquiry respecting the events of the 5th and 6th of October, of which he and Mirabeau were accused as the authors, had been conducted by the Châtelets inquiry, which had been suspended, was now resumed. By this attack the court again displayed its want of foresight; for it ought to have proved the accusation or not to have made it. The assembly having decided on giving up the guilty parties, had it found any such, declared there was no ground for proceeding; and Mirabeau, after an overwhelming outburst against the whole affair, obliged the Right to be silent, and thus arose triumphantly from an accusation which had been made expressly to intimidate him.

They attacked not only a few deputies but the assembly itself. The court intrigued against it, but the Right drove this to exaggeration. "We like its decrees," said the abbé Maury; "we want three or four more of them." Hired libellists sold, at its very doors, papers calculated to deprive it of the respect of the people; the ministers blamed and obstructed its progress. Necker, still haunted by the recollection of his former ascendancy, addressed to it memorials, in which he opposed its decrees and gave it advice. This minister could not accustom himself to a secondary part: he would not fall in with the abrupt plans of the assembly, so entirely opposed to his ideas of gradual reform. At length, convinced or weary of the inutility of his efforts, he left Paris, after resigning, on the 4th of September, 1790, and obscurely traversed those provinces which a year before he had gone through in triumph. In revolutions, men are easily forgotten, for the nation sees many in its varied course. If we would not find them ungrateful, we must not cease for an instant to serve according to their own desire.

On the other hand, the nobility which had found a new subject of discontent in the abolition of titles, continued its anti-revolutionary efforts. As it did not succeed in exciting the people, who, from their position, found the recent changes very beneficial, it had recourse to means which it considered more certain; it quitted the kingdom, with the intention of returning thither with all Europe as its armed ally; but while waiting till a system of emigration could be organised, while waiting for the appearance of foreign foes to the revolution, it continued to arouse enemies to it in the interior of the kingdom. The troops, as we have before observed, had already for some time been tampered with in various ways. The new military code was favourable to the soldiers; promotion formerly granted to the nobility was now granted to seniority. Most of the officers were attached to the ancient régime, nor did they conceal the fact. Compelled to take what had become the common oath, the oath of fidelity to the nation, the law, and the king, some left the army, and increased the number of emigrants, while others endeavoured to win the soldiers over to their party.

General Bouillé was of this number. After having long refused to take the civic oath, he did so at last with this intention. He had a numerous body of troops under his command near the northern frontier; he was clever, resolute, attached to the king, opposed to the revolution, such as it had then become, though the friend of reform; a circumstance that afterwards brought him into suspicion at Coblentz. He kept his army isolated from the citizens, that it might remain faithful, and that it might not be infected with the spirit of insubordination which they communicated to the troops. By skilful management, and the ascendancy of a great mind, he also succeeded in retaining the confidence and attachment of his soldiers. It was not thus elsewhere. The officers were the objects of a general dislike; they were accused of diminishing the pay, and having no concern for the great body of the troops. The prevailing opinions had also something to do with this dissatisfaction. These combined causes led to revolts among the men; that of Nancy, in August, 1790, produced great alarm, and became almost the signal of a civil war. Three regiments, those of Châteauvieux, Maître-de-camp, and the King's own, rebelled against their chiefs. Bouillé was ordered to march against them; he did so at the head of the garrison and national guard of Metz. After an animated skirmish, he subdued them. The assembly congratulated him; but Paris, which saw in Bouillé a conspirator, was thrown into fresh agitation at this intelligence. Crowds collected, and the impeachment of the ministers who had given orders to Bouillé to march upon Nancy was clamorously demanded. Lafayette, however, succeeded in allaying this ebullition, supported by the assembly, which, finding itself placed between a counter- revolution and anarchy, opposed both with equal wisdom and courage.

The aristocracy triumphed at the sight of the difficulties which perplexed the assembly. They imagined that it would be compelled to be dependent on the multitude, or deprive itself entirely of its support; and in either case the return to the ancient régime appeared to them short and easy. The clergy had its share in this work. The sale of church property, which it took every means to impede, was effected at a higher price than that fixed. The people, delivered from tithes and reassured as to the national debt, were far from listening to the angry suggestions of the priests; they accordingly made use of the civil constitution of the clergy to excite a schism. We have seen that this decree of the assembly did not affect either the discipline or the creed of the church. The king sanctioned it on the 26th of December; but the bishops, who sought to cover their interests with the mantle of religion, declared that it encroached on the spiritual authority. The pope, consulted as to this purely political measure, refused his assent to it, which the king earnestly sought, and encouraged the opposition of the priests. The latter decided that they would not concur in the establishment of the civil constitution; that those of them who might be suppressed would protest against this uncanonical act, that every bishopric created without the concurrence of the pope should be null, and that the metropolitans should refuse institution to bishops appointed according to civil forms.

The assembly strengthened this league by attempting to frustrate it. If, contrary to their real desire, it had left the dissentient priests to themselves, they would not have found the elements of a religious war. But the assembly decreed that the ecclesiastics should swear fidelity to the nation, the law, and the king, and to maintain the civil constitution of the clergy. Refusal to take this oath was to be attended by the substitution of others in their bishoprics and cures. The assembly hoped that the higher clergy from interest, and the lower clergy from ambition, would adopt this measure.

The bishops, on the contrary, thought that all the ecclesiastics would follow their example, and that by refusing to swear, they would leave the state without public worship, and the people without priests. The result satisfied the expectations of neither party; the majority of the bishops and curés of the assembly refused to take the oath, but a few bishops and many curés took it. The dissentient incumbents were deprived, and the electors nominated successors to them, who received canonical institution from the bishops of Autun and Lida. But the deprived ecclesiastics refused to abandon their functions, and declared their successors intruders, the sacraments administred by them null, and all Christians who should venture to recognise them excommunicated. They did not leave their dioceses; they issued charges, and excited the people to disobey the laws; and thus an affair of private interest became first a matter of religion and then a matter of party. There were two bodies of clergy, one constitutional, the other refractory; they had each its partisans, and treated each other as rebels and heretics. According to passion or interest, religion became an instrument or an obstacle; and while the priests made fanatics the revolution made infidels. The people, not yet infected with this malady of the upper classes, lost, especially in towns, the faith of their fathers, from the imprudence of those who placed them between the revolution and their religion. "The bishops," said the marquis de Ferrières, who will not be suspected, "refused to fall in with any arrangements, and by their guilty intrigues closed every approach to reconciliation; sacrificing the catholic religion to an insane obstinacy, and a discreditable attachment to their wealth."

Every party sought to gain the people; it was courted as sovereign. After attempting to influence it by religion, another means was employed, that of the clubs. At that period, clubs were private assemblies, in which the measures of government, the business of the state, and the decrees of the assembly were discussed; their deliberations had no authority, but they exercised a certain influence. The first club owed its origin to the Breton deputies, who already met together at Versailles to consider the course of proceeding they should take. When the national representatives were transferred from Versailles to Paris, the Breton deputies and those of the assembly who were of their views held their sittings in the old convent of the Jacobins, which subsequently gave its name to their meetings. It did not at first cease to be a preparatory assembly, but as all things increase in time, the Jacobin club did not confine itself to the influencing the assembly; it sought also to influence the municipality and the people, and received as associates members of the municipality and common citizens. Its organization became more regular, its action more powerful; its sittings were regularly reported in the papers; it created branch clubs in the provinces, and raised by the side of legal power another power which first counselled and then conducted it.

The Jacobin club, as it lost its primitive character and became a popular assembly, had been forsaken by part of its founders. The latter established another society on the plan of the old one, under the name of the club of '89. Sieyès, Chapelier, Lafayette, La Rochefoucauld directed it, as Lameth and Barnave directed that of the Jacobins. Mirabeau belonged to both, and by both was equally courted. These clubs, of which the one prevailed in the assembly and the other amongst the people, were attached to the new order of things, though in different degrees. The aristocracy sought to attack the revolution with its own arms; it opened royalist clubs to oppose the popular clubs. That first established under the name of the *Club des Impartiaux* could not last because it addressed itself to no class opinion. Reappearing under the name of the *Club Monarchique*, it included among its members all those whose views it represented. It sought to render itself popular with the lower classes, and distributed bread; but far from accepting its overtures, the people considered such establishments as a counter-revolutionary movement. The people disturbed their sittings, and obliged them several times to change their place of meeting. At length, the municipal authority found itself obliged, in January, 1791, to close this club, which had been the cause of several riots.

The distrust of the multitude was extreme; the departure of the king's aunts, to which it attached an exaggerated importance, increased its uneasiness, and led it to suppose another departure was preparing. These suspicions were not unfounded, and they occasioned a kind of rising which the anti-revolutionists sought to turn to account by carrying off the king. This project failed, owing to the resolution and skill of Lafayette. While the crowd went to Vincennes to demolish the dungeon which they said communicated with the Tuileries, and would favour the flight of the king, more than six hundred persons armed with swords and daggers entered the Tuileries to compel the king to flee. Lafayette, who had repaired to Vincennes to disperse the multitude, returned to quell the anti- revolutionists of the château, after dissipating the mob of the popular party, and by this second expedition he regained the confidence which his first had lost him.

The attempt rendered the escape of Louis XVI. more feared than ever. Accordingly, a short time after, when he wished to go to Saint Cloud, he was prevented by the crowd and even by his own guard, despite the efforts of Lafayette, who endeavoured to make them respect the law, and the liberty of the monarch. The assembly on its side, after having decreed the inviolability of the prince, after having regulated his constitutional guard, and assigned the regency to the nearest male heir to the crown, declared that his flight from the kingdom would lead to his dethronement. The increasing emigration, the open avowal of its objects, and the threatening attitude of the European cabinets, all cherished the fear that the king might adopt such a determination.

Then, for the first time, the assembly sought to stop the progress of emigration by a decree; but this decree was a difficult question. If they punished those who left the kingdom, they violated the maxims of liberty, rendered sacred by the declaration of rights; if they did not raise obstacles to emigration, they endangered the safety of France, as the nobles merely quitted it in order to invade it. In the assembly, setting aside those who favoured emigration, some looked only at the right, others only at the danger, and every one sided with or opposed the restrictive law, according to his mode of viewing the subject. Those who desired the law, wished it to be mild; but only one law could be practicable at such a moment, and the assembly shrank from enacting it. This law, by the arbitrary order of a committee of three members, was to pronounce a sentence of civil death on the fugitive, and the confiscation of his property. "The horror expressed on the reading of this project," cried Mirabeau, "proves that this is a law worthy of being placed in the code of Draco, and cannot find place among the decrees of the national assembly of France. I proclaim that I shall consider myself released from every oath of fidelity I have made towards those who may be infamous enough to nominate a dictatorial commission. The popularity I covet, and which I have the honour to enjoy, is not a feeble reed; I wish it to take root in the soil, based on justice and liberty." The exterior position was not yet sufficiently alarming for the adoption of such a measure of safety and revolutionary defence.

Mirabeau did not long enjoy the popularity which he imagined he was so sure of. That was the last sitting he attended. A few days afterwards he terminated a life worn out by passions and by toil. His death, which happened on the 2nd of March, 1791, was considered a public calamity; all Paris attended his funeral; there was a general mourning throughout France, and his remains were deposited in the receptacle which had just been consecrated *aux grands hommes*, in the name of *la patrie reconnaissante*. No one succeeded him in power and popularity; and for a long time, in difficult discussions, the eyes of the assembly would turn towards the seat from whence they had been accustomed to hear the commanding eloquence which terminated their debates. Mirabeau, after having assisted the revolution with his daring in seasons of trial, and with his powerful reasoning since its victory, died seasonably. He was revolving vast designs; he wished to strengthen the throne, and consolidate the revolution; two attempts extremely difficult at such a time. It is to be feared that royalty, if he had made it independent, would have put down the revolution; or, if he had failed, that the revolution would have put down royalty. It is, perhaps, impossible to convert an ancient power into a new order; perhaps a revolution must be prolonged in order to become legitimate, and the throne, as it recovers, acquire the novelty of the other institutions.

From the 5th and 6th of October, 1789, to the month of April, 1791, the national assembly completed the reorganization of France; the court gave itself up to petty intrigues and projects of flight; the privileged classes sought for new means of power, those which they formerly possessed having been successively taken from them. They took advantage of all the opportunities of disorder which circumstances furnished them with, to attack the new régime and restore the old, by means of anarchy. At the opening of the law courts the nobility caused the Chambres de vacations to protest; when the provinces were abolished, it made the orders protest. As soon as the departments were formed, it tried new elections; when the old writs had expired, it sought the dissolution of the assembly; when the new military code passed, it endeavoured to excite the defection of the officers; lastly, all these means of opposition failing to effect the success of its designs, it emigrated, to excite Europe against the revolution. The clergy, on its side, discontented with the loss of its possessions still more than with the ecclesiastical constitution, sought to destroy the new order by insurrections, and to bring on insurrections by a schism. Thus it was during this epoch that parties became gradually disunited, and that the two classes hostile to the revolution prepared the elements of civil and foreign war.

CHAPTER IV

FROM APRIL, 1791, TO THE 3OTH SEPTEMBER. THE END OF THE CONSTITUENT ASSEMBLY

Political state of Europe before the French revolution—System of alliance observed by different states—General coalition against the revolution— Motives of each power—Conference of Mantua, and circular of Pavia—Flight to Varennes—Arrest of the king—His suspension—The republican party separate, for the first time, from the party of the constitutional monarchy—The latter re-establishes the king—Declaration of Pilnitz—The king accepts the constitution—End of the constituent assembly—Opinion of it.

The French revolution was to change the political state of Europe, to terminate the strife of kings among themselves, and to commence that between kings and people. This would have taken place much later had not the kings themselves provoked it. They sought to suppress the revolution, and they extended it; for by attacking it they were to render it victorious. Europe had then arrived at the term of the political system which swayed it. The political activity of the several states after being internal under the feudal government, had become external under the monarchical government. The first period terminated almost at the same time among all the great nations of Europe. Then kings who had so long been at war with their vassals, because they were in contact with them, encountered each other on the boundaries of their kingdoms, and fought. As no domination could become universal, neither that of Charles V. nor that of Louis XIV., the weak always uniting against the strong, after several vicissitudes of superiority and alliance, a sort of European equilibrium was established. In order to appreciate ulterior events, I propose to consider this equilibrium before the revolution.

Austria, England, and France had been, from the peace of Westphalia to the middle of the eighteenth century, the three great powers of Europe. Interest had leagued the two first against the third. Austria had reason to dread the influence of France in the Netherlands; England feared it on the sea. Rivalry of power and commerce often set them at variance, and they sought to weaken or plunder each other. Spain, since a prince of the house of Bourbon had been on the throne, was the ally of France against England. This, however, was a fallen power: confined to a corner of the continent, oppressed by the system of Philip II., deprived by the Family Compact of the only enemy that could keep it in action, by sea only had it retained any of its ancient superiority. But France had other allies on all sides of Austria: Sweden on the north; Poland and the Porte on the east; in the south of Germany, Bavaria; Prussia on the west; and in Italy, the kingdom of Naples. These powers, having reason to dread the encroachments of Austria, were naturally the allies of her enemy. Piedmont, placed between the two systems of alliance, sided, according to circumstances and its interests, with either. Holland was united with England or with France, as the party of the stadtholders or that of the people prevailed in the republic. Switzerland was neutral.

In the last half of the eighteenth century, two powers had risen in the north, Russia and Prussia. The latter had been changed from a simple electorate into an important kingdom, by Frederick-William, who had given it a treasure and an army; and by his son Frederick the Great, who had made use of these to extend his territory. Russia, long unconnected with the other states, had been more especially introduced into the politics of Europe by Peter I. and Catharine II. The accession of these two powers considerably modified the ancient alliances. In concert with the cabinet of Vienna, Russia and Prussia had executed the first partition of Poland in 1772; and after the death of Frederick the Great, the empress Catharine and the emperor Joseph united in 1785 to effect that of European Turkey.

The cabinet of Versailles, weakened since the imprudent and unfortunate Seven Years' War, had assisted at the partition of Poland without opposing it, had raised no obstacle to the fall of the Ottoman empire, and even allowed its ally, the republican party in Holland, to sink under the blows of Prussia and England, without assisting it. The latter powers had in 1787 re-established by force the hereditary, stadtholderate of the United Provinces. The only act which did honour to French policy, was the support it had happily given to the emancipation of North America. The revolution of 1789, while extending the moral influence of France, diminished still more its diplomatic influence.

England, under the government of young Pitt, was alarmed in 1788 at the ambitious projects of Russia, and united with Holland and Prussia to put an end to them. Hostilities were on the point of commencing when the emperor Joseph died, in February, 1790, and was succeeded by Leopold, who in July accepted the convention of Reichenbach. This convention, by the mediation of England, Russia, and Holland, settled the terms of the peace between Austria and Turkey, which was signed definitively, on the 4th of August, 1791, at Sistova; it at the same time provided for the pacification of the Netherlands. Urged by England and Prussia, Catharine II. also made peace with the Porte at Jassy, on the 29th of December, 1791. These negotiations, and the treaties they gave rise to, terminated the political struggles of the eighteenth century, and left the powers free to turn their attention to the French Revolution.

The princes of Europe, who had hitherto had no enemies but themselves, viewed it in the light of a common foe. The ancient relations of war and of alliance, already overlooked during the Seven Years' War, now ceased entirely: Sweden united with Russia, and Prussia with Austria. There was nothing now but the kings on one side, and people on the other, waiting for the auxiliaries which its example, or the faults of princes might give it. A general coalition was soon formed against the French revolution. Austria engaged in it with the hope of aggrandizement, England to avenge the American war, and to preserve itself from the spirit of the revolution; Prussia to strengthen the threatened absolute power, and profitably to engage its unemployed army; the German states to restore feudal rights to some of their members who had been deprived of them, by the abolition of the old régime in Alsace; the king of Sweden, who had constituted himself the champion of arbitrary power, to re-establish it in France, as he had just done in his own country; Russia, that it might execute without trouble the partition of Poland, while the attention of Europe was directed elsewhere; finally, all the sovereigns of the house of Bourbon, from the interest of power and family attachments. The emigrants encouraged them in these projects, and excited them to invasion. According to them, France was without an army, or at least without leaders, destitute of money, given up to disorder, weary of the assembly, disposed to the ancient régime, and without either the means or the inclination to defend itself. They flocked in crowds to take a share in the promised short campaign, and formed into organized bodies under the prince de Condé, at Worms, and the count d'Artois, at Coblentz.

The count d'Artois especially hastened the determination of the cabinets. The emperor Leopold was in Italy, and the count repaired to him, with Calonne as minister, and the count Alphonse de Durfort, who had been his mediator with the court of the Tuileries, and who had brought him the king's authority to treat with Leopold. The conference took place at Mantua, and the count de Durfort returned, and delivered to Louis XVI. in the name of the emperor, a secret declaration, in which was announced to him the speedy assistance of the coalition. Austria was to advance thirty- five thousand men on the frontier of Flanders; the German states, fifteen thousand on Alsace; the Swiss, fifteen thousand on the Lyonese frontier; the king of Sardinia, fifteen thousand on that of Dauphiné; Spain was to augment its army in Catalonia to twenty thousand; Prussia was well disposed in favour of the coalition, and the king of England was to take part in it as elector of Hanover. All these troops were to move at the same time, at the end of July; the house of Bourbon was then to make a protest, and the powers were to publish a manifesto; until then, however, it was essential to keep the design secret, to avoid all partial insurrection, and to make no attempt at flight. Such was the result of the conferences at Mantua on the 20th May, 1791.

Louis XVI., either from a desire not to place himself entirely at the mercy of foreign powers, or dreading the ascendency which the count d'Artois, should he return at the head of the victorious emigrants, would assume over the government he had established, preferred restoring the government alone. In general Bouillé he had a devoted and skilful partisan, who at the same time condemned both emigration and the assembly, and promised him refuge and support in his army. For some time past, a secret correspondence had taken place between him and the king. Bouillé prepared everything to receive him. He established a camp at Montmedy, under the pretext of a movement of hostile troops on the frontier; he placed detachments on the route the king was to take, to serve him for escort, and as a motive was necessary for these arrangements, he alleged that of protecting the money despatched for the payment of the troops.

The royal family on its side made every preparation for departure; very few persons were informed of it, and no measures betrayed it. Louis XVI. and the queen, on the contrary, pursued a line of conduct calculated to silence suspicion; and on the night of the 20th of June, they issued at the appointed hour from the château, one by one, in disguise. In this way they eluded the vigilance of the guard, reached the Boulevard, where a carriage awaited them, and took the road to Châlons and Montmedy.

On the following day the news of this escape threw Paris into consternation; indignation soon became the prevailing sentiment; crowds assembled, and the tumult increased. Those who had not prevented the flight were accused of favouring it. Neither Bailly nor Lafayette escaped the general mistrust. This event was considered the precursor of the invasion of France, the triumph of the emigrants; the return of the ancient régime, and a long civil war. But the conduct of the assembly soon restored the public mind to calmness and security. It took every measure which so difficult a conjuncture required. It summoned the ministers and authorities to its bar; calmed the people by a proclamation; used proper precautions to secure public tranquillity; seized on the executive power, commissioned Montmorin, the minister of foreign affairs, to inform the European powers of its pacific intentions; sent commissioners to secure the favour of the troops, and receive their oath, no longer made in the name of the king, but in that of the assembly, and lastly, issued an order through the departments for the arrest of any one attempting to leave the kingdom. "Thus, in less than four hours," says the marquis de Ferrières, "the assembly was invested with every kind of power. The government went on; public tranquillity did not experience the slightest shock; and Paris and France learned from this experience, so fatal to royalty, that the monarch is almost always a stranger to the government that exists in his name."

Meantime Louis XVI. and his family were drawing near the termination of their journey. The success of the first days' journeys, the increasing distance from Paris, rendered the king less reserved and more confident; he had the imprudence to show himself, was recognised, and arrested at Varennes on the 21st. The national guard were under arms instantly; the officers of the detachments posted by Bouillé sought in vain to rescue the king; the dragoons and hussars feared or refused to support them. Bouillé, apprised of this fatal event, hastened himself at the head of a regiment of cavalry. But it was too late; on reaching Varennes, he found that the king had left it several hours before; his squadrons were tired, and refused to advance. The national guard were on all sides under arms, and after the failure of his enterprise, he had no alternative but to leave the army and quit France.

The assembly, on hearing of the king's arrest, sent to him, as commissioners, three of its members, Pétion, Latour-Maubourg, and Barnave. They met the royal family at Epernay and returned with them. It was during this journey, that Barnave, touched by the good sense of Louis XVI., the fascinations of Marie Antoinette, and the fate of this fallen family, conceived for it an earnest interest. From that day he gave it his assiduous counsel and support. On reaching Paris the royal party passed through an immense crowd, which expressed neither applause nor murmurs, but observed a reproachful silence.

The king was provisionally suspended: he had had a guard set over him, as had the queen; and commissioners were appointed to question him. Agitation pervaded all parties. Some desired to retain the king on the throne, notwithstanding his flight; others maintained, that he had abdicated by condemning, in a manifesto addressed to the French on his departure, both the revolution, and the acts which had emanated from him during that period, which he termed a time of captivity.

The republican party now began to appear. Hitherto it had remained either dependent or hidden, because it had been without any existence of its own, or because it wanted a pretext for displaying itself. The struggle, which lay at first between the assembly and the court, then between the constitutionalists and the aristocrats, and latterly among the constitutionalists themselves, was now about to commence between the constitutionalists and the republicans. In times of revolution such is the inevitable course of events. The partisans of the order newly established then met and renounced differences of opinion which were detrimental to their cause, even while the assembly was all powerful, but which had become highly perilous, now that the emigration party threatened it on the one hand, and the multitude on the other. Mirabeau was no more. The Centre, on which this powerful man had relied, and which constituted the least ambitious portion of the assembly, the most attached to principles, might by joining the Lameths, re-establish Louis XVI. and constitutional monarchy, and present a formidable opposition to the popular ebullition.

This alliance took place; the Lameth party came to an understanding with André and the principal members of the Centre, made overtures to the court, and opened the club of the Feuillants in opposition to that of the Jacobins. But the latter could not want leaders; under Mirabeau, they had contended against Mounier; under the Lameths against Mirabeau; under Pétion and Robespierre, they contended against the Lameths. The party which desired a second revolution had constantly supported the most extreme actors in the revolution already accomplished, because this was bringing within its reach the struggle and the victory. At this period, from subordinate it had become independent; it no longer fought for others and for opinions not its own, but for itself, and under its own banner. The court, by its multiplied faults, its imprudent machinations, and, lastly, by the flight of the monarch, had given it a sort of authority to avow its object; and the Lameths, by forsaking it, had left it to its true leaders.

The Lameths, in their turn, underwent the reproaches of the multitude, which saw only their alliance with the court, without examining its conditions. But supported by all the constitutionalists, they were strongest in the assembly; and they found it essential to establish the king as soon as possible, in order to put a stop to a controversy which threatened the new order, by authorizing the public party to demand the abolition of the royal power while its suspension lasted. The commissioners appointed to interrogate Louis XVI. dictated to him a declaration, which they presented in his name to the assembly, and which modified the injurious effect of his flight. The reporter declared, in the name of the seven committees entrusted with the examination of this great question, that there were no grounds for bringing Louis XVI. to trial, or for pronouncing his dethronement. The discussion which followed this report was long and animated; the efforts of the republican party, notwithstanding their pertinacity, were unsuccessful. Most of their orators spoke; they demanded deposition or a regency; that is to say, popular government, or an approach towards it. Barnave, after meeting all their arguments, finished his speech with these remarkable words: "Regenerators of the empire, follow your course without deviation. You have proved that you had courage to destroy the abuses of power; you have proved that you possessed all that was requisite to substitute wise and good institutions in their place; prove now that you have the wisdom to protect and maintain these. The nation has just given a great evidence of its strength and courage; it has displayed, solemnly and by a spontaneous movement, all that it could oppose to the attacks which threatened it. Continue the same precautions; let our boundaries, let our frontiers be powerfully defended. But while we manifest our power, let us also prove our moderation; let us present peace to the world, alarmed by the events which take place amongst us; let us present an occasion for triumph to all those who in foreign lands have taken an interest in our revolution. They cry to us from all parts: you are powerful; be wise, be moderate, therein will lie your highest glory. Thus will you prove that in various circumstances you can employ various means, talents, and virtues."

The assembly sided with Barnave. But to pacify the people, and to provide for the future safety of France, it decreed that the king should be considered as abdicating, *de facto*, if he retracted the oath he had taken to the constitution; if he headed an army for the purpose of making war upon the nation, or permitted any one to do so in his name; and that, in such case, become a simple citizen, he would cease to be inviolable, and might be responsible for acts committed subsequent to his abdication.

On the day that this decree was adopted by the assembly, the leaders of the republican party excited the multitude against it. But the hall in which it sat was surrounded by the national guard, and it could not be assailed or intimidated. The agitators unable to prevent the passing of the decree, aroused the people against it. They drew up a petition, in which they denied the competency of the assembly; appealed from it to the sovereignty of the nation, treated Louis XVI. as deposed since his flight, and demanded a substitute for him. This petition, drawn up by Brissot, author of the *Patriote Français*, and president of the *Comité des Recherches* of Paris, was carried, on the 17th of July, to the altar of the country in the Champ de Mars: an immense crowd flocked to sign it. The assembly, apprized of what was taking place, summoned the municipal authorities to its bar, and directed them to preserve the public tranquillity. Lafayette marched against the crowd, and in the first instance succeeded in dispersing it without bloodshed. The municipal officers took up their quarters in the Invalides; but the same day the crowd returned in greater numbers, and with more determination. Danton and Camille Desmoulins harangued them from the altar of the country. Two Invalides, supposed to be spies, were massacred and their heads stuck on pikes. The insurrection became alarming. Lafayette again repaired to the Champ de Mars, at the head of twelve hundred of the national guard. Bailly accompanied him, and had the red banner unfurled. The crowd was then summoned to disperse in the name of the law; it refused to retire, and, contemning authority, shouted, "Down with the red flag!"

and assailed the national guard with stones. Lafayette ordered his men to fire, but in the air. The crowd was not intimidated with this, and resumed the attack; compelled by the obstinacy of the insurgents, Lafayette then ordered another discharge, a real and effective one. The terrified multitude fled, leaving many dead on the field. The disturbances now ceased, order was restored; but blood had flown, and the people never forgave Bailly or Lafayette the cruel necessity to which the crowd had driven them. This was a regular combat, in which the republican party, not as yet sufficiently strong or established, was defeated by the constitutional monarchy party. The attempt of the Champ de Mars was the prelude of the popular movements which led to the 10th of August.

While this was passing in the assembly and at Paris, the emigrants, whom the flight of Louis XVI. had elated with hope, were thrown into consternation at his arrest. *Monsieur*, who had fled at the same time as his brother, and with better fortune, arrived alone at Brussels with the powers and title of regent. The emigrants thenceforth relied only on the assistance of Europe; the officers quitted their colours; two hundred and ninety members of the assembly protested against its decrees; in order to legitimatize invasion, Bouillé wrote a threatening letter, in the inconceivable hope of intimidating the assembly, and at the same time to take upon himself the sole responsibility of the flight of Louis XVI.; finally, the emperor, the king of Prussia, and the count d'Artois met at Pilnitz, where they made the famous declaration of the 27th of August, preparatory to the invasion of France, and which, far from improving the condition of the king, would have imperilled him, had not the assembly, in its wisdom, continued to follow out its new designs, regardless at once of the clamours of the multitude at home, and the foreign powers.

In the declaration of Pilnitz, the sovereigns considered the cause of Louis XVI. as their own. They required that he should be free to go where he pleased, that is to say, to repair to them that he should be restored to his throne; that the assembly should be dissolved, and that the princes of the empire having possessions in Alsace, should be reinstated in their feudal rights In case of refusal, they threatened France with a war in which all the powers who were guarantees for the French monarchy would concur. This declaration, so far from discouraging, only served to irritate the assembly and the people. Men asked only another, what right the princes of Europe had to interfere in the government of France; by what right they gave orders to great people, and imposed conditions upon it; and since the sovereigns appealed to force, the people of France prepared to resist them. The frontiers were put in a state of defence; the hundred thousand men of the national guard were enrolled, and they awaited in calm serenity the attack of the enemy, well convinced that the French people, on their own soil and in a state of revolution, would be invincible.

Meantime, the assembly approached the close of its labours; civil relations, public taxation, the nature of crimes, their prosecution, and their punishment, had been by it as wisely regulated as were the public and constitutional relations of the country. Equality had been introduced into the laws of inheritance, into taxation, and into punishments; nothing remained but to unite all the constitutional decrees into a body and submit them to the king for his approval. The assembly was growing weary of its labours and of its dissensions; the people itself, who in France ever become tired of that which continues beyond a certain time, desired a new national representation; the convocation of the electoral colleges was therefore fixed for the 5th of August. Unfortunately, the members of the present assembly could not form part of the succeeding one; this had been decided before the flight to Varennes. In this important question, the assembly had been drawn away by the rivalry of some, the disinterestedness of others, the desire for anarchy on the part of the aristocrats, and of domination on that of the republicans. Vainly did Duport exclaim: "While every one is pestering us with new principles of all sorts, how is it overlooked that stability is also a principle of government? Is France, whose children are so ardent and changeable, to be exposed every two years to a revolution in her laws and opinions?" This was the desire of the privileged classes and the Jacobins, though with different views. In all such matters, the constituent assembly was deceived or overruled; when the ministry was in question, it decided, in opposition to Mirabeau, that no deputy could hold office; on the subject of re-election, it decided, in opposition to its own members, that it could not take place; in the same spirit, it prohibited their accepting, for four years, any post offered them by the prince. This mania of disinterestedness soon induced Lafayette to divest himself of the command of the national guard, and Bailly to resign the mayoralty. Thus this remarkable epoch entirely annihilated the constituent body.

The collection of the constitutional decrees into one body led to the idea of revising them. But this idea of revision gave great dissatisfaction, and was almost of no effect; it was not desirable to render the constitution more aristocratic by after measures, lest the multitude should require it to be made more popular. To limit the sovereignty of the nation, and, at the same time, not to overlook it, the assembly declared that France had a right to revise its constitution, but that it was prudent not to exercise this right for thirty years.

The act of the constitution was presented to the king by sixty deputies; the suspension being taken off, Louis XVI. resumed the exercise of his power; and the guard the law had given him was placed under his own command. Thus restored to freedom, the constitution was submitted to him. After examining it for several days, "I accept the constitution," he wrote to the assembly; "I engage to maintain it at home, to defend it from all attacks from abroad; and to cause its execution by all the means it places at my disposal. I declare, that being informed of the attachment of the great majority of the people to the constitution, I renounce my claim to assist in the work, and that being responsible to the nation alone, no other person, now that I have made this renunciation, has a right to complain."

This letter excited general approbation. Lafayette demanded and procured an amnesty in favour of those who were under prosecution for favouring the king's flight, or for proceedings against the revolution. Next day the king came in person to accept the constitution in the assembly. The populace attended him thither with acclamations; he was the object of the enthusiasm of the deputies and spectators, and he regained that day the confidence and affection of his subjects. The 29th of September was fixed for the closing of the assembly; the king was present; his speech was often interrupted by applause, and when he said, "For you, gentlemen, who during a long and arduous career have displayed such indefatigable zeal, there remains one duty to fulfil when you have returned to your homes over the country: to explain to your fellow-citizens the true meaning of the laws you have made for them; to counsel those who slight them; to clarify and unite all opinions by the example you shall afford of your love of order, and of submission to the laws." Cries of "Yes! yes!" were uttered by all the deputies with one common voice. "I rely on your being the interpreters of my sentiments to your fellow-citizens." "Yes! yes!" "Tell them all that the king will always be their first and most faithful friend; that he needs their love; that he can only be happy with them and by their means; the hope of contributing to their happiness will sustain my courage, as the satisfaction of having succeeded will be my sweetest recompense"

"It is a speech worthy of Henry IV.," said a voice, and the king left the hall amidst the loudest testimonials of love.

Then Thouret, in a loud voice, and addressing the people, exclaimed: "The constituent assembly pronounces its mission accomplished, and that its sittings now terminate." Thus closed this first and glorious assembly of the nation. It was courageous, intelligent, just, and had but one passion —a passion for law. It accomplished, in two years, by its efforts, and with indefatigable perseverance, the greatest revolution ever witnessed by one generation of men. Amidst its labours, it repressed despotism and anarchy, by frustrating the conspiracies of the aristocracy and maintaining the multitude in subordination. Its only fault was that it did not confide the guidance of the revolution to those who were its authors; it divested itself of power, like those legislators of antiquity who exiled themselves from their country after giving it a constitution. A new assembly did not apply itself to consolidating its work, and the revolution, which ought to have been finished, was recommenced.

The constitution of 1791 was based on principles adapted to the ideas and situation of France. This constitution was the work of the middle class, then the strongest; for, as is well known, the predominant force ever takes possession of institutions. When it belongs to one man alone, it is despotism; when to several, it is privilege; when to all, it is right; this last state is the limit, as it is the origin, of society. France had at length attained it, after passing through feudalism, which was the aristocratic institution, and absolute power, which was the monarchical institution. Equality was consecrated among the citizens, and delegation recognised among the powers; such were to be, under the new system, the condition of men, and the form of government.

In this constitution the people was the source of all powers, but it exercised none; it was entrusted only with election in the first instance, and its magistrates were selected by men chosen from among the enlightened portions of the community. The latter constituted the assembly, the law courts, the public offices, the corporations, the militia, and thus possessed all the force and all the power of the state. It alone was fit to exercise them, because it alone had the intelligence necessary for the conduct of government. The people was not yet sufficiently advanced to participate in power, consequently, it was only by accident, and in the most casual and evanescent manner, that power fell into its hands; but it received civic education, and was disciplined to government in the primary assemblies, according to the true aim of society, which is not to confer its advantages as a patrimony on one particular class, but to make all share in them, when all are capable of acquiring them. This was the leading characteristic of the constitution of 1791; as each, by degrees, became competent to enjoy the right, he was admitted to it; it extended its limits with the extension of civilization, which every day calls a greater number of men to the administration of the state. In this way it had established true equality, whose real character is admissibility, as that of inequality is exclusion. In rendering power transferable by election, it made it a public magistracy; whilst privilege, in rendering it hereditary by transmission, makes it private property.

The constitution of 1791 established homogeneous powers which corresponded among themselves, and thus reciprocally restrained each other; still, it must be confessed, the royal authority was too subordinate to popular power. It is never otherwise: sovereignty, from whatever source derived, gives itself a feeble counterpoise when it limits itself. A constituent assembly enfeebles royalty; a king who is a legislator limits the prerogatives of an assembly.

This constitution was, however, less democratic than that of the United States, which had been practicable, despite the extent of the territory, proving that it is not the form of institutions, but the assent which they obtain, or the dissent which they excite, which permits or hinders their establishment. In a new country, after a revolution of independence, as in America, any constitution is possible; there is but one hostile party, that of the metropolis, and when that is overcome, the struggle ceases, because defeat leads to its expulsion. It is not so with social revolutions among nations who have long been in existence. Changes attack interests, interests form parties, parties enter into contest, and the more victory spreads the greater grows opposition. This is what happened in France. The work of the constituent assembly perished less from its defects than from the attacks of faction. Placed between the aristocracy and the multitude, it was attacked by the one and invaded by the other. The latter would not have become sovereign, had not civil war and the foreign coalition called for its intervention and aid. To defend the country, it became necessary that it should govern it; then it effected its revolution, as the middle class had effected its own. It had its 14th of July in the 10th of August; its constituent assembly, the convention; its government, which was the committee of public safety; yet, as we shall see, without emigration there would have been no republic.

THE NATIONAL LEGISLATIVE ASSEMBLY

CHAPTER V

FROM THE 1ST OF OCTOBER, 1791, TO THE 21ST OF SEPTEMBER, 1792

Early relations between the legislative assembly and the king—State of parties: the Feuillants rely on the middle classes, the Girondists on the people—Emigration and the dissentient clergy; decree against them; the king's veto—Declarations of war—Girondist ministry; Dumouriez, Roland— Declaration of war against the king of Hungary and Bohemia—Disasters of our armies; decree for a camp of reserve for twenty thousand men at Paris; decree of banishment against the nonjuring priests; veto of the king; fall of the Girondist ministry—Petition of insurgents of the 20th of June to secure the passing of the decrees and the recall of the ministers—Last efforts of the constitutional party—Manifesto of the duke of Brunswick— Events of the 10th of August—Military insurrection of Lafayette against the authors of the events of the 10th of August; it fails—Division of the assembly and the new commune; Danton—Invasion of the Prussians— Massacres of the 2nd of September—Campaign of the Argonne—Causes of the events under the legislative assembly.

The new assembly opened its session on the 1st October, 1791. It declared itself immediately *the national legislative assembly*. From its first appearance, it had occasion to display its attachment to the actual state of things, and the respect it felt for the authors of French liberty. The book of the constitution was solemnly presented to it by the archivist Camus, accompanied by twelve of the oldest members of the national representation. The assembly received the constitutional act standing and uncovered, and on it took the oath, amidst the acclamations of the people who occupied the tribunes, *"to live free or perish!"* A vote of thanks was given by it to the members of the constituent assembly, and it then prepared to commence its labours.

But its first relations with the king had not the same character of union and confidence. The court, doubtless hoping to regain under the legislative, the superior position which it had lost under the constituent assembly, did not employ sufficient management towards a susceptible and anxious popular authority, which was then considered the first of the state. The assembly sent a deputation of sixty of its members to the king to announce its opening. The king did not receive them in person, and sent word by the minister of justice that he could not give them audience till noon on the following day. This unceremonious dismissal, and the indirect communication between the national representatives and the prince, by means of a minister, hurt the deputation excessively. Accordingly, when the audience took place, Duchastel, who headed the deputation, said to him laconically: "Sire, the national legislative assembly is sitting; we are deputed to inform you of this." Louis XVI. replied still more drily: "I cannot visit you before Friday." This conduct of the court towards the assembly was impolitic, and little calculated to conciliate the affection of the people.

The assembly approved of the cold manner assumed by the deputation, and soon indulged in an act of reprisal. The ceremony with which the king was to be received among them was arranged according to preceding laws. A fauteuil in the form of a throne was reserved for him; they used towards him the titles of *sire* and *majesty*, and the deputies, standing and uncovered on his entrance, were to sit down, put on their hats, and rise again, following with deference all the movements of the prince. Some restless and exaggerated minds considered this condescension unworthy of a sovereign assembly. The deputy Grangeneuve required that the words *sire* and *majesty* should be replaced by the "more constitutional and finer" title of *king of the French*. Couthon strongly enforced this motion, and proposed that a simple fauteuil should be assigned to the king, exactly like the president's. These motions excited some slight disapprobation on the part of a few members, but the greater number received them eagerly. "It gives me pleasure to suppose," said Guadet, "that the French people will always venerate the simple fauteuil upon which sits the president of the national representatives, much more than the gilded fauteuil where sits the head of the executive power. I will say nothing, gentlemen, of the titles of *sire* and *majesty*. It astonishes me to find the national assembly deliberating whether they shall be retained. The word *sire* signifies seigneur; it belonged to the feudal system, which has ceased to exist. As for the term *majesty*, it should only be employed in speaking of God and of the people."

The previous question was demanded, but feebly; these motions were put to the vote, and carried by a considerable majority. Yet, as this decree appeared hostile, the constitutional opinion pronounced itself against it, and censured this too excessive rigour in the application of principles. On the following day those who had demanded the previous question moved that the decisions of the day before should be abandoned. A report was circulated, at the same time, that the king would not enter the assembly if the decree were maintained; and the decree was revoked. These petty skirmishes between two powers who had to fear usurpations, assumptions, and more especially ill will between them, terminated here on this occasion, and all recollection of them was effaced by the presence of Louis XVI. in the legislative body, where he was received with the greatest respect and the most lively enthusiasm.

General pacification formed the chief topic of his speech. He pointed out to the assembly the subjects that ought to attract its attention,— finance, civil law, commerce, trade, and the consolidation of the new government; he promised to employ his influence to restore order and discipline in the army, to put the kingdom in a state of defence, and to diffuse ideas respecting the French revolution, calculated to re-establish a good understanding in Europe. He added the following words, which were received with much applause: "Gentlemen, in order that your important labours, as well as your zeal, may produce all the good which may be expected from them, a constant harmony and unchanging confidence should reign between the legislative body and the king. The enemies of our peace seek but too eagerly to disunite us, but let love of country cement our union, and let public interest make us inseparable! Thus public power may develop itself without obstacle; government will not be harassed by vain fears; the possessions and faith of each will be equally protected, and no pretext will remain for any one to live apart from a country where the laws are in vigour, and where the rights of all are respected." Unfortunately there were two classes, without the revolution, that would not enter into composition with it, and whose efforts in Europe and the interior of France were to prevent the realization of these wise and pacific words. As soon as there are displaced parties in a state, a struggle will result, and measures of hostility must be taken against them. Accordingly, the internal troubles, fomented by non-juring priests, the military assemblings of emigrants, and the preparations for the coalition, soon drove the legislative assembly further than the constitution allowed, and than it itself had proposed.

The composition of this assembly was completely popular. The prevailing ideas being in favour of the revolution, the court, nobility, and clergy had exercised no influence over the elections. There were not in this assembly, as in the preceding, partisans of absolute power and of privilege. The two fractions of the Left who had separated towards the close of the constituent assembly were again brought face to face; but no longer in the same proportion of number and strength. The popular minority of the previous assembly became the majority in this. The prohibition against electing representatives already tried, the necessity of choosing deputies from those most distinguished by their conduct and opinions, and especially the active influence of the clubs, led to this result. Opinions and parties soon became known. As in the constituent assembly there was a Right, a Centre, a Left, but of a perfectly different character.

The Right, composed of firm and absolute constitutionalists, composed the Feuillant party. Its principal speakers were Dumas, Ramond, Vaublanc, Beugnot, etc. It had some relations with the court, through Barnave, Duport, and Alexander Lameth, who were its former leaders; but whose counsels were rarely followed by Louis XVI., who gave himself up with more confidence to the advice of those immediately around him. Out of doors, it supported itself on the club of the Feuillants and upon the bourgeoisie. The national guard, the army, the directory of the department, and in general all the constituted authorities, were favourable to it. But this party, which no longer prevailed in the assembly, soon lost a post quite as essential, that of the municipality, which was occupied by its adversaries of the Left.

These formed the party called Girondist, and which in the revolution only formed an intermediate party between the middle class and the multitude. It had then no subversive project; but it was disposed to defend the revolution in every way, and in this differed from the constitutionalists who would only defend it with the law. At its head were the brilliant orators of the Gironde,[1] who gave their name to the party, Vergniaud, Guadet, Gensonné, and the Provençal Isnard, who had a style of still more impassioned eloquence than theirs. Its chief leader was Brissot, who, a member of the corporation of Paris during the last session, had subsequently become a member of the assembly. The opinions of Brissot, who advocated a complete reform; his great activity of mind, which he developed at once in the journal the *Patriote*, in the tribune of the assembly, and at the club of the Jacobins; his exact and extensive knowledge of the position of foreign powers, gave him great ascendancy at the moment of a struggle between parties, and of a war with Europe. Condorcet possessed influence of another description; he owed this to his profound ideas, to his superior reason, which almost procured him the place of Sieyès in this second revolutionary generation. Pétion, of a calm and determined character, was the active man of this party. His tranquil brow, his fluent elocution, his acquaintance with the people, soon procured for him the municipal magistracy, which Bailly had discharged for the middle class.

The Left had in the assembly the nucleus of a party more extreme than itself, and the members of which, such as Chabot, Bazire, Merlin, were to the Girondists what Pétion, Buzot, Robespierre, had been to the Left of the constituent. This was the commencement of the democratic faction which, without, served as auxiliary to the Gironde, and which managed the clubs and the multitude. Robespierre in the society of the Jacobins, where he established his sway after leaving the assembly; Danton, Camille Desmoulins, and Fabre-d'Eglantine at the Cordeliers, where they had founded a club of innovators more extreme than the Jacobins, composed of men of the bourgeoisie; the brewer Santerre in the faubourgs, where the popular power lay; were the true chiefs of this faction, which depended on one whole class, and aspired at founding its own régime.

The Centre of the legislative assembly was sincerely attached to the new order of things. It had almost the same opinions, the same inclination for moderation as the Centre of the constituent assembly; but its power was very different: it was no longer at the head of a class established, and by the aid of which it could master all the extreme parties. Public dangers, making the want of exalted opinions and parties from without again felt, completely annulled the Centre. It was soon won over to the strongest side, the fate of all moderate parties, and the Left swayed it.

The situation of the assembly was very difficult. Its predecessor had left it parties which it evidently could not pacify. From the beginning of the session it was obliged to turn its attention to these, and that in opposing them. Emigration was making an alarming progress: the king's two brothers, the prince de Condé and the duke de Bourbon, had protested against Louis XVI. accepting the consti-

[1] The name of the river Garonne, after its confluence with the Dordogne.

tutional act, that is, against the only means of accommodation; they had said that the king could not alienate the rights of the ancient monarchy; and their protest, circulating throughout France, had produced a great effect on their partisans. Officers quitted the armies, the nobility their châteaux, whole companies deserted to enlist on the frontiers. Distaffs were sent to those who wavered; and those who did not emigrate were threatened with the loss of the position when the nobility should return victorious. In the Austrian Low Countries and the bordering electorates, there was formed what was called *La France extérieure*. The counterrevolution was openly preparing at Brussels, Worms, and Coblentz, under the protection and even with the assistance of foreign courts. The ambassadors of the emigrants were received, while those of the French government were dismissed, ill received, or even thrown into prison, as in the case of M. Duveryer. French merchants and travellers suspected of patriotism and attachment to the revolution were scouted throughout Europe. Several powers had declared themselves without disguise: of this number were Sweden, Russia, and Spain; the latter at that time being governed by the marquis Florida- Blanca, a man entirely devoted to the emigrant party. At the same time, Prussia kept its army prepared for war: the lines of the Spanish and Sardinian troops increased on our Alpine and Pyrenean frontiers, and Gustavus was assembling a Swedish army.

The dissentient ecclesiastics left nothing undone which might produce a diversion in favour of the emigrants at home. "Priests, and especially bishops," says the marquis de Ferrières, "employed all the resources of fanaticism to excite the people, in town and country, against the civil constitution of the clergy." Bishops ordered the priests no longer to perform divine service in the same church with the constitutional priests, for fear the people might confound the two. "Independently," he adds, "of circular letters written to the curés, instructions intended for the people were circulated through the country. They said that the sacraments could not be effectually administered by the constitutional priests, whom they called *Intruders*, and that every one attending their ministrations became by their presence guilty of a mortal sin; that those who were married by Intruders, were not married; that they brought a curse upon themselves and upon their children; that no one should have communication with them, or with those separated from the church; that the municipal officers who installed them, like them became apostates; that the moment of their installation all bell-ringers and sextons ought to resign their situations.... These fanatical addresses produced the effect which the bishops expected. Religious disturbances broke out on all sides."

Insurrection more especially broke out in Calvados, Gevaudan, and La Vendée. These districts were ill-disposed towards the revolution, because they contained few of the middle and intelligent classes, and because the populace, up to that time, had been kept in a state of dependence on the nobility and clergy. The Girondists, taking alarm, wished to adopt rigorous measures against emigration and the dissentient priests, who attacked the new order of things. Brissot proposed putting a stop to emigration, by giving up the mild system hitherto observed towards it. He divided the emigrants into three classes:—1st. The principal leaders, and at their head the brothers of the king. 2ndly. Public functionaries who forsook their posts and country, and sought to entice their colleagues. 3rdly. Private individuals, who, to preserve life, or from an aversion to the revolution, or from other motives, left their native land, without taking arms against it. He required that severe laws should be put in force against the first two classes; but thought it would be good policy to be indulgent towards the last. With respect to non-juring ecclesiastics and agitators, some of the Girondists proposed to confine themselves to a stricter surveillance; others thought there was only one safe line of conduct to be pursued towards them: that the spirit of sedition could only be quelled by banishing them from the country. "All attempts at conciliation," said the impetuous Isnard, "will henceforth be in vain. What, I ask, has been the consequence of these reiterated pardons? The daring of your foes has increased with your indulgence; they will only cease to injure you when deprived of the means of doing so. They must be conquerors or conquered. On this point all must agree; the man who will not see this great truth is, in my opinion, politically blind."

The constitutionalists were opposed to all these measures; they did not deny the danger, but they considered such laws arbitrary. They said, before everything it was necessary to respect the constitution, and from that time to confine themselves to precautionary measures; that it was sufficient to keep on the defensive against the emigrants; and to wait, in order to punish the dissentient priests, till they discovered actual conspiracies on their part. They recommended that the law should not be violated even towards enemies, for fear that once engaging in such a course, it should be impossible to arrest that course, and so the revolution be lost, like the ancient régime, through its injustice. But the assembly, which deemed the safety of the state more important than the strict observance of the law, which saw danger in hesitation, and which, moreover, was influenced by passions which lead to expeditious measures, was not stopped by these considerations. With common consent it again, on the 30th of October, passed a decree relative to the eldest brother of the king, Louis-Stanislaus-Xavier. This prince was required, in the terms of the constitution, to return to France in two months, or at the expiration of that period he would be considered to have forfeited his rights as regent. But agreement ceased as to the decrees against emigrants and priests. On the 9th of November the assembly resolved, that the French gathered together beyond the frontiers were suspected of conspiracy against their country; that if they remained assembled on the 1st of January, 1792, they would be treated as conspirators, be punishable by death, and that after condemnation to death for contumacy, the proceeds of their estates were to be confiscated to the nation, always without prejudice to the rights of their wives, children, and lawful creditors. On the 29th of the same month it passed a similar decree respecting the dissentient priests. They were obliged to take the civic oath, under pain of being deprived of their pensions and suspected of revolt against the law. If they still refused they were to be closely watched; and if any religious disturbances took place in their parishes, they were to be taken to the chief town of the department, and if found to have taken any part in exciting disobedience, they were liable to imprisonment.

The king sanctioned the first decree respecting his brother; he put his veto on the other two. A short time before he had disavowed emigration by public measures, and he had written to the emigrant princes recalling them to the kingdom. He invited them to return in the name of the tranquillity of France, and of the attachment and obedience they owed to him as their brother and their king. "I shall," said he, in concluding the letter, "always be grateful to you for saving me the necessity of acting in opposition to you, through the invariable resolution I have made to maintain what I have announced." These wise invitations had led to no result: but Louis XVI., while he condemned the conduct of the emigrants, would not give his consent to the measures taken against them. In refusing his sanction he was supported by the friends of the constitution and the directory of the department. This support was not without use to him, at a time when, in the eyes of the people, he appeared to be an accomplice of emigration, when he provoked the dissatisfaction of the Girondists, and separated himself from the assembly. He should have united closely with it, since he invoked the constitution against the emigrants in his letters, and against the revolutionist, by the exercise of his prerogative. His position could only become strong by sincerely falling in with the first revolution, and making his own cause one with that of the bourgeoisie.

But the court was not so resigned; it still expected better times, and was thus prevented from pursuing an invariable line of conduct, and induced to seek grounds for hope in every quarter. Now and then disposed to favour the intervention of foreign powers, it continued to correspond with Europe; it intrigued with its ministers against the popular party, and made use of the Feuillants against the Girondists, though with much distrust. At this period its chief resource was in the petty schemes of Bertrand de Moleville, who directed the council; who had established a *French club*, the members of which he paid; who purchased the applause of the tribunes of the assembly, hoping by this imitation of the revolution to conquer the true revolution, his object being to deceive parties, and annul the effects of the constitution by observing it literally.

By this line of conduct the court had even the imprudence to weaken the constitutionalists, whom it ought to have reinforced; at their expense it favoured the election of Pétion to the mayoralty. Through the disinterestedness with which the preceding assembly had been seized, all who had held popular posts under it successively gave them up. On the 18th of October, Lafayette resigned the command of the national guard, and Bailly had just retired from the mayoralty. The constitutional party proposed that Lafayette should replace him in this first post of the state, which, by permitting or restraining insurrections, delivered Paris into the power of him who occupied it. Till then it had been in the hands of the constitutionalists, who, by this means, had repressed the rising of the Champ de Mars. They had lost the direction of the assembly, the command of the national guard; they now lost the corporation. The court gave to Pétion, the Girondist candidate, all the votes at its disposal. "M. de Lafayette," observed the queen to Bertrand de Moleville, "only wishes to be mayor of Paris in order to become mayor of the palace. Pétion is a jacobin, a republican, but he is a fool, incapable of ever leading a party." On the 4th of November, Pétion was elected mayor by a majority of 6708 votes in a total of 10,632.

The Girondists, in whose favour this nomination became decisive, did not content themselves with the acquisition of the mayoralty. France could not remain long in this dangerous and provisional state. The decrees which, justly or otherwise, were to provide for the defence of the revolution, and which had been rejected by the king, were not replaced by any government measure; the ministry manifested either unwillingness or sheer indifference. The Girondists, accordingly, accused Delessart, the minister for foreign affairs, of compromising the honour and safety of the nation by the tone of his negotiations with foreign powers, by his procrastination, and want of skill. They also warmly attacked Duportail, the war minister, and Bertrand de Moleville, minister of the marine, for neglecting to put the coasts and frontiers in a state of defence. The conduct of the Electors of Trèves, Mayence, and the bishop of Spires, who favoured the military preparations of the emigrants, more especially excited the national indignation. The diplomatic committee proposed a declaration to the king, that the nation would view with satisfaction a requisition by him to the neighbouring princes to disperse the military gatherings within three weeks, and his assembling the forces necessary to make them respect international law. By this important measure, they also wished to make Louis XVI. enter into a solemn engagement, and signify to the diet of Ratisbon, as well as to the other courts of Europe, the firm intentions of France.

Isnard ascended the tribune to support this proposition. "Let us," said he, "in this crisis, rise to the full elevation of our mission; let us speak to the ministers, to the king, to all Europe, with the firmness that becomes us. Let us tell our ministers, that hitherto the nation is not well satisfied with the conduct of any of them; that henceforth they will have no choice but between public gratitude and the vengeance of the laws; and that by the word responsibility we understand death. Let us tell the king that it is his interest to defend the constitution; that he only reigns by the people and for the people; that the nation is his sovereign, and that he is subject to the law. Let us tell Europe, that if the French people once draw the sword, they will throw away the scabbard, and will not raise it again till it may be crowned with the laurels of victory; that if cabinets engage kings in a war against the people, we will engage the people in a mortal warfare against kings. Let us tell them, that all the fights the people shall fight at the order of despots"—here he was interrupted by loud applause—"Do not applaud," he cried—"do not applaud; respect my enthusiasm; it is that of liberty! Let us say to Europe, that all the fights which the people shall fight at the command of despots, resemble the blows that two friends, excited by a perfidious instigator, inflict on each other in darkness. When light arrives, they throw down their arms, embrace, and chastise their deceiver. So will it be if, when foreign armies are contending with ours, the light of philosophy shine upon them. The nations will embrace in the presence of dethroned tyrants— of the earth consoled, of Heaven satisfied."

The assembly unanimously, and with transport, passed the proposed measure, and, on the 29th of November, sent a message to the king. Vaublanc was the leader of the deputation. "Sire," said he to Louis XVI., "the national assembly had scarcely glanced at the state of the nation ere it saw that the troubles which still agitate it arise from the criminal preparations of French emigrants. Their audacity is encouraged by German princes, who trample under foot the treaties between them and France, and affect to forget that they are indebted to this empire for the treaty of Westphalia, which secured their rights and their safety. These hostile preparations, these threats of invasion, will require armaments absorbing immense sums, which the nation would joyfully pay over to its creditors. It is for you, sire, to make them desist; it is for you to address to foreign powers the language befitting the king of the French. Tell them, that wherever preparations are permitted to be made against France, there France recognises only foes; that we will religiously observe our oath to make no conquests; that we offer them the good neighbourship, the inviolable friendship of a free and powerful people; that we will respect their laws, their customs, and their constitutions; but that we will have our own respected! Tell them, that if princes of Germany continue to favour preparations directed against the French, the French will carry into their territories, not indeed fire and sword, but liberty. It is for them to calculate the consequences of this awakening of nations."

Louis XVI. replied, that he would give the fullest consideration to the message of the assembly; and in a few days he came in person to announce his resolutions on the subject. They were conformable with the general wish. The king said, amidst vehement applause, that he would cause it to be declared to the elector of Trèves and the other electors, that, unless all gatherings and hostile preparations on the part of the French emigrants in their states ceased before the 15th of January, he would consider them as enemies. He added, that he would write to the emperor to engage him, as chief of the empire, to interpose his authority for the purpose of averting the calamities which the lengthened resistance of a few members of the Germanic body would occasion. "If these declarations are not heeded, then, gentlemen," said he, "it will only remain for me to propose war—war, which a people who have solemnly renounced conquest, never declares without necessity, but which a free and generous nation will undertake and carry on when its honour and safety require it."

The steps taken by the king with the princes of the empire were supported by military preparations. On the 6th of December a new minister of war replaced Duportail; Narbonne, taken from the Feuillants, young, active, ambitious of distinguishing himself by the triumph of his party and the defence of the revolution, repaired immediately to the frontiers. A hundred and fifty thousand men were placed in requisition; for this object the assembly voted an extraordinary supply of twenty millions of francs; three armies were formed under the command of Rochambeau, Luckner, and Lafayette; finally, a decree was passed impeaching *Monsieur*, the count d'Artois, and the prince de Condé as conspirators against the general safety of the state and of the constitution. Their property was sequestrated, and the period previously fixed on for *Monsieur's* return to the kingdom having expired, he was deprived of his claim to the regency.

The elector of Trèves engaged to disperse the gatherings, and not to allow them in future. It was, however, but the shadow of a dispersion. Austria ordered marshal Bender to defend the elector if he were attacked, and ratified the conclusions of the diet of Ratisbon, which required the restoration of the princes' possessions; refused to sanction any pecuniary indemnity for the loss of their rights, and only left France the alternative of restoring feudalism in Alsace, or war. These two measures of the cabinet of Vienna were by no means pacific. Its troops advanced towards the frontiers of France, and gave further proof that it would not be safe to trust to its neutrality. It had fifty thousand men in the Netherlands; six thousand posted in Breisgau; and thirty thousand men on their way from Bohemia. This powerful army of observation might at any moment be converted into an army of attack.

The assembly felt that it was urgently necessary to bring the emperor to a decision. It looked on the electors as merely his agents, and on the emigrants as his instruments; for the prince von Kaunitz recognised as legitimate "the league of sovereigns united for the safety and honour of crowns." The Girondists, therefore, wished to anticipate this dangerous adversary, in order not to give him time for more mature preparations. They required from him, before the 10th of February, a definite and precise explanation of his real intentions with regard to France. They at the same time proceeded against those ministers on whom they could not rely in the event of war. The incapacity of Delessart, and the intrigues of Moleville especially, gave room for attack; Narbonne was alone spared. They were aided by the divisions of the council, which was partly aristocratic in Bertrand de Moleville, Delessart, etc., and partly constitutional, in Narbonne, and Cahier de Gerville, minister of the interior. Men so opposed in character and intentions could scarcely be expected to agree; Bertrand de Moleville had warm contests with Narbonne, who wished his colleagues to adopt a frank, decided line of conduct, and to make the assembly the fulcrum of the throne. Narbonne succumbed in this struggle, and his dismissal involved the disorganization of the ministry. The Girondists threw the blame upon Bertrand de Moleville and Delessart; the former had the address to exonerate himself; but the latter was brought before the high court of Orleans.

The king, intimidated by the assaults of the assembly upon the members of his council, and more especially by the impeachment of Delessart, had no resource but to select his new ministers from amongst the victorious party. An alliance with the actual rulers of the revolution could alone save liberty and the throne, by restoring concord between the assembly, the supreme authority, and the municipality; and if this union had been maintained, the Girondists would have effected with the court that which, after the rupture itself, they considered they could only effect without it. The members of the new ministry were:—minister of the marine, Lacoste; of finance, Clavière; of justice, Duranton; of war, de Grave, soon afterwards replaced by Servan; of foreign affairs, Dumouriez; of the interior, Roland. The two latter were the most important and most remarkable men in the cabinet.

Dumouriez was forty-seven years of age when the revolution began; he had lived till then immersed in intrigue, and he retained his old habits too closely at an epoch when he should have employed small means only to aid great ones, instead of supplying their place. The first part of his political life was spent in seeking those by whom he might rise: the second, those by whom he might maintain his position. A courtier up to 1789, a constitutionalist under the first assembly, a Girondist under the second, a Jacobin under the republic, he was eminently a man of circumstances. But he had all the resources of great men; an enterprising character, indefatigable activity, a ready, sure, and extensive perception, impetuosity of action, and an extraordinary confidence of success; he was, moreover, open, easy, witty, daring; adapted alike for arms and for factions, full of expedients, wonderfully ready, and, in difficult positions, versed in the art of stooping to conquer. It is true that his great qualities were weakened by defects; he was rash, flighty, full of inconsistency of thought and action, owing to his continual thirst for movement and machination. But his great defect was the total absence of a political conviction. In times of revolution, nothing can be done for liberty or power by him who is not decidedly of one party or another, and when he is ambitious, unless he see further than the immediate objects of that party, and have a stronger will than his colleagues. This it was made Cromwell; this it was made Buonaparte; while Dumouriez, the employed of all parties, thought he could get the better of them all by intriguing. He wanted the passion of his time: that which completes a man, and alone enables him to sway.

Roland was the opposite of Dumouriez; his was a character which Liberty found ready formed, as if moulded by herself. Roland had simple manners, austere morals, tried opinions; enthusiastically attached to liberty, he was capable of disinterestedly devoting to her cause his whole life, or of perishing for her, without ostentation and without regret. A man worthy of being born in a republic, but out of place in a revolution, and ill adapted for the agitation and struggle of parties; his talents were not superior, his temper somewhat uncompliant; he was unskilled in the knowledge and management of men; and though laborious, well informed, and active, he would have produced little effect but for his wife. All he wanted she had for him; force, ability, elevation, foresight. Madame Roland was the soul of the Gironde; it was at her house that those brilliant and courageous men assembled to discuss the necessities and dangers of their country; it was she who stimulated to action those whom she saw were qualified for action, and who encouraged to the tribune those whom she knew to be eloquent.

The court named this ministry, which was appointed during the month of March, *le Ministère Sans-Culotte*. The first time Roland appeared at the château with strings in his shoes and a round hat, contrary to etiquette, the master of the ceremonies refused to admit him. Obliged, however, to give way, he said, despairingly, to Dumouriez, pointing to Roland: "*Ah, sir—no buckles in his shoes.*" "Ah, sir, all is lost," replied Dumouriez, with an air of the most sympathising gravity. Such were the trifles which still occupied the attention of the court. The first step of the new ministry was war. The position of France was becoming more and more dangerous; everything was to be feared from the enmity of Europe. Leopold was dead, and this event was calculated to accelerate the decision of the cabinet of Vienna. His young successor, Francis II., was likely to be less pacific or less prudent than he. Moreover, Austria was assembling its troops, forming camps, and appointing generals; it had violated the territory of Bâle, and placed a garrison in Porentruy, to secure for itself the entry of the department of Doubs. There could be no doubt as to its projects. The gatherings at Coblenz had recommenced to a greater extent than before; the cabinet of Vienna had only temporarily dispersed the emigrants assembled in the Belgian provinces, in order to prevent the invasion of that country, at a time when it was not yet ready to repel invasion; it had, however, merely sought to save appearances, and had allowed a staff of general officers, in full uniform, and with the white cockade, to remain at Brussels. Finally, the reply of the prince von Kaunitz to the required explanations was by no means satisfactory. He even refused to negotiate directly, and the baron von Cobenzl was commissioned to reply, that Austria would not depart from the required conditions already set forth. The re-establishment of the monarchy on the basis of the royal sitting of the 23rd of June; the restitution of its property to the clergy; of the territory of Alsace, with all their rights, to the German princes; of Avignon and the Venaissin to the pope; such was the *ultimatum* of Austria. All accord was now impossible; peace could no longer be maintained. France was threatened with the fate which Holland had just experienced, and perhaps with that of Poland. The sole question now was whether to wait for or to initiate war, whether to profit by the enthusiasm of the people or to allow that enthusiasm to cool. The true author of war is not he who declares it, but he who renders it necessary.

On the 20th of April, Louis XVI. went to the assembly, attended by all his ministers. "I come, gentlemen," said he, "to the national assembly for one of the most important objects that can occupy the representatives of the nation. My minister for foreign affairs will read to you the report drawn up in our council, as to our political situation." Dumouriez then rose. He set forth the grounds of complaint that France had against the house of Austria; the object of the conferences of Mantua, Reichenbach and Pilnitz; the coalition it had formed against the French revolution; its armaments becoming more and more considerable; the open protection it afforded to bodies of emigrants; the imperious tone and the undisguised procrastination of its negotiations, lastly, the intolerable conditions of its *ultimatum*; and, after a long series of considerations, founded on the hostile conduct of the king of Hungary and Bohemia (Francis II. was not yet elected emperor); on the urgent circumstances of the nation; on its formally declared resolution to endure no insult, no encroachment on its rights; on the honour and good faith of Louis XVI., the depositary of the dignity and safety of France; he demanded war against Austria. Louis XVI. then said, in a voice slightly tremulous: "You have heard, gentlemen, the result of my negotiations with the court of Vienna. The conclusions of the report are based upon the unanimous opinion of my council; I have myself adopted them. They are conformable with the wishes often expressed to me by the national assembly, and with the sentiments frequently testified by bodies of citizens in different parts of the kingdom; all prefer war, to witnessing the continuance of insult to the French people, and danger threatening the national existence. It was my duty first to try every means of maintaining peace. Having failed in these efforts, I now come, according to the terms of the constitution, to propose to the national assembly war against the king of Hungary and Bohemia." The king's address was received with some applause, but the solemnity of the circumstances, and the grandeur of the decision, filled every bosom with silent and concentrated emotion. As soon as the king had withdrawn, the assembly voted an extraordinary sitting for the evening. In that sitting war was almost unanimously decided upon. Thus was undertaken, against the chief of the confederate powers, that war which was protracted throughout a quarter of a century, which victoriously established the revolution, and which changed the whole face of Europe.

All France received the announcement with joy. War gave a new movement to the people already so much excited. Districts, municipalities, popular societies, wrote addresses; men were enrolled, voluntary gifts offered, pikes forged, and the nation seemed to rise up to await Europe, or to attack it. But enthusiasm, which ensures victory in the end, does not at first supply the place of organization. Accordingly, at the opening of the campaign, the regular troops were all that could be relied upon until the new levies were trained. This was the state of the forces. The vast frontier, from Dunkirk to Huninguen, was divided into three great military districts. On the left, from Dunkirk to Philippeville, the army of the north, of about forty thousand foot, and eight thousand horse, was under the orders of marshal de Rochambeau. Lafayette commanded the army of the centre, composed of forty-five thousand foot, and seven thousand horse, and occupying the district between Philippeville and the lines of Weissemberg. Lastly, the army of the Rhine, consisting of thirty-five thousand foot, and eight thousand horse, extending from the lines of Weissemberg to Bâle, was under the command of marshal Luckner. The frontier of the Alps and Pyrenees was confided to general Montesquiou, whose army was inconsiderable; but this part of France was not as yet in danger.

The marshal de Rochambeau was of opinion that it would be prudent to remain on the defensive, and simply to guard the frontiers. Dumouriez, on the contrary, wished to take the initiative in action, as they had done in declaring war, so as to profit by the advantage of being first prepared. He was very enterprising, and as, although minister of foreign affairs, he directed the military operations, his plan was adopted. It consisted of a rapid invasion of Belgium. This province had, in 1790, essayed to throw off the Austrian yoke, but, after a brief victory, was subdued by superior force. Dumouriez imagined that the Brabant patriots would favour the attack of the French, as a means of freedom for themselves. With this view, he combined a triple invasion. The two generals, Theobald Dillon, and Biron, who commanded in Flanders under Rochambeau, received orders to advance, the one with four thousand men from Lille upon Tournai—the other, with ten thousand, from Valenciennes upon Mons. At the same time, Lafayette, with a part of his army, quitted Metz, and advanced by forced marches upon Namur, by Stenai, Sedan, Mézières, and Givet. But this plan implied in the soldiers a discipline which they had not of course as yet acquired, and on the part of the chiefs a concert very difficult to obtain; besides, the invading columns were not strong enough for such an enterprise. Theobald Dillon had scarcely passed the frontier, when, on meeting the first enemy on the 28th of April, a panic terror seized upon the troops. The cry of *sauve qui peut* ran through the ranks, and the general was carried off, and massacred by his troops. Much the same thing took place, under the same circumstances, in the corps of Biron, who was obliged to retreat in disorder to his previous position. The sudden and concurrent flight of these two columns must be attributed either to fear of the enemy, on the part of troops who had never before stood fire, or to a distrust of their leaders, or to traitors who sounded the alarm of treachery.

Lafayette, on arriving at Bouvines, after travelling fifty leagues of bad roads in two or three days, learnt the disasters of Valenciennes and Lille; he at once saw that the object of the invasion had failed; and he justly thought that the best course would be to effect a retreat. Rochambeau complained of the precipitate and incongruous nature of the measures which had been in the most absolute manner prescribed to him. As he did not choose to remain a passive machine, obliged to fill, at the will of the ministers, a post which he himself ought to have the full direction of, he resigned. From that moment the French army resumed the defensive. The frontier was divided into two general commands only, the one intrusted to Lafayette, extending from the sea to Longwy, and the other, from the Moselle to the Jura, being confided to Luckner. Lafayette placed his left under the command of Arthur Dillon, and with his right reached to Luckner, who had Biron as his lieutenant on the Rhine. In this position they awaited the allies.

Meantime, the first checks increased the rupture between the Feuillants and the Girondists. The generals ascribed them to the plans of Dumouriez, the ministry attributed them to the manner in which its plans had been executed by the generals, who, having been appointed by Narbonne, were of the constitutional party. The Jacobins, on the other hand, accused the anti-revolutionists of having occasioned the flight by the cry of *sauve qui peut!* Their joy, which they did not conceal, the declared hope of soon seeing the confederates in Paris, the emigrants returned, and the ancient regime restored, confirmed these suspicions. It was thought that the court, which had increased the household troops from eighteen hundred to six thousand men, and these carefully selected anti-revolutionists, acted in concert with the coalition. The public denounced, under the name of *comité Autrichien*, a secret committee, the very existence of which could not be proved, and mistrust was at its height.

The assembly at once took decided measures. It had entered upon the career of war, and it was thenceforth condemned to regulate its conduct far more with reference to the public safety than with regard to the mere justice of the case. It resolved upon sitting permanently; it discharged the household troops; on account of the increase of religious disturbances, it passed a decree exiling refractory priests, so that it might not have at the same time to combat a coalition and to appease revolts. To repair the late defeats, and to have an army of reserve near the capital, it voted on the 8th of June, and on the motion of the minister for war, Servan, the formation of a camp outside Paris of twenty thousand men drawn from the provinces. It also sought to excite the public mind by revolutionary fêtes, and began to enroll the multitude and arm them with pikes, conceiving that no assistance could be superfluous in such a moment of peril.

All these measures were not carried without opposition from the constitutionalists. They opposed the establishment of the camp of twenty thousand men, which they regarded as the army of a party directed against the national guard and the throne. The staff of the former protested, and the recomposition of this body was immediately effected in accordance with the views of the dominant party. Companies armed with pikes were introduced into the new national guard. The constitutionalists were still more dissatisfied with this measure, which introduced a lower class into their ranks, and which seemed to them to aim at superseding the bourgeoisie by the populace. Finally, they openly condemned the banishment of the priests, which in their opinion was nothing less than proscription.

Louis XVI. had for some time past manifested a coolness towards his ministers, who on their part had been more exacting with him. They urged him to admit about him priests who had taken the oath, in order to set an example in favour of the constitutional religion, and to remove pretexts for religious agitation; he steadily refused this, determined as he was to make no further religious concession. These last decrees had put an end to his concord with the Gironde; for several days he did not mention the subject, much less make known his intentions respecting it. It was on this occasion that Roland addressed to him his celebrated letter on his constitutional duties, and entreated him to calm the public mind, and to establish his authority, by becoming frankly the king of the revolution. This letter still more highly irritated Louis XVI., already disposed to break with the Girondists. He was supported in this by Dumouriez, who, forsaking his party, had formed with Duranton and Lacoste, a division in the ministry against Roland, Servan, and Clavière. But, able as well as ambitious, Dumouriez advised Louis, while dismissing the ministers of whom he had to complain, to sanction their decrees, in order to make himself popular. He described that against the priests as a precaution in their favour, exile probably removing them from a proscription still more fatal; he undertook to prevent any revolutionary consequences from the camp of twenty thousand men, by marching off each battalion to the army immediately upon its arrival at the camp. On these conditions, Dumouriez took upon himself the post of minister for war, and sustained the attacks of his own party. The king dismissed his ministers on the 13th of June, rejected the decrees on the 29th, and Dumouriez set out for the army, after having rendered himself an object of suspicion. The assembly declared that Roland, Servan, and Clavière carried with them the regrets of the nation.

The king selected his new ministers from among the Feuillants. Scipio Chambonnas was appointed minister of foreign affairs; Terrier de Monceil, of the interior; Beaulieu, of finance; Lajarre, of war; Lacoste and Duranton remained provisionally ministers of justice and of the marine. All these men were without reputation or credit, and their party itself was approaching the term of its existence. The constitutional situation, during which it was to sway, was changing more and more decidedly into a revolutionary situation. How could a legal and moderate party maintain itself between two extreme and belligerent parties, one of which was advancing from without to destroy the revolution, while the other was resolved to defend it at any cost? The Feuillants became superfluous in such a conjuncture. The king, perceiving their weakness, now seemed to place his reliance upon Europe alone, and sent Mallet-Dupan on a secret mission to the coalition.

Meantime, all those who had been outstripped by the popular tide, and who belonged to the first period of the revolution, united to second this slight retrograde movement. The monarchists, at whose head were Lally- Tollendal and Malouet, two of the principal members of the Mounier and Necker party; Feuillants, directed by the old triumvirate, Duport, Lameth, and Barnave; lastly, Lafayette, who had immense reputation as a constitutionalist, tried to put down the clubs, and to re-establish legal order and the power of the king. The Jacobins made great exertions at this period; their influence was becoming enormous; they were at the head of the party of the populace. To oppose them, to check them, the old party of the bourgeoisie was required; but this was disorganised, and its influence grew daily weaker and weaker. In order to revive its courage and strength, Lafayette, on the 16th of June, addressed from the camp at Maubeuge a letter to the assembly, in which he denounced the Jacobin faction, required the cessation of the clubs, the independence and confirmation of the constitutional throne, and urged the assembly in his own name, in that of his army, in that of all the friends of liberty, only to adopt such measures for the public welfare as were sanctioned by law. This letter gave rise to warm debates between the Right and Left in the assembly. Though dictated only by pure and disinterested motives, it appeared, coming as it did from a young general at the head of his army, a proceeding *à la Cromwell*, and from that moment Lafayette's reputation, hitherto respected by his opponents, became the object of attack. In fact, considering it merely in a political point of view, this step was imprudent. The Gironde, driven from the ministry, stopped in its measures for the public good, needed no further goading; and, on the other hand, it was quite undesirable that Lafayette, even for the benefit of his party, should use his influence.

The Gironde wished, for its own safety and that of the nation, to recover power, without, however, departing from constitutional means. Its object was not, as at a later period, to dethrone the king, but to bring him back amongst them. For this purpose it had recourse to the imperious petitions of the multitude. Since the declaration of war, petitioners had appeared in arms at the bar of the national assembly, had offered their services in defence of the country, and had obtained permission to march armed through the house. This concession was blameable, neutralizing all the laws against military gatherings; but both parties found themselves in an extraordinary position, and each employed illegal means; the court having recourse to Europe, and the Gironde to the people. The latter was in a state of great agitation. The leaders of the Faubourgs, among whom were the deputy Chabot, Santerre, Legendre, a butcher, Gonchon, the marquis de Saint Hurugue, prepared them, during several days, for a revolutionary outbreak, similar to the one which failed at the Champ de Mars. The 20th of June was approaching, the anniversary of the oath of the Tennis-court. Under the pretext of celebrating this memorable day by a civic fête, and of planting a May-pole in honour of liberty, an assemblage of about eight thousand men left the Faubourgs Saint Antoine and Saint Marceau, on the 20th of June, and took their way to the assembly.

Roederer, the recorder, brought the tidings to the assembly, but in the meantime the mob had reached the doors of the hall. Their leaders asked permission to present a petition, and to defile before the assembly. A violent debate arose between the Right, who were unwilling to admit the armed petitioners, and the Left, who, on the ground of custom, wished to receive them, Vergniaud declared that the assembly would violate every principle by admitting armed bands among them; but, considering actual circumstances, he also declared that it was impossible to deny a request in the present case, that had been granted in so many others.

It was difficult not to yield to the desires of an enthusiastic and vast multitude, when seconded by a majority of the representatives. The crowd already thronged the passages, when the assembly decided that the petitioners should be admitted to the bar. The deputation was introduced. The spokesman expressed himself in threatening language. He said that the people were astir; that they were ready to make use of great means—the means comprised in the declaration of rights, *resistance of oppression;* that the dissentient members of the assembly, if there were any, *would purge the world of liberty,* and would repair to Coblentz; then returning to the true design of this insurrectional petition, he added: "The executive power is not in union with you; we require no other proof of it than the dismissal of the patriot ministers. It is thus, then, that the happiness of a free nation shall depend on the caprice of a king! But should this king have any other will than that of the law? The people will have it so, and the life of the people is as valuable as that of crowned despots. That life is the genealogical tree of the nation, and the feeble reed must bend before this sturdy oak! We complain, gentlemen, of the inactivity of our armies; we require of you to penetrate into the cause of this; if it spring from the executive power, let that power be destroyed!"

The assembly answered the petitioners that it would take their request into consideration; it then urged them to respect the law and legal authorities, and allowed them to defile before it. This procession, amounting to thirty thousand persons, comprising women, children, national guards, and men armed with pikes, among whom waved revolutionary banners and symbols, sang, as they traversed the hall, the famous chorus, *Ca ira,* and cried: "Vive la nation!" "Vivent les sans-culottes!" "A bas le veto!" It was led by Santerre and the marquis de Saint Hurugue. On leaving the assembly, it proceeded to the château, headed by the petitioners.

The outer doors were opened at the king's command; the multitude rushed into the interior. They ascended to the apartments, and while forcing the doors with hatchets, the king ordered them to be opened, and appeared before them, accompanied by a few persons. The mob stopped a moment before him; but those who were outside, not being awed by the presence of the king, continued to advance. Louis XVI. was prudently placed in the recess of a window. He never displayed more courage than on this deplorable day. Surrounded by national guards, who formed a barrier against the mob, seated on a chair placed on a table, that he might breathe more freely and be seen by the people, he preserved a calm and firm demeanour. In reply to the cries that arose on all sides for the sanction of the decrees, he said: "This is neither the mode nor the moment to obtain it of me." Having the courage to refuse the essential object of the meeting, he thought he ought not to reject a symbol, meaningless for him, but in the eyes of the people, that of liberty; he placed on his head a red cap presented to him on the top of a pike. The multitude were quite satisfied with this condescension. A moment or two afterwards, they loaded him with applause, as, almost suffocated with hunger and thirst, he drank off, without hesitation, a glass of wine presented to him by a half-drunken workman. In the meantime, Vergniaud, Isnard, and a few deputies of the Gironde, had hastened thither to protect the king, to address the people, and put an end to these indecent scenes. The assembly, which had just risen from a sitting, met again in haste, terrified at this outbreak, and despatched several successive deputations to Louis XVI. by way of protection. At length, Pétion, the mayor, himself arrived; he mounted a chair, harangued the people, urged them to retire without tumult, and the people obeyed. These singular insurgents, whose only aim was to obtain decrees and ministers, retired without having exceeded their mission, but without discharging it.

The events of the 20th of June excited the friends of the constitution against its authors. The violation of the royal residence, the insults offered to Louis XVI., the illegality of a petition presented amidst the violence of the multitude, and the display of arms, were subjects of serious censure against the popular party. The latter saw itself reduced for a moment to the defensive; besides being guilty of a riot, it had undergone a complete check. The constitutionalists assumed the tone and superiority of an offended and predominant party; but this lasted only a short time, for they were not seconded by the court. The national guard offered to Louis XVI. to remain assembled round his person; the duc de la Rochefoucauld-Liancourt, who commanded at Rouen, wished to convey him to his troops, who were devoted to his cause. Lafayette proposed to take him to Compiègne, and place him at the head of his army; but Louis XVI. declined all these offers. He conceived that the agitators would be disgusted at the failure of their last attempt; and, as he hoped for deliverance from the coalition of European powers, rendered more active by the events of the 20th of June, he was unwilling to make use of the constitutionalists, because he would have been obliged to treat with them.

Lafayette, however, attempted to make a last effort in favour of legal monarchy. After having provided for the command of his army, and collected addresses protesting against the late events, he started for Paris, and on the 28th of June he unexpectedly presented himself at the bar of the assembly. He required in his name, as well as in that of his army, the punishment of the insurrectionists of the 20th of June, and the destruction of the Jacobin party. His proceeding excited various sentiments in the assembly. The Right warmly applauded it, but the Left protested against his conduct. Guadet proposed that an inquiry should be made as to his culpability in leaving his army and coming to dictate laws to the assembly. Some remains of respect prevented the latter from following Guadet's advice; and after tumultuous debates, Lafayette was admitted to the honours of the sitting, but this was all on the part of the assembly. Lafayette then turned to the national guard, that had so long been devoted to him, and hoped with its aid to close the clubs, disperse the Jacobins, restore to Louis XVI. the authority which the law gave him, and again establish the constitution. The revolutionists were astounded, and dreaded everything from the daring and activity of this adversary of the Champ de Mars. But the court, which feared the triumph of the constitutionalists, caused Lafayette's projects to fail; he had appointed a review, which it contrived to prevent by its influence over the officers of the royalist battalions. The grenadiers and chasseurs, picked companies still better disposed than the rest, were to assemble at his residence and proceed against the clubs; scarcely thirty men came. Having thus vainly attempted to rally in the cause of the constitution, and the common defence, the court and the national guard, and finding himself deserted by those he came to assist, Lafayette returned to his army, after having lost what little influence and popularity remained to him. This attempt was the last symptom of life in the constitutional party.

The assembly naturally returned to the situation of France, which had not changed. The extraordinary commission of twelve presented, through Pastoret, an unsatisfactory picture of the state and divisions of party. Jean Debry, in the name of the same commission, proposed that the assembly should secure the tranquillity of the people, now greatly disturbed, by declaring that when the crisis became imminent, the assembly would declare *the country is in danger*; and that it would then take measures for the public safety. The debate opened upon this important subject. Vergniaud, in a speech which deeply moved the assembly, drew a vivid picture of all the perils to which the country was at that moment exposed. He said that it was in the name of the king that the emigrants were assembled, that the sovereigns of Europe had formed a coalition, that foreign armies were marching on our frontiers, and that internal disturbances were taking place. He accused him of checking the national zeal by his refusals, and of giving France up to the coalition. He quoted the article of the constitution by which it was declared that "if the king placed himself at the head of an army and directed its force against the nation, or if he did not formally oppose such an enterprise, undertaken in his name, he should be considered as having abdicated the throne." Supposing, then, that Louis XVI. voluntarily opposed the means of defending the country, in that case, said he: "have we not a right to say to him: 'O king, who thought, no doubt, with the tyrant Lysander, that truth was of no more worth than falsehood, and that men were to be amused by oaths, as children are diverted by toys; who only feigned obedience to the laws that you might better preserve the power that enables you to defy them; and who only feigned love for the constitution that it might not precipitate you from the throne on which you felt bound to remain in order to destroy the constitution, do you expect to deceive us by hypocritical protestations? Do you think to deceive us as to our misfortunes by the art of your excuses? Was it defending us to oppose to foreign soldiers forces whose known inferiority admitted of no doubt as to their defeat? To set aside projects for strengthening the interior? Was it defending us not to check a general who was violating the constitution, while you repressed the courage of those who sought to serve it? Did the constitution leave you the choice of ministers for our happiness or our ruin? Did it place you at the head of our army for our glory or our shame? Did it give you the right of sanction, a civil list and so many prerogatives, constitutionally to lose the empire and the constitution? No! no! man! whom the generosity of the French could not affect, whom the love of despotism alone actuates, you are now nothing to the constitution you have so unworthily violated, and to the people you have so basely betrayed!'"

The only resource of the Gironde, in its present situation, was the abdication of the king; Vergniaud, it is true, as yet only expressed himself ambiguously, but all the popular party attributed to Louis XVI. projects which Vergniaud had only expressed in the form of suppositions. In a few days, Brissot expressed himself more openly. "Our peril," said he, "exceeds all that past ages have witnessed. The country is in danger, not because we are in want of troops, not because those troops want courage, or that our frontiers are badly fortified, and our resources scanty. No, it is in danger, because its force is paralysed. And who has paralysed it? A man—one man, the man whom the constitution has made its chief, and whom perfidious advisers have made its foe. You are told to fear the kings of Hungary and Prussia; I say, the chief force of these kings is at the court, and it is there that we must first conquer them. They tell you to strike the dissentient priests throughout the kingdom. I tell you to strike at the Tuileries, that is, to fell all the priests with a single blow; you are told to prosecute all factious and intriguing conspirators; they will all disappear if you once knock loud enough at the door of the cabinet of the Tuileries, for that cabinet is the point to which all these threads tend, where every scheme is plotted, and whence every impulse proceeds. The nation is the plaything of this cabinet. This is the secret of our position, this is the source of the evil, and here the remedy must be applied."

In this way the Gironde prepared the assembly for the question of deposition. But the great question concerning the danger of the country was first terminated. The three united committees declared that it was necessary to take measures for the public safety, and on the 5th July the assembly pronounced the solemn declaration: *Citizens, the country is in danger!* All the civil authorities immediately established themselves *en surveillance permanente*. All citizens able to bear arms, and having already served in the national guard, were placed in active service; every one was obliged to make known what arms and ammunition he possessed; pikes were given to those who were unable to procure guns; battalions of volunteers were enrolled on the public squares, in the midst of which banners were placed, bearing the words—"Citizens, the country is in danger!" and a camp was formed at Soissons. These measures of defence, now become indispensable, raised the revolutionary enthusiasm to the highest pitch. It was especially observable on the anniversary of the 14th of July, when the sentiments of the multitude and the federates from the departments were manifested without reserve. Pétion was the object of the people's idolatry, and had all the honours of the federation. A few days before, he had been dismissed, on account of his conduct on the 20th of June by the directory of the department and the council; but the assembly had restored him to his functions, and the only cry on the day of the federation was: *"Pétion or death!"* A few battalions of the national guard, such as that of the Filles-Saint-Thomas, still betrayed attachment to the court; they became the object of popular resentment and mistrust. A disturbance was excited in the Champs Élysées between the grenadiers of the Filles-Saint-Thomas and the federates of Marseilles, in which some grenadiers were wounded. Every day the crisis became more imminent; the party in favour of war could no longer endure that of the constitution. Attacks against Lafayette multiplied; he was censured in the journals, denounced in the assembly. At length hostilities began. The club of the Feuillants was closed; the grenadier and chasseur companies of the national guard which formed the force of the bourgeoisie were disbanded; the soldiers of the line, and a portion of the Swiss, were sent away from Paris, and open preparations were made for the catastrophe of the 10th of August.

The progress of the Prussians and the famous manifesto of Brunswick contributed to hasten this movement. Prussia had joined Austria and the German princes against France. This coalition, to which the court of Turin joined itself, was formidable, though it did not comprise all the powers that were to have joined it at first. The death of Gustavus, appointed at first commander of the invading army, detached Sweden; the substitution of the count d'Aranda, a prudent and moderate man, for the minister Florida- Blanca, prevented Spain from entering it; Russia and England secretly approved the attacks of the European league, without as yet co-operating with it. After the military operations already mentioned, they watched each other rather than fought. During the interval, Lafayette had inspired his army with good habits of discipline and devotedness; and Dumouriez, stationed under Luckner at the camp of Maulde, had inured the troops confided to him by petty engagements and daily successes. In this way they had formed the nucleus of a good army; a desirable thing, as they required organization and confidence to repel the approaching invasion of the coalesced powers.

The duke of Brunswick directed it. He had the chief command of the enemy's army, composed of seventy thousand Prussians, and sixty-eight thousand Austrians, Hessians, or emigrants. The plan of invasion was as follows:— The duke of Brunswick with the Prussians, was to pass the Rhine at Coblentz, ascend the left bank of the Moselle, attack the French frontier by its central and most accessible point, and advance on the capital by way of Longwy, Verdun, and Châlons. The prince von Hohenlohe on his left, was to advance in the direction of Metz and Thionville, with the Hessians and a body of emigrants; while general Clairfayt, with the Austrians and another body of emigrants, was to overthrow Lafayette, stationed before Sedan and Mézieres, cross the Meuse, and march upon Paris by Rheims and Soissons. Thus the centre and two wings were to make a concentrated advance on the capital from the Moselle, the Rhine, and the Netherlands. Other detachments stationed on the frontier of the Rhine and the extreme northern frontier, were to attack our troops on these sides and facilitate the central invasion.

On the 26th of July, when the army began to move from Coblentz, the duke of Brunswick published a manifesto in the name of the emperor and the king of Prussia. He reproached *those who had usurped the reins of administration in France,* with having disturbed order and overturned the legitimate government; with having used daily-renewed violence against the king and his family; with having arbitrarily suppressed the rights and possessions of the German princes in Alsace and Lorraine; and, finally, with having crowned the measure by declaring an unjust war against his majesty the emperor, and attacking his provinces in the Netherlands. He declared that the allied sovereigns were advancing to put an end to anarchy in France, to arrest the attacks made on the altar and the throne; to restore to the king the security and liberty he was deprived of, and to place him in a condition to exercise his legitimate authority. He consequently rendered the national guard and the authorities responsible for all the disorders that should arise until the arrival of the troops of the coalition. He summoned them to return to their ancient fidelity. He said that the inhabitants of towns, *who dared to stand on the defensive,* should instantly be punished as rebels, with the rigour of war, and their houses demolished or burned; that if the city of Paris did not restore the king to full liberty, and render him due respect, the princes of the coalition would make the members of the national assembly, of the department, of the district, the corporation, and the national guard, personally responsible with their heads, to be tried by martial-law, and without hope of pardon; and that if the château were attacked or insulted, the princes would inflict an exemplary and never-to-be-forgotten vengeance, by delivering Paris over to military execution, and total subversion. He promised, on the other hand, if the inhabitants of Paris would promptly obey the orders of the coalition, to secure for them the mediation of the allied princes with Louis XVI. for the pardon of their offences and errors.

This fiery and impolitic manifesto, which disguised neither the designs of the emigrants nor those of Europe, which treated a great nation with a truly extraordinary tone of command and contempt, which openly announced to it all the miseries of an invasion, and, moreover, vengeance and despotism, excited a national insurrection. It more than anything else hastened the fall of the throne, and prevented the success of the coalition. There was but one wish, one cry of resistance, from one end of France to the other; and whoever had not joined in it, would have been looked on as guilty of impiety towards his country and the sacred cause of its independence. The popular party, placed in the necessity of conquering, saw no other way than that of annihilating the power of the king, and in order to annihilate it, than that of dethroning him. But in this party, every one wished to attain the end in his own way: the Gironde by a decree of the assembly; the leaders of the multitude by an insurrection. Danton, Robespierre, Camille Desmoulins, Fabre-d'Eglantine, Marat, etc., were a displaced faction requiring a revolution that would raise it from the midst of the people to the assembly and the corporation. They were the true leaders of the new movement about to take place by the means of the lower class of society against the middle class, to which the Girondists belonged by their habits and position. A division arose from that day between those who only wished to suppress the court in the existing order of things, and those who wished to introduce the multitude. The latter could not fall in with the tardiness of discussion. Agitated by every revolutionary passion, they disposed themselves for an attack by force of arms, the preparations for which were made openly, and a long time beforehand.

Their enterprise had been projected and suspended several times. On the 26th of July, an insurrection was to break out; but it was badly contrived, and Pétion prevented it. When the federates from Marseilles arrived, on their way to the camp at Soissons, the faubourgs were to meet them, and then repair, unexpectedly, to the château. This insurrection also failed. Yet the arrival of the Marseillais encouraged the agitators of the capital, and conferences were held at Charenton between them and the federal leaders for the overthrow of the throne. The sections were much agitated; that of Mauconseil was the first to declare itself in a state of insurrection, and notified this to the assembly. The dethronement was discussed in the clubs, and on the 3rd of August, the mayor Pétion came to solicit it of the legislative body, in the name of the commune and of the sections. The petition was referred to the extraordinary commission of twelve. On the 8th, the accusation of Lafayette was discussed. Some remains of courage induced the majority to support him, and not without danger. He was acquitted; but all who had voted for him were hissed, pursued, and ill treated by the people at the breaking up of the sitting.

The following day the excitement was extreme. The assembly learned by the letters of a large number of deputies, that the day before on leaving the house they had been ill used, and threatened with death, for voting the acquittal of Lafayette. Vaublanc announced that a crowd had invested and searched his house in pursuit of him. Girardin exclaimed: "Discussion is impossible, without perfect liberty of opinion; I declare to my constituents that I cannot deliberate if the legislative body does not secure me liberty and safety." Vaublanc earnestly urged that the assembly should take the strongest measures to secure respect to the law. He also required that the federates, who were defended by the Girondists, should be sent without delay to Soissons. During these debates the president received a message from de Joly, minister of justice. He announced that the mischief was at its height, and the people urged to every kind of excess. He gave an account of those committed the evening before, not only against the deputies, but against many other persons. "I have," said the minister, "denounced these attacks in the criminal court; but law is powerless; and I am impelled by honour and probity to inform you, that without the promptest assistance of the legislative body, the government can no longer be responsible." In the meantime, it was announced that the section of the Quinze-vingts had declared that, if the dethronement were not pronounced that very day, at midnight they would sound the tocsin, would beat the générale and attack the château. This decision had been transmitted to the forty-eight sections, and all had approved it, except one. The assembly summoned the recorder of the department, who assured them of his good-will, but his inability; and the mayor, who replied that, at a time when the sections had resumed their sovereignty, he could only exercise over the people the influence of persuasion. The assembly broke up without adopting any measures.

The insurgents fixed the attack on the château for the morning of the 10th of August. On the 8th, the Marseillais had been transferred from their barracks in the Rue Blanche to the Cordeliers, with their arms, cannon, and standard. They had received five thousand ball cartridges, which had been distributed to them by command of the commissioner of police. The principal scene of the insurrection was the Faubourg Saint Antoine. In the evening, after a very stormy sitting, the Jacobins repaired thither in procession; the insurrection was then organized. It was decided to dissolve the department; to dismiss Pétion, in order to withdraw him from the duties of his place, and all responsibility; and, finally, to replace the general council of the present commune by an insurrectional municipality. Agitators repaired at the same time to the sections of the faubourgs and to the barracks of the federate Marseillais and Bretons.

The court had been apprised of the danger for some time, and had placed itself in a state of defence. At this juncture, it probably thought it was not only able to resist, but also entirely to re-establish itself. The interior of the château was occupied by Swiss, to the number of eight or nine hundred, by officers of the disbanded guard, and by a troop of gentlemen and royalists, who had offered their services, armed with sabres, swords, and pistols. Mandat, the general-in-chief of the national guard, had repaired to the château, with his staff, to defend it; he had given orders to the battalions most attached to the constitution to take arms. The ministers were also with the king; the recorder of the department had gone thither in the evening at the command of the king, who had also sent for Pétion, to ascertain from him the state of Paris, and obtain an authorization to repel force by force.

At midnight, the tocsin sounded; the générale was beaten. The insurgents assembled, and fell into their ranks; the members of the sections broke up the municipality, and named a provisional council of the commune, which proceeded to the Hôtel de Ville to direct the insurrection. The battalions of the national guard, on their side, took the route to the château, and were stationed in the court, or at the principal posts, with the mounted gendarmerie; artillerymen occupied the avenues of the Tuileries, with their pieces; while the Swiss and volunteers guarded the apartments. The defence was in the best condition.

Some deputies, meanwhile, aroused by the tocsin, had hurried to the hall of the legislative body, and had opened the sitting under the presidentship of Vergniaud. Hearing that Pétion was at the Tuileries, and presuming he was detained there, and wanted to be released, they sent for him to the bar of the assembly, to give an account of the state of Paris. On receiving this order, he left the château; he appeared before the assembly, where a deputation again inquired for him, also supposing him to be a prisoner at the Tuileries. With this deputation he returned to the Hôtel de Ville, where he was placed under a guard of three hundred men by the new commune. The latter, unwilling to allow any other authority on this day of disorder than the insurrectional authorities, early in the morning sent for the commandant Mandat, to know what arrangements were made at the château. Mandat hesitated to obey; yet, as he did not know that the municipality had been changed, and as his duty required him to obey its orders, on a second call which he received from the commune, he proceeded to the Hôtel de Ville. On perceiving new faces as he entered, he turned pale. He was accused of authorizing the troops to fire on the people. He became agitated, and was ordered to the Abbaye, and the mob murdered him as he was leaving, on the steps of the Hôtel de Ville. The commune immediately conferred the command of the national guard on Santerre.

The court was thus deprived of its most determined and influential defender. The presence of Mandat, and the order he had received to employ force in case of need, were necessary to induce the national guard to fight. The sight of the nobles and royalists had lessened its zeal. Mandat himself, previous to his departure, had urged the queen in vain to dismiss this troop, which the constitutionalists considered as a troop of aristocrats.

About four in the morning the queen summoned Roederer, the recorder of the department, who had passed the night at the Tuileries, and inquired what was to be done under these circumstances? Roederer replied, that he thought it necessary that the king and the royal family should proceed to the national assembly. "You propose," said Dubouchage, "to take the king to his foes." Roederer replied, that, two days before, four hundred members of that assembly out of six hundred, had pronounced in favour of Lafayette; and that he had only proposed this plan as the least dangerous. The queen then said, in a very positive tone: "Sir, we have forces here: it is at length time to know who is to prevail, the king and the constitution, or faction?" "In that case, madam," rejoined Roederer, "let us see what arrangements have been made for resistance." Laschenaye, who commanded in the absence of Mandat, was sent for. He was asked if he had taken measures to prevent the crowd from arriving at the château? If he had guarded the Carrousel? He replied in the affirmative; and, addressing the queen, he said, in a tone of anger: "I must not allow you to remain in ignorance, madam, that the apartments are filled with people of all kinds, who very much impede the service, and prevent free access to the king, a circumstance which creates dissatisfaction among the national guard." "This is out of season," replied the queen; "I will answer for those who are here; they will advance first or last, in the ranks, as you please; they are ready for all that is necessary; they are sure men." They contented themselves with sending the two ministers, Joly and Champion to the assembly to apprise it of the danger, and ask for its assistance and for commissioners.[2]

Division already existed between the defenders of the château, when Louis XVI. passed them in review at five o'clock in the morning. He first visited the interior posts, and found them animated by the best intentions. He was accompanied by some members of his family, and appeared extremely sad. "I will not," he said, "separate my cause from that of good citizens; we will save ourselves or perish together." He then descended into the yard, accompanied by some general officers. As soon as he arrived, they beat to arms. The cry of "Vive le roi!" was heard, and was repeated by the national guard; but the artillerymen, and the battalion of the Croix Rouge replied by the cry of "Vive la nation!" At the same instant, new battalions, armed with guns and pikes, defiled before the king, and took their places upon the terrace of the Seine, crying; "Vive la nation!" "Vive Pétion!" The king continued the review, not, however, without feeling saddened by this omen. He was received with the strongest evidences of devotion by the battalions of the Filles-Saint-Thomas, and Petits-Pères, who occupied the terrace, extending the length of the château. As he crossed the garden to visit the ports of the Pont Tournant, the pike battalions pursued him with the cry of: "Down with the veto!" "Down with the traitor!" and as he returned, they quitted their position, placed themselves near the Pont Royal, and turned their cannon against the château. Two other battalions stationed in the courts imitated them, and established themselves on the Place du Carrousel in an attitude of attack. On re-entering the château, the king was pale and dejected; and the queen said, "All is lost! This kind of review has done more harm than good."

While all this was passing at the Tuileries, the insurgents were advancing in several columns; they had passed the night in assembling, and becoming organized. In the morning, they had forced the arsenal, and distributed the arms. The column of the Faubourg Saint-Antoine, about fifteen thousand strong, and that of the Faubourg Saint Marceau, amounting to five thousand, began to march about six. The crowd increased as they advanced. Artillerymen had been placed on the

---

[2] *Chronique des Cinquante Jours,* par P. L. Roederer, a writer of the most scrupulous accuracy.

Pont Neuf by the directory of the department, in order to prevent the union of the insurgents from the two sides of the river. But Manuel, the town clerk, had ordered them to be withdrawn, and the passage was accordingly free. The vanguard of the Faubourgs, composed of Marseillais and Breton federates, had already arrived by the Rue Saint Honoré, stationed themselves in battle array on the Carrousel, and turned their cannon against the château. De Joly and Champion returned from the assembly, stating that the attendance was not sufficient in number to debate; that it scarcely amounted to sixty or eighty members, and that their proposition had not been heard. Then Roederer, the recorder of the department, with the members of the department, presented himself to the crowd, observing that so great a multitude could not have access to the king, or to the national assembly, and recommending them to nominate twenty deputies, and entrust them with their requests. But they did not listen to him. He turned to the national guard, reminded them of the article of the law, which enjoined them when attacked, to repel force by force. A very small part of the national guard seemed disposed to do so; and a discharge of cannon was the only reply of the artillerymen. Roederer, seeing that the insurgents were everywhere triumphant, that they were masters of the field, and that they disposed of the multitude, and even of the troops, returned hastily to the château, at the head of the executive directory.

The king held a council with the queen and ministers. A municipal officer had just given the alarm by announcing that the columns of the insurgents were advancing upon the Tuileries. "Well, and what do they want?" asked Joly, keeper of the seals. "Abdication," replied the officer. "To be pronounced by the assembly," added the minister. "And what will follow abdication?" inquired the queen. The municipal officer bowed in silence. At this moment Roederer arrived, and increased the alarm of the court by announcing that the danger was extreme; that the insurgents would not be treated with, and that the national guard could not be depended upon. "Sire," said he, urgently, "your majesty has not five minutes to lose: your only safety is in the national assembly; it is the opinion of the department that you ought to repair thither without delay. There are not sufficient men in the court to defend the château; nor are we sure of them. At the mention of defence, the artillerymen discharged their cannon." The king replied, at first, that he had not observed many people on the Carrousel; and the queen rejoined with vivacity, that the king had forces to defend the château. But, at the renewed urgency of Roederer, the king after looking at him attentively for a few minutes, turned to the queen, and said, as he rose: "Let us go." "Monsieur Roederer," said Madame Elizabeth, addressing the recorder, "you answer for the life of the king?" "Yes, madame, with my own," he replied. "I will walk immediately before him."

Louis XVI. left his chamber with his family, ministers, and the members of the department, and announced to the persons assembled for the defence of the château that he was going to the national assembly. He placed himself between two ranks of national guards, summoned to escort him, and crossed the apartments and garden of the Tuileries. A deputation of the assembly, apprised of his approach, came to meet him: "Sire," said the president of this deputation, "the assembly, eager to provide for your safety, offers you and your family an asylum in its bosom." The procession resumed its march, and had some difficulty in crossing the terrace of the Tuileries, which was crowded with an animated mob, breathing forth threats and insults. The king and his family had great difficulty in reaching the hall of the assembly, where they took the seats reserved for the ministers. "Gentlemen," said the king, "I come here to avoid a great crime; I think I cannot be safer than with you." "Sire," replied Vergniaud, who filled the chair, "you may rely on the firmness of the national assembly. Its members have sworn to die in maintaining the rights of the people, and the constituted authorities." The king then took his seat next the president. But Chabot reminded him that the assembly could not deliberate in the presence of the king, and Louis XVI. retired with his family and ministers into the reporter's box behind the president, whence all that took place could be seen and heard.

All motives for resistance ceased with the king's departure. The means of defence had also been diminished by the departure of the national guards who escorted the king. The gendarmerie left their posts, crying "Vive la nation!" The national guard began to move in favour of the insurgents. But the foes were confronted, and, although the cause was removed, the combat nevertheless commenced. The column of the insurgents surrounded the château. The Marseillais and Bretons who occupied the first rank had just forced the Porte Royale on the Carrousel, and entered the court of the château. They were led by an old subaltern, called Westermann, a friend of Danton, and a very daring man. He ranged his force in battle array, and approaching the artillerymen, induced them to join the Marseillais with their pieces. The Swiss filled the windows of the château, and stood motionless. The two bodies confronted each other for some time without making an attack. A few of the assailants advanced amicably, and the Swiss threw some cartridges from the windows in token of peace. They penetrated as far as the vestibule, where they were met by other defenders of the château. A barrier separated them. Here the combat began, but it is unknown on which side it commenced. The Swiss discharged a murderous fire on the assailants, who were dispersed. The Place du Carrousel was cleared. But the Marseillais and Bretons soon returned with renewed force; the Swiss were fired on by the cannon, and surrounded. They kept their posts until they received orders from the king to cease firing. The exasperated mob did not cease, however, to pursue them, and gave itself up to the most sanguinary reprisals. It now became a massacre rather than a combat; and the crowd perpetrated in the château all the excesses of victory.

All this time the assembly was in the greatest alarm. The first cannonade filled them with consternation. As the firing became more frequent, the agitation increased. At one moment, the members considered themselves lost. An officer entering the hall, hastily exclaimed: "To your places, legislators; we are forced!" A few rose to go out. "No, no," cried others, "this is our post." The spectators in the gallery exclaimed instantly, "Vive l'assemblée nationale!" and the assembly replied, "Vive la nation!" Shouts of victory were then heard without, and the fate of monarchy was decided.

The assembly instantly made a proclamation to restore tranquillity, and implore the people to respect justice, their magistrates, the rights of man, liberty, and equality. But the multitude and their chiefs had all the power in their hands, and were determined to use it. The new municipality came to assert its authority. It was preceded by three banners, inscribed with the words, "Patrie, liberté, egalité." Its address was imperious, and concluded by demanding the deposition of the king, and a national convention. Deputations followed, and all expressed the same desire, or rather issued the same command.

The assembly felt itself compelled to yield; it would not, however, take upon itself the deposition of the king. Vergniaud ascended the tribune, in the name of the commission of twelve, and said: "I am about to propose to you a very rigorous measure; I appeal to the affliction of your hearts to judge how necessary it is to adopt it immediately." This measure consisted of the convocation of a national assembly, the dismissal of the ministers, and the suspension of the king. The assembly adopted it unanimously. The Girondist ministers were recalled; the celebrated decrees were carried into execution, about four thousand non-juring priests were exiled, and commissioners were despatched to the armies to make sure of them. Louis XVI., to whom the assembly had at first assigned the Luxembourg as a residence, was transferred as a prisoner to the Temple, by the all- powerful commune, under the pretext that it could not otherwise be answerable for the safety of his person. Finally, the 23rd of September was appointed for opening the extraordinary assembly, destined to decide the fate of royalty. But royalty had already fallen on the 10th of August, that day marked by the insurrection of the multitude against the middle classes and the constitutional throne, as the 14th of July had seen the insurrection of the middle class against the privileged class and the absolute power of the crown. On the 10th of August began the dictatorial and arbitrary epoch of the revolution. Circumstances becoming more and more difficult to encounter, a vast warfare arose, requiring still greater energy than ever, and that energy irregular, because popular, rendered the domination of the lower class restless, cruel, and oppressive. The nature of the question was then entirely changed; it was no longer a matter of liberty, but of public safety; and the conventional period, from the end of the constitution of 1791, to the time when the constitution of the year III. established the directory, was only a long campaign of the revolution against parties and against Europe. It was scarcely possible it should be otherwise. "The revolutionary movement once established," says M. de Maîstre, in his *Considerations sur la France.*[3] "France and the monarchy could only be saved by Jacobinism. Our grandchildren, who will care little for our sufferings, and will dance on our graves, will laugh at our present ignorance; they will easily console themselves for the excesses we have witnessed, and which will have preserved the integrity of the finest of kingdoms."

The departments adhered to the events of the 10th of August. The army, which shortly afterwards came under the influence of the revolution, was at yet of constitutional royalist principles; but as the troops were subordinate to parties, they would easily submit to the dominant opinion. The generals, second in rank, such as Dumouriez, Custines, Biron, Kellermann, and Labourdonnaie, were disposed to adopt the last changes. They had not yet declared for any particular party, look-

---

[3] Lausanne, 1796.

ing to the revolution as a means of advancement. It was not the same with the two generals in chief. Luckner floated undecided between the insurrection of the 10th of August, which he termed, "a little accident that had happened to Paris and his friend, Lafayette." The latter, head of the constitutional party, firmly adhering to his oaths, wished still to defend the overturned throne, and a constitution which no longer existed. He commanded about thirty thousand men, who were devoted to his person and his cause. His head-quarters were near Sedan. In his project of resistance in favour of the constitution, he concerted with the municipality of that town, and the directory of the department of Ardennes, to establish a civil centre round which all the departments might rally. The three commissioners, Kersaint, Antonelle, and Péraldy, sent by the legislature to his army, were arrested and imprisoned in the tower of Sedan. The reason assigned for this measure was, that the assembly having been intimidated, the members who had accepted such a mission were necessarily but the leaders or instruments of the faction which had subjugated the national assembly and the king. The troops and the civil authorities then renewed their oath to the constitution, and Lafayette endeavoured to enlarge the circle of the insurrection of the army against the popular insurrection.

General Lafayette at that moment thought, possibly, too much on the past, on the law, and the common oath, and not enough on the really extraordinary position in which France then was. He only saw the dearest hopes of the friends of liberty destroyed, the usurpation of the state by the multitude, and the anarchical reign of the Jacobins; he did not perceive the fatality of a situation which rendered the triumph of the latest comer in the revolution indispensable. It was scarcely possible that the bourgeoisie, which had been strong enough to overthrow the old system and the privileged classes, but which had reposed after that victory, could resist the emigrants and all Europe. For this a new shock, a new faith were necessary; there was need of a numerous, ardent, inexhaustible class, as enthusiastic for the 10th of August, as the bourgeoisie had been for the 14th of July. Lafayette could not associate with this party; he had combated it, under the constituent assembly, at the Champ de Mars, before and after the 20th of June. He could not continue to play his former part, nor defend a cause just in itself, but condemned by events, without compromising his country, and the results of a revolution to which he was sincerely attached. His resistance, if continued, would have given rise to a civil war between the people and the army, at a time when it was not certain that the combination of all parties would suffice against a foreign war.

It was the 19th of August, and the army of invasion having left Coblentz on the 30th of July, was ascending the Moselle, and advancing on that frontier. In consideration of the common danger, the troops were disposed to resume their obedience to the assembly; Luckner, who at first approved of Lafayette's views, retracted, weeping and swearing, before the municipality of Metz; and Lafayette himself saw the necessity of yielding to a more powerful destiny. He left his army, taking upon himself all the responsibility of the whole insurrection. He was accompanied by Bureau-de- Pusy, Latour-Maubourg, Alexander Lameth, and some officers of his staff. He proceeded through the enemy's posts towards Holland, intending to go to the United States, his adopted country. But he was discovered and arrested with his companions. In violation of the rights of nations, he was treated as a prisoner of war, and confined first in the dungeons of Magdeburg, and then by the Austrians at Olmütz. The English parliament itself took steps in his favour; but it was not until the treaty of Campo-Formio that Bonaparte released him from prison. During four years of the hardest captivity, subject to every description of privation, kept in ignorance of the state of his country and of liberty, with no prospect before him but that of perpetual and harsh imprisonment, he displayed the most heroic courage. He might have obtained his liberty by making certain retractations, but he preferred remaining buried in his dungeon to abandoning in the least degree the sacred cause he had embraced.

There have been in our day few lives more pure than Lafayette's; few characters more beautiful; few men whose popularity has been more justly won and longer maintained. After defending liberty in America at the side of Washington, he desired to establish it in the same manner in France; but this noble part was impossible in our revolution. When a people in the pursuit of liberty has no internal dissension, and no foes but foreigners, it may find a deliverer; may produce, in Switzerland a William Tell, in the Netherlands a prince of Orange, in America a Washington; but when it pursues it against its own countrymen and foreigners, at once amidst factions and battles, it can only produce a Cromwell or a Bonaparte, who become the dictators of revolutions when the struggle subsides and parties are exhausted. Lafayette, an actor in the first epoch of the crisis, enthusiastically declared for its results. He became the general of the middle class, at the head of the national guard under the constituent assembly, in the army under the legislative assembly. He had risen by it, and he would end with it. It may be said of him, that if he committed some faults of position, he had ever but one object, liberty, and that he employed but one means, the law. The manner in which, when yet quite young, he devoted himself to the deliverance of the two worlds, his glorious conduct and his invariable firmness, will transmit his name with honour to posterity, with whom a man cannot have two reputations, as in the time of party, but his own alone.

The authors of the events of the 10th of August became more and more divided, having no common views as to the results which should arise from that revolution. The more daring party, which had got hold of the commune or municipality, wished by means of that commune to rule Paris; by means of Paris, the national assembly; and by means of the assembly, France. After having effected the transference of Louis XVI. to the Temple, it threw down all the statues of the kings, and destroyed all the emblems of the monarchy. The department exercised a right of superintendence over the municipality; to be completely independent, it abrogated this right. The law required certain conditions to constitute a citizen; it decreed the cessation of these, in order that the multitude might be introduced into the government of the state. At the same time, it demanded the establishment of an extraordinary tribunal to try *the conspirators of the 10th of August*. As the assembly did not prove sufficiently docile, and endeavoured by proclamations to recall the people to more just and moderate sentiments, it received threatening messages from the Hôtel de Ville. "As a citizen," said a member of the commune, "as a magistrate of the people, I come to announce to you that this evening, at midnight, the tocsin will sound, the drum beat to arms. The people are weary of not being avenged; tremble lest they administer justice themselves." "If, before two or three hours pass, the foreman of the jury be not named," said another, "and if the jury be not itself in a condition to act, great calamities will befall Paris." To avert the threatened outbreaks, the assembly was obliged to appoint an extraordinary criminal tribunal. This tribunal condemned a few persons, but the commune having conceived the most terrible projects, did not consider it sufficiently expeditious.

At the head of the commune were Marat, Panis, Sergent, Duplain, Lenfent, Lefort, Jourdeuil, Collot d'Herbois, Billaud-Varennes, Tallien, etc.; but the chief leader of the party at that time was Danton. He, more than any other person, had distinguished himself on the 10th of August. During the whole of that night he had rushed about from the sections to the barracks of the Marseillais and Bretons, and from these to the Faubourgs. A member of the revolutionary commune, he had directed its operations, and had afterwards been appointed minister of justice.

Danton was a gigantic revolutionist; he deemed no means censurable so they were useful, and, according to him, men could do whatever they dared attempt. Danton, who has been termed the Mirabeau of the populace bore a physical resemblance to that tribune of the higher classes; he had irregular features, a powerful voice, impetuous gesticulation, a daring eloquence, a lordly brow. Their vices, too, were the same; only Mirabeau's were those of a patrician, Danton's those of a democrat; that which there was of daring in the conceptions of Mirabeau, was to be found in Danton, but in another way, because, in the revolution, he belonged to another class and another epoch. Ardent, overwhelmed with debts and wants, of dissolute habits, given up now to his passions, now to his party, he was formidable while in the pursuit of an object, but became indifferent as soon as he had obtained it. This powerful demagogue presented a mixture of the most opposite vices and qualities. Though he had sold himself to the court, he did not seem sordid; he was one of those who, so to speak, give an air of freedom even to baseness. He was an absolute exterminator, without being personally ferocious; inexorable towards masses, humane, generous even towards individuals.[4] Revolution, in his opinion, was a game at which the conqueror, if he required it, won the life of the conquered. The welfare of his party was, in his eyes, superior to law and even to humanity; this will explain his endeavours after the 10th of August, and his return to moderation when he considered the republic established.

At this period the Prussians, advancing on the plan of invasion described above, passed the frontier, after a march of twenty days. The army of Sedan was without a leader, and incapable of resisting a force so superior in numbers and so much better organised. On the 20th of August, Longwy was invested by the Prussians; on the 21st it was bombarded, and on the 24th it capitulated. On the 30th the hostile army arrived before Verdun, invested it, and began to bombard it. Verdun taken, the road to the capital was open. The capture of Longwy, and the approach

---

[4] At the time the commune was arranging the massacre of the 2nd September, he saved all who applied to him; he, of his own accord, released from prison Duport, Barnave, and Ch. Lameth, his personal antagonists.

of so great a danger, threw Paris into the utmost agitation and alarm. The executive council, composed of the ministers, was summoned by the committee of general defence, to deliberate on the best measures to be adopted in this perilous conjuncture. Some proposed to wait for the enemy under the walls of the capital, others to retire to Saumur. "You are not ignorant," said Danton, when his turn to speak arrived, "that France is Paris; if you abandon the capital to the foreigner, you surrender yourselves, and you surrender France. It is in Paris that we must defend ourselves by every possible means. I cannot sanction any plan tending to remove you from it. The second project does not appear to me any better. It is impossible to think of fighting under the walls of the capital. The 10th of August has divided France into two parties, the one attached to royalty, the other desiring a republic. The latter, the decided minority of which in the state cannot be concealed, is the only one on which you can rely to fight; the other will refuse to march; it will excite Paris in favour of the foreigner, while your defenders, placed between two fires, will perish in repelling him. Should they fall, which seems to me beyond a doubt, your ruin and that of France are certain; if, contrary to all expectation, they return victorious over the coalition, this victory will still be a defeat for you; for it will have cost you thousands of brave men, while the royalists, more numerous than you, will have lost nothing of their strength and influence. It is my opinion, that to disconcert their measures and stop the enemy, we must make the royalists fear." The committee, at once understanding the meaning of these words, were thrown into a state of consternation. "Yes, I tell you," resumed Danton, "we must make them fear." As the committee rejected this proposition by a silence full of alarm, Danton concerted with the commune. His aim was to put down its enemies by terror, to involve the multitude more and more by making them his accomplices, and to leave the revolution no other refuge than victory.

Domiciliary visits were made with great and gloomy ceremony; a large number of persons whose condition, opinions, or conduct rendered them objects of suspicion, were thrown into prison. These unfortunate persons were taken especially from the two dissentient classes, the nobles and the clergy, who were charged with conspiracy under the legislative assembly. All citizens capable of bearing arms were enrolled in the Champ de Mars, and departed on the first of September for the frontier. The générale was beat, the tocsin sounded, cannon were fired, and Danton, presenting himself to the assembly to report the measures taken to save the country, exclaimed: "The cannon you hear are no alarm cannon, but the signal for attacking the enemy! To conquer them, to prostrate them, what is necessary? Daring, again daring, and still again and ever daring!" Intelligence of the taking of Verdun arrived during the night of the 1st of September. The commune availed themselves of this moment, when Paris, filled with terror, thought it saw the enemy already at its gates, to execute their fearful projects. The cannon were again fired, the tocsin sounded, the barriers were closed, and the massacre began.

During three days, the prisoners confined in the Carmes, the Abbaye, the Conciergérie, the Force, etc., were slaughtered by a band of about three hundred assassins, directed and paid by the commune. This body, with a calm fanaticism, prostituting to murder the sacred forms of justice, now judges, now executioners, seemed rather to be practising a calling than to be exercising vengeance; they massacred without question, without remorse, with the conviction of fanatics and the obedience of executioners. If some peculiar circumstances seemed to move them, and to recall them to sentiments of humanity, to justice, and to mercy, they yielded to the impression for a moment, and then began anew. In this way a few persons were saved; but they were very few. The assembly desired to prevent the massacres, but were unable to do so. The ministry were as incapable as the assembly; the terrible commune alone could order and do everything; Pétion, the mayor, had been cashiered; the soldiers placed in charge of the prisoners feared to resist the murderers, and allowed them to take their own course; the crowd seemed indifferent, or accomplices; the rest of the citizens dared not even betray their consternation. We might be astonished that so great a crime should, with such deliberation, have been conceived, executed, and endured, did we not know what the fanaticism of party will do, and what fear will suffer. But the chastisement of this enormous crime fell at last upon the heads of its authors. The majority of them perished in the storm they had themselves raised, and by the same violent means that they had themselves employed. Men of party seldom escape the fate they have made others undergo.

The executive council, directed, as to military operations by general Servan, advanced the newly-levied battalions towards the frontier. As a man of judgment, he was desirous of placing a general at the threatened point; but the choice was difficult. Among the generals who had declared in favour of the late political events, Kellermann seemed only adapted for a subordinate command, and the authorities had therefore merely placed him in the room of the vacillative and incompetent Luckner. Custine was but little skilled in his art; he was fit for any dashing *coup de main*, but not for the conduct of a great army intrusted with the destiny of France. The same military inferiority was chargeable upon Biron, Labourdonnaie, and the rest, who were therefore left at their old stations, with the corps under their command. Dumouriez alone remained, against whom the Girondists still retained some rancour, and in whom they, moreover, suspected the ambitious views, the tastes, and character of an adventurer, while they rendered justice to his superior talents. However, as he was the only general equal to so important a position, the executive council gave him the command of the army of the Moselle.

Dumouriez repaired in all haste from the camp at Maulde to that of Sedan. He assembled a council of war, in which the general opinion was in favour of retiring towards Châlons or Rheims, and covering themselves with the Marne. Far from adopting this dangerous plan, which would have discouraged the troops, given up Lorraine, Trois Evêchés, and a part of Champagne, and thrown open the road to Paris, Dumouriez conceived a project full of genius. He saw that it was necessary, by a daring march, to advance on the forest of Argonne, where he might infallibly stop the enemy. This forest had four issues; that of the Chêne-Populeux on the left; those of the Croix-au-Bois and of Grandpré in the centre, and that of Les Islettes on the right, which opened or closed the passage into France. The Prussians were only six leagues from the forest, and Dumouriez had twelve to pass over, and his design of occupying it to conceal, if he hoped for success. He executed his project skilfully and boldly. General Dillon, advancing on the Islettes, took possession of them with seven thousand men; he himself reached Grandpré, and there established a camp of thirteen thousand men. The Croix-au-Bois, and the Chêne-Populeux were in like manner occupied and defended by some troops. It was here that he wrote to the minister of war, Servan:—"Verdun is taken; I await the Prussians. The camps of Grandpré and Les Islettes are the Thermopylae of France; but I shall be more fortunate than Leonidas."

In this position, Dumouriez might have stopped the enemy, and himself have securely awaited the succours which were on their road to him from every part of France. The various battalions of volunteers repaired to the camps in the interior, whence they were despatched to his army, as soon as they were at all in a state of discipline. Beurnonville, who was on the Flemish frontier, had received orders to advance with nine thousand men, and to be at Rhétel, on Dumouriez's left, by the 13th of September. Duval was also on the 7th to march with seven thousand men to the Chêne-Populeux; and Kellermann was advancing from Metz, on his right, with a reinforcement of twenty-two thousand men. Time, therefore, was all that was necessary.

The duke of Brunswick, after taking Verdun, passed the Meuse in three columns. General Clairfait was operating on his right, and prince Hohenlohe on his left. Renouncing all hope of driving Dumouriez from his position by attacking him in front, he tried to turn him. Dumouriez had been so imprudent as to place nearly his whole force at Grandpré and the Islettes, and to put only a small corps at Chêne-Populeux and Coix-au- Bois—posts, it is true, of minor importance. The Prussians, accordingly, seized upon these, and were on the point of turning him in his camp at Grandpré, and of thus compelling him to lay down his arms. After this grand blunder, which neutralized his first manoeuvres, he did not despair of his situation. He broke up his camp secretly during the night of the 14th September, passed the Aisne, the approach to which might have been closed to him, made a retreat as able as his advance on the Argonne had been, and concentrated his forces in the camp at Sainte-Menehould. He had already delayed the advance of the Prussians at Argonne. The season, as it advanced, became bad. He had now only to maintain his post till the arrival of Kellermann and Beurnonville, and the success of the campaign would be certain. The troops had become disciplined and inured, and the army amounted to about seventy thousand men, after the arrival of Beurnonville and Kellermann, which took place on the 17th.

The Prussian army had followed the movements of Dumouriez. On the 20th, it attacked Kellermann at Valmy, in order to cut off from the French army the retreat on Châlons. There was a brisk cannonade on both sides. The Prussians advanced in columns towards the heights of Valmy, to carry them. Kellermann also formed his infantry in columns, enjoined them not to fire, but to await the approach of the enemy, and charge them with the bayonet. He gave this command, with the cry of *Vive la nation!* and this cry, repeated from one end of the line to the other, startled the Prussians still more than the firm attitude of our troops. The duke of Brunswick made his somewhat shaken battalions fall back; the firing continued till the evening; the enemy attempted a fresh attack, but were repulsed. The day was ours;

and the success of Valmy, almost insignificant in itself, produced on our troops, and upon opinion in France, the effect of the most complete victory.

From the same epoch may be dated the discouragement and retreat of the enemy. The Prussians had entered upon this campaign on the assurance of the emigrants that it would be a mere military promenade. They were without magazines or provisions; in the midst of a perfectly open country, they encountered a resistance each day more energetic; the incessant rains had broken up the roads; the soldiers marched knee-deep in mud, and, for four days past, boiled corn had been their only food. Diseases, produced by the chalky water, want of clothing, and damp, had made great ravages in the army. The duke of Brunswick advised a retreat, contrary to the opinion of the king of Prussia and the emigrants, who wished to risk a battle, and get possession of Châlons. But as the fate of the Prussian monarchy depended on its army, and the entire ruin of that army would be the inevitable consequence of a defeat, the duke of Brunswick's opinion prevailed. Negotiations were opened, and the Prussians, abating their first demands, now only required the restoration of the king upon the constitutional throne. But the convention had just assembled; the republic had been proclaimed, and the executive council replied, "that the French republic could listen to no proposition until the Prussian troops had entirely evacuated the French territory." The Prussians, upon this, commenced their retreat on the evening of the 30th of September. It was slightly disturbed by Kellermann, whom Dumouriez sent in pursuit, while he himself proceeded to Paris to enjoy his triumph, and concert measures for the invasion of Belgium. The French troops re-entered Verdun and Longwy; and the enemy, after having crossed the Ardennes and Luxembourg, repassed the Rhine at Coblentz, towards the end of October. This campaign had been marked by general success. In Flanders, the duke of Saxe-Teschen had been compelled to raise the siege of Lille, after seven days of a bombardment, contrary, both in its duration and in its useless barbarity, to all the usages of war. On the Rhine, Custine had taken Trèves, Spires, and Mayence. In the Alps, general Montesquiou had invaded Savoy, and general Anselme the territory of Nice. Our armies, victorious in all directions, had everywhere assumed the offensive, and the revolution was saved.

If we were to present the picture of a state emerging from a great crisis, and were to say: "There were in this state an absolute government whose authority has been restricted; two privileged classes which have lost their supremacy; a vast population, already freed by the effect of civilization and intelligence, but without political rights, and who have been obliged, by reason of repeated refusals, to gain these for themselves"; if we were to add: "The government, after opposing this revolution, submitted to it, but the privileged classes constantly opposed it,"—the following would probably be concluded from these data:

"The government will be full of regret, the people will exhibit distrust, and the privileged classes will attack the new order of things, each in its own way. The nobility, unable to do so at home, from its weakness there, will emigrate, in order to excite foreign powers, who will make preparations for attack; the clergy, who would lose its means of action abroad, will remain at home, where it will seek out foes to the revolution. The people, threatened from without, in danger at home, irritated against the emigrants who seek to arm foreign powers, against foreign powers about to attack its independence, against the clergy, who excite the country to insurrection, will treat as enemies clergy, emigrants, and foreign powers. It will require first surveillance over, then the banishment of the refractory priests; confiscation of the property of the emigrants; war against allied Europe, in order to forestall it. The first authors of the revolution will condemn such of these measures as shall violate the law; the continuators of the revolution will, on the contrary, regard them as the salvation of the country; and discord will arise between those who prefer the constitution to the state, and those who prefer the state to the constitution. The monarch, induced by his interests as king, his affections and his conscience, to reject such a course of policy, will pass for an accomplice of the counter-revolution, because he will appear to protect it. The revolutionists will then seek to gain over the king by intimidation, and failing in this, will overthrow his authority."

Such was the history of the legislative assembly. Internal disturbances led to the decree against the priests; external menaces to that against the emigrants; the coalition of foreign powers to war against Europe; the first defeat of our armies, to the formation of the camp of twenty thousand. The refusal of Louis XVI. to adopt most of these decrees, rendered him an object of suspicion to the Girondists; the dissensions between the latter and the constitutionalists, who desired some of them to be legislators, as in time of peace, others, enemies, as in time of war, disunited the partisans of the revolution. With the Girondists the question of liberty was involved in victory, and victory in the decrees. The 20th of June was an attempt to force their acceptance; but having failed in its effect, they deemed that either the crown or the revolution must be renounced, and they brought on the 10th of August. Thus, but for emigration which induced the war, but for the schism which induced the disturbances, the king would probably have agreed to the constitution, and the revolutionists would not have dreamed of the republic.

THE NATIONAL CONVENTION

CHAPTER VI

FROM THE 20TH OF SEPTEMBER, 1792, TO THE 21ST OF JANUARY, 1793

First measures of the Convention—Its composition—Rivalry of the Gironde and of the Mountain—Strength and views of the two parties—Robespierre: the Girondists accuse him of aspiring to the dictatorship—Marat—Fresh accusation of Robespierre by Louvet; Robespierre's defence; the Convention passes to the order of the day—The Mountain, victorious in this struggle, demand the trial of Louis XVI.—Opinions of parties on this subject—The Convention decides that Louis XVI. shall be tried, and by itself—Louis XVI. at the Temple; his replies before the Convention; his defence; his condemnation; courage and serenity of his last moments—What he was, and what he was not, as a king.

The convention was constituted on the 20th of September, 1792, and commenced its deliberations on the 21st. In its first sitting it abolished royalty, and proclaimed the republic. On the 22nd, it appropriated the revolution to itself, by declaring it would not date from *year IV. of Liberty*; but from *year I. of the French Republic*. After these first measures, voted by acclamation, with a sort of rivalry in democracy and enthusiasm in the two parties, which had become divided at the close of the legislative assembly, the convention, instead of commencing its labours, gave itself up to intestine quarrels. The Girondists and the Mountain, before they established the new revolution, desired to know to which of them it was to belong, and the enormous dangers of their position did not divert them from this contest. They had more than ever to fear the efforts of Europe. Austria, Prussia, and some of the German princes having attacked France before the 10th of August, there was every reason to believe that the other sovereigns of Europe would declare against it after the fall of the monarchy, the imprisonment of the king, and the massacres of September. Within, the enemies of the revolution had increased. To the partisans of the ancient regime, of the aristocracy and clergy, were now to be added the friends of constitutional monarchy, with whom the fate of Louis XVI. was an object of earnest solicitude, and those who imagined liberty impossible without order, or under the empire of the multitude. Amidst so many obstacles and adversaries, at a moment when their strictest union was requisite, the Gironde and the Mountain attacked each other with the fiercest animosity. It is true that these two parties were wholly incompatible, and that their respective leaders could not combine, so strong and varied were the grounds of separation in their rivalry for power, and in their designs.

Events had compelled the Girondists to become republicans. It would have suited them far better to have remained constitutionalists. The integrity of their purposes, their distaste for the multitude, their aversion for violent measures, and especially the prudence which counselled them only to attempt that which seemed possible—every circumstance made this imperative upon them; but they had not been left free to remain what they at first were. They had followed the bias which led them onward to the republic, and they had gradually habituated themselves to this form of government. They now desired it ardently and sincerely, but they felt how difficult it would be to establish and consolidate it. They deemed it a great and noble thing; but they felt that the men for it were wanting. The multitude had neither the intelligence nor the virtue proper for this kind of government. The revolution effected by the constituent assembly was legitimate, still more because it was possible than because it was just; it had its constitution and its citizens. But a new revolution, which should call the lower classes to the conduct of the state, could not be durable. It would injuriously affect too many interests, and have but momentary defenders, the lower class being capable of sound action and conduct in a crisis, but not for a permanency. Yet, in consenting to this second revolution, it was this inferior class which must be looked to for support. The Girondists did not adopt this course, and they found themselves placed in a position altogether false; they lost the assistance of the constitutionalists without procuring that of the democrats; they had a hold upon neither extreme of society. Accordingly, they only formed a half party, which was soon overthrown, because it had no root. The Girondists, after the 10th of August, were, between the middle class and the multitude, what the monarchists, or the Mounier and Necker party, had been after the 24th of July, between the privileged classes and the bourgeoisie.

The Mountain, on the contrary, desired a republic of the people. The leaders of this party, annoyed at the credit of the Girondists, sought to overthrow and to supersede them. They were less intelligent, and less eloquent, but abler, more decided, and in no degree scrupulous as to means. The extremest democracy seemed to them the best of governments, and what they termed the people, that is, the lowest populace, was the object of their constant adulation, and most ardent solicitude. No party was more dangerous; most consistently it laboured for those who fought its battle.

Ever since the opening of the convention, the Girondists had occupied the right benches, and the Mountain party the summit of the left, whence the name by which they are designated. The Girondists were the strongest in the assembly; the elections in the departments had generally been in their favour. A great number of the deputies of the legislative assembly had been re-elected, and as at that time connexion effected much, the members who had been united with the deputation of the Gironde and the commune of Paris before the 10th of August, returned with the same opinions. Others came without any particular system or party, without enmities or attachments: these formed what was then called the *Plaine* or the *Marais*. This party, taking no interest in the struggles between the Gironde and the Mountain, voted with the side they considered the most just, so long as they were allowed to be moderate; that is to say, so long as they had no fears for themselves.

The Mountain was composed of deputies of Paris, elected under the influence of the commune of the 10th of August, and of some very decided republicans from the provinces; it, from time to time, increased its ranks with those who were rendered enthusiastic by circumstances, or who were impelled by fear. But though inferior in the convention in point of numbers, it was none the less very powerful, even at this period. It swayed Paris; the commune was devoted to it, and the commune had managed to constitute itself the supreme authority in the state. The Mountain had sought to master the departments, by endeavouring to establish an identity of views and conduct between the municipality of Paris and the provincial municipalities; they had not, however, completely succeeded in this, and the departments were for the most part favourable to their adversaries, who cultivated their good will by means of pamphlets and journals sent by the minister Roland, whose house the Mountain called a *bureau d'esprit public*, and whose friends they called *intrigants*. But besides this junction of the communes, which sooner or later would take place, they were adopted by the Jacobins. This club, the most influential as well as the most ancient and extensive, changed its views at every crisis without changing its name; it was a framework ready for every dominating power, excluding all dissentients. That at Paris was the metropolis of Jacobinism, and governed the others almost imperiously. The Mountain had made themselves masters of it; they had already driven the Girondists from it, by denunciation and disgust, and replaced the members taken from the bourgeoisie by sans-culottes. Nothing remained to the Girondists but the ministry, who, thwarted by the commune, were powerless in Paris. The Mountain, on the contrary, disposed of all the effective force of the capital, of the public mind by the Jacobins, of the sections and faubourgs by the sans-culottes, of the insurrectionists by the municipality.

The first measure of parties after having decreed the republic, was to contend with each other. The Girondists were indignant at the massacres of September, and they beheld with horror on the benches of the convention the men who had advised or ordered them. Above all others, two inspired them with antipathy and disgust; Robespierre, whom they suspected of aspiring to tyranny; and Marat, who from the commencement of the revolution had in his writings constituted himself the apostle of murder. They denounced Robespierre with more animosity than prudence; he was not yet sufficiently formidable to incur the accusation of aspiring to the dictatorship. His enemies by reproaching him with intentions then improbable, and at all events incapable of proof, themselves augmented his popularity and importance.

Robespierre, who played so terrible a part in our revolution, was beginning to take a prominent position. Hitherto, despite his efforts, he had had superiors in his own party: under the constituent assembly, its famous leaders; under the legislative, Brissot and Pétion; on the 10th of August, Danton. At these different periods he had declared himself against those whose renown or popularity offended him. Only able to distinguish himself among the celebrated personages of the first assembly by the singularity of his opinions, he had shown himself an exaggerated reformer; during the second, he became a constitutionalist, because his rivals were innovators, and he had talked in favour of peace to the Jacobins, because his rivals advocated war. From the 10th of August he essayed in that club to ruin the Girondists, and to supplant Danton, always associating the cause of his vanity with that of the multitude. This man, of ordinary talents and vain character, owed it to his inferiority to rank with the last, a great advantage in times of revolution; and his conceit drove him to aspire to the first rank, to do all to reach it, to dare all to maintain himself there.

Robespierre had the qualifications for tyranny; a soul not great, it is true, but not common; the advantage of one sole passion, the appearance of patriotism, a deserved reputation for incorruptibility, an austere life, and no aversion to the effusion of blood. He was a proof that amidst civil troubles it is not mind but conduct that leads to political fortune, and that persevering mediocrity is more powerful than wavering genius. It must also be observed that Robespierre had the support of an immense and fanatical sect, whose government he had solicited, and whose principles he had defended since the close of the constituent assembly. This sect derived its origin from the eighteenth century, certain opinions of which it represented. In politics, its symbol was the absolute sovereignty of the *Contrat social* of J.J. Rousseau, and for creed, it held the deism of *la Profession de foi du Vicaire Savoyard*; at a later period it succeeded in realizing these for a moment in the constitution of '93, and the worship of the Supreme Being. More fanaticism and system existed in the different epochs of the revolution than is generally supposed.

Whether the Girondists distinctly foresaw the dominion of Robespierre, or whether they suffered themselves to be carried away by their indignation, they accused him, with republicans, of the most serious of crimes. Paris was agitated by the spirit of faction; the Girondists wished to pass a law against those who excited disorders and violence, and at the same time to give the convention an independent force derived from the eighty-three departments. They appointed a commission to present a report on this subject. The Mountain attacked this measure as injurious to Paris; the Gironde defended it, by pointing out the project of a triumvirate formed by the deputation of Paris. "I was born in Paris," said Osselin; "I am deputy for that town. It is announced that a party is formed in the very heart of it, desiring a dictatorship, triumvirs, tribunes, etc. I declare that extreme ignorance or profound wickedness alone could have conceived such a project. Let the member of the deputation of Paris who has conceived such an idea be anathematized!" "Yes," exclaimed Rebecqui of Marseilles, "yes, there exists in this assembly a party which aspires at the dictatorship, and I will name the leader of this party; Robespierre. That is the man whom I denounce." Barbaroux supported this denunciation by his evidence; he was one of the chief authors of the 10th of August; he was the leader of the Marseillais, and he possessed immense influence in the south. He stated that about the 10th of August, the Marseillais were much courted by the two parties who divided the capital; he was brought to Robespierre's, and there he was told to ally himself to those citizens who had acquired most popularity, and that Paris expressly named to him, *Robespierre, as the virtuous man who was to be dictator of France.* Barbaroux was a man of action. There were some members of the Right who thought with him, that they ought to conquer their adversaries, in order to avoid being conquered by them. They wished, making use of the convention against the commune, to oppose the departments to Paris, and while they remained weak, by no means to spare enemies, to whom they would otherwise be granting time to become stronger. But the greater number dreaded a rupture, and trembled at the idea of energetic measures.

This accusation against Robespierre had no immediate consequences; but it fell back on Marat, who had recommended a dictatorship, in his journal "L'Ami du Peuple," and had extolled the massacres. When he ascended the tribune to justify himself, the assembly shuddered. "*A bas! à bas!*" resounded from all sides. Marat remained imperturbable. In a momentary pause, he said: "I have a great number of personal enemies in this assembly. (*Tous! tous!*) I beg of them to remember decorum; I exhort them to abstain from all furious clamours and indecent threats against a man who has served liberty and themselves more than they think. For once let them learn to listen." And this man delivered in the midst of the convention, astounded at his audacity and sangfroid, his views of the proscriptions and of the dictatorship. For some time he had fled from cellar to cellar to avoid public anger, and the warrants issued against him. His sanguinary journal alone appeared; in it he demanded heads, and prepared the multitude for the massacres of September. There is no folly which may not enter a man's head, and what is worse, which may not be realized for a moment. Marat was possessed by certain fixed ideas. The revolution had enemies, and, in his opinion, it could not last unless freed from them; from that moment he deemed nothing could be more simple than to exterminate them, and appoint a dictator, whose functions should be limited to proscribing; these two measures he proclaimed aloud, with a cynical cruelty, having no more regard for propriety than for the lives of men, and despising as weak minds all those who called his projects atrocious, instead of considering them profound. The revolution had actors really more sanguinary than he, but none exercised a more fatal influence over his times. He depraved the morality of parties already sufficiently corrupt; and he had the two leading ideas which the committee of public safety subsequently realized by its commissioners or its government— extermination in mass, and the dictatorship.

Marat's accusation was not attended with any results; he inspired more disgust, but less hatred than Robespierre; some regarded him as a madman; others considered these debates as the quarrels of parties, and not as an object of interest for the republic. Moreover, it seemed dangerous to attempt to purify the convention, or to dismiss one of its members, and it was a difficult step to get over, even for parties. Danton did not exonerate Marat. "I do not like him," said he; "I have had experience of his temperament; it is volcanic, crabbed and unsociable. But why seek for the language of a faction in what he writes? Has the general agitation any other cause than that of the revolutionary movement itself?" Robespierre, on his part, protested that he knew very little of Marat; that, previous to the 10th of August, he had only had one conversation with him, after which Marat, whose violent opinions he did not approve, had considered his political views so narrow, that he had stated in his journal, *that he had neither the higher views nor the daring of a statesman.*

But he was the object of much greater indignation because he was more dreaded. The first accusation of Rebecqui and Barbaroux had not succeeded. A short time afterwards, the Minister Roland made a report on the state of France and Paris; in it he denounced the massacres of September, the encroachments of the commune, and the proceedings of the agitators. "When," said he, "they render the wisest and most intrepid defenders of liberty odious or suspected, when principles of revolt and slaughter are boldly professed and applauded in the assemblies, and clamours arise against the convention itself, I can no longer doubt that partisans of the ancient regime, or false friends of the people, concealing their extravagance or wickedness under a mask of patriotism, have conceived the plan of an overthrow in which they hope to raise themselves on ruins and corpses, and gratify their thirst for blood, gold, and atrocity."

He cited, in proof of his report, a letter in which the vice-president of the second section of the criminal tribunal informed him, that he and the most distinguished Girondists were threatened; that, in the words of their enemies, *another bleeding was wanted*; and that these men would hear of no one but Robespierre.

At these words the latter hastened to the tribune to justify himself. "No one," he cried, "dare accuse me to my face!" "I dare!" exclaimed Louvet, one of the most determined men of the Gironde. "Yes, Robespierre," he continued, fixing his eye upon him; "I accuse you!" Robespierre, hitherto full of assurance, became moved. He had once before, at the Jacobins, measured his strength with this formidable adversary, whom he knew to be witty, impetuous, and uncompromising. Louvet now spoke, and in a most eloquent address spared neither acts nor names. He traced the course of Robespierre to the Jacobins, to the commune, to the electoral assembly: "calumniating the best patriots; lavishing the basest flatteries on a few hundred citizens, at first designated as the people of Paris, afterwards as the people absolutely, and then as the sovereign; repeating the eternal enumeration of his own merits, perfections, and virtues; and never failing, after he had dwelt on the strength, grandeur, and sovereignty of the people, to protest that he was the people too." He then described him concealing himself on the 10th of August, and afterwards swaying the conspirators of the commune. Then he came to the massacres of September, and exclaimed: "The revolution of the 10th of August belongs to all!" he added, pointing out a few of the members of the Mountain in the commune, "but that of the 2nd of September, that belongs to them—and to none but them! Have they not glorified themselves by it? They themselves, with brutal contempt, only designated us as the patriots of the 10th of August. With ferocious pride they called themselves the patriots of the 2nd of September! Ah, let them retain this distinction worthy of the courage peculiar to them; let them retain it as our justification, and for their lasting shame! These pretended friends of the people wish to cast on the people of Paris the horrors that stained the first week of September. They have basely slandered them. The people of Paris can fight; they cannot murder! It is true, they were assembled all the day long before the château of the Tuileries on the glorious 10th of August; it is false that they were seen before the prisons on the horrible 2nd of September. How many executioners were there within? Two hundred; probably not two hundred. And without, how many spectators could be reckoned drawn thither by truly incomprehensible curiosity? At most, twice the number. But, it is asked, why, if the people did not assist in these murders, did they not hinder them? Why? Because Pétion's tutelary authority was fettered; because Roland spoke in vain; because Danton, the minister of justice, did not speak at all,… because the presidents of the forty-eight sections waited for orders which the general in command did not give; because municipal officers, wearing their scarfs, presided at these atrocious executions. But the legislative assembly? The legislative assembly! representatives of the people, you will avenge it! The powerless state into which your predecessors were reduced is, in the midst of such crimes, the greatest for which these ruffians, whom I denounce, must be punished." Returning to Robespierre, Louvet pointed out his ambition, his efforts, his extreme ascendancy over the people, and terminated his fiery philippic by a series of facts, each one of which was preceded by this terrible form: *"Robespierre, I accuse thee!"*

Louvet descended from the tribune amidst applause, Robespierre mounted it to justify himself; he was pale, and was received with murmurs. Either from agitation or fear of prejudice, he asked for a week's delay. The time arrived; he appeared less like one accused than as a triumpher; he repelled with irony Louvet's reproaches, and entered into a long apology for himself. It must be admitted that the facts were vague, and it required little trouble to weaken or overturn them. Persons were placed in the gallery to applaud him; even the convention itself, who regarded this quarrel as the result of a private pique, and, as Barrère said, did not fear *a man of a day, a petty leader of riots*, was disposed to close these debates. Accordingly, when Robespierre observed, as he finished: "For my part, I will draw no personal conclusions; I have given up the easy advantage of replying to the calumnies of my adversaries by more formidable denunciations; I wished to suppress the offensive part of my justification. I renounce the just vengeance I have a right to pursue against my calumniators; I ask for no other than the return of peace and triumph of liberty!" he was applauded, and the convention passed to the order of the day. Louvet in vain sought to reply; he was not allowed. Barbaroux as vainly presented himself as accuser and Lanjuinais opposed the motion for the order without obtaining the renewal of the discussion. The Girondists themselves supported it: they committed one fault in commencing the accusation, and another in not continuing it. The Mountain carried the day, since they were not conquered, and Robespierre was brought nearer the assumption of the part he had been so far removed from. In times of revolution, men very soon become what they are supposed to be, and the Mountain adopted him for their leader because the Girondists pursued him as such.

But what was much more important than personal attacks, were the discussions respecting the means of government, and the management of authorities and parties. The Girondists struck, not only against individuals but against the commune. Not one of their measures succeeded; they were badly proposed or badly sustained. They should have supported the government, replaced the municipality, maintained their post among the Jacobins and swayed them, gained over the multitude, or prevented its acting; and they did nothing of all this. One among them, Buzot, proposed giving the convention a guard of three thousand men, taken from the departments. This measure, which would at least have made the assembly independent, was not supported with sufficient vigour to be adopted. Thus the Girondists attacked the Mountain without weakening them, the commune without subduing it, the Faubourgs without suppressing them. They irritated Paris by invoking the aid of the departments, without procuring it; thus acting in opposition to the most common rules of prudence, for it is always safer to do a thing than to threaten to do it.

Their adversaries skilfully turned this circumstance to advantage. They secretly circulated a report which could not but compromise the Girondists; it was, that they wished to remove the republic to the south, and give up the rest of the empire. Then commenced that reproach of federalism, which afterwards became so fatal. The Girondists disdained it because they did not see the consequences; but it necessarily gained credit in proportion as they became weak and their enemies became daring. What had given rise to the report was the project of defending themselves behind the Loire, and removing the government to the south, if the north should be invaded and Paris taken, and the predilection they manifested for the provinces, and their indignation against the agitators of the capital. Nothing is more easy than to change the appearance of a measure by changing the period in which the measure was adopted, and discover in the disapprobation expressed at the irregular acts of a city, an intention to form the other cities of the state into a league against it. Accordingly, the Girondists were pointed out to the multitude as federalists. While they denounced the commune, and accused Robespierre and Marat, the Mountain decreed *the unity and indivisibility of the republic*. This was a way of attacking them and bringing them into suspicion, although they themselves adhered so eagerly to these propositions that they seemed to regret not having made them.

But a circumstance, apparently unconnected with the disputes of these two parties, served still better the cause of the Mountain. Already emboldened by the unsuccessful attempts which had been directed against them, they only waited for an opportunity to become assailants in their turn. The convention was fatigued by these long discussions. Those members who were not interested in them, and even those of the two parties who were not in the first rank, felt the need of concord, and wished to see men occupy themselves with the republic. There was an apparent truce, and the attention of the assembly was directed for a moment to the new constitution, which the Mountain caused it to abandon, in order to decide on the fate of the fallen prince. The leaders of the extreme Left were driven to this course by several motives: they did not want the Girondists, and the moderate members of the Plain, who directed the committee of the constitution, the former by Pétion, Condorcet, Brissot, Vergniaud, Gensonné, the others by Barrère, Sieyès, and Thomas Paine, to organize the republic. They would have established the system of the bourgeoisie, rendering it a little more democratic than that of

1791, while they themselves aspired at constituting the people. But they could only accomplish their end by power, and they could only obtain power by protracting the revolutionary state in France. Besides the necessity of preventing the establishment of legal order by a terrible coup d'état, such as the condemnation of Louis XVI., which would arouse all passions, rally round them the violent parties, by proving them to be the inflexible guardians of the republic, they hoped to expose the sentiments of the Girondists, who did not conceal their desire to save Louis XVI., and thus ruin them in the estimation of the multitude. There were, without a doubt, in this conjuncture, a great number of the Mountain, who, on this occasion, acted with the greatest sincerity and only as republicans, in whose eyes Louis XVI. appeared guilty with respect to the revolution; and a dethroned king was dangerous to a young democracy. But this party would have been more clement, had it not had to ruin the Gironde at the same time with Louis XVI.

For some time past, the public mind had been prepared for his trial. The Jacobin club resounded with invectives against him; the most injurious reports were circulated against his character; his condemnation was required for the firm establishment of liberty. The popular societies in the departments addressed petitions to the convention with the same object. The sections presented themselves at the bar of the assembly, and they carried through it, on litters, the men wounded on the 10th of August, who came to cry for vengeance on Louis Capet. They now only designated Louis XVI. by this name of the ancient chief of his race, thinking to substitute his title of king by his family name.

Party motives and popular animosities combined against this unfortunate prince. Those who, two months before, would have repelled the idea of exposing him to any other punishment than that of dethronement, were stupefied; so quickly does man lose in moments of crisis the right to defend his opinions! The discovery of the iron chest especially increased the fanaticism of the multitude, and the weakness of the king's defenders. After the 10th of August, there were found in the offices of the civil list documents which proved the secret correspondence of Louis XVI. with the discontented princes, with the emigration, and with Europe. In a report, drawn up at the command of the legislative assembly, he was accused of intending to betray the state and overthrow the revolution. He was accused of having written, on the 16th April, 1791, to the bishop of Clermont, that if he regained his power he would restore the former government and the clergy to the state in which they previously were; of having afterwards proposed war, merely to hasten the approach of his deliverers; of having been in correspondence with men who wrote to him— "War will compel all the powers to combine against the seditious and abandoned men who tyrannize over France, in order that their punishment may speedily serve as an example to all who shall be induced to trouble the peace of empires. You may rely on a hundred and fifty thousand men, Prussians, Austrians, and Imperialists, and on an army of twenty thousand emigrants;" of having been on terms with his brothers, whom his public measures had discountenanced: and, lastly, of having constantly opposed the revolution.

Fresh documents were soon brought forward in support of this accusation. In the Tuileries, behind a panel in the wainscot, there was a hole wrought in the wall, and closed by an iron door. This secret closet was pointed out by the minister, Roland, and there were discovered proofs of all the conspiracies and intrigues of the court against the revolution; projects with the popular leaders to strengthen the constitutional power of the king, to restore the ancient régime and the aristocrats; the manoeuvres of Talon, the arrangements with Mirabeau, the proposition accepted by Bouillé, under the constituent assembly, and some new plots under the legislative assembly. This discovery increased the exasperation against Louis XVI. Mirabeau's bust was broken by the Jacobins, and the convention covered the one which stood in the hall where it held its sittings.

For some time there had been a question in the assembly as to the trial of this prince, who, having been dethroned, could no longer be proceeded against. There was no tribunal empowered to pronounce his sentence, no punishment which could be inflicted on him: accordingly, they plunged into false interpretations of the inviolability granted to Louis XVI., in order to condemn him legally. The greatest error of parties, next to being unjust, is the desire not to appear so. The committee of legislation, commissioned to draw up a report on the question as to whether Louis XVI. could be tried, and whether he could be tried by the convention, decided in the affirmative. The deputy Mailhe opposed, in its name, the dogma of inviolability; but as this dogma had influenced the preceding epoch of the revolution, he contended that Louis XVI. was inviolable as king, but not as an individual. He maintained that the nation, unable to give up its guarantee respecting acts of power, had supplied the inviolability of the monarch by the responsibility of his ministers; and that, when Louis XVI. had acted as a simple individual, his responsibility devolving on no one, he ceased to be inviolable. Thus Mailhe limited the constitutional safeguard given to Louis XVI. to the acts of the king. He concluded that Louis XVI. could be tried, the dethronement not being a punishment, but a change of government; that he might be brought to trial, by virtue of the penal code relative to traitors and conspirators; that he could be tried by the convention, without observing the process of other tribunals, because, the convention representing the people—the people including all interests, and all interests constituting justice—it was impossible that the national tribunal could violate justice, and that, consequently, it was useless to subject it to forms. Such was the chain of sophistry, by means of which the committee transformed the convention into a tribunal. Robespierre's party showed itself much more consistent, dwelling only on state reasons, and rejecting forms as deceptive.

The discussion commenced on the 13th of November, six days after the report of the committee. The partisans of inviolability, while they considered Louis XVI. guilty, maintained that he could not be tried. The principal of these was Morrison. He said, that inviolability was general; that the constitution had anticipated more than secret hostility on the part of Louis XVI., an open attack, and even in that case had only pronounced his deposition; that in this respect the nation had pledged its sovereignty; that the mission of the convention was to change the government, not to judge Louis XVI.; that, restrained by the rules of justice, it was so also by the usages of war, which only permitted an enemy to be destroyed during the combat—after a victory, the law vindicates him; that, moreover, the republic had no interest in condemning Louis; that it ought to confine itself with respect to him, to measures of general safety, detain him prisoner, or banish him from France. This was the opinion of the Right of the convention. The Plain shared the opinion of the committee; but the Mountain repelled, at the same time, the inviolability and the trial of Louis XVI.

"Citizens," said Saint-Just, "I engage to prove that the opinion of Morrison, who maintains the king's inviolability, and that of the committee which requires his trial as a citizen, are equally false; I contend that we should judge the king as an enemy; that we have less to do with trying than with opposing him: that having no place in the contract which unites Frenchmen, the forms of the proceeding are not in civil law, but in the law of the right of nations; thus, all delay or reserve in this case are sheer acts of imprudence, and next to the imprudence which postpones the moment that should give us laws, the most fatal will be that which makes us temporize with the king." Reducing everything to considerations of enmity and policy, Saint-Just added, "The very men who are about to try Louis have a republic to establish: those who attach any importance to the just chastisement of a king, will never found a republic. Citizens, if the Roman people, after six hundred years of virtue and of hatred towards kings; if Great Britain after the death of Cromwell, saw kings restored in spite of its energy, what ought not good citizens, friends of liberty, to fear among us, when they see the axe tremble in your hands, and a people, from the first day of their freedom, respect the memory of their chains?"

This violent party, who wished to substitute a coup d'état for a sentence, to follow no law, no form, but to strike Louis XVI. like a conquered prisoner, by making hostilities even survive victory, had but a very feeble majority in the convention; but without, it was strongly supported by the Jacobins and the commune. Notwithstanding the terror which it already inspired, its murderous suggestions were repelled by the convention; and the partisans of inviolability, in their turn, courageously asserted reasons of public interest at the same time as rules of justice and humanity. They maintained that the same men could not be judges and legislators, the jury and the accusers. They desired also to impart to the rising republic the lustre of great virtues, those of generosity and forgiveness; they wished to follow the example of the people of Rome, who acquired their freedom and retained it five hundred years, because they proved themselves magnanimous; because they banished the Tarquins instead of putting them to death. In a political view, they showed the consequences of the king's condemnation, as it would affect the anarchical party of the kingdom, rendering it still more insolent; and with regard to Europe, whose still neutral powers it would induce to join the coalition against the republic.

But Robespierre, who during this long debate displayed a daring and perseverance that presaged his power, appeared at the tribune to support Saint-Just, to reproach the convention with involving in doubt what the insurrection had decided, and with restoring, by sympathy and the publicity of a defence, the fallen royalist party. "The assembly," said Robespierre, "has involuntarily been led far away from the real question. Here we have nothing to do with trial: Louis is not an accused man; you are not judges, you are, and can only be, statesmen. You have no sentence to pronounce for or against a man, but you are called on to adopt a measure of public safety; to perform an act of national precaution. A dethroned king is only fit for two purposes, to disturb the tranquillity of the state, and shake its freedom, or to strengthen one or the other of them.

"Louis was king; the republic is founded; the famous question you are discussing is decided in these few words. Louis cannot be tried; he is already tried, he is condemned, or the republic is not absolved." He required that the convention should declare Louis XVI. a traitor towards the French, criminal towards humanity, and sentence him at once to death, by virtue of the insurrection.

The Mountain by these extreme propositions, by the popularity they attained without, rendered condemnation in a measure inevitable. By gaining an extraordinary advance on the other parties, it obliged them to follow it, though at a distance. The majority of the convention, composed in a large part of Girondists, who dared not pronounce Louis XVI. inviolable, and of the Plain, decided, on Pétion's proposition, against the opinion of the fanatical Mountain and against that of the partisans of inviolability, that Louis XVI. should be tried by the convention. Robert Lindet then made, in the name of the commission of the twenty-one, his report respecting Louis XVI. The arraignment, setting forth the offences imputed to him, was drawn up, and the convention summoned the prisoner to its bar.

Louis had been confined in the Temple for four months. He was not at liberty, as the assembly at first wished him to be in assigning him the Luxembourg for a residence. The suspicious commune guarded him closely; but, submissive to his destiny, prepared for everything, he manifested neither impatience, regret, nor indignation. He had only one servant about his person, Cléry, who at the same time waited on his family. During the first months of his imprisonment, he was not separated from his family; and he still found solace in meeting them. He comforted and supported his two companions in misfortune, his wife and sister; he acted as preceptor to the young dauphin, and gave him the lessons of an unfortunate man, of a captive king. He read a great deal, and often turned to the History of England, by Hume; there he read of many dethroned kings, and one of them condemned by the people. Man always seeks destinies similar to his own. But the consolation he found in the sight of his family did not last long; as soon as his trial was decided, he was separated from them. The commune wished to prevent the prisoners from concerting their justification; the surveillance it exercised over Louis XVI. became daily more minute and severe.

In this state of things, Santerre received the order to conduct Louis XVI. to the bar of the convention. He repaired to the Temple, accompanied by the mayor, who communicated his mission to the king, and inquired if he was willing to descend. Louis hesitated a moment, then said: "This is another violence. I must yield!" and he decided on appearing before the convention; not objecting to it, as Charles I. had done with regard to his judges. "Representatives," said Barrère, when his approach was announced, "you are about to exercise the right of national justice. Let your attitude be suited to your new functions;" and turning to the gallery, he added, "Citizens, remember the terrible silence which accompanied Louis on his return from Varennes; a silence which was the precursor of the trial of kings by nations." Louis XVI. appeared firm as he entered the hall, and he took a steady glance round the assembly. He was placed at the bar, and the president said to him in a voice of emotion: "Louis, the French nation accuses you. You are about to hear the charges of the indictment. Louis, be seated." A seat had been prepared for him; he sat in it. During a long examination, he displayed much calmness and presence of mind, he replied to each question appropriately, often in an affecting and triumphant manner. He repelled the reproaches addressed to him respecting his conduct before the 14th of July, reminding them that his authority was not then limited; before the journey to Varennes, by the decree of the constituent assembly, which had been satisfied with his replies; and after the 10th of August, by throwing all public acts on ministerial responsibility, and by denying all the secret measures which were personally attributed to him. This denial did not, however, in the eyes of the convention, overthrow facts, proved for the most part by documents written or signed by the hand of Louis XVI. himself; he made use of the natural right of every accused person. Thus he did not admit the existence of the iron chest, and the papers that were brought forward. Louis XVI. invoked a law of safety, which the convention did not admit, and the convention sought to protect itself from anti-revolutionary attempts, which Louis XVI. would not admit.

When Louis had returned to the Temple, the convention considered the request he had made for a defender. A few of the Mountain opposed the request in vain. The convention determined to allow him the services of a counsel. It was then that the venerable Malesherbes offered himself to the convention to defend Louis XVI. "Twice," he wrote, "have I been summoned to the council of him who was my master, at a time when that function was the object of ambition to every man; I owe him the same service now, when many consider it dangerous." His request was granted, Louis XVI. in his abandonment, was touched by this proof of devotion. When Malesherbes entered his room, he went towards him, pressed him in his arms, and said with tears:—"Your sacrifice is the more generous, since you endanger your own life without saving mine." Malesherbes and Tronchet toiled uninterruptedly at his defence, and associated M. Desèze with them; they sought to reanimate the courage of the king, but they found the king little inclined to hope. "I am sure they will take my life; but no matter, let us attend to my trial as if I were about to gain it. In truth, I shall gain it, for I shall leave no stain on my memory."

At length the day for the defence arrived; it was delivered by M. Desèze; Louis was present. The profoundest silence pervaded the assembly and the galleries. M. Desèze availed himself of every consideration of justice and innocence in favour of the royal prisoner. He appealed to the inviolability which had been granted him; he asserted that as king he could not be tried; that as accusers, the representatives of the people could not be his judges. In this he advanced nothing which had not already been maintained by one party of the assembly. But he chiefly strove to justify the conduct of Louis XVI. by ascribing to him intentions always pure and irreproachable. He concluded with these last and solemn words:— "Listen, in anticipation, to what History will say to Fame; Louis ascending the throne at twenty, presented an example of morals, justice, and economy; he had no weakness, no corrupting passion: he was the constant friend of the people. Did the people desire the abolition of an oppressive tax? Louis abolished it: did the people desire the suppression of slavery? Louis suppressed it: did the people solicit reforms? he made them: did the people wish to change its laws? he consented to change them: did the people desire that millions of Frenchmen should be restored to their rights? he restored them: did the people wish for liberty? he gave it them. Men cannot deny to Louis the glory of having anticipated the people by his sacrifices; and it is he whom it is proposed to slay. Citizens, I will not continue, I leave it to History; remember, she will judge your sentence, and her judgment will be that of ages." But passion proved deaf and incapable of foresight.

The Girondists wished to save Louis XVI., but they feared the imputation of royalism, which was already cast upon them by the Mountain. During the whole transaction, their conduct was rather equivocal; they dared not pronounce themselves in favour of or against the accused; and their moderation ruined them without serving him. At that moment his cause, not only that of his throne, but of his life, was their own. They were about to determine, by an act of justice or by a coup d'état, whether they should return to the legal regime, or prolong the revolutionary regime. The triumph of the Girondists or of the Mountain was involved in one or the other of these solutions. The latter became exceedingly active. They pretended that, while following forms, men were forgetful of republican energy, and that the defence of Louis XVI. was a lecture on monarchy addressed to the nation. The Jacobins powerfully seconded them, and deputations came to the bar demanding the death of the king.

Yet the Girondists, who had not dared to maintain the question of inviolability, proposed a skilful way of saving Louis XVI. from death, by appealing from the sentence of the convention to the people. The extreme Right still protested against the erection of the assembly into a tribunal; but the competence of the assembly having been previously decided, all their efforts were turned in another direction. Salles proposed that the king should be pronounced guilty, but that the application of the punishment should be left to the primary assembly. Buzot, fearing that the convention would incur the reproach of weakness, thought that it ought to pronounce the sentence, and submit the judgment it pronounced to the decision of the people. This advice was vigorously opposed by the Mountain, and even by a great number of the more moderate members of the convention, who saw, in the convocation of the primary assemblies, the germ of civil war.

The assembly had unanimously decided that Louis was guilty, when the appeal to the people was put to the question. Two hundred and eighty-four voices voted for, four hundred and twenty-four against it; ten declined voting. Then came the terrible question as to the nature of the punishment. Paris was in a state of the greatest excitement: deputies were threatened at the very door of the assembly; fresh excesses on the part of the populace were dreaded; the Jacobin clubs resounded with extravagant invectives against Louis XVI., and the Right. The Mountain, till then the weakest party in the convention, sought to obtain the majority by terror, determined, if it did not succeed, none the less to sacrifice Louis XVI. Finally, after four hours of nominal appeal, the president, Vergniaud, said:

"Citizens, I am about to proclaim the result of the scrutiny. When justice has spoken, humanity should have its turn." There were seven hundred and twenty-one voters. The actual majority was three hundred and sixty-one. The death of the king was decided by a majority of twenty-six votes. Opinions were very various: Girondists voted for his death, with a reservation, it is true; most of the members of the Right voted for imprisonment or exile; a few of the Mountain voted with the Girondists. As soon as the result was known, the president said, in a tone of grief: "In the name of the convention, I declare the punishment, to which it condemns Louis Capet, to be death." Those who had undertaken the defence appeared at the bar; they were deeply affected. They endeavoured to bring back the assembly to sentiments of compassion, in consideration of the small majority in favour of the sentence. But this subject had already been discussed and decided. "Laws are only made by a simple majority," said one of the Mountain. "Yes," replied a voice, "but laws may be revoked; you cannot restore the life of a man." Malesherbes wished to speak, but could not. Sobs prevented his utterance; he could only articulate a few indistinct words of entreaty. His grief moved the assembly. The request for a reprieve was received by the Girondists as a last resource; but this also failed them, and the fatal sentence was pronounced.

Louis expected it. When Malesherbes came in tears to announce the sentence, he found him sitting in the dark, his elbows resting on a table, his face hid in his hands, and in profound meditation. At the noise of his entrance, Louis rose and said: "For two hours I have been trying to discover if, during my reign, I have deserved the slightest reproach from my subjects. Well, M. de Malesherbes, I swear to you, in the truth of my heart, as a man about to appear before God, that I have constantly sought the happiness of my people, and never indulged a wish opposed to it." Malesherbes urged that a reprieve would not be rejected, but this Louis did not expect. As he saw Malesherbes go out, Louis begged him not to forsake him in his last moments; Malesherbes promised to return; but he came several times, and was never able to gain access to him. Louis asked for him frequently, and appeared distressed at not seeing him. He received without emotion the formal announcement of his sentence from the minister of justice. He asked three days to prepare to appear before God; and also to be allowed the services of a priest, and permission to communicate freely with his wife and children. Only the last two requests were granted.

The interview was a distressing scene to this desolate family; but the moment of separation was far more so. Louis, on parting with his family, promised to see them again the next day; but, on reaching his room, he felt that the trial would be too much, and, pacing up and down violently, he exclaimed, "I will not go!" This was his last struggle; the rest of his time was spent in preparing for death. The night before the execution he slept calmly. Cléry awoke him, as he had been ordered, at five, and received his last instructions. He then communicated, commissioned Cléry with his dying words, and all he was allowed to bequeath, a ring, a seal, and some hair. The drums were already beating, and the dull sound of travelling cannon, and of confused voices, might be heard. At length Santerre arrived. "You are come for me," said Louis; "I ask one moment." He deposited his will in the hands of the municipal officer, asked for his hat, and said, in a firm tone: "Let us go."

The carriage was an hour on its way from the Temple to the Place de la Revolution. A double row of soldiers lined the road; more than forty thousand men were under arms. Paris presented a gloomy aspect. The citizens present at the execution manifested neither applause nor regret; all were silent. On reaching the place of execution, Louis alighted from the carriage. He ascended the scaffold with a firm step, knelt to receive the benediction of the priest, who is recorded to have said, "Son of Saint Louis, ascend to heaven!" With some repugnance he submitted to the binding of his hands, and walked hastily to the left of the scaffold; "I die innocent," said he; "I forgive my enemies; and you, unfortunate people..." Here, at a signal, the drums and trumpets drowned his voice, and the three executioners seized him. At ten minutes after ten he had ceased to live.

Thus perished, at the age of thirty-nine, after a reign of sixteen years and a half, spent in endeavouring to do good, the best but weakest of monarchs. His ancestors bequeathed to him a revolution. He was better calculated than any of them to prevent and terminate it; for he was capable of becoming a reformer-king before it broke out, or of becoming a constitutional king afterwards. He is, perhaps, the only prince who, having no other passion, had not that of power, and who united the two qualities which make good kings, fear of God and love of the people. He perished, the victim of passions which he did not share; of those of the persons about him, to which he was a stranger, and to those of the multitude, which he had not excited. Few memories of kings are so commendable. History will say of him, that, with a little more strength of mind, he would have been an exemplary king.

CHAPTER VII

FROM THE 21ST OF JANUARY, 1793, TO THE 2ND OF JUNE

Political and military situation of France—England, Holland, Spain, Naples, and all the circles of the empire fall in with the coalition—Dumouriez, after having conquered Belgium, attempts an expedition into Holland—He wishes to re-establish constitutional monarchy—Reverses of our armies—Struggle between the Gironde and the Mountain—Conspiracy of the 10th of March—Insurrection of La Vendée; its progress—Defection of Dumouriez—The Gironde accused of being his accomplices—New conspiracies against them—Establishment of the Commission of Twelve to frustrate the conspirators—Insurrections of the 27th and 31st of May against the Commission of Twelve; its suppression—Insurrection of the 2nd of June against the two-and-twenty leading Girondists; their arrest—Total defeat of that party.

The death of Louis XVI. rendered the different parties irreconcilable, and increased the external enemies of the revolution. The republicans had to contend with all Europe, with several classes of malcontents, and with themselves. But the Mountain, who then directed the popular movement, imagined that they were too far involved not to push matters to extremity. To terrify the enemies of the revolution, to excite the fanaticism of the people by harangues, by the presence of danger, and by insurrections; to refer everything to it, both the government and the safety of the republic; to infuse into it the most ardent enthusiasm, in the name of liberty, equality, and fraternity; to keep it in this violent state of crisis for the purpose of making use of its passions and its power; such was the plan of Danton and the Mountain, who had chosen him for their leader. It was he who augmented the popular effervescence by the growing dangers of the republic, and who, under the name of revolutionary government, established the despotism of the multitude, instead of legal liberty. Robespierre and Marat went even much further than he. They sought to erect into a permanent government what Danton considered as merely transitory. The latter was only a political chief, while the others were true sectarians; the first, more ambitious, the second, more fanatical.

The Mountain had, by the catastrophe of the 21st of January, gained a great victory over the Girondists, whose politics were much more moral than theirs, and who hoped to save the revolution, without staining it with blood. But their humanity, their spirit of justice, proved of no service, and even turned against them. They were accused of being the enemies of the people, because they opposed their excesses; of being the accomplices of the tyrant, because they had sought to save Louis XVI.; and of betraying the republic, because they recommended moderation. It was with these reproaches that the Mountain persecuted them with constant animosity in the bosom of the convention, from the 21st of January till the 31st of May and the 2nd of June. The Girondists were for a long time supported by the Centre, which sided with the Right against murder and anarchy, and with the Left for measures of public safety. This mass, which, properly speaking, formed the spirit of the convention, displayed some courage, and balanced the power of the Mountain and the Commune as long as it possessed those intrepid and eloquent Girondists, who carried with them to prison and to the scaffold all the generous resolutions of the assembly.

For a moment, union existed among the various parties of the assembly. Lepelletier Saint Fargeau was stabbed by a retired member of the household guard, named Pâris, for having voted the death of Louis XVI. The members of the convention, united by common danger, swore on his tomb to forget their enmities; but they soon revived them. Some of the murderers of September, whose punishment was desired by the more honourable republicans, were proceeded against at Meaux. The Mountain, apprehensive that their past conduct would be inquired into, and that their adversaries would take advantage of a condemnation to attack them more openly themselves, put a stop to these proceedings. This impunity further emboldened the leaders of the multitude; and Marat, who at that period had an incredible influence over the multitude, excited them to pillage the dealers, whom he accused of monopolizing provisions. He wrote and spoke violently, in his pamphlets and at the Jacobins, against the aristocracy of the burghers, merchants, and *statesmen* (as he designated the Girondists), that is to say, against those who, in the assembly or the nation at large, still opposed the reign of the Sans-culottes and the Mountain. There was something frightful in the fanaticism and invincible obstinacy of these sectaries. The name given by them to the Girondists from the beginning of the convention, was that of Intrigants, on account of the ministerial and rather stealthy means with which they opposed in the departments the insolent and public conduct of the Jacobins.

Accordingly, they denounced them regularly in the club. "At Rome, an orator cried daily: 'Carthage must be destroyed!' well, let a Jacobin mount this tribune every day, and say these single words, 'The intrigants must be destroyed!' Who could withstand us? We oppose crime, and the ephemeral power of riches; but we have truth, justice, poverty, and virtue in our cause. With such arms, the Jacobins will soon have to say: 'We had only to pass on, they were already extinct.'" Marat, who was much more daring than Robespierre, whose hatred and projects still concealed themselves under certain forms, was the patron of all denouncers and lovers of anarchy. Several of the Mountain reproached him with compromising their cause by his extreme counsels, and by unseasonable excesses; but the entire Jacobin people supported him even against Robespierre, who rarely obtained the advantage in his disputes with him. The pillage recommended in February, in

L'Ami du Peuple, with respect to some dealers, "by way of example," took place, and Marat was denounced to the convention, who decreed his accusation after a stormy sitting. But this decree had no result, because the ordinary tribunals had no authority. This double effort of force on one side, and weakness on the other, took place in the month of February. More decisive events soon brought the Girondists to ruin.

Hitherto, the military position of France had been satisfactory. Dumouriez had just crowned the brilliant campaign of Argonne by the conquest of Belgium. After the retreat of the Prussians, he had repaired to Paris to concert measures for the invasion of the Austrian Netherlands. Returning to the army on the 20th of October, 1792, he began the attack on the 28th. The plan attempted so inappropriately, with so little strength and success, at the commencement of the war, was resumed and executed with superior means. Dumouriez, at the head of the army of Belgium, forty thousand strong, advanced from Valenciennes upon Mons, supported on the right by the army of the Ardennes, amounting to about sixteen thousand men, under general Valence, who marched from Givet upon Namur; and on his left, by the army of the north, eighteen thousand strong, under general Labourdonnaie, who advanced from Lille upon Tournai. The Austrian army, posted before Mons, awaited battle in its intrenchments. Dumouriez completely defeated it; and the victory of Jemappes opened Belgium to the French, and again gave our arms the ascendancy in Europe. A victor on the 6th of November, Dumouriez entered Mons on the 7th, Brussels on the 14th, and Liége on the 28th. Valence took Namur, Labourdonnaie Antwerp; and by the middle of December, the invasion of the Netherlands was completely achieved. The French army, masters of the Meuse and the Scheldt, went into their winter quarters, after driving beyond the Roër the Austrians, whom they might have pushed beyond the Lower Rhine.

From this moment hostilities began between Dumouriez and the Jacobins. A decree of the convention, dated the 15th of September, abrogated the Belgian customs, and democratically organized that country. The Jacobins sent agents to Belgium to propagate revolutionary principles, and establish clubs on the model of the parent society; but the Flemings, who had received us with enthusiasm, became cool at the heavy demands made upon them, and at the general pillage and insupportable anarchy which the Jacobins brought with them. All the party that had opposed the Austrian army, and hoped to be free under the protection of France, found our rule too severe, and regretted having sought our aid, or supported us. Dumouriez, who had projects of independence for the Flemings, and of ambition for himself, came to Paris to complain of this impolitic conduct with regard to the conquered countries. He changed his hitherto equivocal course; he had employed every means to keep on terms with the two factions; he had ranged himself under the banner of neither, hoping to make use of the Right through his friend Gensonné, and the Mountain through Danton and Lacroix, whilst he awed both by his victories. But in this second journey he tried to stop the Jacobins and save Louis XVI.; not having been able to attain his end, he returned to the army to begin the second campaign, very dissatisfied, and determined to make his new victories the means of suspending the revolution and changing its government.

This time all the frontiers of France were to be attacked by the European powers. The military successes of the revolution, and the catastrophe of the 21st of January, had made most of the undecided or neutral governments join the coalition.

The court of St. James', on learning the death of Louis XVI., dismissed the ambassador Chauvelin, whom it had refused to acknowledge since the 10th of August and the dethronement of the king. The convention, finding England already leagued with the coalition, and consequently all its promises of neutrality vain and elusive, on the 1st of February, 1793, declared war against the king of Great Britain and the stadtholder of Holland, who had been entirely guided by the English cabinet since 1788. England had hitherto preserved the appearances of neutrality, but it took advantage of this opportunity to appear on the scene of hostilities. For some time disposed for a rupture, Pitt employed all his resources, and in the space of six months concluded seven treaties of alliance, and six treaties of subsidies.[5] England thus became the soul of the coalition against France; her fleets were ready to sail; the minister had obtained 3,200,000l. extraordinary, and Pitt designed to profit by our revolution by securing the preponderance of Great Britain, as Richelieu and Mazarin had taken advantage of the crisis in England in 1640, to establish the French domination in Europe. The court of St. James' was only influenced by motives of English interests; it desired at any cost to effect the consolidation of the aristocratical power at home, and the exclusive empire in the two Indies, and on the seas.

The court of St. James' then made the second levy of the coalition. Spain had just undergone a ministerial change; the famous Godoy, duke of Alcudia, afterwards Prince of the Peace, had been placed at the head of the government by means of an intrigue of England and the emigrants. This power came to a rupture with the republic, after having interceded in vain for Louis XVI., and made its neutrality the price of the life of the king. The German empire entirely adopted the war; Bavaria, Suabia, and the elector palatine joined the hostile circles of the empire. Naples followed the example of the Holy See; and the only neutral powers were Venice, Switzerland, Sweden, Denmark, and Turkey. Russia was still engaged with the second partition of Poland.

The republic was threatened on all sides by the most warlike troops of Europe. It would soon have to face forty-five thousand Austro-Sardinians in the Alps; fifty thousand Spaniards on the Pyrenees; seventy thousand Austrians or Imperialists, reinforced by thirty-eight thousand English and Dutch troops, on the Lower Rhine and in Belgium; thirty-three thousand four hundred Austrians between the Meuse and the Moselle; a hundred and twelve thousand six hundred Prussians, Austrians

[5] These treaties were as follows: the 4th March, articles between Great Britain and Hanover; 25th March, treaty of alliance at London between Russia and Great Britain; 10th April, treaty of subsidies with the landgrave of Hesse Cassel; 25th April, treaty of subsidies with Sardinia; 25th May, treaty of alliance at Madrid with Spain; 12th July, treaty of alliance with Naples, the kingdom of the Two Sicilies; 14th July, treaty of alliance at the camp before Mayence with Prussia; 30th August, treaty of alliance at London with the emperor; 21st September, treaty of subsidies with the margrave of Baden; 26th September, treaty of alliance at London with Portugal. By these treaties England gave considerable subsidies, more especially to Austria and Prussia.

and Imperialists on the Middle and Upper Rhine. In order to confront so many enemies, the convention decreed a levy of three hundred thousand men. This measure of external defence was accompanied by a party measure for the interior. At the moment the new battalions, about to quit Paris, presented themselves to the assembly, the Mountain demanded the establishment of an extraordinary tribunal to maintain the revolution at home, which the battalions were going to defend on the frontiers. This tribunal, composed of nine members, was to try without jury or appeal. The Girondists arose with all their power against so arbitrary and formidable an institution, but it was in vain; for they seemed to be favouring the enemies of the republic by rejecting a tribunal intended to punish them. All they obtained was the introduction of juries into it, the removal of some violent men, and the power of annulling its acts, as long as they maintained any influence.

The principal efforts of the coalition were directed against the vast frontier extending from the north sea to Huninguen. The prince of Coburg, at the head of the Austrians, was to attack the French army on the Roër and the Meuse, to enter Belgium; while the Prussians, on the other point, should march against Custine, give him battle, surround Mayence, and after taking it, renew the preceding invasion. These two armies of operation were sustained in the intermediate position by considerable forces. Dumouriez, engrossed by ambitious and reactionary designs, at a moment when he ought only to have thought of the perils of France, proposed to himself to re-establish the monarchy of 1791, in spite of the convention and Europe. What Bouillé could not do for an absolute, nor Lafayette for a constitutional throne, Dumouriez, at a less propitious time, hoped alone to carry through in the interest of a destroyed constitution and a monarchy without a party. Instead of remaining neutral among factions, as circumstances dictated to a general, and even to an ambitious man, Dumouriez preferred a rupture, in order to sway them. He conceived a design of forming a party out of France; of entering Holland by means of the Dutch republicans opposed to the stadtholdership, and to English influence; to deliver Belgium from the Jacobins; to unite these countries in a single independent state, and secure for himself their political protectorate after having acquired all the glory of a conqueror. To intimidate parties, he was to gain over his troops, march on the capital, dissolve the convention, put down popular meetings, re-establish the constitution of 1791, and give a king to France.

This project, impracticable amidst the great shock between the revolution and Europe, appeared easy to the fiery and adventurous Dumouriez. Instead of defending the line, threatened from Mayence to the Roër, he threw himself on the left of the operations, and entered Holland at the head of twenty thousand men. By a rapid march he was to reach the centre of the United Provinces, attack the fortresses from behind, and be joined at Nymegen by twenty-five thousand men under General Miranda, who would probably have made himself master of Maestricht. An army of forty thousand men was to observe the Austrians and protect his right.

Dumouriez vigorously prosecuted his expedition into Holland; he took Breda and Gertruydenberg, and prepared to pass the Biesbos, and capture Dordrecht. But the army of the right experienced in the meantime the most alarming reverses on the Lower Meuse. The Austrians assumed the offensive, passed the Roër, beat Miazinski at Aix-la-Chapelle; made Miranda raise the blockade of Maestricht, which he had uselessly bombarded; crossed the Meuse, and at Liège put our army, which had fallen back between Tirlemont and Louvain, wholly to the rout. Dumouriez received from the executive council orders to leave Holland immediately, and to take the command of the troops in Belgium; he was compelled to obey, and to renounce in part his wildest but dearest hopes.

The Jacobins, at the news of these reverses, became much more intractable; unable to conceive a defeat without treachery, especially after the brilliant and unexpected victories of the last campaign, they attributed these military disasters to party combinations. They denounced the Girondists, the ministers, and generals who, they supposed, had combined to abandon the republic, and clamoured for their destruction. Rivalry mingled with suspicion, and they desired as much to acquire an exclusive domination, as to defend the threatened territory; they began with the Girondists. As they had not yet accustomed the multitude to the idea of the proscription of representatives, they at first had recourse to a plot to get rid of them; they resolved to strike them in the convention, where they would all be assembled, and the night of the 10th of March was fixed on for the execution of the plot. The assembly sat permanently on account of the public danger. It was decided on the preceding day at the Jacobins and Cordeliers to shut the barriers, sound the tocsin, and march in two bands on the convention and the ministers. They started at the appointed hour, but several circumstances prevented the conspirators from succeeding. The Girondists, apprised, did not attend the evening sitting; the sections declared themselves opposed to the plot, and Beurnonville, minister for war, advanced against them at the head of a battalion of Brest federalists; these unexpected obstacles, together with the ceaseless rain, obliged the conspirators to disperse. The next day Vergniaud denounced the insurrectional committee who had projected these murders, demanded that the executive council should be commissioned to make inquiries respecting the conspiracy of the 10th of March, to examine the registers of the clubs, and to arrest the members of the insurrectional committee. "We go," said he, "from crimes to amnesties, from amnesties to crimes. Numbers of citizens have begun to confound seditious insurrections with the great insurrection of liberty; to look on the excitement of robbers as the outburst of energetic minds, and robbery itself as a measure of general security. We have witnessed the development of that strange system of liberty, in which we are told: 'you are free; but think with us, or we will denounce you to the vengeance of the people; you are free, but bow down your head to the idol we worship, or we will denounce you to the vengeance of the people; you are free, but join us in persecuting the men whose probity and intelligence we dread, or we will denounce you to the vengeance of the people.' Citizens, we have reason to fear that the revolution, like Saturn, will devour successively all its children, and only engender despotism and the calamities which accompany it." These prophetic words produced some effect in the assembly; but the measures proposed by Vergniaud led to nothing.

The Jacobins were stopped for a moment by the failure of their first enterprise against their adversaries; but the insurrection of La Vendée gave them new courage. The Vendéan war was an inevitable event in the revolution. This country, bounded by the Loire and the sea, crossed by few roads, sprinkled with villages, hamlets, and manorial residences, had retained its ancient feudal state. In La Vendée there was no civilization or intelligence, because there was no middle class; and there was no middle class because there were no towns, or very few. At that time the peasants had acquired no other ideas than those few communicated to them by the priests, and had not separated their interests from those of the nobility. These simple and sturdy men, devotedly attached to the old state of things, did not understand a revolution, which was the result of a faith and necessities entirely foreign to their situation. The nobles and priests, being strong in these districts, had not emigrated; and the ancient regime really existed there, because there were its doctrines and its society. Sooner or later, a war between France and La Vendée, countries so different, and which had nothing in common but language, was inevitable. It was inevitable that the two fanaticisms of monarchy and of popular sovereignty, of the priesthood and human reason, should raise their banners against each other, and bring about the triumph of the old or of the new civilization.

Partial disturbances had taken place several times in La Vendée. In 1792 the count de la Rouairie had prepared a general rising, which failed on account of his arrest; but all yet remained ready for an insurrection, when the decree for raising three hundred thousand men was put into execution. This levy became the signal of revolt. The Vendéans beat the gendarmerie at Saint Florent, and took for leaders, in different directions, Cathelineau, a waggoner, Charette, a naval officer, and Stofflet, a gamekeeper. Aided by arms and money from England, the insurrection soon overspread the country; nine hundred communes flew to arms at the sound of the tocsin; and then the noble leaders Bonchamps, Lescure, La Rochejaquelin, d'Elbée, and Talmont, joined the others. The troops of the line and the battalions of the national guard who advanced against the insurgents were defeated. General Marcé was beaten at Saint Vincent by Stofflet; general Gauvilliers at Beaupréau, by d'Elbée and Bonchamps; general Quetineau at Aubiers, by La Rochejaquelin; and general Ligonnier at Cholet. The Vendéans, masters of Châtillon, Bressuire, and Vihiers, considered it advisable to form some plan of organization before they pushed their advantages further. They formed three corps, each from ten to twelve thousand strong, according to the division of La Vendée, under three commanders; the first, under Bonchamps, guarded the banks of the Loire, and was called the *Armée d'Anjou*; the second, stationed in the centre, formed the *Grande armée* under d'Elbée; the third, in Lower Vendée, was styled the *Armée du Marais*, under Charette. The insurgents established a council to determine their operations, and elected Cathelineau generalissimo. These arrangements, with this division of the country, enabled them to enrol the insurgents, and to dismiss them to their fields, or call them to arms.

The intelligence of this formidable insurrection drove the convention to adopt still more rigorous measures against priests and emigrants. It outlawed all priests and nobles who took part in any gathering, and disarmed all who had belonged to the privileged classes. The former emigrants were banished for ever; they could not return, under penalty of death; their property was confiscated. On the door of every house, the names of all its inmates were to be inscribed; and the revolution-ary tribunal, which had been adjourned, began its terrible functions.

At the same time, tidings of new military disasters arrived, one after the other. Dumouriez, returned to the army of Belgium, concentrated all his forces to resist the Austrian general, the prince of Coburg. His troops were greatly discouraged, and in want of everything; he wrote to the convention a threatening letter against the Jacobins, who denounced him. After having again restored to his army a part of its former confidence by some minor advantages, he ventured a general action at Neerwinden, and lost it. Belgium was evacuated, and Dumouriez, placed between the Austrians and Jacobins, beaten by the one and assailed by the other, had recourse to the guilty project of defection, in order to realize his former designs. He had conferences with Colonel Mack, and agreed with the Austrians to march upon Paris for the purpose of re-establishing the monarchy, leaving them on the frontiers, and having first given up to them several fortresses as a guarantee. It is probable that Dumouriez wished to place on the constitutional throne the young duc de Chartres, who had distinguished himself throughout this campaign; while the prince of Coburg hoped that if the counter-revolution reached that point, it would be carried further and restore the son of Louis XVI. and the ancient mon-archy. A counter-revolution will not halt any more than a revolution; when once begun, it must exhaust itself. The Jacobins were soon informed of Dumouriez's arrangements; he took little precaution to conceal them; whether he wished to try his troops, or to alarm his enemies, or whether he merely followed his natural lev-ity. To be more sure of his designs, the Jacobin club sent to him a deputation, con-sisting of Proly, Péreira, and Dubuisson, three of its members. Taken to Dumou-riez's presence, they received from him more admissions than they expected: "The convention," said he, "is an assembly of seven hundred and thirty-five tyrants. While I have four inches of iron I will not suffer it to reign and shed blood with the revolutionary tribunal it has just created; as for the republic," he added, "it is an idle word. I had faith in it for three days. Since Jemappes, I have deplored all the successes I obtained in so bad a cause. There is only one way to save the coun-try—that is, to re-establish the constitution of 1791, and a king." "Can you think of it, general?" said Dubuisson; "the French view royalty with horror—the very name of Louis—" "What does it signify whether the king be called Louis, Jacques, or Philippe?" "And what are your means?" "My army—yes, my army will do it, and from my camp, or the stronghold of some fortress, it will express its desire for a king." "But your project endangers the safety of the prisoners in the Temple." "Should the last of the Bourbons be killed, even those of Coblentz, France shall still have a king, and if Paris were to add this murder to those which have already dis-honoured it, I would instantly march upon it." After thus unguardedly disclosing his intentions, Dumouriez proceeded to the execution of his impracticable design. He was really in a very difficult position; the soldiers were very much attached to him, but they were also devoted to their country. He was to surrender some fortresses which he was not master of, and it was to be supposed that the generals under his orders, either from fidelity to the republic, or from ambition, would treat him as he had treated Lafayette. His first attempt was not encouraging; after having established himself at Saint Amand, he essayed to possess himself of Lille,

Condé, and Valenciennes; but failed in this enterprise. The failure made him hesitate, and prevented his taking the initiative in the attack.

It was not so with the convention; it acted with a promptitude, a boldness, a firmness, and, above all, with a precision in attaining its object, which rendered success certain. When we know what we want, and desire it strongly and speedily, we nearly always attain our object. This quality was wanting in Dumouriez, and the want impeded his audacity and deterred his partisans. As soon as the convention was informed of his projects, it summoned him to its bar. He refused to obey; without, however, immediately raising the standard of revolt. The convention instantly despatched four representatives: Camus, Quinette, Lamarque, Bancal, and Beurnonville, the war minister, to bring him before it, or to arrest him in the midst of his army. Dumouriez received the commissioners at the head of his staff. They presented to him the decree of the convention; he read it and returned it to them, saying that the state of his army would not admit of his leaving it. He offered to resign, and promised in a calmer season to demand judges himself, and to give an account of his designs and of his conduct. The commissioners tried to induce him to submit, quoting the example of the ancient Roman generals. "We are always mistaken in our quotations," he replied; "and we disfigure Roman history by taking as an excuse for our crimes the example of their virtues. The Romans did not kill Tarquin; the Romans had a well ordered republic and good laws; they had neither a Jacobin club nor a revolutionary tribunal. We live in a time of anarchy. Tigers wish for my head; I will not give it them." "Citizen general," said Camus then, "will you obey the decree of the national convention, and repair to Paris?" "Not at present." "Well, then, I declare that I suspend you; you are no longer a general; I order your arrest." "This is too much," said Dumouriez; and he had the commissioners arrested by German hussars, and delivered them as hostages to the Austrians. After this act of revolt he could no longer hesitate. Dumouriez made another attempt on Condé, but it succeeded no better than the first. He tried to induce the army to join him, but was forsaken by it. The soldiers were likely for a long time to prefer the republic to their general; the attachment to the revolution was in all its fervour, and the civil power in all its force. Dumouriez experienced, in declaring himself against the convention, the fate which Lafayette experienced when he declared himself against the legislative assembly, and Bouillé when he declared against the constituent assembly. At this period, a general, combining the firmness of Bouillé with the patriotism and popularity of Lafayette, with the victories and resources of Dumouriez, would have failed as they did. The revolution, with the movement imparted to it, was necessarily stronger than parties, than generals, and than Europe. Dumouriez went over to the Austrian camp with the duc de Chartres, colonel Thouvenot, and two squadrons of Berchiny. The rest of his army went to the camp at Famars, and joined the troops commanded by Dampierre.

The convention, on learning the arrest of the commissioners, established itself as a permanent assembly, declared Dumouriez a traitor to his country, authorized any citizen to attack him, set a price on his head, decreed the famous committee of public safety, and banished the duke of Orleans and all the Bourbons from the republic. Although the Girondists had assailed Dumouriez as warmly as the Mountain, they were accused of being his accomplices, and this was a new cause of complaint added to the rest. Their enemies became every day more powerful; and it was in moments of public danger that they were especially dangerous. Hitherto, in the struggle between the two parties, they had carried the day on every point. They had stopped all inquiries into the massacres of September; they had maintained the usurpation of the commune; they had obtained, first the trial, then the death of Louis XVI.; through their means the plunderings of February and the conspiracy of the 10th of March, had remained unpunished; they had procured the erection of the revolutionary tribunal despite the Girondists; they had driven Roland from the ministry, in disgust; and they had just defeated Dumouriez. It only remained now to deprive the Girondists of their last asylum—the assembly; this they set about on the 10th of April, and accomplished on the 2nd of June.

Robespierre attacked by name Brissot, Guadet, Vergniaud, Pétion, and Gensonné, in the convention; Marat denounced them in the popular societies. As president of the Jacobins, he wrote an address to the departments, in which he invoked the thunder of petitions and accusations against the traitors and faithless delegates who had sought to save the tyrant by an appeal to the public or his imprisonment. The Right and the Plain of the convention felt that it was necessary to unite. Marat was sent before the revolutionary tribunal. This news set the clubs in motion, the people, and the commune. By way of reprisal, Pache, the mayor, came in the name of the thirty-five sections and of the general council, to demand the expulsion of the principal Girondists. Young Boyer Fonfrède required to be included in the proscription of his colleagues, and the members of the Right and the Plain rose, exclaiming, "All! all!" This petition, though declared calumnious, was the first attack upon the convention from without, and it prepared the public mind for the destruction of the Gironde.

The accusation of Marat was far from intimidating the Jacobins who accompanied him to the revolutionary tribunal. Marat was acquitted, and borne in triumph to the assembly. From that moment the approaches to the hall were thronged with daring sans-culottes, and the partisans of the Jacobins filled the galleries of the convention. The clubists and Robespierre's *tricoteuses* (knitters) constantly interrupted the speakers of the Right, and disturbed the debate; while without, every opportunity was sought to get rid of the Girondists. Henriot, commandant of the section of sans-culottes, excited against them the battalions about to march for La Vendée. Gaudet then saw that it was time for something more than complaints and speeches; he ascended the tribune. "Citizens," said he, "while virtuous men content themselves with bewailing the misfortunes of the country, conspirators are active for its ruin. With Caesar they say: 'Let them talk, we will act.' Well, then, do you act also. The evil consists in the impunity of the conspirators of the 10th of March; the evil is in anarchy; the evil is in the existence of the authorities of Paris—authorities striving at once for gain and dominion. Citizens, there is yet time; you may save the republic and your compromised glory. I propose to abolish the Paris authorities, to replace within twenty-four hours the municipality by the presidents of the sections, to assemble the convention at Bourges with the least possible delay, and to transmit this decree to the departments by extraordinary couriers." The Mountain was surprised for a moment by Guadet's motion. Had his measures been at once adopted, there would have been an end to the domination of the commune, and to the projects of the conspirators; but it is also probable that the agitation of parties would have brought on a civil war, that the convention would have been dissolved by the assembly at Bourges, that all centre of action would have been destroyed, and that the revolution would not have been sufficiently strong to contend against internal struggles and the attacks of Europe. This was what the moderate party in the assembly feared. Dreading anarchy if the career of the commune was not stopped, and counter-revolution if the multitude were too closely kept down, its aim was to maintain the balance between the two extremes of the convention. This party comprised the committees of general safety and of public safety. It was directed by Barrère, who, like all men of upright intentions but weak characters, advocated moderation so long as fear did not make him an instrument of cruelty and tyranny. Instead of Guadet's decisive measures, he proposed to nominate an extraordinary commission of twelve members, deputed to inquire into the conduct of the municipality; to seek out the authors of the plots against the national representatives, and to secure their persons. This middle course was adopted; but it left the commune in existence, and the commune was destined to triumph over the convention.

The Commission of Twelve threw the members of the commune into great alarm by its inquiries. It discovered a new conspiracy, which was to be put into execution on the 22nd of May, and arrested some of the conspirators, and among others, Hébert, the deputy recorder, author of *Père Duchesne*, who was taken in the very bosom of the municipality. The commune, at first astounded, began to take measures of defence. From that moment, not conspiracy, but insurrection was the order of the day. The general council, encouraged by the Mountain, surrounded itself with the agitators of the capital; it circulated a report that the Twelve wished to purge the convention, and to substitute a counter-revolutionary tribunal for that which had acquitted Marat. The Jacobins, the Cordeliers, the sections sat permanently. On the 26th of May, the agitation became perceptible; on the 27th; it was sufficiently decided to induce the commune to open the attack. It accordingly appeared before the convention and demanded the liberation of Hébert and the suppression of the Twelve; it was accompanied by the deputies of the sections, who expressed the same desire, and the hall was surrounded by a large mob. The section of the City even presumed to require that the Twelve should be brought before the revolutionary tribunal. Isnard, president of the assembly, replied in a solemn tone: "Listen to what I am about to say. If ever by one of those insurrections, of such frequent recurrence since the 10th of March, and of which the magistrates have never apprised the assembly, a hostile hand be raised against the national representatives, I declare to you in the name of all France, Paris will be destroyed. Yes, universal France would rise to avenge such a crime, and soon it would be matter of doubt on which side of the Seine Paris had stood." This reply became the signal for great tumult. "And I declare to you," exclaimed Danton, "that so much impudence begins to be intolerable; we will resist you." Then turning to the Right, he added: "No truce between the Mountain and the cowards who wished to save the tyrant."

The utmost confusion now reigned in the hall. The strangers' galleries vociferated denunciations of the Right; the Mountain broke forth into menaces; every moment deputations arrived without, and the convention was surrounded by an immense multitude. A few sectionaries of the Mail and of the Butte-des-Moulins, commanded by Raffet, drew up in the passages and avenues to defend it. The Girondists withstood, as long as they could, the deputations and the Mountain. Threatened within, besieged without, they would have availed themselves of this violence to arouse the indignation of the assembly. But the minister of the interior, Garat, deprived them of this resource. Called upon to give an account of the state of Paris, he declared that the convention had nothing to fear; and the opinion of Garat, who was considered impartial, and whose conciliatory turn of mind involved him in equivocal proceedings, emboldened the members of the Mountain. Isnard was obliged to resign the chair, which was taken by Hérault de Séchelles, a sign of victory for the Mountain. The new president replied to the petitioners, whom Isnard had hitherto kept in the background. "The power of reason and the power of the people are the same thing. You demand from us a magistrate and justice. The representatives of the people will give you both." It was now very late; the Right was discouraged, some of its members had left. The petitioners had moved from the bar to the seats of the representatives, and there, mixed up with the Mountain, with outcry and disorder, they voted, all together, for the dismissal of the Twelve, and the liberation of the prisoners. It was at half-past twelve, amidst the applause of the galleries and the people outside, that this decree was passed.

It would, perhaps, have been wise on the part of the Girondists, since they were really not the strongest party, to have made no recurrence to this matter. The movement of the preceding day would have had no other result than the suppression of the Twelve, if other causes had not prolonged it. But animosity had attained such a height, that it had become necessary to bring the quarrel to an issue; since the two parties could not endure each other, the only alternative was for them to fight; they must needs go on from victory to defeat, and from defeat to victory, growing more and more excited every day, until the stronger finally triumphed over the weaker party. Next day, the Right regained its position in the convention, and declared the decree of the preceding day illegally passed, in tumult and under compulsion, and the commission was re- established. "You yesterday," said Danton, "did a great act of justice; but I declare to you, if the commission retains the tyrannical power it has hitherto exercised; if the magistrates of the people are not restored to their functions; if good citizens are again exposed to arbitrary arrest; then, after having proved to you that we surpass our enemies in prudence, in wisdom, we shall surpass them in audacity and revolutionary vigour." Danton feared to commence the attack; he dreaded the triumph of the Mountain as much as he did that of the Girondists: he accordingly sought, by turns, to anticipate the 31st of May, and to moderate its results. But he was reduced to join his own party during the conflict, and to remain silent after the victory.

The agitation, which had been a little allayed by the suppression of the Twelve, became threatening at the news of their restoration. The benches of the sections and popular societies resounded with invectives, with cries of danger, with calls to insurrection. Hébert, having quitted his prison, reappeared at the commune. A crown was placed on his brow, which he transferred to the bust of Brutus, and then rushed to the Jacobins to demand vengeance on the Twelve. Robespierre, Marat, Danton, Chaumette, and Pache then combined in organising a new movement. The insurrection was modelled on that of the 10th of August. The 29th of May was occupied in preparing the public mind. On the 30th, members of the electoral college, commissioners of the clubs, and deputies of sections assembled at the Evêché, declared themselves in a state of insurrection, dissolved the general council of the commune, and immediately reconstituted it, making it take a new oath; Henriot received the title of commandant-general of the armed force, and the sans-culottes were assigned forty sous a day while under arms. These preparations made, early on the morning of the 31st the tocsin rang, the drums beat to arms, the troops were assembled, and all marched towards the convention, which for some time past had held its sittings at the Tuileries.

The assembly had met at the sound of the tocsin. The minister of the interior, the administrators of the department, and the mayor of Paris had been summoned, in succession, to the bar. Garat had given an account of the agitated state of Paris, but appeared to apprehend no dangerous result. Lhuillier, in the name of the department, declared it was only a *moral* insurrection. Pache, the mayor, appeared last, and informed them, with an hypocritical air, of the operations of the insurgents; he pretended that he had employed every means to maintain order; assured them that the guard of the convention had been doubled, and that he had prohibited the firing of the alarm cannon; yet, at the same moment, the cannon was heard in the distance. The surprise and excitement of the assembly were extreme. Cambon exhorted the members to union, and called upon the people in the strangers' gallery to be silent. "Under these extraordinary circumstances," said he, "the only way of frustrating the designs of the malcontents is to make the national convention respected." "I demand," said Thuriot, "the immediate abolition of the Commission of Twelve." "And I," cried Tallien, "that the sword of the law may strike the conspirators who profane the very bosom of the convention." The Girondists, on their part, required that the audacious Henriot should be called to the bar, for having fired the alarm cannon without the permission of the convention. "If a struggle take place," said Vergniaud, "be the success what it may, it will be the ruin of the republic. Let every member swear to die at his post." The entire assembly rose, applauding the proposition. Danton rushed to the tribune: "Break up the Commission of Twelve! you have heard the thunder of the cannon. If you are politic legislators, far from blaming the outbreak of Paris, you will turn it to the profit of the republic, by reforming your own errors, by dismissing your commission.—I address those," he continued, on hearing murmurs around him, "who possess some political talent, not dullards, who can only act and speak in obedience to their passions.—Consider the grandeur of your aim; it is to save the people from their foes, from the aristocrats, to save them from their own blind fury. If a few men, really dangerous, no matter to what party they belong, should then seek to prolong a movement, become useless, by your act of justice, Paris itself will hurl them back into their original insignificance. I calmly, simply, and deliberately demand the suppression of the commission, on political grounds." The commission was violently attacked on one side, feebly defended on the other; Barrère and the committee of public safety, who were its creators proposed its suppression, in order to restore peace, and to save the assembly from being left to the mercy of the multitude. The moderate portion of the Mountain were about to adopt this concession, when the deputations arrived. The members of the department, those of the municipality, and the commissaries of sections, being admitted to the bar, demanded not merely the suppression of the Twelve, but also the punishment of the moderate members, and of all the Girondist chiefs.

The Tuileries was completely blockaded by the insurgents; and the presence of their commissaries in the convention emboldened the extreme Mountain, who were desirous of destroying the Girondist party. Robespierre, their leader and orator, spoke: "Citizens, let us not lose this day in vain clamours and unnecessary measures; this is, perhaps, the last day in which patriotism will combat with tyranny. Let the faithful representatives of the people combine to secure their happiness." He urged the convention to follow the course pointed out by the petitioners, rather than that proposed by the committee of public safety. He was thundering forth a lengthened declamation against his adversaries, when Vergniaud interfered: "Conclude this!"—"I am about to conclude, and against you! Against you, who, after the revolution of the 10th of August, sought to bring to the scaffold those who had effected it. Against you, who have never ceased in a course which involved the destruction of Paris. Against you, who desired to save the tyrant. Against you, who conspired with Dumouriez. Against you, who fiercely persecuted the same patriots whose heads Dumouriez demanded. Against you, whose criminal vengeance provoked those cries of vengeance which you seek to make a crime in your victims. I conclude my conclusion is—I propose a decree of accusation against all the accomplices of Dumouriez, and against those who are indicated by the petitioners." Notwithstanding the violence of this outbreak, Robespierre's party were not victorious. The insurrection had only been directed against the Twelve, and the committee of public safety, who proposed their suppression prevailed over the commune. The assembly adopted the decree of Barrère, which dissolved the Twelve, placed the public force in permanent requisition, and, to satisfy the petitioners, directed the committee of public safety to inquire into the conspiracies which they denounced. As soon as the multitude surrounding the assembly was informed of these measures, it received them with applause, and dispersed.

But the conspirators were not disposed to rest content with this half triumph: they had gone further on the 30th of May than on the 29th; and on the 2nd of June they went further than on the 31st of May. The insurrection, from being moral, as they termed it, became personal; that is to say, it was no longer directed against a power, but against the deputies; it passed from Danton and the Mountain, to Robespierre, Marat, and the commune. On the evening of the 31st, a Jacobin deputy said: "We have had but half the game yet; we must complete it, and not allow the people to cool." Henriot offered to place the armed force at the disposition of the club. The insurrectional committee openly took up its quarters near the convention. The whole of the 1st of June was devoted to the preparation of a great movement. The commune wrote to the sections: "Citizens, remain under arms: the danger of the country renders this a supreme law." In the evening, Marat, who was the chief author of the 2nd of June, repaired to the Hôtel de Ville, ascended the clock-tower himself, and rang the tocsin; he called upon the members of the council not to separate till they had obtained a decree of accusation against the traitors and the "statesmen." A few deputies assembled at the convention, and the conspirators came to demand the decree against the proscribed parties; but they were not yet sufficiently strong to enforce it from the convention.

The whole night was spent in making preparations; the tocsin rang, drums beat to arms, the people gathered together. On Sunday morning, about eight o'clock, Henriot presented himself to the general council, and declared to his accomplices, in the name of the insurrectionary people, that they would not lay down their arms until they had obtained the arrest of the conspiring deputies. He then placed himself at the head of the vast crowd assembled in the Place de l'Hôtel de Ville, harangued them, and gave the signal for their departure. It was nearly ten o'clock when the insurgents reached the Place du Carrousel. Henriot posted round the château bands of the most devoted men, and the convention was soon surrounded by eighty thousand men, the greater part ignorant of what was required of them and more disposed to defend than to attack the deputation.

The majority of the proscribed members had not proceeded to the assembly. A few, courageous to the last, had come to brave the storm for the last time. As soon as the sitting commenced, the intrepid Lanjuinais ascended the tribune. "I demand," said he, "to speak respecting the general call to arms now beating throughout Paris." He was immediately interrupted by cries of "Down! down! He wants civil war! He wants a counter-revolution! He calumniates Paris! He insults the people." Despite the threats, the insults, the clamours of the Mountain and the galleries, Lanjuinais denounced the projects of the commune and of the malcontents; his courage rose with the danger. "You accuse us," he said, "of calumniating Paris! Paris is pure; Paris is good; Paris is oppressed by tyrants who thirst for blood and dominion." These words were the signal for the most violent tumult; several Mountain deputies rushed to the tribune to tear Lanjuinais from it; but he, clinging firmly to it, exclaimed, in accents of the most lofty courage, "I demand the dissolution of all the revolutionist authorities in Paris. I demand that all they have done during the last three days may be declared null. I demand that all who would arrogate to themselves a new authority contrary to law, be placed without the law, and that every citizen be at liberty to punish them." He had scarcely concluded, when the insurgent petitioners came to demand his arrest, and that of his colleagues. "Citizens," said they, "the people are weary of seeing their happiness still postponed; they leave it once more in your hands; save them, or we declare that they will save themselves."

The Right moved the order of the day on the petition of the insurgents, and the convention accordingly proceeded to the previous question. The petitioners immediately withdrew in a menacing attitude; the strangers quitted the galleries; cries to arms were shouted, and a great tumult was heard without: "Save the people!"

cried one of the Mountain. "Save your colleagues, by decreeing their provisional arrest." "No, no!" replied the Right, and even a portion of the Left. "We will all share their fate!" exclaimed La Réveillère-Lépaux. The committee of public safety, called upon to make a report, terrified at the magnitude of the danger, proposed, as on the 31st of May, a measure apparently conciliatory, to satisfy the insurgents, without entirely sacrificing the proscribed members. "The committee," said Barrère, "appeal to the generosity and patriotism of the accused members. It asks of them the suspension of their power, representing to them that this alone can put an end to the divisions which afflict the republic, can alone restore to it peace." A few among them adopted the proposition. Isnard at once gave in his resignation; Lanthénas, Dussaulx, and Fauchet followed his example; Lanjuinais would not. He said: "I have hitherto, I believe, shown some courage; expect not from me either suspension or resignation. When the ancients," he continued, amidst violent interruption, "prepared a sacrifice, they crowned the victim with flowers and chaplets, as they conducted it to the altar; but they did not insult it." Barbaroux was as firm as Lanjuinais. "I have sworn," he said, "to die at my post; I will keep my oath." The conspirators of the Mountain themselves protested against the proposition of the committee. Marat urged that those who make sacrifices should be pure; and Billaud-Varennes demanded the trial of the Girondists, not their suspension.

While this was going on, Lacroix, a deputy of the Mountain, rushed into the house, and to the tribune, and declared that he had been insulted at the door, that he had been refused egress, and that the convention was no longer free. Many of the Mountain expressed their indignation at Henriot and his troops. Danton said it was necessary vigorously to avenge this insult to the national majesty. Barrère proposed to the convention to present themselves to the people. "Representatives," said he, "vindicate your liberty; suspend your sitting; cause the bayonets that surround you to be lowered." The whole convention arose, and set forth in procession, preceded by its sergeants, and headed by the president, who was covered, in token of his affliction. On arriving at a door on the Place du Carrousel, they found there Henriot on horseback, sabre in hand. "What do the people require?" said the president, Hérault de Séchelles; "the convention is wholly engaged in promoting their happiness." "Hérault," replied Henriot, "the people have not risen to hear phrases; they require twenty-four traitors to be given up to them." "Give us all up!" cried those who surrounded the president. Henriot then turned to his people, and exclaimed: "Cannoneers, to your guns." Two pieces were directed upon the convention, who, retiring to the gardens, sought an outlet at various points, but found all the issues guarded. The soldiers were everywhere under arms. Marat ran through the ranks, encouraging and exciting them. "No weakness," said he; "do not quit your posts till they have given them up." The convention then returned within the house, overwhelmed with a sense of their powerlessness, convinced of the inutility of their efforts, and entirely subdued. The arrest of the proscribed members was no longer opposed. Marat, the true dictator of the assembly, imperiously decided the fate of its members. "Dussaulx," said he, "is an old twaddler, incapable of leading a party; Lathénas is a poor creature, unworthy of a thought; Ducos is merely chargeable with a few absurd notions, and is not at all a man to become a counter-revolutionary leader. I require that these be struck out of the list, and their names replaced by that of Valazé." These names were accordingly struck out, and that of Valazé substituted, and the list thus altered was agreed to, scarcely one half of the assembly taking part in the vote.

These are the names of the illustrious men proscribed: the Girondists Gensonné, Guadet, Brissot, Gorsas, Pétion, Vergniaud, Salles, Barbaroux, Chambon, Buzot, Birotteau, Lidon, Rabaud, Lasource, Lanjuinais, Grangeneuve, Lehardy, Lesage, Louvet, Valazé, Lebrun, minister of foreign affairs, Clavières, minister of taxes; and the members of the Council of Twelve, Kervelegan, Gardien, Rabaud Saint-Etienne, Boileau, Bertrand, Vigée, Molleveau, Henri La Rivière, Gomaire, and Bergoing. The convention placed them under arrest at their own houses, and under the protection of the people. The order for keeping the assembly itself prisoners was at once withdrawn, and the multitude dispersed, but from that moment the convention ceased to be free.

Thus fell the Gironde party, a party rendered illustrious by great talents and great courage, a party which did honour to the young republic by its horror of bloodshed, its hatred of crime and anarchy, its love of order, justice, and liberty; a party unfitly placed between the middle class, whose revolution it had combated, and the multitude, whose government it rejected. Condemned to inaction, it could only render illustrious certain defeat, by a courageous struggle and a glorious death. At this period, its fate might readily be foreseen; it had been driven from post to post; from the Jacobins by the invasion of the Mountain; from the commune by the outbreak of Pétion; from the ministry by the retirement of Roland and his colleagues; from the army by the defection of Dumouriez. The convention alone remained to it, there it threw up its intrenchments, there it fought, and there it fell. Its enemies employed against it, in turn, insurrection and conspiracy. The conspiracies led to the creation of the Commission of Twelve, which seemed to give a momentary advantage to the Gironde, but which only excited its adversaries the more violently against it. These aroused the people, and took from the Girondists, first, their authority, by destroying the Twelve; then, their political existence, by proscribing their leaders.

The consequences of this disastrous event did not answer the expectations of any one. The Dantonists thought that the dissensions of parties were at an end: civil war broke out. The moderate members of the committee of public safety thought that the convention would resume all its power: it was utterly subdued. The commune thought that the 31st of May would secure to it domination; domination fell to Robespierre, and to a few men devoted to his fortune, or to the principle of extreme democracy. Lastly, there was another party to be added to the parties defeated, and thenceforth hostile; and as after the 10th of August the republic had been opposed to the constitutionalists, after the 31st of May the Reign of Terror was opposed to the moderate party of the republic.

CHAPTER VIII

FROM THE 2ND OF JUNE, 1793, TO APRIL, 1794

Insurrection of the departments against the 31st of May—Protracted reverses on the frontiers—Progress of the Vendéans—The *Montagnards* decree the constitution of 1793, and immediately suspend it to maintain and strengthen the revolutionary government—*Levée en masse*; law against suspected persons—Victories of the *Montagnards* in the interior, and on the frontiers—Death of the queen, of the twenty-two Girondists, etc.— Committee of public safety; its power; its members—Republican calendar— The conquerors of the 31st of May separate—The ultra-revolutionary faction of the commune, or the Hébertists, abolish the catholic religion, and establish the worship of Reason; its struggle with the committee of public safety; its defeat—The moderate faction of the *Montagnards*, or the Dantonists, wish to destroy the revolutionary dictatorship, and to establish the legal government; their fall—The committee of public safety remains alone, and triumphant.

It was to be presumed that the Girondists would not bow to their defeat, and that the 31st of May would be the signal for the insurrection of the departments against the Mountain and the commune of Paris. This was the last trial left them to make, and they attempted it. But, in this decisive measure, there was seen the same want of union which had caused their defeat in the assembly. It is doubtful whether the Girondists would have triumphed, had they been united, and especially whether their triumph would have saved the revolution. How could they have done with just laws what the Mountain effected by violent measures? How could they have conquered foreign foes without fanaticism, restrained parties without the aid of terror, fed the multitude without a *maximum*, and supplied the armies without requisition. If the 31st of May had had a different result, what happened at a much later period would probably have taken place immediately, namely, a gradual abatement of the revolutionary movement, increased attacks on the part of Europe, a general resumption of hostilities by all parties, the days of Prairial, without power to drive back the multitude; the days of Vendémiaire, without power to repel the royalists; the invasion of the allies, and, according to the policy of the times, the partition of France. The republic was not sufficiently powerful to meet so many attacks as it did after the reaction of Thermidor.

However this may be, the Girondists who ought to have remained quiet or fought all together, did not do so, and, after the 2nd of June, all the moderate men of the party remained under the decree of arrest: the others escaped. Vergniaud, Gensonné, Ducos, Fonfrède, etc., were among the first; Pétion, Barbaroux, Guadet, Louvet, Buzot, and Lanjuinais, among the latter. They repaired to Evreux, in the department de l'Eure, where Buzot had much influence, and thence to Caen, in Calvados. These made this town the centre of the insurrection. Brittany soon joined them. The insurgents, under the name of the *assembly of the departments assembled at Caen*, formed an army, appointed general Wimpfen commander, arrested Romme and Prieur de la Marne, who were members of the Mountain and commissaries of the convention, and prepared to march on Paris. From there, a young, beautiful, and courageous woman, Charlotte Corday, went to punish Marat, the principal author of the 31st of May, and the 2nd of June. She hoped to save the republic by sacrificing herself to its cause. But tyranny did not rest with one man; it belonged to a party, and to the violent situation of the republic. Charlotte Corday, after executing her generous but vain design, died with unchanging calmness, modest courage, and the satisfaction of having done well.[6] But Marat, after his assassination, became a greater object of enthusiasm with the people than he had been while living. He was invoked on all the public squares; his bust was placed in all the popular societies, and the convention was obliged to grant him the honours of the Panthéon.

At the same time Lyons arose, Marseilles and Bordeaux took arms, and more than sixty departments joined the insurrection. This attack soon led to a general rising among all parties, and the royalists for the most part took advantage of the movement which the Girondists had commenced. They sought, especially, to direct the insurrection of Lyons, in order to make it the centre of the movement in the south. This city was strongly attached to the ancient order of things. Its manufactures of silver and gold and silken embroidery, and its trade in articles of luxury, made it dependent on the upper classes. It therefore declared at an early period against a social change, which destroyed its former connexions, and ruined its manufactures, by destroying the nobility and clergy. Lyons, accordingly, in 1790, even under the constituent assembly, when the emigrant princes were in that neighbourhood, at the court of Turin, had made attempts at a rising. These attempts, directed by priests and nobles, had been repressed, but the spirit remained the same. There, as elsewhere, after the 10th of August, men had wished to bring about the revolution of the multitude, and to establish its government. Châlier, the fanatical imitator of Marat, was at the head of the Jacobins, the sans-culottes, and the municipality of Lyons. His audacity increased after the massacres of September and the 21st of January. Yet nothing had as yet been decided between the lower republican class, and the middle royalist class, the one having its seat of

---

[6] The following are a few of the replies of this heroic girl before the revolutionary tribunal:—"What were your intentions in killing Marat?"—"To put an end to the troubles of France."—"Is it long since you conceived this project?"—"Since the proscription of the deputies of the people on the 31st of May."—"You learned then by the papers that Marat was a friend of anarchy?"—"Yes, I knew he was perverting France. I have killed," she added, raising her voice, "a man to save a thousand; a villain, to save the innocent; a wild beast, to give tranquility to my country. I was a republican before the revolution, and I have never been without energy."

power in the municipality, and the other in the sections. But the disputes became greater towards the end of May; they fought, and the sections carried the day. The municipality was besieged, and taken by assault. Châlier, who had fled, was apprehended and executed. The sections, not as yet daring to throw off the yoke of the convention, endeavoured to excuse themselves on the score of the necessity of arming themselves, because the Jacobins and the members of the corporation had forced them to do so. The convention, which could only save itself by means of daring, losing everything if it yielded, would listen to nothing. Meanwhile the insurrection of Calvados became known, and the people of Lyons, thus encouraged, no longer feared to raise the standard of revolt. They put their town in a state of defence; they raised fortifications, formed an army of twenty thousand men, received emigrants among them, entrusted the command of their forces to the royalist Précy and the marquis de Virieux, and concerted their operations with the king of Sardinia.

The revolt of Lyons was so much the more to be feared by the convention, as its central position gave it the support of the south, which was in arms, while there was also a rising in the west. At Marseilles, the news of the 31st of May had aroused the partisans of the Girondists: Rebecqui repaired thither in haste. The sections were assembled; the members of the revolutionary tribunal were outlawed; the two representatives, Baux and Antiboul, were arrested, and an army of ten thousand men raised to advance on Paris. These measures were the work of the royalists, who, there as elsewhere, only waiting for an opportunity to revive their party, had at first assumed a republican appearance, but now acted in their own name. They had secured the sections; and the movement was no longer effected in favour of the Girondists, but for the counter-revolutionists. Once in a state of revolt, the party whose opinions are the most violent, and whose aim is the clearest, supplants its allies. Rebecqui, perceiving this new turn of the insurrection, threw himself in despair into the port of Marseilles. The insurgents took the road to Lyons; their example was rapidly imitated at Toulon, Nîmes, Montauban, and the principal towns in the south. In Calvados, the insurrection had had the same royalist character, since the marquis de Puisaye, at the head of some troops, had introduced himself into the ranks of the Girondists. The towns of Bordeaux, Nantes, Brest, and L'Orient, were favourable to the persons proscribed on the 2nd of June, and a few openly joined them; but they were of no great service, because they were restrained by the Jacobin party, or by the necessity of fighting the royalists of the west.

The latter, during this almost general rising of the departments, continued to extend their enterprises. After their first victories, the Vendéans seized on Bressuire, Argenton, and Thouars. Entirely masters of their own country, they proposed getting possession of the frontiers, and opening a way into revolutionary France, as well as communications with England. On the 6th of June, the Vendéan army, composed of forty thousand men, under Cathelineau, Lescure, Stofflet, and La Rochejaquelin, marched on Saumur, which it took by storm. It then prepared to attack and capture Nantes, to secure the possession of its own country, and become master of the course of the Loire. Cathelineau, at the head of the Vendéan troops, left a garrison in Saumur, took Angers, crossed the Loire, pretended to advance upon Tours and Le Mans, and then rapidly threw himself upon Nantes, which he attacked on the right bank, while Charette was to attack it on the left.

Everything seemed combined for the overthrow of the convention. Its armies were beaten on the north and on the Pyrenees, while it was threatened by the people of Lyons in the centre, those of Marseilles in the south, the Girondists in one part of the west, the Vendéans in the other, and while twenty thousand Piedmontese were invading France. The military reaction which, after the brilliant campaigns of Argonne and Belgium, had taken place, chiefly owing to the disagreement between Dumouriez and the Jacobins, between the army and the government, had manifested itself in a most disastrous manner since the defection of the commander-in-chief. There was no longer unity of operation, enthusiasm in the troops, or agreement between the convention, occupied with its quarrels, and the discouraged generals. The remains of Dumouriez's army had assembled at the camp at Famars, under the command of Dampierre; but they had been obliged to retire, after a defeat, under the cannon of Bouchain. Dampierre was killed. The frontier from Dunkirk to Givet was threatened by superior forces. Custine was promptly called from the Moselle to the army of the north, but his presence did not restore affairs. Valenciennes, the key to France, was taken; Condé shared the same fate; the army, driven from position to position, retired beyond the Scarpe, before Arras, the last post between the Scarpe and Paris. Mayence, on the other side, sorely pressed by the enemy and by famine, gave up all hope of being assisted by the army of the Moselle, reduced to inaction; and despairing of being able to hold out long, capitulated. Lastly, the English Government, seeing that Paris and the departments were distressed by famine, after the 31st of May and the 2nd of June, pronounced all the ports of France in a state of blockade, and that all neutral ships attempting to bring a supply of provisions would be confiscated. This measure, new to the annals of history, and destined to starve an entire people, three months afterwards originated the law of the *maximum*. The situation of the republic could not be worse.

The convention was, as it were, taken by surprise. It was disorganized, because emerging from a struggle, and because the conquerors had not had time to establish themselves. After the 2nd of June, before the danger became so pressing both on the frontiers and in the departments, the Mountain had sent commissioners in every direction, and immediately turned its attention to the constitution, which had so long been expected, and from which it entertained great hopes. The Girondists had wished to decree it before the 21st of January, in order to save Louis XVI., by substituting legal order for the revolutionary state of things; they returned to the subject previous to the 31st of May, in order to prevent their own ruin. But the Mountain, on two occasions, had diverted the assembly from this discussion by two coups d'état, the trial of Louis XVI., and the elimination of the Gironde. Masters of the field, they now endeavoured to secure the republicans by decreeing the constitution. Hérault de Séchelles was the legislator of the Mountain, as Condorcet had been of the Gironde. In a few days, this new constitution was adopted in the convention, and submitted to the approval of the primary assemblies. It is easy to conceive its nature, with the ideas that then prevailed respecting democratic government. The constituent assembly was considered as aristocratical: the law it had established was regarded as a violation of the rights of the people, because it imposed conditions for the exercise of political rights; because it did not recognise the most absolute equality; because it had deputies and magistrates appointed by electors, and these electors by the people; because, in some cases, it put limits to the national sovereignty, by excluding a portion of active citizens from high public functions, and the proletarians from the functions of acting citizens; finally, because, instead of fixing on population as the only basis of political rights, it combined it, in all its operations, with property. The constitutional law of 1793 established the pure régime of the multitude: it not only recognised the people as the source of all power, but also delegated the exercise of it to the people; an unlimited sovereignty; extreme mobility in the magistracy; direct elections, in which every one could vote; primary assemblies, that could meet without convocation, at given times, to elect representatives and control their acts; a national assembly, to be renewed annually, and which, properly speaking, was only a committee of the primary assemblies; such was this constitution. As it made the multitude govern, and as it entirely disorganized authority, it was impracticable at all times; but especially in a moment of general war. The Mountain, instead of extreme democracy, needed a stern dictatorship. The constitution was suspended as soon as made, and the revolutionary government strengthened and maintained until peace was achieved.

Both during the discussion of the constitution and its presentation to the primary assemblies, the Mountain learned the danger which threatened them. These daring men, having three or four parties to put down in the interior, several kinds of civil war to terminate, the disasters of the armies to repair, and all Europe to repel, were not alarmed at their position. The representatives of the forty-four thousand municipalities came to accept the constitution. Admitted to the bar of the assembly, after making known the assent of the people, they required *the arrest of all suspected persons, and a levy en masse of the people.* "Well," exclaimed Danton, "let us respond to their wishes. The deputies of the primary assemblies have just taken the initiative among us, in the way of inspiring terror! I demand that the convention, which ought now to be penetrated with a sense of its dignity, for it has just been invested with the entire national power, I demand that it do now, by a decree, invest the primary assemblies with the right of supplying the state with arms, provisions, and ammunition; of making an appeal to the people, of exciting the energy of citizens, and of raising four hundred thousand men. It is with cannon-balls that we must declare the constitution to our foes! Now is the time to take the last great oath, that we will destroy tyranny, or perish!" This oath was immediately taken by all the deputies and citizens present. A few days after, Barrère, in the name of the committee of public safety, which was composed of revolutionary members, and which became the centre of operations and the government of the assembly, proposed measures still more general: "Liberty," said he, "has become the creditor of every citizen; some owe her their industry; others their fortune; these their counsel; those their arms; all owe her their blood. Accordingly, all the French, of every age and of either sex, are summoned by their country to defend liberty; all faculties, physical or moral; all means, political or commercial; all metal, all the elements are her tributaries. Let each maintain his post in the national and military movement about to take place. The young men will fight; the married men will forge arms, transport the baggage and artillery, and prepare provisions; the women will make tents and clothes for the soldiers, and exercise their hospitable care in the asylums of the wounded; children will make lint from old linen; and the aged, resuming the mission they discharged among the ancients, shall cause themselves to be carried to the public places, where they shall excite the courage of the young warriors, and propagate the doctrine of hatred to kings, and the unity of the republic. National buildings shall be converted into barracks, public squares into workshops; the ground of the cellars will serve for the preparation of saltpetre; all saddle horses shall be placed in requisition for the cavalry; all draught horses for the artillery; fowling-pieces, pistols, swords and pikes, belonging to individuals, shall be employed in the service of the interior. The republic being but a large city, in a state of necessity, France must be converted into a vast camp."

The measures proposed by Barrère were at once decreed. All Frenchmen, from eighteen to five-and-twenty, took arms, the armies were recruited by levies of men, and supported by levies of provisions. The republic had very soon fourteen armies, and twelve hundred thousand soldiers. France, while it became a camp and a workshop for the republicans, became at the same time a prison for those who did not accept the republic. While marching against avowed enemies, it was thought necessary to make sure of secret foes, and the famous law, *des suspects*, was passed. All foreigners were arrested, on the ground of their hostile machinations, and the partisans of constitutional monarchy and a limited republic were imprisoned, to be kept close, until the peace was effected. At the time, this was so far only a reasonable measure of precaution. The bourgeoisie, the mercantile people, and the middle classes, furnished prisoners after the 31st of May, as the nobility and clergy had done after the 10th of August. A revolutionary army of six thousand soldiers and a thousand artillerymen was formed for the interior. Every indigent citizen was allowed forty sous a day, to enable him to be present at the sectionary meetings. Certificates of citizenship were delivered, in order to make sure of the opinions of all who co-operated in the revolutionary movement. The functionaries were placed under the surveillance of the clubs, a revolutionary committee was formed in each section, and thus they prepared to face the enemy on all sides, both abroad and at home.

The insurgents in Calvados were easily suppressed; at the very first skirmish at Vernon, the insurgent troops fled. Wimpfen endeavoured to rally them in vain. The moderate class, those who had taken up the defence of the Girondists, displayed little ardour or activity. When the constitution was accepted by the other departments, it saw the opportunity for admitting that it had been in error, when it thought it was taking arms against a mere factious minority. This retractation was made at Caen, which had been the headquarters of the revolt. The Mountain commissioners did not sully this first victory with executions. General Carteaux, on the other hand, marched at the head of some troops against the sectionary army of the south; he defeated its force, pursued it to Marseilles, entered the town after it, and Provence would have been brought into subjection like Calvados, if the royalists, who had taken refuge at Toulon, after their defeat, had not called in the English to their aid, and placed in their hands this key to France. Admiral Hood entered the town in the name of Louis XVII., whom he proclaimed king, disarmed the fleet, sent for eight thousand Spaniards by sea, occupied the surrounding forts, and forced Carteaux, who was advancing against Toulon, to fall back on Marseilles.

Notwithstanding this check, the conventionalists succeeded in isolating the insurrection, and this was a great point. The Mountain commissioners had made their entry into the rebel capitals; Robert Lindet into Caen; Tallien into Bordeaux; Barras and Fréron into Marseilles. Only two towns remained to be taken—Toulon and Lyons.

A simultaneous attack from the south, west, and centre was no longer apprehended, and in the interior the enemy was only on the defensive. Lyons was besieged by Kellermann, general of the army of the Alps; three corps pressed the town on all sides. The veteran soldiers of the Alps, the revolutionary battalions and the newly-levied troops, reinforced the besiegers every day. The people of Lyons defended themselves with all the courage of despair. At first, they relied on the assistance of the insurgents of the south; but these having been repulsed by Carteaux, the Lyonnais placed their last hope in the army of Piedmont, which attempted a diversion in their favour, but was beaten by Kellermann. Pressed still more energetically, they saw their first positions carried. Famine began to be felt, and courage forsook them. The royalist leaders, convinced of the inutility of longer resistance, left the town, and the republican army entered the walls, where they awaited the orders of the convention. A few months after, Toulon itself, defended by veteran troops and formidable fortifications, fell into the power of the republicans. The battalions of the army of Italy, reinforced by those which the taking of Lyons left disposable, pressed the place closely. After repeated attacks and prodigies of skill and valour, they made themselves masters of it, and the capture of Toulon finished what that of Lyons had begun.

Everywhere the convention was victorious. The Vendéans had failed in their attempt upon Nantes, after having lost many men, and their general-in- chief, Cathelineau. This attack put an end to the aggressive and previously promising movement of the Vendéan insurrection. The royalists repassed the Loire, abandoned Saumur, and resumed their former cantonments. They were, however, still formidable; and the republicans, who pursued them, were again beaten in La Vendée. General Biron, who had succeeded general Berruyer, unsuccessfully continued the war with small bodies of troops; his moderation and defective system of attack caused him to be replaced by Canclaux and Rossignol, who were not more fortunate than he. There were two leaders, two armies, and two centres of operation—the one at Nantes, and the other at Saumur, placed under contrary influences. General Canclaux could not agree with general Rossignol, nor the moderate Mountain commissioner Philippeaux with Bourbotte, the commissioner of the committee of public safety; and this attempt at invasion failed like the preceding attempts, for want of concert in plan and action. The committee of public safety soon remedied this, by appointing one sole general-in- chief, Lechelle, and by introducing war on a large scale into La Vendée. This new method, aided by the garrison of Mayence, consisting of seventeen thousand veterans, who, relieved from operations against the allied nations after the capitulation, were employed in the interior, entirely changed the face of the war. The royalists underwent four consecutive defeats, two at Châtillon, two at Cholet. Lescure, Bonchamps, and d'Elbée were mortally wounded, and the insurgents, completely beaten in Upper Vendée, and fearing that they should be exterminated if they took refuge in Lower Vendée, determined to leave their country to the number of eighty thousand persons. This emigration through Brittany, which they hoped to arouse to insurrection, became fatal to them. Repulsed before Granville, utterly routed at Mans, they were destroyed at Savenay, and barely a few thousand men, the wreck of this vast emigration, returned to Vendée. These disasters, irreparable for the royalist cause, the taking of the island of Noirmoutiers from Charette, the dispersion of the troops of that leader, the death of La Rochejaquelin, rendered the republicans masters of the country. The committee of public safety, thinking, not without reason, that its enemies were beaten but not subjugated, adopted a terrible system of extermination to prevent them from rising again. General Thurreau surrounded Vendée with sixteen entrenched camps; twelve moveable columns, called the *infernal columns*, overran the country in every direction, sword and fire in hand, scoured the woods, dispersed the assemblies, and diffused terror throughout this unhappy country.

The foreign armies had also been driven back from the frontiers they had invaded. After having taken Valenciennes and Condé, blockaded Maubeuge and Le Quesnoy, the enemy advanced on Cassel, Hondschoote, and Furnes, under the command of the duke of York. The committee of public safety, dissatisfied with Custine, who was further regarded with suspicion as a Girondist, superseded him by general Houchard. The enemy, hitherto successful, was defeated at Hondschoote, and compelled to retreat. The military reaction began with the daring measures of the committee of public safety. Houchard himself was dismissed. Jourdan took the command of the army of the north, gained the important victory of Watignies over the prince of Coburg, raised the siege of Maubeuge, and resumed the offensive on that frontier. Similar successes took place on all the others. The immortal campaign of 1793-1794 opened. What Jourdan had done with the army of the north, Hoche and Pichegru did with the army of the Moselle, and Kellermann with that of the Alps. The enemy was repulsed, and kept in check on all sides. Then took place, after the 31st of May, that which had followed the 10th of August. The want of union between the generals and the leaders of the assembly was removed; the revolutionary movement, which had slackened, increased; and victories recommenced. Armies have had their crises, as well as parties, and these crises have brought about successes or defeat, always by the same law.

In 1792, at the beginning of the war, the generals were constitutionalists, and the ministers Girondists. Rochambeau, Lafayette, and Luckner, did not at all agree with Dumouriez, Servan, Clavière, and Roland. There was, besides, little enthusiasm in the army; it was beaten. After the 10th of August, the Girondist generals, Dumouriez, Custine, Kellermann, and Dillon, replaced the constitutionalist generals. There was unity of views, confidence, and co-operation, between the army and the government. The catastrophe of the 10th of August augmented this energy, by increasing the necessity for victory; and the results were the plan of the campaign of Argonne, the victories of Valmy and Jemappes, and the invasion of Belgium. The struggle between the Mountain and the Gironde, between Dumouriez and the Jacobins, again created discord between the army and government, and destroyed the confidence of the troops, who experienced immediate and numerous reverses. There was defection on the part of Dumouriez, as there had been withdrawal on the part of Lafayette. After the 31st of May, which overthrew the Gironde party, after the committee of public safety had become established, and had replaced the Girondist generals, Dumouriez, Custine, Houchard, and Dillon, by the Mountain generals, Jourdan, Hoche, Pichegru, and Moreau; after it had restored the revolutionary movement by the daring measures we have described, the campaign of Argonne and of Belgium was renewed in that of 1794, and the genius of Carnot equalled that of Dumouriez, if it did not surpass it.

During this war, the committee of public safety permitted a frightful number of executions. Armies confine themselves to slaughter in battle; it is not so with parties, who, under violent circumstances, fearing to see the combat renewed after the victory, secure themselves from new attacks by inexorable rigour. The usage of all governments being to make their own preservation a matter of right, they regard those who attack them as enemies so long as they fight, as conspirators when they are defeated; and thus destroy them alike by means of war and of law.

All these views at once guided the policy of the committee of public safety, a policy of vengeance, of terror, and of self-preservation. This was the maxim upon which it proceeded in reference to insurgent towns: "The name of Lyons," said Barrère, "must no longer exist. You will call it *Ville Affranchie*, and upon the ruins of that famous city there shall be raised a monument to attest the crime and the punishment of the enemies of liberty. Its history shall be told in these words: '*Lyons warred against liberty; Lyons exists no more.*'" To realise this terrible anathema, the committee sent to this unfortunate city Collot-d'Herbois, Fouché, and Couthon, who slaughtered the inhabitants with grape shot and demolished its buildings. The insurgents of Toulon underwent at the hands of the representatives, Barras and Fréron, a nearly similar fate. At Caen, Marseilles, and Bordeaux, the executions were less general and less violent, because they were proportioned to the gravity of the insurrection, which had not been undertaken in concert with foreign foes.

In the interior, the dictatorial government struck at all the parties with which it was at war, in the persons of their greatest members. The condemnation of queen Marie-Antoinette was directed against Europe; that of the twenty-two against the Girondists; of the wise Bailly against the old constitutionalists; lastly, that of the duke of Orleans against certain members of the Mountain who were supposed to have plotted his elevation. The unfortunate widow of Louis XVI. was first sentenced to death by this sanguinary revolutionary tribunal. The proscribed of the 2nd of June soon followed her. She perished on the 16th of October, and the Girondist deputies on the 31st. They were twenty-one in number: Brissot, Vergniaud,

Gensonné, Fonfrède, Ducos, Valazé, Lasource, Silléry, Gardien, Carra, Duperret, Duprat, Fauchet, Beauvais, Duchâtel, Mainvielle, Lacaze, Boileau, Lehardy, Antiboul, and Vigée. Seventy-three of their colleagues, who had protested against their arrest, were also imprisoned, but the committee did not venture to inflict death upon them.

During the debates, these illustrious prisoners displayed uniform and serene courage. Vergniaud raised his eloquent voice for a moment, but in vain. Valazé stabbed himself with a poignard on hearing the sentence, and Lasource said to the judges: "I die at a time when the people have lost their senses; you will die when they recover them." They went to execution displaying all the stoicism of the times, singing the *Marseillaise*, and applying it to their own case:

> "Allons, enfants de la patrie,
> Le jour de gloire est arrivé:
> Contre nous de la tyrannie
> Le couteau sanglant est levé," etc.

Nearly all the other leaders of this party had a violent end. Salles, Guadet, and Barbaroux, were discovered in the grottos of Saint-Emilion, near Bordeaux, and died on the scaffold. Pétion and Buzot, after wandering about some time, committed suicide; they were found, dead in a field, half devoured by wolves. Rabaud-Saint-Etienne was betrayed by an old friend; Madame Roland was also condemned to death, and displayed the courage of a Roman matron. Her husband, on hearing of her death, left his place of concealment, and killed himself on the high road. Condorcet, outlawed soon after the 2nd of June, was taken while endeavouring to escape, and saved himself from the executioner's knife only by poison. Louvet, Kervelegan, Lanjuinais, Henri La Rivière, Lesage, La Réveillère-Lépeaux, were the only leading Girondists who, in secure retreat, awaited the end of the furious storm.

The revolutionary government was formed; it was proclaimed by the convention on the 10th of October. Before the 31st of May, power had been nowhere, neither in the ministry, nor in the commune, nor in the convention. It was natural that power should become concentrated in this extreme situation of affairs, and at a moment when the need for unity and promptitude of action was deeply felt. The assembly being the most central and extensive power, the dictatorship would as naturally become placed in its bosom, be exercised there by the dominant faction, and in that faction by a few men. The committee of public safety of the convention created on the 6th of April, in order, as the name indicates, to provide for the defence of the revolution by extraordinary measures, was in itself a complete framework of government. Formed during the divisions of the Mountain and the Gironde, it was composed of neutral members of the convention till the 31st of May; and at its first renewal, of members of the extreme Mountain. Barrère remained in it; but Robespierre acceded, and his party dominated in it by Saint-Just, Couthon, Collot-d'Herbois, and Billaud-Varennes. He set aside some Dantonists who still remained in it, such as Hérault de Séchelles and Robert Lindet, gained over Barrère, and usurped the lead by assuming the direction of the public mind and of police. His associates divided the various departments among themselves.

Saint-Just undertook the surveillance and denouncing of parties; Couthon, the violent propositions which required to be softened in form; Billaud-Varennes and Collot-d'Herbois directed the missions into the departments; Carnot took the war department; Cambon, the exchequer; Prieur de la Côte-d'Or, Prieur de la Marne, and several others, the various branches of internal administration; and Barrère was the daily orator, the panegyrist ever prepared, of the dictatorial committee. Below these, assisting in the detail of the revolutionary administration, and of minor measures, was placed the committee of general safety, composed in the same spirit as the great committee, having, like it, twelve members, who were re-eligible every three months, and always renewed in their office.

The whole revolutionary power was lodged in the hands of these men. Saint-Just, in proposing the establishment of the decemviral power until the restoration of peace, did not conceal the motives nor the object of this dictatorship. "You must no longer show any lenity to the enemies of the new order of things," said he. "Liberty must triumph at any cost. In the present circumstances of the republic, the constitution cannot be established; it would guarantee impunity to attacks on our liberty, because it would be deficient in the violence necessary to restrain them. The present government is not sufficiently free to act. You are not near enough to strike in every direction at the authors of these attacks; the sword of the law must extend everywhere; your arm must be felt everywhere." Thus was created that terrible power, which first destroyed the enemies of the Mountain, then the Mountain and the Commune, and, lastly, itself. The committee did everything in the name of the convention, which it used as an instrument. It nominated and dismissed generals, ministers, representatives, commissioners, judges, and juries. It assailed factions; it took the initiative in all measures. Through its commissioners, armies and generals were dependent upon it, and it ruled the departments with sovereign sway. By means of the law touching suspected persons, it disposed of men's liberties; by the revolutionary tribunal, of men's lives; by levies and the *maximum*, of property; by decrees of accusation in the terrified convention, of its own members. Lastly, its dictatorship was supported by the multitude, who debated in the clubs, ruled in the revolutionary committees: whose services it paid by a daily stipend, and whom it fed with the *maximum*. The multitude adhered to a system which inflamed its passions, exaggerated its importance, assigned it the first place, and appeared to do everything for it.

The innovators, separated by war and by their laws from all states and from all forms of government, determined to widen the separation. By an unprecedented revolution they established an entirely new era; they changed the divisions of the year, the names of the months and days; they substituted a republican for the Christian calendar, the decade for the week, and fixed the day of rest not on the sabbath, but on the tenth day. The new era dated from the 22nd of September, 1792, the epoch of the foundation of the republic. There were twelve equal months of thirty days, which began on the 22nd of September, in the following order:—*Vendémiaire, Brumaire, Frimaire*, for the autumn; *Nivôse, Pluviôse, Ventôse*, for the winter; *Germinal, Floréal, Prairial*, for the spring; *Messidor, Thermidor, Fructidor*, for the summer. Each month had three décades, each décade ten days, and each day was named from its order in the décade:—*Primidi, Duodi, Tridi, Quartidi, Quinti-di, Sextidi, Septidi, Octidi, Nonidi, Decadi*. The surplus five days were placed at the end of the year; they received the name of *Sans-culottides*, and were consecrated, the first, to the festival of genius; the second, to that of labour; the third, to that of actions; the fourth, to that of rewards; the fifth, to that of opinion. The constitution of 1793 led to the establishment of the republican calendar, and the republican calendar to the abolition of Christian worship. We shall soon see the commune and the committee of public safety each proposing a religion of its own; the commune, the worship of reason; the committee of public safety, the worship of the Supreme Being. But we must first mention a new struggle between the authors of the catastrophe of the 31st of May themselves.

The Commune and the Mountain had effected this revolution against the Gironde, and the committee alone had benefited by it. During the five months from June to November, the committee, having taken all the measures of defence, had naturally become the first power in the republic. The actual struggle being, as it were, over, the commune sought to sway the committee, and the Mountain to throw off its yoke. The most intense manifestation of the revolution was found in the municipal faction. With an aim opposed to that of the committee of public safety, it desired instead of the conventional dictatorship, the most extreme local democracy; and instead of religion, the consecration of materialism. Political anarchy and religious atheism were the symbols of this party, and the means by which it aimed at establishing its own rule. A revolution is the effect of the different systems which have agitated the age which has originated it. Thus, during the continuance of the crisis in France, ultra-montane catholicism was represented by the nonjuring clergy; Jansenism by the constitutionist clergy; philosophical deism by the worship of the Supreme Being, instituted by the committee of public safety; and the materialism of Holbach's school by the worship of Reason and of Nature, decreed by the commune. It was the same with political opinions, from the royalty of the *Ancien Régime* to the unlimited democracy of the municipal faction. The latter had lost, in Marat, its principal support, its true leader, while the committee of public safety still retained Robespierre. It had at its head men who enjoyed great popularity with the lower classes; Chaumette, and his substitute Hébert, were its political leaders; Ronsin, commandant of the revolutionary army, its general; the atheist, Anacharsis Clootz, its apostle. In the sections it relied on the revolutionary committees, in which there were many obscure foreigners, supposed, and not without probability, to be agents of England, sent to destroy the republic by driving it into anarchy and excess. The club of the Cordeliers was composed entirely of its partisans. The *Vieux Cordeliers* of Danton, who had contributed so powerfully to the 10th of August, and who constituted the commune of that period, had entered the government and the convention, and had been replaced in the club by members whom they contemptuously designated the *patriotes de la troisième réquisition*.

Hébert's faction, which, in a work entitled *Père Duchêsne*, popularised obscene language and low and cruel sentiments, and which added derision of the victims to the executions of party, in a short time made terrible progress. It compelled the bishop of Paris and his vicars to abjure Christianity at the bar of the convention, and forced the convention to decree, that *the worship of Reason should be substituted for the catholic religion*. The churches were shut up or converted into temples of reason, and fêtes were established in every town, which became scandalous scenes of atheism. The committee of public safety grew alarmed at the power of this ultra-revolutionary faction, and hastened to stop and to destroy it. Robespierre soon attacked it in the assembly, (15th Frimaire, year II., 5th Dec., 1793). "Citizens, representatives of the people," said he, "the kings in alliance against the republic are making war against us with armies and intrigues; we will oppose their armies by braver ones; their intrigues, by vigilance and the terror of national justice. Ever intent on renewing their secret plots, in proportion as they are destroyed by the hand of patriotism, ever skilful in directing the arms of liberty against liberty itself, the emissaries of the enemies of France are now labouring to overthrow the republic by republicanism, and to rekindle civil war by philosophy." He classed the ultra-revolutionists of the commune with the external enemies of the republic. "It is your part," said he to the convention, "to prevent the follies and extravagancies which coincide with the projects of foreign conspiracy. I require you to prohibit particular authorities (the commune) from serving our enemies by rash measures, and that no armed force be allowed to interfere in questions of religious opinions." And the convention, which had applauded the abjurations at the demand of the commune, decreed, on Robespierre's motion, that *all violence and all measures opposed to the liberty of religion are prohibited*.

The committee of public safety was too strong not to triumph over the commune; but, at the same time, it had to resist the moderate party of the Mountain, which demanded the cessation of the revolutionary government and the dictatorship of the committees. The revolutionary government had only been created to restrain, the dictatorship to conquer; and as Danton and his party no longer considered restraint and victory essential, they sought to establish legal order, and the independence of the convention; they wished to throw down the faction of the commune, to stop the operation of the revolutionary tribunal, to empty the prisons now filled with suspected persons, to reduce or destroy the powers of the committees. This project in favour of clemency, humanity, and legal government, was conceived by Danton, Philippeaux, Camille Desmoulins, Fabre-d'Eglantine, Lacroix, general Westermann, and all the friends of Danton. Before all things they wanted *that the republic should secure the field of battle*; but after conquest, they wished to conciliate.

This party, become moderate, had renounced power; it had withdrawn from the government, or suffered itself to be excluded by Robespierre's party. Moreover, since the 31st of May, zealous patriots had considered Danton's conduct equivocal. He had acted mildly on that day, and had subsequently disapproved the condemnation of the twenty-two. They began to reproach him with his disorderly life, his venal passions, his change of party, and untimely moderation. To avoid the storm, he had retired to his native place, Arcis-sur-Aube, and there he seemed to have forgotten all in retirement. During his absence, the Hébert faction made immense progress; and the friends of Danton hastily summoned him to their aid. He returned at the beginning of Frimaire (December). Philippeaux immediately denounced the manner in which the Vendéan war had been carried on; general Westermann, who had greatly distinguised himself in that war, and who had just been dismissed by the committee of public safety, supported Philippeaux, and Camille Desmoulins published the first numbers of his *Vieux Cordelier*. This brilliant and fiery young man had followed all the movements of the revolution, from the 14th of July to the 31st of May, approving all its exaggerations and all its measures. His heart, however, was gentle and tender, though his opinions were violent, and his humour often bitter. He had praised the revolutionary régime because he believed it indispensable for the establishment of the republic; he had co-operated in the ruin of the Gironde, because he feared the dissensions of the republic. For the republic he had sacrificed even his scruples and the desires of his heart, even justice and humanity; he had given all to his party, thinking that he gave it to the republic; but now he was able neither to praise nor to keep silent; his energetic activity, which he had employed for the republic, he now directed against those who were ruining it by bloodshed. In his *Vieux Cordelier* he spoke of liberty with the depth of Machiavelli, and of men with the wit of Voltaire. But he soon raised the fanatics and dictators against him, by calling the government to sentiments of moderation, compassion, and justice.

He drew a striking picture of present tyranny, under the name of a past tyranny. He selected his examples from Tacitus. "At this period," said he, "words became state crimes: there wanted but one step more to render mere glances, sadness, pity, sighs—even silence itself criminal. It soon became high-treason, or an anti-revolutionary crime, for Cremutius Cordus to call Brutus and Cassius the last of the Romans; a counter-revolutionary crime in a descendant of Cassius to possess a portrait of his ancestor; a counter-revolutionary crime in Mamercus Scaurus to write a tragedy in which there were lines capable of a double meaning; a counter- revolutionary crime in Torquatus Silanus to be extravagant; a counter- revolutionary crime in Pomponius, because a friend of Sejanus had sought an asylum in one of his country houses; a counter-revolutionary crime to bewail the misfortunes of the time, for this was accusing the government; a counter-revolutionary crime for the consul Fusius Geminus to bewail the sad death of his son.

"If a man would escape death himself, it became necessary to rejoice at the death of his friend or relative. Under Nero, many went to return thanks to the gods for their relatives whom he had put to death. At least, an assumed air of contentment was necessary; for even fear was sufficient to render one guilty. Everything gave the tyrant umbrage. If a citizen was popular, he was considered a rival to the prince, and capable of exciting a civil war, and he was suspected. Did he, on the contrary, shun popularity, and keep by his fireside; his retired mode of life drew attention, and he was suspected. Was a man rich; it was feared the people might be corrupted by his bounty, and he was suspected. Was he poor; it became necessary to watch him closely, as none are so enterprising as those who have nothing, and he was suspected. If his disposition chanced to be sombre and melancholy, and his dress neglected, his distress was supposed to be occasioned by the state of public affairs, and he was suspected. If a citizen indulged in good living to the injury of his digestion, he was said to do so because the prince lived ill, and he was suspected. If virtuous and austere in his manners, he was thought to censure the court, and he was suspected. Was he philosopher, orator, or poet; it was unbecoming to have more celebrity than the government, and he was suspected. Lastly, if any one had obtained a reputation in war, his talent only served to make him dangerous; it became necessary to get rid of the general, or to remove him speedily from the army; he was suspected.

"The natural death of a celebrated man, or of even a public official, was so rare, that historians handed it down to posterity as an event worthy to be remembered in remote ages. The death of so many innocent and worthy citizens seemed less a calamity than the insolence and disgraceful opulence of their murderers and denouncers. Every day the sacred and inviolable informer made his triumphant entry into the palace of the dead, and received some rich heritage. All these denouncers assumed illustrious names, and called themselves Cotta, Scipio, Regulus, Saevius, Severus. To distinguish himself by a brilliant début, the marquis Serenus brought an accusation of anti-revolutionary practices against his aged father, already in exile, after which he proudly called himself Brutus. Such were the accusers, such the judges; the tribunals, the protectors of life and property, became slaughter-houses, in which theft and murder bore the names of punishment and confiscation."

Camille Desmoulins did not confine himself to attacking the revolutionary and dictatorial regime; he required its abolition. He demanded the establishment of a committee of mercy, as the only way of terminating the revolution and pacifying parties. His journal produced a great effect upon public opinion; it inspired some hope and courage: Have you read the *Vieux Cordelier*? was asked on all sides. At the same time Fabre- d'Eglantine, Lacroix, and Bourdon de l'Oise, excited the convention to throw off the yoke of the committee; they sought to unite the Mountain and the Right, in order to restore the freedom and power of the assembly. As the committees were all powerful, they tried to ruin them by degrees, the best course to follow. It was important to change public opinion, and to encourage the assembly, in order to support themselves by a moral force against revolutionary force, by the power of the convention against the power of the committees. The Dantonist in the Mountain endeavoured to detach Robespierre from the other Decemvirs; Billaud-Varennes, Collot- d'Herbois and Saint-Just, alone appeared to them invincibly attached to the Reign of Terror. Barrère adhered to it through weakness—Couthon from his devotion to Robespierre. They hoped to gain over the latter to the cause of moderation, through his friendship for Danton, his ideas of order, his austere habits, his profession of public virtue, and his pride. He had defended seventy-three imprisoned Girondist deputies against the committees and the Jacobins; he had dared to attack Clootz and Hébert as ultra-revolutionists; and he had induced the convention to decree the existence of the Supreme Being. Robespierre was the most popularly renowned man of that time; he was, in a measure, the moderator of the republic and the dictator of opinion: by gaining him, they hoped to overcome both the committees and the commune, without compromising the cause of the revolution.

Danton saw him on his return from Arcis-sur-Aube, and they seemed to understand one another; attacked at the Jacobins, he was defended by him. Robespierre himself read and corrected the *Vieux Cordelier*, and approved of it. At the same time he professed some principles of moderation; but then all those who exercised the revolutionary government, or who thought it indispensable, became aroused. Billaud-Varennes and Saint-Just openly maintained the policy of the committees. Desmoulins had said of the latter: "He so esteems himself, that he carries his head on his shoulders with as much respect as if it were the holy sacrament." "And I," replied Saint-Just, "will make him carry his like another Saint Denis." Collot-d'Herbois, who was on a mission, arrived while matters were in this state. He protected the faction of the anarchists, who had been intimidated for a moment, and who derived fresh audacity from his presence. The Jacobins expelled Camille Desmoulins from their society, and Barrère attacked him at the convention in the name of the government. Robespierre himself was not spared; he was accused of *moderatism*, and murmurs began to circulate against him.

However, his credit being immense, as they could not attack or conquer without him, he was sought on both sides. Taking advantage of this superior position, he adopted neither party, and sought to put down the leaders of each, one after the other.

Under these circumstances, he wished to sacrifice the commune and the anarchists; the committees wished to sacrifice the Mountain and the Moderates. They came to an understanding: Robespierre gave up Danton, Desmoulins, and their friends to the members of the committee; and the members of the committee gave up Hébert, Clootz, Chaumette, Ronsin, and their accomplices. By favouring the Moderates at first, he prepared the ruin of the anarchists, and he attained two objects favourable to his domination or to his pride—he overturned a formidable faction, and he got rid of a revolutionary reputation, the rival of his own.

Motives of public safety, it must be admitted, mingled with these combinations of party. At this period of general fury against the republic, and of victories not yet definitive on its part, the committees did not think the moment for peace with Europe and the internal dissentients had arrived; and they considered it impossible to carry on the war without a dictatorship. They, moreover, regarded the Hébertists as an obscene faction, which corrupted the people, and served the foreign foe by anarchy; and the Dantonists as a party whose political moderation and private immorality compromised and dishonoured the republic. The government accordingly proposed to the assembly, through the medium of Barrère, the continuation of the war, with additional activity in its pursuit; while Robespierre, a few days afterwards, demanded the continuance of the revolutionary government. In the Jacobins he had already expressed himself opposed to the *Vieux Cordelier*, which he had hitherto supported. He rejected legal government in the following terms:—

"Without," said he, "all the tyrants surround us; within, all the friends of tyranny conspire against us; they will continue to conspire till crime is left without hope. We must destroy the infernal and external enemies of the republic or perish with it. Now, in such a situation, the first maxim of your policy should be, to lead the people by reason, and the enemies of the people by terror. If, during peace, virtue be the mainspring of a popular government, its mainspring in the times of revolution is both virtue and terror; virtue, without which terror becomes fatal, terror, without which virtue is powerless. Subdue, then, the enemies of liberty by terror; and, as the founders of the republic, you will act rightly. The government of the revolution is the despotism of liberty against tyranny."

In this speech he denounced the *moderates* and the *ultra- revolutionists*, as both of them desiring the downfall of the republic. "They advance," said he, "under different banners and by different roads, but they advance towards the same goal; that goal is the disorganization of the popular government, the ruin of the convention, and the triumph of tyranny. One of these two factions reduces us to weakness, the other drives us to excesses." He prepared the public mind for their proscription; and his speech, adopted without discussion, was sent to all the popular societies, to all the authorities, and to all the armies.

After this beginning of hostilities, Danton, who had not given up his connexion with Robespierre, asked for an interview with him. It took place at the residence of Robespierre himself. They were cold and bitter; Danton complained violently, and Robespierre was reserved. "I know," said Danton, "all the hatred the committee bear me; but I do not fear it." "You are wrong," replied Robespierre; "it entertains no ill designs against you; but you would do well to have an explanation." "An explanation?" rejoined Danton, "an explanation? That requires good faith!" Seeing that Robespierre looked grave at these words, he added: "No doubt it is necessary to put down the royalists, but we ought only to strike blows which will benefit the republic; we must not confound the innocent with the guilty." "And who says," exclaimed Robespierre, sharply, "that an innocent person has been put to death?" Danton turned to one of his friends who had accompanied him, and said, with a bitter smile: "What do you say to this? Not one innocent person has perished!" They then separated, and all friendship ceased between them.

A few days afterwards, Saint-Just ascended the tribune, and threatened more openly than had yet been done all dissentients, moderates, or anarchists. "Citizens," said he, "you wished for a republic; if you do not at the same time desire all that constitutes it, you will overwhelm the people in its ruins. What constitutes a republic is the destruction of all that is opposed to it. We are guilty towards the republic because we pity the prisoners; we are guilty towards the republic because we do not desire virtue; we are guilty to the republic because we do not desire terror. What is it you want, those of you who do not wish for virtue, that you may be happy? (The Anarchists.) What is it you want, those of you who do not wish to employ terror against the wicked? (The Moderates.) What is it you want, those of you who haunt public places to be seen, and to have it said of you: 'Do you see such a one pass?' (Danton.) You will perish, those of you who seek fortune, who assume haggard looks, and affect the patriot that the foreigner may buy you up, or the government give you a place; you of the indulgent faction, who seek to save the guilty; you of the foreign faction, who direct severity against the defenders of the people. Measures are already taken to secure the guilty; they are hemmed in on all sides. Let us return thanks to the genius of the French people, that liberty has triumphed over one of the most dangerous attacks ever meditated against it. The development of this vast plot, the panic it will create, and the measures about to be proposed to you, will free the republic and the world of all the conspirators."

Saint-Just caused the government to be invested with the most extensive powers against the conspirators of the commune. He had it decreed that justice and probity were the order of the day. The anarchists were unable to adopt any measure of defence; they veiled for a moment the Rights of Man at the club of the Cordeliers, and they made an attempt at insurrection, but without vigour or union. The people did not stir, and the committee caused its commandant, Henriot, to seize the substitute Hébert, Ronsin, the revolutionary general, Anacharsis Clootz, Monmoro the orator of the human race, Vincent, etc. They were brought before the revolutionary tribunal, as *the agents of foreign powers, and, as having conspired to place a tyrant over the state*. That tyrant was to have been Pache, under the title of *Grand Juge*. The anarchist leaders lost their audacity as soon as they were arrested; they defended themselves, and, for the most part, died, without any display of courage. The committee of public safety disbanded the revolutionary army, diminished the power of the sectionary committees, and obliged the commune to appear at the bar of the convention, and give thanks for the arrest and punishment of the conspirators, its accomplices.

It was now time for Danton to defend himself; the proscription, after striking the commune, threatened him. He was advised to be on his guard, and to take immediate steps; but not having been able to overturn the dictatorial power, by arousing public opinion and the assembly by the means of the public journals, and his friends of the Mountain, on what could he depend for support? The convention, indeed, was inclined to favour him and his cause; but it was wholly subject to the revolutionary power of the committee. Danton having to support him, neither the government, nor the assembly, nor the commune, nor the clubs, awaited proscription, without making any effort to avoid it.

His friends implored him to defend himself. "I would rather," said he, "be guillotined, than be a guillotiner; besides, my life is not worth the trouble; and I am sick of the world." "The members of the committee seek thy death." "Well," he exclaimed, impatiently, "should Billaud, should Robespierre kill me, they will be execrated as tyrants; Robespierre's house will be razed to the ground; salt will be strewn upon it; a gallows will be erected on it, devoted to the vengeance of crime! But my friends will say of me, that I was a good father, a good friend, a good citizen; they will not forget me." "Thou mayst avert…" "I would rather be guillotined than be a guillotiner." "Well, then, thou shouldst depart." "Depart!" he repeated, curling his lip disdainfully, "depart! Can we carry our country away on the sole of our shoe?"

Danton's only resource now was to make trial of his so well known and potent eloquence, to denounce Robespierre and the committee, and to arouse the convention against their tyranny. He was earnestly entreated to do this; but he knew too well how difficult a thing it is to overthrow an established domination, he knew too well the complete subjection and terror of the assembly, to rely on the efficacy of such means. He accordingly waited, thinking, he who had dared so much, that his enemies would shrink from proscribing him.

On the 10th of Germinal, he was informed that his arrest was being discussed in the committee of public safety, and he was again entreated to save himself by flight. After a moment's reflection, he exclaimed, "They dare not." During the night his house was surrounded, and he was taken to the Luxembourg with Camille Desmoulins, Philippeaux, Lacroix, and Westermann. On his arrival, he accosted with cordiality the prisoners who crowded round him. "Gentlemen," said he, "I had hoped in a short time to liberate you, but here I am come to join you, and I know not how the matter may end." In about an hour he was placed in solitary confinement in the cell in which Hébert had been imprisoned, and which Robespierre was so soon to occupy. There, giving way to reflection and regret, he exclaimed: "It was at this time I instituted the revolutionary tribunal. I implore forgiveness from God and man for having done so; but I designed it not for the scourge of humanity."

His arrest gave rise to general excitement, to a sombre anxiety. The following day, at the opening of the sittings in the assembly, men spoke in whispers; they inquired with alarm, what was the pretext for this new proceeding against the representatives of the people. "Citizens," at length exclaimed Legendre, "four members of this assembly have been arrested during the night. Danton is one, I know not the others. Citizens, I declare that I believe Danton to be as pure as myself, yet he is in a dungeon. They feared, no doubt, that his replies would overturn the accusations brought against him: I move, therefore, that before you listen to any report, you send for the prisoners, and hear them." This motion was favourably received, and inspired the assembly with momentary courage: a few members desired it might be put to the vote, but this state of things did not last long. Robespierre ascended the tribune. "By the excitement, such as for a long time has been unknown in this the assembly," said he, "by the sensation the words of the speaker you have just heard have produced, it is easy to see that a question of great interest is before us; a question whether two or three individuals shall be preferred to the country. We shall see to-day whether the convention can crush to atoms a mock idol, long since decayed, or whether its fall shall overwhelm both the convention and the French people." And a few words from him sufficed to restore silence and subordination to the assembly, to restrain the friends of Danton, and to make Legendre himself retract. Soon after, Saint-Just entered the house, followed by other members of the committees. He read a long report against the members under arrest, in which he impugned their opinions, their political conduct, their private life, their projects; making them appear, by improbable and subtle combinations, accomplices in every conspiracy, and the servants of every party. The assembly, after listening without a murmur, with a bewildered sanction unanimously decreed, and with applause even, the impeachment of Danton and his friends. Every one sought to gain time with tyranny, and gave up others' heads to save his own.

The accused were brought before the revolutionary tribunal; their attitude was haughty, and full of courage. They displayed an audacity of speech, and a contempt of their judges, wholly unusual: Danton replied to the president Dumas, who asked him the customary questions as to his name, his age, his residence: "I am Danton, tolerably well known in the revolution; I am thirty-five years old. My residence will soon be nothing. My name will live in the Panthéon of history." His disdainful or indignant replies, the cold and measured answers of Lacroix, the austere dignity of Philippeaux, the vigour of Desmoulins, were beginning to move the people. But the accused were silenced, under the pretext that they were wanting in respect to justice, and were immediately condemned without a hearing. "We are immolated," cried Danton, "to the ambition of a few miserable brigands, but they will not long enjoy the fruit of their criminal victory. I draw Robespierre after me—Robespierre will follow me." They were taken to the Conciergerie, and thence to the scaffold.

They went to death with the intrepidity usual at that epoch. There were many troops under arms, and their escort was numerous. The crowd, generally loud in its applause, was silent. Camille Desmoulins, when in the fatal cart, was still full of astonishment at his condemnation, which he could not comprehend. "This, then," said he, "is the reward reserved for the first apostle of liberty." Danton stood erect, and looked proudly and calmly around. At the foot of the scaffold he betrayed a momentary emotion. "Oh, my best beloved—my wife!" he cried, "I shall not see thee again." Then suddenly interrupting himself: "No weakness, Danton!" Thus perished the last defenders of humanity and moderation; the last who sought to promote peace among the conquerors of the revolution and pity for the conquered. For a long time after them no voice was raised against the dictatorship of terror; and from one end of France to the other it struck silent and redoubled blows. The Girondists had sought to prevent this violent reign,—the Dantonists to stop it; all perished, and the conquerors had the more victims to strike the more foes arose around them. In so sanguinary a career, there is no stopping until the tyrant is himself slain. The Decemvirs, after the definitive fall of the Girondists, had made *terror* the order of the day; after the fall of the Hébertists, *justice* and *probity*, because these were *impure men of faction*; after the fall of the Dantonists, *terror* and *all virtues*, because these Dantonists were, according to their phraseology, *indulgents and immorals*.

CHAPTER IX

FROM THE DEATH OF DANTON, APRIL, 1794, TO THE 9TH THERMIDOR, (27TH JULY, 1794)

Increase of terror; its cause—System of the democrats; Saint-Just—
Robespierre's power—Festival of the Supreme Being—Couthon
presents the law of the 22nd Prairial, which reorganizes the revolutionary tribunal; disturbances; debates; final obedience of the
convention—The active members of the committee have a division—Robespierre, Saint-Just, and Couthon on one side; Billaud-Varennes, Collot-d'Herbois, Barrère, and the members of the
committee of general safety on the other—Conduct of Robespierre—He absents himself from the committee, and rests on the
Jacobins and the commune—On the 8th of Thermidor he demands the renewal of the committees; the motion is rejected—
Sitting of the 9th Thermidor; Saint-Just denounces the committees; is interrupted by Tallien; Billaud- Varennes violently attacks
Robespierre; general indignation of the convention against the
triumvirate; they are arrested—The commune rises and liberates
the prisoners—Peril and courage of the convention; it outlaws the
insurgents—The sections declare for the convention—Defeat and
execution of Robespierre.

During the four months following the fall of the Danton party, the committees
exercised their authority without opposition or restraint. Death became the only
means of governing, and the republic was given up to daily and systematic executions. It was then were invented the alleged conspiracies of the inmates of the
prisons, crowded under the law *des suspects*, or emptied by that of the 22nd Prairial, which might be called the law *des condamnés*; then the emissaries of the committee of public safety entirely replaced in the departments those of the Mountain;
and Carrier, the protégé of Billaud, was seen in the west; Maigret, the protégé of
Couthon, in the south; and Joseph Lebon, the protégé of Robespierre, in the north.
The extermination *en masse* of the enemies of the democratic dictatorship, which
had already been effected at Lyons and Toulon by grape-shot, became still more
horrible, by the noyades of Nantes, and the scaffolds of Arras, Paris, and Orange.

May this example teach men a truth, which for their good ought to be generally known, that in a revolution all depends on a first refusal and a first struggle.
To effect a pacific innovation, it must not be contested; otherwise war is declared

and the revolution spreads, because the whole nation is aroused to its defence. When society is thus shaken to its foundations, it is the most daring who triumph, and instead of wise and temperate reformers, we find only extreme and inflexible innovators. Engendered by contest, they maintain themselves by it; with one hand they fight to maintain their sway, with the other they establish their system with a view to its consolidation; they massacre in the name of their doctrines: virtue, humanity, the welfare of the people, all that is holiest on earth, they use to sanction their executions, and to protect their dictatorship. Until they become exhausted and fall, all perish indiscriminately, both the enemies and the partisans of reform. The tempest dashes a whole nation against the rock of revolution. Inquire what became of the men of 1789 in 1794, and it will be found that they were all alike swept away in this vast shipwreck. As soon as one party appeared on the field of battle, it summoned all the others thither, and all like it were in turn conquered and exterminated; constitutionalists, Girondists, the Mountain, and the Decemvirs themselves. At each defeat, the effusion of blood became greater, and the system of tyranny more violent. The Decemvirs were the most cruel, because they were the last.

The committee of public safety, being at once the object of the attacks of Europe, and of the hatred of so many conquered parties, thought that any abatement of violence would occasion its destruction; it wished at the same time to subdue its foes, and to get rid of them. "The dead alone do not return," said Barrère. "The more freely the social body perspires, the more healthy it becomes," added Collot-d'Herbois. But the Decemvirs, not suspecting their power to be ephemeral, aimed at founding a democracy, and sought in institutions a security for its permanence in the time when they should cease to employ executions. They possessed in the highest degree the fanaticism of certain social theories, as the millenarians of the English revolution, with whom they may be compared, had the fanaticism of certain religious ideas. The one originated with the people, as the other looked to God; these desired the most absolute political equality, as those sought evangelical equality; these aspired to the reign of virtue, as those to the reign of the saints. Human nature flies to extremes in all things, and produces, in a religious epoch, democratic Christians—in a philosophical epoch, political democrats.

Robespierre and Saint-Just had produced the plan of that democracy, whose principles they professed in all their speeches; they wished to change the manners, mind, and customs of France, and to make it a republic after the manner of the ancients; they sought to establish the dominion of the people; to have magistrates free from pride; citizens free from vice; fraternity of intercourse, simplicity of manners, austerity of character, and the worship of virtue. The symbolical words of the sect may be found in the speeches of all the reporters of the committee, and especially in those of Robespierre and Saint-Just. *Liberty and equality* for the government of the republic; *indivisibility* for its form; *public safety* for its defence and preservation; *virtue* for its principle; *the Supreme Being* for its religion; as for the citizens, *fraternity* for their daily intercourse; *probity* for their conduct; *good sense* for their mental qualities; *modesty* for their public actions, which were to have for object the welfare of the state, and not their own: such was the symbol of this democracy. Fanaticism could not go further. The authors of this system did not inquire into its practicability; they thought it just and natural; and having power, they tried to establish it by violence. Not one of these words but served to condemn a party or individuals. The royalists and aristocrats were hunted down in the name of *liberty and equality*; the Girondists in the name of *indivisibility*; Philippeaux, Camille Desmoulins, and the moderate party, in the name of *public safety*; Chaumette, Anacharsis Clootz, Gobet, Hébert, all the anarchical and atheistical party, in the name of *virtue and the Supreme Being*; Chabot, Bazire, Fabre-d'Eglantine, in the name of *probity*; Danton in the name of *virtue and modesty*. In the eyes of fanatics, these *moral crimes* necessitated their destruction, as much as the conspiracies which they were accused of.

Robespierre was the patron of this sect, which had in the committee a more zealous, disinterested, and fanatic partisan than himself, in the person of Saint-Just, who was called the Apocalyptic. His features were bold but regular, and marked by an expression determined, but melancholy. His eye was steady and piercing; his hair black, straight, and long. His manners cold, though his character was ardent; simple in his habits, austere and sententious, he advanced without hesitation towards the completion of his system. Though scarcely twenty-five years old, he was the boldest of the Decemvirs, because his convictions were the deepest. Passionately devoted to the republic, he was indefatigable in the committees, intrepid on his missions to the armies, where he set an example of courage, sharing the marches and dangers of the soldiers. His predilection for the multitude did not make him pay court to their propensities; and far from adopting their dress and language with Hébert, he wished to confer on them ease, gravity, and dignity. But his policy made him more terrible than his popular sentiments. He had much daring, coolness, readiness, and decision. Rarely susceptible to pity, he reduced to form his measures for the public safety, and put them into execution immediately. If he considered victory, proscription, the dictatorship necessary, he at once demanded them. Unlike Robespierre, he was completely a man of action. The latter, comprehending all the use he might make of him, early gained him over in the convention. Saint-Just, on his part, was drawn towards Robespierre by his reputation for incorruptibility, his austere life, and the conformity of their ideas.

The terrible effects of their association may be conceived when we consider their popularity, the envious and tyrannical passions of the one, and the inflexible character and systematic views of the other. Couthon had joined them; he was personally devoted to Robespierre. Although he had a mild look and a partially paralysed frame, he was a man of merciless fanaticism. They formed, in the committee, a triumvirate which soon sought to engross all power. This ambition alienated the other members of the committee, and caused their own destruction. In the meantime, the triumvirate imperiously governed the convention and the committee itself. When it was necessary to intimidate the assembly, Saint-Just was intrusted with the task; when they wished to take it by surprise, Couthon was employed. If the assembly murmured or hesitated, Robespierre rose, and restored silence and terror by a single word.

During the first two months after the fall of the commune and the Danton party, the Decemvirs, who were not yet divided, laboured to secure their domination: their commissioners kept the departments in restraint, and the armies of the republic were victorious on all the frontiers. The committee took advantage of this moment of security and union to lay the foundation of new manners and new institutions. It must never be forgotten, that in a revolution men are moved by two tendencies, attachment to their ideas, and a thirst for command. The members of the committee, at the beginning, agreed in their democratic sentiments; at the end, they contended for power.

Billaud-Varennes presented the theory of popular government and the means of rendering the army always subordinate to the nation. Robespierre delivered a discourse on the moral sentiments and solemnities suited to a republic: he dedicated festivals *to the Supreme Being, to Truth, Justice, Modesty, Friendship, Frugality, Fidelity, Immortality, Misfortune, etc.,* in a word, to all the moral and republican virtues. In this way he prepared the establishment of the new worship *of the Supreme Being.* Barrère made a report on the extirpation of mendicity, and the assistance the republic owed to indigent citizens. All these reports passed into decrees, agreeably to the wishes of the democrats. Barrère, whose habitual speeches in the convention were calculated to disguise his servitude from himself, was one of the most supple instruments of the committee; he belonged to the régime of terror, neither from cruelty nor from fanaticism. His manners were gentle, his private life blameless, and he possessed great moderation of mind. But he was timid; and after having been a constitutional royalist before the 10th of August, a moderate republican prior to the 31st of May, he became the panegyrist and the co- operator of the decemviral tyranny. This shows that, in a revolution, no one should become an actor without decision of character. Intellect alone is not inflexible enough; it is too accommodating; it finds reasons for everything, even for what terrifies and disgusts it; it never knows when to stop, at a time when one ought always to be prepared to die, and to end one's part or end one's opinions.

Robespierre, who was considered the founder of this moral democracy, now attained the highest degree of elevation and of power. He became the object of the general flattery of his party; he was *the great man* of the republic. Men spoke of nothing but *of his virtue, of his genius, and of his eloquence.* Two circumstances contributed to augment his importance still further. On the 3rd Prairial, an obscure but intrepid man, named l'Admiral, was determined to deliver France from Robespierre and Collot- d'Herbois. He waited in vain for Robespierre all day, and at night he resolved to kill Collot. He fired twice at him with pistols, but missed him. The following day, a young girl, name Cécile Renaud, called at Robespierre's house, and earnestly begged to speak with him. As he was out, and as she still insisted upon being admitted, she was detained. She carried a small parcel, and two knives were found on her person. "What motive brought you to Robespierre's?" inquired her examiners. "I wanted to speak to him." "On what business?" "That depended on how I might find him." "Do you know citizen Robespierre?" "No, I sought to know him; I went to his house to see what a tyrant was like." "What did you propose doing with your two knives?" "Nothing, having no intention to injure any one." "And your parcel?" "Contains a change of linen for my use in the place I shall be sent to." "Where is that?" "To prison; and from thence to the guillotine." The unfortunate girl was ultimately taken there, and her family shared her fate.

Robespierre received marks of the most intoxicating adulation. At the Jacobins and in the convention his preservation was attributed to the *good genius of the republic*, and to *the Supreme Being*, whose existence he had decreed on the 18th Floréal. The celebration of the new religion had been fixed for the 20th Prairial throughout France. On the 16th, Robespierre was unanimously appointed president of the convention, in order that he might officiate as the pontiff at the festival. At that ceremony he appeared at the head of the assembly, his face beaming with joy and confidence, an unusual expression with him. He advanced alone, fifteen feet in advance of his colleagues, attired in a magnificent dress, holding flowers and ears of corn in his hand, the object of general attention. Expectation was universally raised on this occasion: the enemies of Robespierre foreboded attempts at usurpation, the persecuted looked forward to a milder régime. He disappointed every one. He harangued the people in his capacity of high priest, and concluded his speech, in which all expected to find a hope of happier prospects, with these discouraging words:—"*People, let us to-day give ourselves up to the transports of pure delight! To-morrow we will renew our struggle against vices and against tyrants.*"

Two days after, on the 22nd Prairial, Couthon presented a new law to the convention. The revolutionary tribunal had dutifully struck all those who had been pointed out to it: royalists, constitutionalists, Girondists, anarchists, and Mountain, had been all alike despatched to execution. But it did not proceed expeditiously enough to satisfy the systematic exterminators, who wished promptly, and at any cost, to get rid of all their prisoners. It still observed some forms; these were suppressed. "All tardiness," said Couthon, "is a crime, all indulgent formality a public danger; there should be no longer delay in punishing the enemies of the state than suffices to recognise them." Hitherto the prisoners had counsel; they had them no longer:—*The law furnishes patriot jurymen for the defence of calumniated patriots; it grants none to conspirators.* They tried them, at first, individually; now they tried them *en masse.* There had been some precision in the crimes, even when revolutionary; now *all the enemies of the people* were declared guilty, and all were pronounced enemies of the people *who sought to destroy liberty by force or stratagem.* The jury before had the law to guide their determinations, they *now only had their conscience.* A single tribunal, Fouquier-Tinville and a few jurymen, were not sufficient for the increase of victims the new law threatened to bring before it; the tribunal was divided into four sections, the number of judges and juries was increased, and the public accuser had four substitutes appointed to assist him. Lastly, the deputies of the people could not before be brought to trial without a decree of the convention; but the law was now so drawn up that they could be tried on an order from the committees. The law respecting suspected persons gave rise to that of Prairial.

As soon as Couthon had made his report, a murmur of astonishment and alarm pervaded the assembly. "If this law passes," cried Ruamps, "all we have to do is to blow our brains out. I demand an adjournment." This motion was supported; but Robespierre ascended the tribunal. "For a long time," said he, "the national assembly has been accustomed to discuss and decree at the same time, because it has long been delivered from the thraldom of faction. I move that without considering the question of adjournment, the convention debate, till eight in the evening if necessary, on the proposed law." The discussion was immediately begun, and in thirty minutes after the second reading, the decree was carried. But the following day, a few members, more afraid of the law than of the committee, returned to the debate of the day before. The Mountain, friends of Danton, fearing, for their own sakes, the new provisions, which left the representatives at the mercy of the Decemvirs, proposed to the convention to provide for the safety of its members. Bourdon de l'Oise was the first to speak on this subject; he was supported. Merlin, by a skilful amendment, restored the old safeguard of the conventionalists, and the assembly adopted Merlin's measure. Gradually, objections were made to the decree; the courage of the Mountain increased, and the discussion became very animated. Couthon attacked the Mountain. "Let them know," replied Bourdon de l'Oise—"let the members of the committee know that if they are patriots, we are patriots too. Let them know that I shall not reply with bitterness to their reproaches. I esteem Couthon, I esteem the committee; but I also esteem the unshaken Mountain which has saved our liberty." Robespierre, surprised at this unexpected resistance, hurried to the tribune. "The convention," said he, "the Mountain, and the committee are the same thing! Every representative of the people who sincerely loves liberty, every representative of the people who is ready to die for his country, belongs to the Mountain! We should insult our country, assassinate the people, did we allow a few intriguing persons, more contemptible than others, because they are more hypocritical, to draw off a portion of the Mountain, and make themselves the leaders of a party." "If was never my intention," said Bourdon, "to make myself leader of a party." "It would be the height of opprobrium," continued Robespierre, "if a few of our colleagues, led away by calumny respecting our intentions and the object of our labours...." "I insist on your proving what you assert," rejoined Bourdon. "I have been very plainly called a scoundrel." "I did not name Bourdon. Woe to the man who names himself! Yes, the Mountain is pure, it is sublime; intriguers do not belong to the Mountain!" "Name them!" "I will name them when it is necessary." The threats and the imperious tone of Robespierre, the support of the other Decemvirs, and the feeling of fear which went round caused profound silence. The amendment of Merlin was revoked as insulting to the committee of public safety, and the whole law was adopted. From that time executions took place in batches; and fifty persons were sent to death daily. This *Terror* within terror lasted about two months.

But the end of this system drew near. The sittings of Prairial were the term of union for the member of the committees. From that time, silent dissensions existed among them. They had advanced together, so long as they had to contend together; but this ceased to be the case when they found themselves alone in the arena, with habits of contest and the desire for dominion. Moreover, their opinions were no longer entirely the same: the democratic party were divided by the fall of the old commune; Billaud- Varennes, Collot-d'Herbois, and the principal members of the committee of general safety, Vadier, Amar, Vouland, clung to this overthrown faction, and preferred *the worship of Reason* to that of *the Supreme Being*. They were also jealous of the fame, and anxious at the power of Robespierre, who, in his turn, was irritated at their secret disapprobation and the obstacles they opposed to his will. At this period, the latter conceived the design of putting down the most enterprising members of the Mountain, Tallien, Bourdon, Legendre, Fréron, Rovère, etc., and his rivals of the committee.

Robespierre had a prodigious force at his disposal, the common people, who considered the revolution as depending on him, supported him as the representative of its doctrines and interests; the armed force of Paris, commanded by Henriot, was at his command. He had entire sway over the Jacobins, whom he admitted and ejected at pleasure; all important posts were occupied by his creatures; he had formed the revolutionary tribunal and the new committee himself, substituting Payan, the national agent, for Chaumette, the attorney-general; and Fleuriot for Pache, in the office of mayor. But what was his design in granting the most influential places to new men, and in separating himself from the committees? Did he aspire to the dictatorship? Did he only seek to establish his democracy *of virtue* by the ruin of the remaining *immoral* members of the Mountain, and the *factious* of the committee? Each party had lost its leaders: the Gironde had lost the *twenty-two*; the commune, Hébert, Chaumette, and Ronsin; the Mountain, Danton, Chabot, Lacroix, and Camille Desmoulins. But while thus proscribing the leaders, Robespierre had carefully protected the sects. He had defended the *seventy-three prisoners* against the denunciations of the Jacobins and the hatred of the committees; he had placed himself at the head of the new commune; he had no longer reason to fear opposition to his projects, whatever they might be, except from a few of the Mountain and the members of the conventional government. It was against this double obstacle that he directed his efforts during the last moments of his career. It is probable that he did not separate the republic from his protectorate, and that he thought to establish both on the overthrow of the other parties.

The committees opposed Robespierre in their own way. They secretly strove to bring about his fall by accusing him of tyranny; they caused the establishment of his religion to be considered as the presage of his usurpation; they recalled the haughty attitude he assumed on the 20th Priarial, and the distance at which he kept even the national convention. Among themselves, they called him *Pisistratus*, and this name already passed from mouth to mouth. A circumstance, insignificant enough at any other time, gave them an opportunity of attacking him indirectly. An old woman, called *Catherine Théot*, played the prophetess in an obscure habitation, surrounded by a few mystic sectaries: they styled her *the Mother of God*, and she announced the immediate coming of a *Messiah*. Among her followers there was on old associate of Robespierre in the constituent assembly, the Chartreux Dom Gerle, who had a civic certificate from Robespierre himself. When the committees discovered *the mysteries of the Mother of God*, and her predictions, they believed or pretended to believe, that Robespierre made use of her instrumentality to gain over the fanatics, or to announce his elevation. They altered her name of *Théot* into that of *Théos*, signifying God; and they craftily insinuated that Robespierre was the Messiah she announced. The aged Vadier, in the name of the committee of general safety, was deputed to bring forward a motion against this new sect. He was vain and subtle; he denounced those who were initiated into these mysteries, turned the worship into derision, implicated Robespierre in it without naming him, and had the fanatics sent to prison. Robespierre wished to save them. The conduct of the committee of general safety greatly irritated him, and in the Jacobin club he spoke of the speech of Vadier with contempt and anger. He experienced fresh opposition from the committee of public safety, which refused to proceed against the persons he pointed out to them. From that time he ceased to join his colleagues in the government, and was rarely present at the sittings of the convention. But he attended the Jacobins regularly; and from the tribune of that club he hoped to overthrow his enemies as he had hitherto done.

Naturally sad, suspicious and timid, he became more melancholy and mistrustful than ever. He never went out without being accompanied by several Jacobins armed with sticks, who were called his body-guard. He soon commenced his denunciations in the popular assembly. "*All corrupt men,*" said he, "*must be expelled the convention.*" This was designating the friends of Danton. Robespierre had them watched with the most minute anxiety. Every day spies followed all their motions, observing their actions, haunts, and conversation. Robespierre not only attacked the Dantonists at the Jacobins, he even arose against the committee itself, and for that purpose he chose a day when Barrère presided in the popular assembly. At the close of the sitting, the latter returned home discouraged; "I am disgusted with men," said he to Villate. "What could be his motive for attacking you?" inquired the other. "Robespierre is insatiable," rejoined Barrère; "because we will not do all he wishes, he must break with us. If he talked to us about Thuriot, Guffroi, Rovère Lecointre, Panis, Cambon, Monestier, and the rest of the Dantonists, we might agree with him; let him even require Tallien, Bourdon de l'Oise, Legendre, Fréron, well; but Duval, Audoin, Leonard Bourdon, Vadier, Vouland—it is impossible to consent." To give up members of the committee of general safety, was to expose themselves; accordingly, while fearing, they firmly awaited the attack. Robespierre was very formidable, with respect to his power, his hatred, and his designs; it was for him to begin the combat.

But how could he set about it? For the first time he was the author of a conspiracy; hitherto he had taken advantage of all popular movements. Danton, the Cordeliers, and the faubourgs had made the insurrection of the 10th of August against the throne; Marat, the Mountain, and the commune had made that of the 31st of May against the Gironde; Billaud, Saint-Just, and the committees had effected the ruin of the commune, and weakened the Mountain. Robespierre remained alone. Unable to procure assistance from the government, since he had declared against the committees, he had recourse to the populace and the Jacobins. The principal conspirators were Saint-Just, and Couthon in the committee; Fleuriot the mayor, and Payan the national agent in the commune; Dumas the president, and Coffinhal the vice-president, in the revolutionary tribunal; Henriot, the commander of the armed force, and the popular society. On the 15th Messidor, three weeks after the law of Prairial, and twenty-four days before the 9th Thermidor, the resolution was already taken; at that time, and under that date, Henriot wrote to the mayor: "You shall be satisfied with me, comrade, and with the way in which I shall proceed;

trust me, men who love their country, easily agree in directing all their steps to the benefit of public affairs. I would have wished, and I do wish, that the *secret of the operation* rested with us two; the wicked should know nothing of it. Health and brotherhood."

Saint-Just was on a mission to the army of the north; Robespierre hastily recalled him. While waiting his return, he prepared the public mind at the Jacobins. In the sitting of the 3rd Thermidor, he complained of the conduct of the committees, and of the *persecution of the patriots*, whom he swore to defend. "There must no longer be traces of crime or faction," said he, "in any place whatever. A few scoundrels disgrace the convention; but it will not allow itself to be swayed by them." He then urged his colleagues, the Jacobins, to prevent *their reflections* to the national assembly. This was the transaction of the 31st of May. On the 4th, he received a deputation from the department of l'Aisne, who came to complain to him of the operations of the government, to which, for a month past, he had been a stranger. "The convention," said Robespierre, in his reply to the deputation, "in the situation in which it now stands, gangrened by corruption, and being wholly unable to recover itself, cannot save the republic-both must perish. The proscription of patriots is the order of the day. As for me I have one foot in the tomb; in a few days the other will follow it. The rest is in the hands of Providence." He was then slightly indisposed, and he purposely exaggerated his discouragement, his fears, and the dangers of the republic, in order to inflame the patriots, and again bind the fate of the revolution with his own.

In the meantime. Saint-Just arrived from the army. He ascertained the state of affairs from Robespierre. He presented himself to the committees, the members of which received him coldly; every time he entered, they ceased to deliberate. Saint-Just, who, from their silence, a few chance words, and the expression of perplexity or hostility on their countenances, saw there was no time to be lost, pressed Robespierre to act. His Maxim was to strike at once, and resolutely. "Dare," said he, "that is the secret of revolutions." But he wished to prevail on Robespierre to take a measure, which was impossible, by urging him to strike his foes, without apprising them. The force at his disposal was a force of revolutionary opinion, and not an organized force. It was necessary for him to seek the assistance of the convention or of the commune, the legal authority of government, or the extraordinary authority of insurrection. Such was the custom, and such must be all coups-d'état. They could not even have recourse to insurrection, until after they had received the refusal of the assembly, otherwise a pretext was wanting for the rising. Robespierre was therefore obliged to commence the attack in the convention itself. He hoped to obtain everything from it by his ascendancy, or if, contrary to its custom, it resisted, he reckoned on the people, urged by the commune, rising on the 9th Thermidor against the proscribed of the Mountain, and the committee of public safety, as it had risen on the 31st of May against the proscribed of the Gironde and the Commission of Twelve. It is almost always by the past that man regulates his conduct and his hopes.

On the 8th Thermidor, he entered the convention at an early hour. He ascended the tribunal and denounced the committee in a most skilful speech. "I am come," said he, "to defend before you your authority insulted, and liberty violated. I will also defend myself; you will not be surprised at this; you do not resemble the tyrants you contend with. The cries of outraged innocence do not importune your ears, and you know that this cause is not foreign to your interests." After this opening, he complained of those who had calumniated him; he attacked those who sought the ruin of the republic, either by excesses or moderation; those who persecuted pacific citizens, meaning the committees, and those who persecuted true patriots, meaning the Mountain. He associated himself with the intentions, past conduct, and spirit of the convention; he added that its enemies were his: "What have I done to merit persecution, if it entered not into the general system of their conspiracy against the convention? Have you not observed that, to isolate you from the nation, they have given out that you are dictators, reigning by means of terror, and disavowed by the silent wishes of all Frenchmen? For myself, what faction do I belong to? To yourselves. What is that faction that, from the beginning of the revolution, has overthrown all factions, and got rid of acknowledged traitors. It is you, it is the people, it is principles. That is the faction to which I am devoted, and against which all crimes are leagued. For at least six weeks, my inability to do good and to check evil has obliged me absolutely to renounce my functions as a member of the committee of public safety. Has patriotism been better protected? Have factions been more timid? Or the country more happy? At all times my influence has been confined to pleading the cause of my country before the national representation, and at the tribunal of public opinion." After having attempted to confound his cause with that of the convention, he tried to excite it against the committees by dwelling on the idea of its independence. "Representatives of the people," said he, "it is time to resume the pride and elevation of character which befits you. You are not made to be ruled, but to rule the depositaries of your confidence."

While he thus endeavoured to tempt the assembly by the return of its power and the end of its slavery, he addressed the moderate party, by reminding them that they were indebted to him for the lives of the Seventy-Three, and by holding forth hopes of returning order, justice, and clemency. He spoke of changing the devouring and trickster system of finance, of softening the revolutionary government, of guiding its influence, and punishing its prevaricating agents. Lastly, he invoked the people, talked of their necessities, and of their power. And when he had recalled all that could act upon the interests, hopes, or fears of the convention, he added: "We say, then, that there exists a conspiracy against public liberty; that it owes its strength to a criminal coalition which intrigues in the very heart of the convention; that this coalition has accomplices in the committee of general safety; that the enemies of the republic have opposed this committee to the committee of public safety, and have thus constituted two governments; that members of the committee of public safety are concerned in this plot; that the coalition thus formed seeks the ruin both of patriots and of the country; What remedy is there for this evil? Punish the traitors; compose anew the committee of general safety; purify this committee, and make it subordinate to the committee of public safety; purify the latter committee itself; constitute the unity of the government under the supreme authority of the convention; crush every faction under the weight of national authority, and establish on their ruins the power of justice and liberty."

Not a murmur, not a mark of applause welcomed this declaration of war. The silence with which Robespierre was heard continued long after he had ceased speaking. Anxious looks were exchanged in all parts of the doubting assembly. At length Lecointre of Versailles arose and proposed that the speech should be printed. This motion was the signal for agitation, discussion, and resistance. Bourdon de l'Oise opposed the motion for printing the speech, as a dangerous measure. He was applauded. But Barrère, in his ambiguous manner, having maintained that all speeches ought to be published, and Couthon having moved that it should be sent to all the communes of the republic, the convention, intimidated by this apparent concord of the two opposite factions, decreed both the printing and circulation of the speech.

The members of the two committees thus attacked, who had hitherto remained silent, seeing the Mountain thwarted, and the majority undecided, thought it time to speak. Vadier first opposed Robespierre's speech and Robespierre himself. Cambon went further. "It is time," he cried, "to speak the whole truth: one man paralyzed the resolution of the national assembly; that man is Robespierre." "The mask must be torn off," added Billaud-Varennes, "whatever face it may cover; I would rather my corpse should serve an ambitious man for his throne, than by my silence to become the accomplice of his crimes." Panis, Bentabole, Charlier, Thirion, Amar, attacked him in turn. Fréron proposed to the convention to throw off the fatal yoke of the committees. "The time is come," said he, "to revive liberty of opinion; I move that the assembly revoke the decree which gives the committee power to arrest the representatives of the people. Who can speak freely while he fears an arrest?" Some applause was heard; but the moment for the entire deliverance of the convention was not yet arrived. It was necessary to contend with Robespierre from behind the committees, in order subsequently to attack the committees more easily. Fréron's motion was accordingly rejected. "The man who is prevented by fear from delivering his opinion," said Billaud-Varennes, looking at him, "is not worthy the title of a representative of the people." Attention was again drawn to Robespierre. The decree ordering his speech to be printed was recalled, and the convention submitted the speech to the examination of the committees. Robespierre who had been surprised at this fiery resistance, then said: "What! I had the courage to place before the assembly truths which I think necessary to the safety of the country, and you send my discourse for the examination of the members whom I accuse." He retired, a little discouraged, but hoping to bring back the assembly to his views, or rather, bring it into subjection with the aid of the conspirators of the Jacobins and the commune.

In the evening he repaired to the popular society. He was received with enthusiasm. He read the speech which the assembly had just condemned, and the Jacobins loaded him with applause. He then recounted to them the attacks which had been directed against him, and to increase their excitement he added: "If necessary, I am ready to drink the cup of Socrates." "Robespierre," cried a deputy, "I will drink it with you." "The enemies of Robespierre," cried numbers on all sides, "are the enemies of the country; let them be named, and they shall cease to live."

During the whole night Robespierre prepared his partisans for the following day. It was agreed that they should assemble at the commune and the Jacobins, in order to be ready for every event, while he, accompanied by his friends, repaired to the assembly.

The committees had also spent the night in deliberation. Saint-Just had appeared among them. His colleagues tried to disunite him from the triumvirate; they deputed him to draw up a report on the events of the preceding day, and submit it to them. But, instead of that, he drew up an act of accusation, which he would not communicate to them, and said, as he withdrew: "You have withered my heart; I am going to open it to the convention." The committees placed all their hope in the courage of the assembly and the union of parties. The Mountain had omitted nothing to bring about this salutary agreement. They had addressed themselves to the most influential members of the Right and of the Marais. They had entreated Boissy d'Anglas and Durand de Maillane, who were at their head, to join them against Robespierre. They hesitated at first: they were so alarmed at his power, so full of resentment against the Mountain, that they dismissed the Dantonists twice without listening to them. At last the Dantonists returned to the charge a third time, and then the Right and the Plain engaged to support them. There was thus a conspiracy on both sides. All the parties of the assembly were united against Robespierre, all the accomplices of the triumvirs were prepared to act against the convention. In this state of affairs the sitting of the ninth Thermidor began.

The members of the assembly repaired there earlier than usual. About half-past eleven they gathered in the passages, encouraging each other. The Bourdon de l'Oise, one of the Mountain, approached Durand de Maillane, a moderate, pressed his hand, and said—"The people of the Right are excellent men." Rovère and Tallien came up and mingled their congratulations with those of Bourdon. At twelve they saw, from the door of the hall, Saint-Just ascend the tribune. "*Now is the time*," said Tallien, and they entered the hall. Robespierre occupied a seat in front of the tribune, doubtless in order to intimidate his adversaries with his looks. Saint-Just began: "I belong," he said, "to no faction; I will oppose them all. The course of things has perhaps made this tribune the Tarpeian rock for him who shall tell you that the members of the government have quitted the path of prudence." Tallien then interrupted Saint-Just, and exclaimed violently: "No good citizen can restrain his tears at the wretched state of public affairs. We see nothing but divisions. Yesterday a member of the government separated himself from it to accuse it. To-day another does the same. Men still seek to attack each other, to increase the woes of the country, to precipitate it into the abyss. Let the veil be wholly torn asunder." "It must! it must!" resounded on every side.

Billaud-Varennes spoke from his seat—"Yesterday," said he, "the society of Jacobins was filled with hired men, for no one had a card; yesterday the design of assassinating the members of the national assembly was developed in that society; yesterday I saw men uttering the most atrocious insults against those who have never deviated from the revolution. I see on the Mountain one of those men who threatened the republic; there he is." "Arrest him! arrest him!" was the general cry.

The serjeant seized him, and took him to the committee of general safety. "The time is come for speaking the truth," said Billaud. "The assembly would form a wrong judgment of events and of the position in which it is placed, did it conceal from itself that it is placed between two massacres. It will perish, if feeble." "No! no! It will not perish!" exclaimed all the members, rising from their seats. They swore to save the republic. The spectators in the gallery applauded, and cried—"Vive la Convention Rationale!" The impetuous Lebas attempted to speak in defence of the triumvirs; he was not allowed to do so, and Billaud continued. He warned the convention of its dangers, attacked Robespierre, pointed out his accomplices, denounced his conduct and his plans of dictatorship. All eyes were directed towards him. He faced them firmly for some time; but at length, unable to contain himself, he rushed to the tribune. The cry of "Down with the tyrant," instantly became general, and drowned his voice.

"Just now," said Tallien, "I required that the veil should be torn asunder. It gives me pleasure to see that it is wholly sundered. The conspirators are unmasked; they will soon be destroyed, and liberty will triumph. I was present yesterday at the sitting of the Jacobins; I trembled for my country. I saw the army of this new Cromwell forming, and I armed myself with a poignard to stab him to the heart, if the national convention wanted courage to decree his impeachment." He drew out his poignard, brandished it before the indignant assembly, and moved before anything else, the arrest of Henriot, the permanent sitting of the assembly; and both motions were carried, in the midst of cries of—"Vive la république!" Billaud also moved the arrest of three of Robespierre's most daring accomplices, Dumas, Boulanger, and Dufrèse. Barrère caused the convention to be placed under the guard of the armed sections, and drew up a proclamation to be addressed to the people. Every one proposed a measure of precaution. Vadier diverted the assembly for a moment, from the danger which threatened it, to the affair of Catherine Théos. "Let us not be diverted from the true object of debate," said Tallien. "I will undertake to bring you back to it," said Robespierre. "Let us turn our attention to the tyrant," rejoined Tallien, attacking him more warmly than before.

Robespierre, after attempting to speak several times, ascending and descending the stairs of the tribune, while his voice was drowned by cries of "Down with the tyrant!" and the bell which the president Thuriot continued ringing, now made a last effort to be heard. "President of assassins," he cried, "for the last time, will you let me speak?" But Thuriot continued to ring his bell. Robespierre, after glancing at the spectators in the public gallery, who remained motionless, turned towards the Right. "Pure and virtuous men," said he, "I have recourse to you; give me the hearing which these assassins refuse." No answer was returned; profound silence prevailed. Then, wholly dejected, he returned to his place, and sank on his seat exhausted by fatigue and rage. He foamed at the mouth, and his utterance was choked. "Wretch!" said one of the Mountain, "the blood of Danton chokes thee." His arrest was demanded and supported on all sides. Young Robespierre now arose: "I am as guilty as my brother," said he. "I share his virtues, and I will share his fate." "I will not be involved in the opprobrium of this decree," added Lebas; "I demand my arrest too." The assembly unanimously decreed the arrest of the two

Robespierres, Couthon, Lebas, and Saint-Just. The latter, after standing for some time at the tribune with unchanged countenance, descended with composure to his place. He had faced this protracted storm without any show of agitation. The triumvirs were delivered to the gendarmerie, who removed them amidst general applause. Robespierre exclaimed, as he went out—"The republic is lost, the brigands triumph." It was now half-past five, and the sitting was suspended till seven.

During this stormy contest the accomplices of the triumvirs had assembled at the Commune and the Jacobins. Fleuriot the mayor, Payan the national agent, and Henriot the commandant, had been at the Hôtel de Ville since noon. They had assembled the municipal officers by the sound of the drum, hoping that Robespierre would be triumphant in the assembly, and that they should not require the general council to decree the insurrection, or the sections to sustain it. A few hours after, a serjeant of the convention arrived to summon the mayor to the bar of the assembly to give a report of the state of Paris. "Go, and tell your scoundrels," said Henriot, "that we are discussing how to purge them. Do not forget to tell Robespierre to be firm, and to fear nothing." About half-past four they learned of the arrest of the triumvirs, and the decree against their accomplices. The tocsin was immediately sounded, the barriers closed, the general council assembled, and the sectionaries called together. The cannoneers were ordered to bring their pieces to the commune, and the revolutionary committees to take the oath of insurrection. A message was sent to the Jacobins, who sat permanently. The municipal deputies were received with the greatest enthusiasm. "The society watches over the country," they were told. "It has sworn to die rather than live under crime." At the same time they concerted together, and established rapid communications between these two centres of the insurrection. Henriot, on his side, to arouse the people, ran through the streets, pistol in hand, at the head of his staff, crying "to arms!" haranguing the multitude, and instigating all he met to repair to the commune to *save the country*. While on this errand, two members of the convention perceived him in the Rue Saint Honoré. They summoned, in the name of the law, a few gendarmes to execute the order for his arrest; they obeyed, and Henriot was pinioned and conveyed to the committee of general safety.

Nothing, however, was decided as yet on either side. Each party made use of its means of power; the convention of its decrees, the commune of the insurrection; each party knew what would be the consequences of defeat, and this rendered them both so active, so full of foresight and decision. Success was long uncertain. From noon till five the convention had the upper hand; it caused the arrest of the triumvirs, Payan the national agent, and Henriot the commandant. It was already assembled, and the commune had not yet collected its forces; but from six to eight the insurgents regained their position, and the cause of the convention was nearly lost. During this interval, the national representatives had separated, and the commune had redoubled its efforts and audacity.

Robespierre had been transferred to the Luxembourg, his brother to Saint-Lazare, Saint-Just to the Écossais, Couthon to La Bourbe, Lebas to the Conciergerie. The commune, after having ordered the gaolers not to receive them, sent municipal officers with detachments to bring them away. Robespierre was liberated first, and conducted in triumph to the Hôtel de Ville. On arriving, he was received with the greatest enthusiasm; "Long live Robespierre! Down with the traitors!" resounded on all sides. A little before, Coffinhal had departed, at the head of two hundred cannoneers, to release Henriot, who was detained at the committee of general safety. It was now seven o'clock, and the convention had resumed its sitting. Its guard, at the most, was a hundred men. Coffinhal arrived, made his way through the outer courts, entered the committee chamber, and delivered Henriot. The latter repaired to the Place du Carrousel, harangued the cannoneers, and ordered them to point their pieces on the convention.

The assembly was just then discussing the danger to which it was exposed. It had just heard of the alarming success of the conspirators, of the insurrectional orders of the commune, the rescue of the triumvirs, their presence at the Hôtel de Ville, the rage of the Jacobins, the successive convocation of the revolutionary council and of the sections. It was dreading a violent invasion every moment, when the terrified members of the committees rushed in, fleeing from Coffinhal. They learned that the committees were surrounded, and Henriot released. This news caused great agitation. The next moment Amar entered precipitately, and announced that the cannoneers, acted upon by Henriot, had turned their pieces upon the convention. "Citizens," said the president, putting on his hat, in token of distress, "the hour is come to die at our posts!" "Yes, yes! we will die there!" exclaimed all the members. The people in the galleries rushed out, crying, "To arms! Let us drive back the scoundrels!" And the assembly courageously outlawed Henriot.

Fortunately for the assembly, Henriot could not prevail upon the cannoneers to fire. His influence was limited to inducing them to accompany him, and he turned his steps to the Hôtel de Ville. The refusal of the cannoneers decided the fate of the day. From that moment the commune, which had been on the point of triumphing, saw its affairs decline. Having failed in a surprise by main force, it was reduced to the slow measures of the insurrection; the point of attack was changed, and soon it was no longer the commune which besieged the Tuileries, but the convention which marched upon the Hôtel de Ville. The assembly instantly outlawed the conspiring deputies and the insurgent commune. It sent commissioners to the sections, to secure their aid, named the representative Barras commandant of the armed force, joining with him Fréron, Rovère, Bourdon de l'Oise, Féraud, Leonard Bourdon, Legendre, all men of decision: and made the committees the centre of operation.

The sections, on the invitation of the commune, had assembled about nine o'clock; the greater part of the citizens, in repairing thither, were anxious, uncertain, and but vaguely informed of the quarrels between the commune and the convention. The emissaries of the insurgents urged them to join them and to march their battalions to the Hôtel de Ville. The sections confined themselves to sending a deputation, but as soon as the commissioners of the convention arrived among them, had communicated to them the decrees and invitations of the assembly, and informed them that there was a leader and a rallying point, they hesitated no longer. Their battalions presented themselves in succession to the assembly;

they swore to defend it, and they passed in files through the hall, amid shouts of enthusiasm and sincere applause. "The moments are precious," said Fréron; "we must act; Barras is gone to take the orders of the committees; we will march against the rebels; we will summon them in the name of the convention to deliver up the traitors, and if they refuse, we will reduce the building in which they are to ashes." "Go," said the president, "and let not day appear before the heads of the conspirators have fallen." A few battalions and some pieces of artillery were placed round the assembly, to guard it from attack, and the sections then marched in two columns against the commune. It was now nearly midnight.

The conspirators were still assembled. Robespierre, after having been received with cries of enthusiasm, promises of devotedness and victory, had been admitted into the general council between Payan and Fleuriot. The Place de Grève was filled with men, and glittered with bayonets, pikes, and cannon. They only waited the arrival of the sections to proceed to action. The presence of their deputies, and the sending of municipal commissioners in their midst, had inspired reliance on their aid. Henriot answered for everything. The conspirators looked for certain victory; they appointed an executive commission, prepared addresses to the armies, and drew up various lists. Half-past midnight, however, arrived, and no section had yet appeared, no order had yet been given, the triumvirs were still sitting, and the crowd on the Place de Grève became discouraged by this tardiness and indecision. A report spread in whispers that the sections had declared in favour of the convention, that the commune was outlawed, and that the troops of the convention were advancing. The eagerness of the armed multitude had already abated, when a few emissaries of the assembly glided among them, and raised the cry, "Vive la convention!" Several voices repeated it. They then read the proclamation of outlawry against the commune; and after hearing it, the whole crowd dispersed. The Place de Grève was deserted in a moment. Henriot came down a few minutes after, sabre in hand, to excite their courage; but finding no one: "What!" cried he; "is it possible? Those rascals of cannoneers, who saved my life five hours ago, now forsake me." He went up again. At that moment, the columns of the convention arrived, surrounded the Hôtel de Ville, silently took possession of all its outlets, and then shouted, "Vive la convention nationale!"

The conspirators, finding they were lost, sought to escape the violence of their enemies. A gendarme named Méda, who first entered the room where the conspirators were assembled, fired a pistol at Robespierre and shattered his jaw; Lebas wounded himself fatally; Robespierre the younger jumped from a window on the third story, and survived his fall; Couthon hid himself under a table; Saint-Just awaited his fate; Coffinhal, after reproaching Henriot with cowardice, threw him from a window into a drain and fled. Meantime, the conventionalists penetrated into the Hôtel de Ville, traversed the desolate halls, seized the conspirators, and carried them in triumph to the assembly. Bourdon entered the hall crying "Victory! victory! the traitors are no more!" "The wretched Robespierre is there," said the president; "they are bringing him on a litter. Doubtless you would not have him brought in." "No! no!" they cried; "carry him to the Place de la Révolution!" He was deposited for some time at the committee of general safety before he was transferred to the Conciergerie; and here, stretched on a table, his face disfigured and bloody, exposed to the looks, the invectives, the curses of all, he beheld the various parties exulting in his fall, and charging upon him all the crimes that had been committed. He displayed much insensibility during his last moments. He was taken to the Conciergerie, and afterwards appeared before the revolutionary tribunal, which, after identifying him and his accomplices, sent them to the scaffold. On the 10th Thermidor, about five in the evening, he ascended the death cart, placed between Henriot and Couthon, mutilated like himself. His head was enveloped in linen saturated with blood; his face was livid, his eyes almost visionless. An immense crowd thronged around the cart, manifesting the most boisterous and exulting joy. They congratulated and embraced each other, loading him with imprecations, and pressed near to view him more closely. The gendarmes pointed him out with their sabres. As to him, he seemed to regard the crowd with contemptuous pity; Saint-Just looked calmly at them; the rest, in number twenty-two, were dejected. Robespierre ascended the scaffold last; when his head fell, shouts of applause arose in the air, and lasted for some minutes.

With him ended the reign of terror, although he was not the most zealous advocate of that system in his party. If he sought for supremacy, after obtaining it, he would have employed moderation; and the reign of terror, which ceased at his fall, would also have ceased with his triumph. I regard his ruin to have been inevitable; he had no organized force; his partisans, though numerous, were not enrolled; his instrument was the force of opinion and of terror; accordingly, not being able to surprise his foes by a strong hand, after the fashion of Cromwell, he sought to intimidate them. Terror not succeeding, he tried insurrection. But as the convention with the support of the committees had become courageous, so the sections, relying on the courage of the convention, would naturally declare against the insurgents. By attacking the government, he aroused the assembly; by arousing the assembly, he aroused the people, and this coalition necessarily ruined him. The convention on the 9th of Thermidor was no longer, as on the 31st of May, divided, undecided, opposed to a compact, numerous, and daring faction. All parties were united by defeat, misfortune, and the proscription ever threatening them, and would naturally cooperate in the event of a struggle. It did not, therefore, depend on Robespierre himself to escape defeat; and it was not in his power to secede from the committees. In the position to which he had attained, one is consumed by one's passions, deceived by hopes and by fortune, hitherto good; and when once the scaffolds have been erected, justice and clemency are as impossible as peace, tranquillity, and the dispensing of power when war is declared. One must then fall by the means by which one has arisen; the man of faction must perish by the scaffold, as conquerors by war.

CHAPTER X

FROM THE 9TH THERMIDOR TO THE 1ST PRAIRIAL, YEAR III. (20TH MAY, 1795). EPOCH OF THE RISE AND FALL OF THE DEMOCRATIC PARTY

The convention, after the fall of Robespierre; party of the committees; Thermidorian party; their constitution and object—Decay of the democratic party of the committees—Impeachment of Lebon and Carrier—State of Paris —The Jacobins and the Faubourgs declare for the old committees; the *jeunesse dorée*, and the sections for the Thermidorians—Impeachment of Billaud-Varennes, Collot-d'Herbois, Barrère, and Vadier—Movement of Germinal—Transportation of the accused, and of a few of the Mountain, their partisans—Insurrection of the 1st Prairial—Defeat of the democratic party; disarming of the Faubourgs—The lower class is excluded from the government, deprived of the constitution of '93, and loses its material power.

The 9th of Thermidor was the first day of the revolution in which those fell who attacked. This indication alone manifested that the ascendant revolutionary movement had reached its term. From that day the contrary movement necessarily began. The general rising of all parties against one man was calculated to put an end to the compression under which they laboured. In Robespierre the committees subdued each other, and the decemviral government lost the prestige of terror which had constituted its strength. The committees liberated the convention, which gradually liberated the entire republic. Yet they thought they had been working for themselves, and for the prolongation of the revolutionary government, while the greater part of those who had supported them had for their object the overthrow of the dictatorship, the independence of the assembly, and the establishment of legal order. From the day after the 9th of Thermidor there were, therefore, two opposite parties among the conquerors, that of the committees, and that of the Mountain, which was called the Thermidorian party.

The former was deprived of half its forces; besides the loss of its chief, it no longer had the commune, whose insurgent members, to the number of seventy-two, had been sent to the scaffold, and, which, after its double defeat under Hébert and under Robespierre, was not again re-organized, and remained without direct influence. But this party retained the direction of affairs through the committees. All its members were attached to the revolutionary system; some, such as Billaud-Varennes, Collot-d'Herbois, Barrère, Vadier, Amar, saw it was their only safety; others, such as Carnot, Cambon, the two Prieurs, de la Marne, and de la Côte-d'Or, etc., feared the counter-revolution, and the punishment of their colleagues. In the convention it reckoned all the commissioners hitherto sent on missions, several of the Mountain who had signalized themselves on the 9th Thermidor, and the remnant of Robespierre's party. Without, the Jacobins were attached to it; and it still had the support of the faubourgs and of the lower class.

The Thermidorian party was composed of the greater number of the conventionalists. All the centre of the assembly, and what remained of the Right, joined the Mountain, who had abated their former exaggeration of views. The coalition of the Moderates, Boissy d'Anglas, Sieyès, Cambacérès, Chénier, Thibeaudeau, with the Dantonists, Tallien, Fréron, Legendre, Barras, Bourdon de l'Oise, Rovère, Bentabole, Dumont, and the two Merlins, entirely changed the character of the assembly. After the 9th of Thermidor, the first step of this party was to secure its empire in the convention. Soon it found its way into the government, and succeeded in excluding the previous occupants. Sustained by public opinion, by the assembly, by the committees, it advanced openly towards its object; it proceeded against the principal decemvirs, and some of their agents. As these had many partisans in Paris, it sought the aid of the young men against the Jacobins, of the sections against the faubourgs. At the same time, to strengthen it, it recalled to the assembly all the deputies whom the committee of public safety had proscribed; first, the seventy-three who had protested against the 31st of May, and then the surviving victims of that day themselves. The Jacobins exhibited excitement: it closed their club; the faubourgs raised an insurrection: it disarmed them. After overthrowing the revolutionary government, it directed its attention to the establishment of another, and to the introduction, under the constitution of the year III., of a feasible, liberal, regular, and stable order of things, in place of the extraordinary and provisional state in which the convention had been from its commencement until then. But all this was accomplished gradually.

The two parties were not long before they began to differ, after their common victory. The revolutionary tribunal was an especial object of general horror. On the 11th Thermidor it was suspended; but Billaud- Varennes, in the same sitting, had the decree of suspension rescinded. He maintained that the accomplices of Robespierre alone were guilty, that the majority of the judges and jurors being men of integrity, it was desirable to retain them in their offices. Barrère presented a decree to that effect: he urged that the triumvirs had done nothing for the revolutionary government; that they had often even opposed its measures; that their only care had been to place their creatures in it, and to give it a direction favourable to their own projects; he insisted, in order to strengthen that government, upon retaining the law *des suspects* and the tribunal, with its existing members, including Fouquier-Tinville. At this name a general murmur rose in the assembly. Fréron, rendering himself the organ of the general indignation, exclaimed: "I demand that at last the earth be delivered from that monster, and that Fouquier be sent to hell, there to wallow in the blood he has shed." His proposition was applauded, and Fouquier's accusation decreed. Barrère, however, did not regard himself as defeated; he still retained toward the convention the imperious language which the old committee had made use of with success; this was at once habit and calculation on his part; for he well knew that nothing is so easily continued as that which has been successful.

But the political tergiversations of Barrère, a man of noble birth, and who was a royalist Feuillant before the 10th of August, did not countenance his assuming this imperious and inflexible tone. "Who is this president of the Feuillants," said Merlin de Thionville, "who assumes to dictate to us the law?" The hall resounded with applause. Barrère became confused, left the tribune, and this first check of the committees indicated their decline in the convention. The revolutionary tribunal continued to exist, but with other members and another organization. The law of the 22nd Prairial was abolished, and there were now as much deliberation and moderation, as many protecting forms in trials, as before there had been precipitation and inhumanity. This tribunal was no longer made use of against persons formerly suspected, who were still detained in prison, though under milder treatment, and who, by degrees, were restored to liberty on the plan proposed by Camille Desmoulins for his Committee of Clemency.

On the 13th of Thermidor the government itself became the subject of discussion. The committee of public safety was deficient in many members; Hérault de Séchelles had never been replaced; Jean-Bon-Saint-André and Prieur de la Marne were on missions; Robespierre, Couthon, and Saint-Just had perished on the scaffold. In the places of these were appointed Tallien, Bréard, Echassériaux, Treilhard, Thuriot, and Laloi, whose accession lessened still more the influence of the old members. At the same time, were reorganized the two committees, so as to render them more dependent on the assembly, and less so on one another. The committee of public safety was charged with military and diplomatic operations; that of general safety with internal administration. As it was desired, by limiting the revolutionary power, to calm the fever which had excited the multitude; and gradually to disperse them, the daily meetings of the sections were reduced to one in every ten days; and the pay of forty sous a day, lately given to every indigent citizen who attended them, was discontinued.

These measures being carried into effect, on the 11th of Fructidor, one month after the death of Robespierre, Lecointre of Versailles denounced Billaud, Collot, Barrère, of the committee of public safety; and Vadier, Amar, and Vouland, of the committee of general safety. The evening before, Tallien had vehemently assailed the reign of terror, and Lecointre was. encouraged to his attack by the sensation which Tallien's speech had produced. He brought twenty-three charges against the accused; he imputed to them all the measures of cruelty or tyranny which they threw on the triumvirs, and called them the successors of Robespierre. This denunciation agitated the assembly, and more especially those who supported the committees, or who wished that divisions might cease in the republic. "If the crimes Lecointre reproaches us with were proved," said Billaud-Varennes—"if they were as real as they are absurd and chimerical, there is, doubtless, not one of us but would deserve to lose his head on the scaffold. But I defy Lecointre to prove, by documents or any evidence worthy of belief, any of the facts he has charged us with." He repelled the charges brought against him by Lecointre; he reproached his enemies with being corrupt and intriguing men, who wished to sacrifice him to the memory of Danton, *an odious conspirator, the hope of all parricidal factions.* "What seek these men," he continued—"what seek these men who call us the successors of Robespierre? Citizens, know you what they seek? To destroy liberty on the tomb of the tyrant." Lecointre's denunciation was premature; almost all the convention pronounced it calumnious. The accused and their friends gave way to outbursts of unrestrained and still powerful indignation, for they were now attacked for the first time; the accuser, scarcely supported by any one, was silenced. Billaud-Varennes and his friends triumphed for the time.

A few days after, the period for renewing a third of the committee arrived. The following members were fixed on by lot to retire: Barrère, Carnot, Robert Lindet, in the committee of public safety; Vadier, Vouland, Moise Baile in the committee of general safety. They were replaced by Thermidorians; and Collot-d'Herbois, as well as Billaud-Varennes, finding themselves too weak, resigned. Another circumstance contributed still more to the fall of their party, by exciting public opinion against it; this was the publicity given to the crimes of Joseph Lebon and Carrier, two of the proconsuls of the committee. They had been sent, the one to Arras and to Cambrai, the frontier exposed to invasion; the other to Nantes, the limit of the Vendéan war. They had signalized their mission by, beyond all others, displaying a cruelty and a caprice of tyranny, which are, however, generally found in those who are invested with supreme human power. Lebon, young and of a weak constitution, was naturally mild. On a first mission, he had been humane; but he was censured for this by the committee, and sent to Arras, with orders to show himself *somewhat more revolutionary.* Not to fall short of the inexorable policy of the committee, he gave way to unheard of excesses; he mingled debauchery with extermination; he had the guillotine always in his presence, and called it holy. He associated with the executioner, and admitted him to his table. Carrier, having more victims to strike, surpassed even Lebon; he was bilious, fanatical, and naturally blood-thirsty. He had only awaited the opportunity to execute enormities that the imagination even of Marat would not have dared to conceive. Sent to the borders of an insurgent country, he condemned to death the whole hostile population—priests, women, children, old men, and girls. As the scaffold did not suffice for his cruelty, he substituted a company of assassins, called Marat's company, for the revolutionary tribune, and, for the guillotine, boats, with false bottoms, by means of which he drowned his victims in the Loire. Cries of vengeance and justice were raised against these enormities. After the 9th of Thermidor, Lebon was attacked first, because he was more especially the agent of Robespierre. Carrier, who was that of the committee of public safety, and of whose conduct Robespierre had disapproved, was prosecuted subsequently.

There were in the prisons of Paris ninety-four people of Nantes, sincerely attached to the revolution, and who had defended their town with courage during the attack made on it by the Vendéans. Carrier had sent them to Paris as federalists. It had not been deemed safe to bring them before the revolutionary tribunal until the ninth of Thermidor; they were then taken there for the purpose of unmasking, by their trial, the crimes of Carrier. They were tried purposely with prolonged solemnity; their trial lasted nearly a month; there was time given for public opinion to declare itself; and on their acquittal, there was a general demand for justice on the revolutionary committee of Nantes, and on the proconsul Carrier. Legendre renewed Lecointre's impeachment of Billaud, Barrère, Collot, and Vadier, who were generously defended by Carnot, Prieur, and Cambon, their former colleagues, who demanded to share their fate. Lecointre's motion was not attended with any result; and, for the present, they only brought to trial the members of the revolutionary committee of Nantes; but we may observe the progress of the Thermidorian party. This time the members of the committee were obliged to have recourse to defence, and the convention simply passed to the order of the day, on the question of the denunciation made by Legendre, without voting it calumnious, as they had done that of Lecointre.

The revolutionary democrats were, however, still very powerful in Paris: if they had lost the commune, the tribunal, the convention, and the committee, they yet retained the Jacobins and the faubourgs. It was in these popular societies that their party concentrated, especially for the purpose of defending themselves. Carrier attended them assiduously, and invoked their assistance; Billaud-Varennes, and Collot-d'Herbois also resorted to them; but these being somewhat less threatened were circumspect. They were accordingly censured for their silence. "*The lion sleeps*," replied Billaud-Varennes, "*but his waking will be terrible.*" This club had been expurgated after the 10th Thermidor, and it had congratulated the convention in the name of the regenerated societies, on the fall of Robespierre and of tyranny. About this time, as many of its leaders were proceeded against, and many Jacobins were imprisoned in the departments, it came in the name of the united societies "*to give utterance to the cry of grief that resounded from every part of the republic, and to the voice of oppressed patriots, plunged in the dungeons which the aristocrats had just left.*"

The convention, far from yielding to the Jacobins, prohibited, for the purpose of destroying their influence, all collective petitions, branch- associations, correspondence, etc., between the parent society and its off-sets, and in this way disorganized the famous confederation of the clubs. The Jacobins, rejected from the convention, began to agitate Paris, where they were still masters. Then the Thermidorians also began to convoke their people, by appealing to the support of the sections. At the same time Fréron called the young men at arms, in his journal *l'Orateur du Peuple*, and placed himself at their head. This new and irregular militia called itself *La jeunesse dorée de Fréron*. All those who composed it belonged to the rich and the middle class; they had adopted a particular costume, called *Costume à la victime*. Instead of the blouse of the Jacobins, they wore a square open coat and very low shoes; the hair, long at the sides, was turned up behind, with tresses called *cadenettes*; they were armed with short sticks, leadened and formed like bludgeons. Some of these young men and some of the sectionaries were royalists; others followed the impulse of the moment, which was anti- revolutionary. The latter acted without object or ambition, declaring in favour of the strongest party, especially when the triumph of that party promised to restore order, the want of which was generally felt. The other contended under the Thermidorians against the old committees, as the Thermidorians had contended under the old committees against Robespierre; it waited for an opportunity of acting on its own account, which occurred after the entire downfall of the revolutionary party. In the violent situation of the two parties, actuated by fear and resentment, they pursued each other ruthlessly and often came to blows in the streets to the cry of "Vive la Montagne!" or "Vive la Convention!" The *jeunesse dorée* were powerful in the Palais Royal, where they were supported by the shopkeepers; but the Jacobins were the strongest in the garden of the Tuileries, which was near their club.

These quarrels became more animated every day; and Paris was transformed into a field of battle, where the fate of the parties was left to the decision of arms. This state of war and disorder would necessarily have an end; and since the parties had not the wisdom to come to an understanding, one or the other must inevitably carry the day. The Thermidorians were the growing party, and victory naturally fell to them. On the day following that on which Billaud had spoken of the *waking of the lion* in the popular society, there was great agitation throughout Paris. It was wished to take the Jacobin club by assault. Men shouted in the streets—"The great Jacobin conspiracy! Outlaw the Jacobins!" At this period the revolutionary committee of Nantes were being tried. In their defence they pleaded that they had received from Carrier the sanguinary orders they had executed; which led the convention to enter into an examination of his conduct. Carrier was allowed to defend himself before the decree was passed against him. He justified his cruelty by the cruelty of the Vendéans, and the maddening; fury of civil war. "When I acted," he said, "the air still seemed to resound with the civic songs of twenty thousand martyrs, who had shouted 'Vive la république!' in the midst of tortures. How could the voice of humanity, which had died in this terrible crisis, be heard? What would my adversaries have done in my place? I saved the republic at Nantes; my life has been devoted to my country, and I am ready to die for it." Out of five hundred voters, four hundred and ninety-eight were for the impeachment; the other two voted for it, but conditionally.

The Jacobins finding their opponents were going from subordinate agents to the representatives themselves, regarded themselves as lost. They endeavoured to rouse the multitude, less to defend Carrier than for the support of their party, which was threatened more and more. But they were kept in check by the *jeunesse dorée* and the sectionaries, who eventually proceeded to the place of their sittings to dissolve the club. A sharp conflict ensued. The besiegers broke the windows with stones, forced the doors, and dispersed the Jacobins after some resistance on their part. The latter complained to the convention of this violence. Rewbell, deputed to make a report on the subject, was not favourable to them. "Where was tyranny organized?" said he. "At the Jacobin club. Where had it its supports and its satellites? At the Jacobin club. Who covered France with mourning, threw families into despair, filled the republic with bastilles, made the republican system so odious, that a slave laden with fetters would have refused to live under it? The Jacobins. Who regret the terrible reign we have lived under? The Jacobins. If you have not courage to decide in a moment like this, the republic is at an end, because you have Jacobins." The convention suspended them provisionally, in order to expurgate and reorganize them, not daring to destroy them at once. The Jacobins, setting the decree at defiance, assembled in arms at their usual place of meeting; the Thermidorian troop who had already besieged them there, came again to assail them. It surrounded the club with cries of "Long live the convention! Down with the Jacobins!" The latter prepared for defence; they left their seats, shouting, "Long live the republic!" rushed to the doors, and attempted a sortie. At first they made a few prisoners; but soon yielding to superior numbers, they submitted, and traversed the ranks of the victors, who, after disarming them, covered them with hisses, insults, and even blows. These illegal expeditions were accompanied by all the excesses which attend party struggles.

The next day commissioners of the convention came to close the club, and put seals on its registers and papers, and from that moment the society of the Jacobins ceased to exist. This popular body had powerfully served the revolution, when, in order to repel Europe, it was necessary to place the government in the multitude, and to give the republic all the energy of defence; but now it only obstructed the progress of the new order of things.

The situation of affairs was changed; liberty was to succeed the dictatorship, now that the salvation of the revolution had been effected, and that it was necessary to revert to legal order, in order to preserve it. An exorbitant and extraordinary power, like the confederation of the clubs, would necessarily terminate with the defeat of the party which had supported it, and that party itself expire with the circumstances which had given it rise.

Carrier, brought before the revolutionary tribunal, was tried without interruption, and condemned with the majority of his accomplices. During the trial, the seventy-three deputies, whose protest against the 31st of May had excluded them from the assemblies, were reinstated. Merlin de Douai moved their recall in the name of the committee of public safety; his motion was received with applause, and the seventy-three resumed their seats in the convention. The seventy-three, in their turn, tried to obtain the return of the outlawed deputies; but they met with warm opposition. The Thermidorians and the members of the new committees feared that such a measure would be calling the revolution itself into question. They were also afraid of introducing a new party into the convention, already divided, and of recalling implacable enemies, who might cause, with regard to themselves, a reaction similar to that which had taken place against the old committees. Accordingly they vehemently opposed the motion, and Merlin de Douai went so far as to say: "Do you want to throw open the doors of the Temple?" The young son of Louis XVI. was confined there, and the Girondists, on account of the results of the 31st of May, were confounded with the Royalists; besides, the 31st of May still figured among the revolutionary dates beside the 10th of August and the 14th of July. The retrograde movement had yet some steps to take before it reached that period. The republican counter-revolution had turned back from the 9th Thermidor, 1794, to the 3rd of October, 1793, the day on which the seventy-three had been arrested, but not to the 2nd of June, 1793, when the twenty-two were arrested. After overthrowing Robespierre, and the committee, it had to attack Marat and the Mountain. In the almost geometrical progression of popular movement, a few months were still necessary to effect this.

They went on to abolish the decemviral system. The decree against the priests and nobles, who had formed two proscribed classes under the reign of terror, was revoked; the *maximum* was abolished, in order to restore confidence by putting an end to commercial tyranny; the general and earnest effort was to substitute the most elevated liberty for the despotic pressure of the committee of public safety. This period was also marked by the independence of the press, the restoration of religious worship, and the return of the property confiscated from the federalists during the reign of the committees.

Here was a complete reaction against the revolutionary government; it soon reached Marat and the Mountain. After the 9th of Thermidor, it had been considered necessary to oppose a great revolutionary reputation to that of Robespierre, and Marat had been selected for this purpose. To him were decreed the honours of the Panthéon, which Robespierre, while in power, had deferred granting him. He, in his turn, was now attacked. His bust was in the convention, the theatres, on the public squares, and in the popular assemblies. The *jeunesse dorée* broke that in the Théâtre Feydeau. The Mountain complained, but the convention decreed that no citizen could obtain the honours of the Panthéon, nor his bust be placed in the convention, until he had been dead ten years. The bust of Marat disappeared from the hall of the convention, and as the excitement was very great in the faubourgs, the sections, the usual support of the assembly, defiled through it. There was, also, opposite the Invalides, an elevated mound, a *Mountain*, surmounted by a colossal group, representing Hercules crushing a hydra. The section of the Halle-au-blé demanded that this should be removed. The left of the assembly murmured. "The giant," said a member, "is an emblem of the people." "All I see in it is a mountain," replied another, "and what is a Mountain but an eternal protest against equality." These words were much applauded, and sufficed to carry the petition and overthrow the monument of the victory and domination of a party.

Next were recalled the proscribed conventionalists; already, some time since, their outlawry had been reversed. Isnard and Louvet wrote to the assembly to be reinstated in their rights; they were met by the objection as to the consequences of the 31st of May, and the insurrections of the departments. "I will not," said Chénier, who spoke in their favour, "I will not so insult the national convention as to bring before them the phantom of federalism, which has been preposterously made the chief charge against your colleagues. They fled, it will be said; they hid themselves. This, then, is their crime! would that this, for the welfare of the republic, had been the crime of all! Why were there not caverns deep enough to preserve to the country the meditations of Condorcet, the eloquence of Vergniaud? Why did not some hospitable land, on the 10th Thermidor, give back to light that colony of energetic patriots and virtuous republicans? But projects of vengeance are apprehended from these men, soured by misfortune. Taught in the school of suffering, they have learnt only to lament human errors. No, no, Condorcet, Rabaud-Saint-Etienne, Vergniaud, Camille Desmoulins seek not holocausts of blood; their manes are not to be appeased by hecatombs." The Left opposed Chénier's motion. "You are about," cried Bentabole, "to rouse every passion; if you attack the insurrection of the 31st of May, you attack the eighty thousand men who concurred in it." "Let us take care," replied Sieyès, "not to confound the work of tyranny with that of principles. When men, supported by a subordinate authority, the rival of ours, succeeded in organizing the greatest of crimes, on the fatal 31st of May, and 2nd of June, it was not a work of patriotism, but an outrage of tyranny; from that time you have seen the convention domineered over, the majority oppressed, the minority dictating laws. The present session is divided into three distinct periods; till the 31st of May, there was oppression of the convention by the people; till the 9th Thermidor, oppression of the people by the convention, itself the object of tyranny; and lastly, since the 9th of Thermidor, justice, as regards the convention, has resumed its rights." He demanded the recall of the proscribed members, as a pledge of union in the assembly, and of security for the republic. Merlin de Douai immediately proposed their return in the name of the committee of public safety; it was granted, and after eighteen months' proscription, the twenty-two conventionalists resumed their seats; among them were Isnard, Louvet, Lanjuinais, Kervelegan, Henri La Rivière, La Réveillère-Lépaux, and Lesage, all that remained of the brilliant but unfortunate Gironde. They joined the moderate party, which was composed daily more and more of the remains of different parties. For old enemies, forgetting their resentments and their contest for domination, because they had now the same interests and the same object, became allies. It was the commencement of pacification between those who wished for a republic against the royalists, and a practicable constitution, in opposition to the revolutionists. At this period all measures against the federalists were rescinded, and the Girondists assumed the lead of the republican counter- revolution.

The convention was, however, carried much too far by the partisans of reaction; in its desire to repair all and to punish all, it fell into excesses of justice. After the abolition of the decemviral régime, the past should have been buried in oblivion, and the revolutionary abyss closed after a few expiatory victims had been thrown into it. Security alone brings about pacification; and pacification only admits of liberty. By again entering upon a course characterized by passion, they only effected a transference of tyranny, violence, and calamity. Hitherto the bourgeoisie had been sacrificed to the multitude, to the consumers now it was just the reverse. Stock-jobbing was substituted for the *maximum*, and informers of the middle class altogether surpassed the popular informers. All who had taken part in the dictatorial government were proceeded against with the fiercest determination. The sections, the seat of the middle class, required the disarming and punishment of the members of their revolutionary committees, composed of sans-culottes. There was a general hue and cry against the *terrorists*, who increased in number daily. The departments denounced all the former proconsuls, thus rendering desperate a numerous party, in reality no longer to be feared, since it had lost all power, by thus threatening it with great and perpetual reprisals.

Dread of proscription, and several other reasons, disposed them for revolt. The general want was terrible. Labour and its produce had been diminished ever since the revolutionary period, during which the rich had been imprisoned and the poor had governed; the suppression of the *maximum* had occasioned a violent crisis, which the traders and farmers turned to account, by disastrous monopoly and jobbing. To increase the difficulty, the assignats were falling into discredit, and their value diminished daily. More than eight milliards worth of them had been issued. The insecurity of this paper money, by reason of the revolutionary confiscations, which had depreciated the national property, the want of confidence on the part of the merchants, tradesmen, etc., in the stability of the revolutionary government, which they considered merely provisional, all this had combined to reduce the real value of the assignats to one- fifteenth of their nominal value. They were received reluctantly, and specie was hoarded up with all the greater care, in proportion to the increasing demand for it, and the depreciation of paper money. The people, in want of food, and without the means of buying it, even when they held assignats, were in utter distress. They attributed this to the merchants, the farmers, the landed and other proprietors, to the government, and dwelt with regret upon the fact that before, under the committee of public safety, they had enjoyed both power and food. The convention had indeed appointed a committee of subsistence to supply Paris with provisions, but this committee had great difficulty and expense in procuring from day to day the supply of fifteen hundred sacks of flour necessary to support this immense city; and the people, who waited in crowds for hours together before the bakers' shops, for the pound of bad bread, distributed to each inhabitant, were loud in their complaints, and violent in their murmurs. They called Boissy d'Anglas, president of the committee of subsistence, *Boissy-Famine*. Such was the state of the fanatical and exasperated multitude, when its former leaders were brought to trial.

On the 12th Ventôse, a short time after the return of the remaining Girondists, the assembly had decreed the arrest of Billaud-Varennes, Collot-d'Herbois, Barrère and Vadier. Their trial before the convention was appointed to commence on the 3rd Germinal. On the 1st (20th of March, 1795), the Décade day, and that on which the sections assembled, their partisans organized a riot to prevent their being brought to trial; the outer sections of the faubourgs Saint Antoine and Saint Marceau were devoted to their cause. From these quarters they proceeded, half petitioners, half insurgents, towards the convention, to demand bread, the constitution of '93, and the liberation of the imprisoned patriots. They met a few young men on their way, whom they threw into the basins of the Tuileries. The news, however, soon spread that the convention was exposed to danger, and that the Jacobins were about to liberate their leaders, and the *jeunesse dorée*, followed by about five thousand citizens of the inner sections, came, dispersed the men of the faubourgs, and acted as a guard for the assembly. The latter, warned by this new danger, revived, on the motion of Sieyès, the old martial law, under the name of *loi de grande police*.

This rising in favour of the accused having failed, they were brought before the convention on the 3rd Germinal. Vadier alone was contumacious. Their conduct was investigated with the greatest solemnity; they were charged with having tyrannized over the people and oppressed the convention. Though proofs were not wanting to support this charge, the accused defended themselves with much address. They ascribed to Robespierre the oppression of the assembly, and of themselves; they endeavoured to palliate their own conduct by citing the measures taken by the committee, and adopted by the convention, by urging the excitement of the period, and the necessity of securing the defence and safety of the republic. Their former colleagues appeared as witnesses in their favour, and wished to make common cause with them. The *Crêtois* (the name then given to the remnant of the Mountain) also supported them warmly. Their trial had lasted nine days, and each sitting had been occupied by the prosecution and the defence. The sections of the faubourgs were greatly excited. The mobs which had collected every day since the 1st Germinal, increased twofold on the 12th, and a new rising took place, in order to suspend the trial, which the first rising had failed to prevent. The agitators, more numerous and bold on this occasion, forced their way through the guard of the convention, and entered the hall, having written with chalk on their hats the words, "Bread," "The constitution of '93," "Liberty for the patriots." Many of the deputies of the *Crête* declared in their favour; the other members, astounded at the tumult and disorder of this popular invasion, awaited the arrival of the inner sections for their deliverance. All debating was at an end. The tocsin, which had been removed from the commune after its defeat, and placed on the top of the Tuileries, where the convention sat, sounded the alarm. The committee ordered the drums to beat to arms. In a short time the citizens of the nearest sections assembled, marched in arms to assist the convention, and rescued it a second time. It sentenced the accused, whose cause was the pretext for this rising, to transportation, and decreed the arrest of seventeen members of the *Crête* who had favoured the insurgents, and might therefore be regarded as their accomplices. Among these were Cambon, Ruamps, Leonard Bourdon, Thuriot, Chasle, Amar, and Lecointre, who, since the recall of the Girondists, had returned to the Mountain. On the following day they, and the persons sentenced to transportation, were conveyed to the castle of Ham.

The events of the 12th of Germinal decided nothing. The faubourgs had been repulsed, but not conquered; and both power and confidence must be taken from a party by a decisive defeat, before it is effectually destroyed. After so many questions decided against the democratists, there still remained one of the utmost importance—the constitution. On this depended the ascendancy of the multitude or of the bourgeoisie. The supporters of the revolutionary government then fell back on the democratic constitution of '93, which presented to them the means of resuming the authority they had lost. Their opponents, on the other hand, endeavoured to replace it by a constitution which would secure all the advantage to them, by concentrating the government a little more, and giving it to the middle class. For a month, both parties were preparing for this last contest. The constitution of 1793, having been sanctioned by the people, enjoyed a great prestige. It was accordingly attacked with infinite precaution. At first its assailants engaged to carry it into execution without restriction; next they appointed a commission of eleven members to prepare the *lois organiques*, which were to render it practicable; by and by, they ventured to suggest objections to it on the ground that it distributed power too loosely, and only recognised one assembly dependent on the people, even in its measures of legislation. At last, a deputation of the sectionaries went so far as to call the constitution of '93 a decemviral constitution, dictated by terror.

All its partisans, at once indignant and filled with fears, organized an insurrection to maintain it. This was another 31st of May, as terrible as the first, but which, not having the support of an all-powerful commune, not being directed by a general commandant, and not having a terrified convention and submissive sections to deal with, had not the same result.

The conspirators, warned by the failure of the risings of the 1st and 12th Germinal, omitted nothing to make up for their want of direct object and of organization. On the 1st Prairial (20th of May) in the name of the people, insurgent for the purpose of obtaining bread and their rights, they decreed the abolition of the revolutionary government, the establishment of the democratic constitution of '93, the dismissal and arrest of the members of the existing government, the liberation of the patriots, the convocation of the primary assemblies on the 25th Prairial, the convocation of the legislative assembly, destined to replace the convention, on the 25th Messidor, and the suspension of all authority not emanating from the people. They determined on forming a new municipality, to serve as a common centre; to seize on the barriers, telegraph, cannon, tocsins, drums, and not to rest till they had secured repose, happiness, liberty, and means of subsistence for all the French nation. They invited the artillery, gendarmes, horse and foot soldiers, to join the banners of the people, and marched on the convention.

Meantime, the latter was deliberating on the means of preventing the insurrection. The daily assemblages occasioned by the distribution of bread and the popular excitement, had concealed from it the preparations for a great rising, and it had taken no steps to prevent it. The committees came in all haste to apprise it of its danger; it immediately declared its sitting permanent, voted Paris responsible for the safety of the representatives of the republic, closed its doors, outlawed all the leaders of the mob, summoned the citizens of the sections to arms, and appointed as their leaders eight commissioners, among whom were Legendre, Henri La Rivière, Kervelegan, etc. These deputies had scarcely gone, when a loud noise was heard without. An outer door had been forced, and numbers of women rushed into the galleries, crying, "Bread and the constitution of '93!" The convention received them firmly. "Your cries," said the president Vernier, "will not alter our position; they will not accelerate by one moment the arrival of supplies. They will only serve to hinder it." A fearful tumult drowned the voice of the president, and interrupted the proceedings. The galleries were then cleared; but the insurgents of the faubourgs soon reached the inner doors, and finding them closed, forced them with hatchets and hammers, and then rushed in amidst the convention.

The hall now became a field of battle. The veterans and gendarmes, to whom the guard of the assembly was confided, cried, "To arms!" The deputy Auguis, sword in hand, headed them, and succeeded in repelling the assailants, and even made a few of them prisoners. But the insurgents, more numerous, returned to the charge, and again rushed into the house. The deputy Féraud entered precipitately, pursued by the insurgents, who fired some shots in the house. They took aim at Boissy d'Anglas, who was occupying the president's chair, in place of Vernier. Féraud ran to the tribune, to shield him with his body; he was struck at with pikes and sabres, and fell dangerously wounded.

The insurgents dragged him into the lobby, and, mistaking him for Fréron, cut off his head, and placed it on a pike.

After this skirmish, they became masters of the hall. Most of the deputies had taken flight. There only remained the members of the *Crête* and Boissy d'Anglas, who, calm, his hat on, heedless of threat and insult, protested in the name of the convention against this popular violence. They held out to him the bleeding head of Féraud; he bowed respectfully before it. They tried to force him, by placing pikes at his breast, to put the propositions of the insurgents to the vote; he steadily and courageously refused. But the *Crêtois*, who approved of the insurrection, took possession of the bureaux and of the tribune, and decreed, amidst the applause of the multitude, all the articles contained in the manifesto of the insurrection. The deputy Romme became their organ. They further appointed an executive commission, composed of Bourbotte, Duroy, Duquesnoy, Prieur de la Marne, and a general-in-chief of the armed force, the deputy Soubrany. In this way they prepared for the return of their domination. They decreed the recall of their imprisoned colleagues, the dismissal of their enemies, a democratic constitution, the re- establishment of the Jacobin club. But it was not enough for them to have usurped the assembly for a short time; it was necessary to conquer the sections, for it was only with these they could really contend there.

The commissioners despatched to the sections had quickly gathered them together. The battalions of the *Butte des Moulins, Lepelletier, des Piques, de la Fontaine-Grenelle*, who were the nearest, soon occupied the Carrousel and its principal avenues. The aspect of affairs then underwent a change; Legendre, Kervelegan, and Auguis besieged the insurgents, in their turn, at the head of the sectionaries. At first they experienced some resistance. But with fixed bayonets they soon entered the hall, where the conspirators were still deliberating, and Legendre cried out: *"In the name of the law, I order armed citizens to withdraw."* They hesitated a moment, but the arrival of the battalions, now entering at every door, intimidated them, and they hastened from the hall in all the disorder of flight. The assembly again became complete; the sections received a vote of thanks, and the deliberations were resumed. All the measures adopted in the interim were annulled, and fourteen representatives, to whom were afterwards joined fourteen others, were arrested, for organizing the insurrection, or approving it in their speeches. It was then midnight; at five in the morning the prisoners were already six leagues from Paris.

Despite this defeat, the faubourgs did not consider themselves beaten; and the next day they advanced *en masse* with their cannon against the convention. The sections, on their side, marched for its defence. The two parties were on the point of engaging; the cannons of the faubourg which were mounted on the Place du Carrousel, were directed towards the château, when the assembly sent commissioners to the insurgents. Negotiations were begun. A deputy of the faubourgs, admitted to the convention, first repeated the demand made the preceding day, adding: "We are resolved to die at the post we now occupy, rather than abate our present demands. I fear nothing! My name is Saint-Légier. Vive la République! Vive la Convention! if it is attached to principles, as I believe it to be." The deputy was favourably received, and they came to friendly terms with the faubourgs, without, however, granting them anything positive. The latter having no longer a general council of the commune to support their resolutions, nor a commander like Henriot to keep them under arms, till their propositions were decreed, went no further. They retired after having received an assurance that the convention would assiduously attend to the question of provisions, and would soon publish the organic laws of the constitution of '93. That day showed that immense physical force and a decided object are not the only things essential to secure success; leaders and an authority to support and direct the insurrection are also necessary. The convention was the only remaining legal power: the party which it held in favour triumphed.

Six democratic members of the Mountain, Goujon, Bourbotte, Romme, Duroy, Duquesnoy, and Soubrany, were brought before a military commission. They behaved firmly, like men fanatically devoted to their cause, and almost all free from excesses. The Prairial movement was the only thing against them; but that was sufficient in times of party strife, and they were condemned to death. They all stabbed themselves with the same knife, which was transferred from one to the other, exclaiming, *"Vive la République!"* Romme, Goujon, and Duquesnoy were fortunate enough to wound themselves fatally; the other three were conducted to the scaffold in a dying state, but faced death with serene countenances.

Meantime, the faubourgs, though repelled on the 1st, and diverted from their object on the 2nd of Prairial, still had the means of rising. An event of much less importance than the preceding riots occasioned their final ruin. The murderer of Féraud was discovered, condemned, and on the 4th, the day of his execution, a mob succeeded in rescuing him. There was a general outcry against this attempt; and the convention ordered the faubourgs to be disarmed. They were encompassed by all the interior sections. After attempting to resist, they yielded, giving up some of their leaders, their arms, and artillery. The democratic party had lost its chiefs, its clubs, and its authorities; it had nothing left but an armed force, which rendered it still formidable, and institutions by means of which it might yet regain everything. After the last check, the inferior class was entirely excluded from the government of the state, the revolutionary committees which formed its assemblies were destroyed; the cannoneers forming its armed force were disarmed; the constitution of '93, which was its code, was abolished; and here the rule of the multitude terminated.

From the 9th Thermidor to the 1st Prairial, the Mountain was treated as the Girondist party had been treated from the 2nd of June to the 9th Thermidor. Seventy-six of its members were sentenced to death or arrest. In its turn, it underwent the destiny it had imposed on the other; for in times when the passions are called into play, parties know not how to come to terms, and seek only to conquer. Like the Girondists, they resorted to insurrection, in order to regain the power which they had lost; and like them, they fell. Vergniaud, Brissot, Guadet, etc., were tried by a revolutionary tribunal; Bourbotte, Duroy, Soubrany, Romme, Goujon, Duquesnoy, by a military commission. They all died with the same courage; which shows that all parties are the same, and are guided by the same maxims, or, if you please, by the same necessities. From that period, the middle class resumed the management of the revolution without, and the assembly was as united under the Girondists as it had been, after the 2nd of June, under the Mountain.

CHAPTER XI

FROM THE 1ST PRAIRIAL (20TH OF MAY, 1795) TO THE 4TH BRUMAIRE (26TH OF OCTOBER), YEAR IV., THE CLOSE OF THE CONVENTION

Campaign of 1793 and 1794—Disposition of the armies on hearing the news of the 9th Thermidor—Conquest of Holland; position on the Rhine—Peace of Basel with Prussia—Peace with Spain—Descent upon Quiberon—The reaction ceases to be conventional, and becomes royalist—Massacre of the revolutionists, in the south—Directorial constitution of the year III.— Decrees of Fructidor, which require the re-election of two-thirds of the convention—Irritation of the sectionary royalist party—It becomes insurgent—The 13th of Vendémiaire—Appointment of the councils and of the directory—Close of the convention; its duration and character.

The exterior prosperity of the revolution chiefly contributed to the fall of the dictatorial government and of the Jacobin party. The increasing victories of the republic to which they had very greatly contributed by their vigorous measures, and by their enthusiasm, rendered their power superfluous. The committee of public safety, by crushing with its strong and formidable hand the interior of France, had developed resources, organized armies, found generals and guided them to victories which ultimately secured the triumph of the revolution in the face of Europe. A prosperous position no longer required the same efforts; its mission was accomplished, the peculiar province of such a dictatorship being to save a country and a cause, and to perish by the very safety it has secured. Internal events have prevented our rapidly describing the impulse which the committee of public safety gave to the armies after the 31st of May, and the results which it obtained from it.

The levy en masse that took place in the summer of 1793, formed the troops of the Mountain. The leaders of that party soon selected from the secondary ranks generals belonging to the Mountain to replace the Girondist generals. Those generals were Jourdan, Pichegru, Hoche, Moreau, Westermann, Dugommier, Marceau, Joubert, Kléber, etc. Carnot, by his admission to the committee of public safety, became minister of war and commander-in-chief of all the republican armies. Instead of scattered bodies, acting without concert upon isolated points, he proceeded with strong masses, concentrated on one object. He commenced the practice of a great plan of warfare, which he tried with decided success at Watignies, in his capacity of commissioner of the convention. This important victory, at which he assisted in person, drove the allied generals, Clairfait and the prince of Coburg, behind the Sambre, and raised the siege of Maubeuge. During the winter of 1793 and 1794 the two armies continued in presence of each other without undertaking anything.

At the opening of the campaign, they each conceived a plan of invasion. The Austrian army advanced upon the towns on the Somme, Péronne, Saint- Quentin, Arras, and threatened Paris, while the French army again projected the conquest of Belgium. The plan of the committee of public safety was combined in a very different way to the vague design of the coalition. Pichegru, at the head of fifty thousand men of the army of the north, entered Flanders, resting on the sea and the Scheldt. On his right, Moreau advanced with twenty thousand men upon Menin and Courtrai. General Souham, with thirty thousand men, remained under Lille, to sustain the extreme right of the invading army against the Austrians; while Jourdan, with the army of the Moselle, directed his course towards Charleroi by Arlon and Dinan, to join the army of the north.

The Austrians, attacked in Flanders, and threatened with a surprise in the rear by Jourdan, soon abandoned their positions on the Somme. Clairfait and the duke of York allowed themselves to be beaten at Courtrai and Hooglède by the army of Pichegru; Coburg at Fleurus by that of Jourdan, who had just taken Charleroi. The two victorious generals rapidly completed the invasion of the Netherlands. The Anglo-Dutch army fell back on Antwerp, and from thence upon Breda, and from Breda to Bois-le-Duc, receiving continual checks. It crossed the Waal, and fell back upon Holland. The Austrians endeavoured with the same want of success, to cover Brussels and Maëstricht: they were pursued and beaten by the army of Jourdan, which since its union had taken the name of the army of the *Sambre et Meuse*, and which did not leave them behind the Roër, as Dumouriez had done, but drove them beyond the Rhine. Jourdan made himself master of Cologne and Bonn, and communicated by his left with the right of the army of the Moselle, which had advanced into the country of Luxembourg, and which, conjointly with him, occupied Coblentz. A general and concerted movement of all the French armies had taken place, all of them marching towards the Rhenish frontier. At the time of the defeats, the lines of Weissenburg had been forced. The committee of public safety employed in the army of the Rhine the expeditious measures peculiar to its policy. The commissioners, Saint-Just and Lebas, gave the chief command to Hoche, made terror and victory the order of the day; and generals Brunswick and Wurmser were very soon driven from Haguenau on the lines of the Lauter, and not being able even to maintain that position, passed the Rhine at Philipsburg. Spire and Worms were retaken. The republican troops, everywhere victorious, occupied Belgium, that part of Holland situated on the left of the Meuse, and all the towns on the Rhine, except Mayence and Mannheim, which were closely beset.

The army of the Alps did not make much progress in this campaign. It tried to invade Piedmont, but failed. On the Spanish frontier, the war had commenced under ill auspices: the two armies of the eastern and western Pyrenees, few in number and badly disciplined, were constantly beaten; one had retired under Perpignan, the other under Bayonne. The committee of public safety turned its attention and efforts but tardily on this point, which was not the most dangerous for it. But as soon as it had introduced its system, generals, and organization into the two armies, the appearance of things changed. Dugommier, after repeated successes, drove the Spaniards from the French territory, and entered the peninsula by Catalonia. Moncey also invaded it by the valley of Bastan, the other opening of the Pyrenees, and became master of San Sebastian and Fontarabia. The coalition was everywhere conquered, and some of the confederated powers began to repent of their over-confident adhesion.

In the meantime, news of the revolution of the 9th Thermidor reached the armies. They were entirely republican, and they feared that Robespierre's fall would lead to that of the popular government; and they, accordingly, received this intelligence with marked disapprobation; but, as the armies were submissive to the civil authority, none of them rebelled. The insurrections of the army only took place from the 14th of July to the 31st of May; because, being the refuge of the conquered parties, their leaders had at every crisis the advantage of political precedence, and contended with all the ardour of compromised factions. Under the committee of public safety, on the contrary, the most renowned generals had no political influence, and were subject to the terrible discipline of parties. While occasionally thwarting the generals, the convention had no difficulty in keeping the armies in obedience.

A short time afterwards the movement of invasion was prolonged in Holland and in the Spanish peninsula. The United Provinces were attacked in the middle of winter, and on several sides, by Pichegru, who summoned the Dutch patriots to liberty. The party opposed to the stadtholderate seconded the victorious efforts of the French army, and the revolution and conquest took place simultaneously at Leyden, Amsterdam, the Hague, and Utrecht. The stadtholder took refuge in England, his authority was abolished, and the assembly of the states-general proclaimed the sovereignty of the people, and constituted the Dutch Republic, which formed a close alliance with France, to which it ceded, by the treaty of Paris, of the 16th of May, 1795, Dutch Flanders, Maëstricht, Venloo, and their dependencies. The navigation of the Rhine, the Scheldt, and the Meuse was left free to both nations. Holland, by its wealth, powerfully contributed towards the continuance of the war against the coalition. This important conquest at the same time deprived the English of a powerful support, and compelled Prussia, threatened on the Rhine and by Holland, to conclude, at Basle, with the French Republic, a peace, for which its reverses and the affairs of Poland had long rendered it disposed. A peace was also made at Basle, on the 10th of July, with Spain, alarmed by our progress on its territory. Figuières and the fortress of Rosas had been taken; and Perignon was advancing into Catalonia; while Moncey, after becoming master of Villa Réal, Bilbao, and Vittoria, marched against the Spaniards who had retired to the frontiers of Old Castile. The cabinet of Madrid demanded peace. It recognised the French Republic, which restored its conquests, and which received in exchange the portion of San Domingo possessed by Spain. The two disciplined armies of the Pyrenees joined the army of the Alps, which by this means soon overran Piedmont, and entered Italy—Tuscany only having made peace with the republic on the 9th of

February, 1795.

These partial pacifications and the reverses of the allied troops gave another direction to the efforts of England and the emigrant party. The time had arrived for making the interior of France the fulcrum of the counter-revolutionary movement. In 1791, when unanimity existed in France, the royalists placed all their hopes in foreign powers; now, dissensions at home and the defeat of their allies in Europe left them no resource but in conspiracies. Unsuccessful attempts, as we have seen, never make vanquished parties despair: victory alone wearies and enervates, and sooner or later restores the dominion of those who wait.

The events of Prairial and the defeat of the Jacobin party, had decided the counter-revolutionary movement. At this period, the reaction, hitherto conducted by moderate republicans, became generally royalist. The partisans of monarchy were still as divided as they had been from the opening of the states-general to the 10th of August. In the interior, the old constitutionalists, who had their sittings in the sections, and who consisted of the wealthy middle classes, had not the same views of monarchy with the absolute royalists. They still felt the rivalry and opposition of interest, natural to the middle against the privileged classes. The absolute royalists themselves did not agree; the party beaten in the interior had little sympathy with that enrolled among the armies of Europe; but besides the divisions between the emigrants and Vendéans, dissensions had arisen among the emigrants from the date of their departure from France. Meantime, all these royalists of different opinions, not having yet to contend for the reward of victory, came to an agreement to attack the convention in common. The emigrants and the priests, who for some months past had returned in great numbers, took the banner of the sections, quite certain, if they carried the day by means of the middle class, to establish their own government; for they had a leader, and a definite object, which the sectionaries had not.

This reaction, of a new character, was restrained for some time in Paris, where the convention, a strong and neutral power, wished to prevent the violence and usurpation of both parties. While overthrowing the sway of the Jacobins, it suppressed the vengeance of the royalists. Then it was that the greater part of *la troupe dorée* deserted its cause, that the leaders of the sections prepared the bourgeoisie to oppose the assembly, and that the confederation of the Journalists succeeded that of the Jacobins. La Harpe, Richer-de-Sérizy, Poncelin, Tronçon-du-Coudray, Marchéna, etc., became the organs of this new opinion, and were the literary clubists. The active but irregular troops of this party assembled at the Théâtre Feydeau. the Boulevard des Italiens, and the Palais Royal, and began *the chase of the Jacobins*, while they sang the *Réveil du Peuple*. The word of proscription, at that time, was Terrorist, in virtue of which an *honest man* might with good conscience attack a revolutionist. The Terrorist class was extended at the will or the passions of the new reactionaries, who wore their hair *à la victime*, and who, no longer fearing to avow their intentions, for some time past had adopted the Chouan uniform—a grey turned-back coat with a green or black collar.

But this reaction was much more ardent in the departments where there was no authority to interpose in the prevention of bloodshed. Here there were only two parties, that which had dominated and that which had suffered under the Mountain. The intermediate class was alternately governed by the royalists and by the democrats. The latter, foreseeing the terrible reprisals to which they would be subject if they fell, held out as long as they could; but their defeat at Paris led to their downfall in the departments. Party executions then took place, similar to those of the proconsuls of the committee of public safety. The south was, more especially, a prey to wholesale massacres and acts of personal vengeance. Societies, called *Compagnies de Jésus* and *Compagnies du Soleil*, which were of royalists origin, were organized, and executed terrible reprisals. At Lyons, Aix, Tarascon, and Marseilles, they slew in the prisons those who had taken part in the preceding régime. Nearly all the south had its 2nd of September. At Lyons, after the first revolutionary massacres, the members of the *compagnie* hunted out those who had not been taken; and when they met one, without any other form than the exclamation, "There's a Matavon," (the name given to them), they slew and threw him into the Rhone. At Tarascon, they threw them from the top of the tower on a rock on the bank of the Rhone. During this new reign of terror, and this general defeat of the revolutionists, England and the emigrants attempted the daring enterprise of Quiberon.

The Vendéans were exhausted by their repeated defeats, but they were not wholly reduced. Their losses, however, and the divisions between their principal leaders, Charette and Stofflet, rendered them an extremely feeble succour. Charette had even consented to treat with the republic, and a sort of pacification had been concluded between him and the convention at Jusnay. The marquis de Puisaye, an enterprising man, but volatile and more capable of intrigue than of vigorous party conceptions, intended to replace the almost expiring insurrection of La Vendée by that of Brittany. Since the enterprise of Wimpfen, in which Puisaye had a command, there already existed, in Calvados and Morbihan, bands of Chouans, composed of the remains of parties, adventurers, men without employment, and daring smugglers, who made expeditions, but were unable to keep the field, like the Vendéans. Puisaye had recourse to England to extend the *Chouanerie*, leading it to hope for a general rising in Brittany, and from thence in the rest of France, if it would land the nucleus of an army, with ammunition and guns.

The ministry of Great Britain, deceived as to the coalition, desired nothing better than to expose the republic to fresh perils, while it sought to revive the courage of Europe. It confided in Puisaye, and in the spring of 1795 prepared an expedition, in which the most energetic emigrants took a share, nearly all the officers of the former navy, and all who, weary of the part of exiles and of the distresses of a life of wandering, wished to try their fortunes for the last time.

The English fleet landed, on the peninsula of Quiberon, fifteen hundred emigrants, six thousand republican prisoners who had embraced the cause of the emigrants to return to France, sixty thousand muskets, and the full equipment for an army of forty thousand men. Fifteen hundred Chouans joined the army on its landing, but it was soon attacked by General Hoche. His attack proved successful; the republican prisoners who were in the ranks deserted, and it was defeated after a most energetic resistance. In the mortal warfare between the emigrants and the republic, the vanquished, being considered as *outlaws*, were mercilessly massacred. Their loss inflicted a deep and incurable wound on the emigrant party.

The hopes founded on the victories of Europe, on the progress of insurrection and the attempt of the emigrants, being thus overthrown, recourse was had to the discontented sections. It was hoped to make a counter-revolution by means of the new constitution decreed by the convention on the 22nd of August, 1795. This constitution was, indeed, the work of the moderate republican party; but as it restored the ascendancy of the middle class, the royalist leaders thought that by it they might easily enter the legislative body and the government.

This constitution was the best, the wisest, and most liberal, and the most provident that had as yet been established or projected; it contained the result of six years' revolutionary and legislative experience. At this period, the convention felt the necessity of organizing power, and of rendering the people settled, while the first assembly, from its position, only felt the necessity of weakening royalty and agitating the nation. All had been exhausted, from the throne to the people; existence now depended on reconstructing and restoring order, at the same time keeping the nation in great activity. The new constitution accomplished this. It differed but little from that of 1791, with respect to the exercise of sovereignty; but greatly in everything relative to government. It confided the legislative power to two councils; that of the *Cinq-cents* and that of the *Anciens*; and the executive power to a directory of five members. It restored the two degrees of elections destined to retard the popular movement, and to lead to a more enlightened choice than immediate elections. The wise but moderate qualifications with respect to property, required in the members of the primary assemblies and the electoral assemblies, again conferred political importance on the middle class, to which it became imperatively necessary to recur after the dismissal of the multitude and the abandonment of the constitution of '93.

In order to prevent the despotism or the servility of a single assembly, it was necessary to place somewhere a power to check or defend it. The division of the legislative body into two councils, which had the same origin, the same duration, and only differed in functions, attained the twofold object of not alarming the people by an aristocratic institution, and of contributing to the formation of a good government. The Council of Five Hundred, whose members were required to be thirty years old, was alone entrusted with the initiative and the discussion of laws. The Council of Ancients, composed of two hundred and fifty members, who had completed their fortieth year, was charged with adopting or rejecting them.

In order to avoid precipitation in legislative measures, and to prevent a compulsory sanction from the Council of Ancients in a moment of popular excitement, they could not come to a decision until after three readings, at a distance of five days at least from each other. In *urgent cases* this formality was dispensed with; and the council had the right of determining such urgency. This council acted sometimes as a legislative power, when it did not thoroughly approve a measure, and made use of the form *"Le Conseil des Anciens ne peut pas adopter,"* and sometimes as a conservative power, when it only considered a measure in its legal bearing, and said *"La Constitution annule."* For the first time, partial re-elections were adopted, and the renewing of half of the council every two years was fixed, in order to avoid that rush of legislators who came with an immoderate desire for innovation, and suddenly changed the spirit of an assembly.

The executive power was distinct from the councils, and no longer existed in the committees. Monarchy was still too much feared to admit of a president of the republic being named. They, therefore, confined themselves to the creation of a directory of five members, nominated by the council of ancients, at the recommendation of that of the Five Hundred. The directors might be brought to trial by the councils, but could not be dismissed by them. They were entrusted with a general and independent power of execution, but it was wished also to prevent their abusing it, and especially to guard against the danger of a long habit of authority leading to usurpation. They had the management of the armed force and of the finances; the nomination of functionaries, the conduct of negotiations, but they could do nothing of themselves; they had ministers and generals, for whose conduct they were responsible. Each member was president for three months, holding the seals and affixing his signature. Every year, one of the members was to go out. It will be seen by this account that the functions of royalty as they were in 1791, were shared by the council of ancients, who had the *veto*, and the directory, which held the executive power. The directory had a guard, a national palace, the Luxembourg, for a residence, and a kind of civil list. The council of the ancients, destined to check the encroachments of the legislative power, was invested with the means of restraining the usurpations of the directory; it could change the residence of the councils and of the government.

The foresight of this constitution was infinite: it prevented popular violence, the encroachments of power, and provided for all the perils which the different crises of the revolution had displayed. If any constitution could have become firmly established at that period, it was the directorial constitution. It restored authority, granted liberty, and offered the different parties an opportunity of peace, if each, sincerely renouncing exclusive dominion, and satisfied with the common right, would have taken its proper place in the state. But it did not last longer than the others, because it could not establish legal order in spite of parties. Each of them aspired to the government, in order to make its system and its interests prevail, and instead of the reign of law, it was still necessary to relapse into that of force, and of coups-d'état. When parties do not wish to terminate a revolution— and those who do not dominate never wish to terminate it—a constitution, however excellent it may be, cannot accomplish it.

The members of the Commission of Eleven, who, previously to the events of Prairial, had no other mission than to prepare the organic laws of the constitution of '93, and who, after those events, made the constitution of the year III., were at the head of the conventional party. This party neither belonged to the old Gironde nor to the old Mountain. Neutral up to the 31st of May, subject till the 9th Thermidor, it had been in the possession of power since that period, because the twofold defeat of the Girondists and the Mountain had left it the strongest. The men of the extreme sides, who had begun the fusion of parties, joined it. Merlin de Douai represented the party of that mass which had yielded to circumstances, Thibaudeau, the party that continued inactive, and Daunou, the courageous party. The latter had declared himself opposed to all coups-d'état, ever since the opening of the assembly, both the 21st of January, and to the 31st of May, because he wished for the régime of the convention, without party violence and measures. After the 9th Thermidor, he blamed the fury displayed towards the chiefs of the revolutionary government, whose victim he had been, as one of the *seventy-three*. He had obtained great ascendancy, as men gradually approached towards a legal system. His enlightened attachment to the revolution, his noble independence, the solidity and extent of his ideas, and his imperturbable fortitude, rendered him one of the most influential actors of this period. He was the chief author of the constitution of the year III., and the convention deputed him, with some others of its members, to undertake the defence of the republic, during the crisis of Vendémiaire.

The reaction gradually increased; it was indirectly favoured by the members of the Right, who, since the opening of that assembly, had only been incidentally republican. They were not prepared to repel the attacks of the royalists with the same energy as that of the revolutionists. Among this number were Boissy d'Anglas, Lanjuinais, Henri La Rivière, Saladin, Aubry, etc.; they formed in the assembly the nucleus of the sectionary party. Old and ardent members of the Mountain, such as Rovère, Bourdon de l'Oise, etc., carried away by the counter-revolutionary movement, suffered the reaction to be prolonged, doubtless in order to make their peace with those whom they had so violently combated.

But the conventional party, reassured with respect to the democrats, set itself to prevent the triumph of the royalists. It felt that the safety of the republic depended on the formation of the councils, and that the councils being elected by the middle class, which was directed by royalists, would be composed on counter-revolutionary principles. It was important to entrust the guardianship of the régime they were about to establish to those who had an interest in defending it. In order to avoid the error of the constituent assembly, which had excluded itself from the legislature that succeeded it, the convention decided by a decree, that two-thirds of its members should be re-elected. By this means it secured the majority of the councils and the nomination of the directory; it could accompany its constitution into the state, and consolidate it without violence. This re-election of two-thirds was not exactly legal, but it was politic, and the only means of saving France from the rule of the democrats or counter-revolutionists. The convention granted itself a moderate dictatorship, by the decrees of the 5th and 13th Fructidor (22nd and 30th of August, 1795), one of which established the re-election, and the other fixed the manner of it. But these two exceptional decrees were submitted to the ratification of the primary assemblies, at the same time as the constitutional act.

The royalist party was taken by surprise by the decrees of Fructidor. It hoped to form part of the government by the councils, of the councils by elections, and to effect a change of system when once in power. It inveighed against the convention. The royalist committee of Paris, whose agent was an obscure man, named Lemaître, the journalists, and the leaders of the sections coalesced. They had no difficulty in securing the support of public opinion, of which they were the only organs; they accused the convention of perpetuating its power, and of assailing the sovereignty of the people. The chief advocates of the two-thirds, Louvet, Daunou, and Chénier, were not spared, and every preparation was made for a grand movement. The Faubourg Saint Germain, lately almost deserted, gradually filled; emigrants flocked in, and the conspirators, scarcely concealing their plans, adopted the Chouan uniform.

The convention, perceiving the storm increase, sought support in the army, which, at that time, was the republican class, and a camp was formed at Paris. The people had been disbanded, and the royalists had secured the bourgeoisie. In the meantime, the primary assemblies met on the 20th Fructidor, to deliberate on the constitutional act, and the decrees of the two-thirds, which were to be accepted or rejected together. The Lepelletier section (formerly Filles Saint Thomas) was the centre of all the others. On a motion made by that section, it was decided that the power of all constituent authority ceased in the presence of the assembled people. The Lepelletier section, directed by Richer-Sérizy, La Harpe, Lacretelle junior, Vaublanc, etc., turned its attention to the organization of the insurrectional government, under the name of the central committee. This committee was to replace in Vendémiaire, against the convention, the committee of the 10th of August against the throne, and of the 31st of May against the Girondists. The majority of the sections adopted this measure, which was annulled by the convention, whose decree was in its turn rejected by the majority of the sections. The struggle now became open; and in Paris they separated the constitutional act, which was adopted, from the decrees of re-election, which were rejected.

On the 1st Vendémiaire, the convention proclaimed the acceptance of the decrees by the greater number of the primary assemblies of France. The sections assembled again to nominate the electors who were to choose the members of the legislature. On the 10th they determined that the electors should assemble in the Théâtre Français (it was then on the other side of the bridges); that they should be accompanied there by the armed force of the sections, after having sworn to defend them till death. On the 11th, accordingly, the electors assembled under the presidency of the duc de Nivernois, and the guard of some detachments of chasseurs and grenadiers.

The convention, apprised of the danger, sat permanently, stationed round its place of sitting the troops of the camp of Sablons, and concentrated its powers in a committee of five members, who were entrusted with all measures of public safety. These members were Colombel, Barras, Daunou, Letourneur, and Merlin de Douai. For some time the revolutionists had ceased to be feared, and all had been liberated who had been imprisoned for the events of Prairial. They enrolled, under the name of *Battalion of Patriots of '89*, about fifteen or eighteen hundred of them, who had been proceeded against, in the departments or in Paris, by the friends of the reaction. In the evening of the 11th, the convention sent to dissolve the assembly of electors by force, but they had already adjourned to the following day.

During the night of the 11th, the decree which dissolved the college of electors, and which armed the battalion of patriots of '89, caused the greatest agitation. Drums beat to arms; the Lepelletier section declaimed against the despotism of the convention, against the return of the *Reign of Terror*, and during the whole of the 12th prepared the other sections for the contest. In the evening, the convention, scarcely less agitated, decided on taking the initiative, by surrounding the conspiring section, and terminating the crisis by disarming it. Menou, general of the interior, and Laporte the representative, were entrusted with this mission. The convent of the Filles Saint Thomas was the headquarters of the sectionaries, before which they had seven or eight hundred men in battle array. These were surrounded by superior forces, from the Boulevards on each side, and the Rue Vivienne opposite. Instead of disarming them, the leaders of the expedition began to parley. Both parties agreed to withdraw; but the conventional troops had no sooner retired than the sectionaries returned reinforced. This was a complete victory for them, which being exaggerated in Paris, as such things always are, increased their number, and gave them courage to attack the convention the next day.

About eleven at night the convention learned the issue of the expedition and the dangerous effect which it had produced; it immediately dismissed Menou, and gave the command of the armed force to Barras, the general in command on the 9th Thermidor. Barras asked the committee of five to appoint as his second in command, a young officer who had distinguished himself at the siege of Toulon, but had been dismissed by Aubry of the reaction party; a young man of talent and resolution, calculated to do good service to the republic in a moment of peril. This young officer was Bonaparte. He appeared before the committee, but there was nothing in his appearance that announced his astonishing destiny. Not a man of party, summoned for the first time to this great scene of action, his demeanour exhibited a timidity and a want of assurance, which disappeared entirely in the preparations for battle, and in the heat of action. He immediately sent for the artillery of the camp of Sablons, and disposed them, with the five thousand men of the conventional army, on all the points from which the convention could be assailed. At noon on the 13th Vendémiaire, the enclosure of the convention had the appearance of a fortified place, which could only be taken by assault. The line of defence extended, on the left side of the Tuileries along the river, from the Pont Neuf to the Pont Louis XV.; on the right, in all the small streets opening on the Rue Saint Honoré, from the Rues de Rohan, de l'Échelle and the Cul-de-sac Dauphin, to the Place de la Révolution. In front, the Louvre, the Jardin de l'Infante, and the Carrousel were planted with cannon; and behind, the Pont Tournant and the Place de la Révolution formed a park of reserve. In this position the convention awaited the insurgents.

The latter soon encompassed it on several points. They had about forty thousand men under arms, commanded by generals Danican, Duhoux, and the ex-garde-du-corps Lafond. The thirty-two sections which formed the majority, had supplied their military contingent. Of the other sixteen, several sections of the faubourgs had their troops in the battalion of '89. A few, those of the Quinze-vingts and Montreuil, sent assistance during the action; others, though favourably disposed, as that of Popincourt, could not do so; and lastly, others remained neutral, like that of L'Indivisibilité. From two to three o'clock, general Carteaux, who occupied the Pont Neuf with four hundred men and two four-pounders, was surrounded by several columns of sectionaries, who obliged him to retire on the Louvre. This advantage emboldened the insurgents, who were strong on all points. General Danican summoned the convention to withdraw its troops, and disarm the terrorists. The officer entrusted with the summons was led into the assembly blindfold, and his message occasioned some agitation, several members declaring in favour of conciliatory measures. Boissy d'Anglas advised a conference with Danican; Gamon proposed a proclamation in which they should call upon the citizens to retire, promising then to disarm the battalion of '89. This address excited violent murmurs. Chénier rushed to the tribune. "I am surprised," said he, "that the demands of sections in a state of revolt should be discussed here. Negotiation must not be heard of; there is only victory or death for the national convention." Lanjuinais wished to support the address, by dwelling on the danger and misery of civil war; but the convention would not hear him, and on the motion of Fermond, passed to the order of the day. The debates respecting measures of peace or war with the sections were continued for some time, when, about half-past four several discharges of musketry were heard, which put an end to all discussion. Seven hundred guns were brought in, and the convention took arms as a body of reserve.

The conflict had now commenced in the Rue Saint Honoré, of which the insurgents were masters. The first shots were fired from the Hôtel de Noailles, and a murderous fire extended the whole length of this line. A few moments after, on the other side, two columns of sectionaries, about four thousand strong, commanded by the count de Maulevrier, advanced by the quays, and attacked the Pont Royal. The action then became general, but it could not last long; the place was too well defended to be taken by assault. After an hour's fighting, the sectionaries were driven from Saint Roch and Rue Saint Honoré, by the cannon of the convention and the battalion of patriots. The column of the Pont Royal received three discharges of artillery in front and on the side, from the bridge and the quays, which put it entirely to flight. At seven o'clock the conventional troops, victorious on all sides, took the offensive; by nine o'clock they had dislodged the sectionaries from the Théâtre de la République and the posts they still occupied in the neighbourhood of the Palais Royal. They prepared to make barricades during the night, and several volleys were fired in the Rue de la Loi (Richelieu), to prevent the works. The next day, the 14th, the troops of the convention disarmed the Lepelletier section, and compelled the others to return to order.

The assembly, which had only fought in its own defence, displayed much moderation. The 13th Vendémiaire was the 10th of August of the royalists against the republic, except that the convention resisted the bourgeoisie much better than the throne resisted the faubourgs. The position of France contributed very much to this victory. Men now wished for a republic without a revolutionary government, a moderate regime without a counter- revolution. The convention, which was a mediatory power, pronounced alike against the exclusive domination of the lower class, which it had thrown off in Prairial, and the reactionary domination of the bourgeoisie, which it repelled in Vendémiaire, seemed alone capable of satisfying this twofold want, and of putting an end to the state of warfare between the two parties, which was prolonged by their alternate entrance into the government.

This situation, as well as its own dangers, gave it courage to resist, and secured its triumph. The sections could not take it by surprise, and still less by assault.

After the events of Vendémiaire, the convention occupied itself with forming the councils and the directory. The third part, freely elected, had been favourable to reaction. A few conventionalists, headed by Tallien, proposed to annul the elections of this *third*, and wished to suspend, for a longer time, the conventional government. Thibaudeau exposed their design with much courage and eloquence. The whole conventional party adopted his opinion. It rejected all superfluous arbitrary sway, and showed itself impatient to leave the provisional state it had been in for the last three years. The convention established itself as a *national electoral assembly*, in order to complete the *two-thirds* from among its members. It then formed the councils; that of the *Ancients* of two hundred and fifty members, who according to the new law had completed forty years; that of *The Five Hundred* from among the others. The councils met in the Tuileries. They then proceeded to form the government.

The attack of Vendémiaire was quite recent; and the republican party, especially dreading the counter-revolution, agreed to choose the directors only, from the conventionalists, and further from among those of them who had voted for the death of the king. Some of the most influential members, among whom was Daunou, opposed this view, which restricted the choice, and continued to give the government a dictatorial and revolutionary character; but it prevailed. The conventionalists thus elected were La Réveillère-Lépaux, invested with general confidence on account of his courageous conduct on the 31st of May, for his probity and his moderation; Sieyès, the man who of all others enjoyed the greatest celebrity of the day; Rewbell, possessed of great administrative activity; Letourneur, one of the members of the commission of five during the last crisis; and Barras, chosen for his two pieces of good fortune of Thermidor and Vendémiaire. Sieyès, who had refused to take part in the legislative commission *of the eleven*, also refused to enter upon the directory. It is difficult to say whether this reluctance arose from calculation or an insurmountable antipathy for Rewbell. He was replaced by Carnot, the only member of the former committee whom they were disposed to favour, on account of his political purity, and his great share in the victories of the republic. Such was the first composition of the directory. On the 4th Brumaire, the convention passed a law of amnesty, in order to enter on legal government; changed the name of the Place de la Révolution into Place de la Concorde, and declared its session closed.

The convention lasted three years, from the 21st of September, 1792, to October 26, 1795 (4th Brumaire, year IV.). It took several directions. During the six first months of its existence it was drawn into the struggle which arose between the legal party of the Gironde, and the revolutionary party of the Mountain. The latter had the lead from the 31st of May, 1793, to the 9th Thermidor, year II. (26th July, 1794). The convention then obeyed the committee of public safety, which first destroyed its old allies of the commune and of the Mountain, and afterwards perished through its own divisions. From the 9th Thermidor to the month of Brumaire, year IV., the convention conquered the revolutionary and royalist parties, and sought to establish a moderate republic in opposition to both.

During this long and terrible period, the violence of the situation changed the revolution into a war, and the assembly into a field of battle. Each party wished to establish its sway by victory, and to secure it by founding its system. The Girondist party made the attempt, and perished; the Mountain made the attempt, and perished; the party of the commune made the attempt, and perished; Robespierre's party made the attempt, and perished. They could only conquer, they were unable to found a system. The property of such a storm was to overthrow everything that attempted to become settled. All was provisional; dominion, men, parties, and systems, because the only thing real and possible was—war. A year was necessary to enable the conventional party, on its return to power, to restore the revolution to a legal position; and it could only accomplish this by two victories—that of Prairial and that of Vendémiaire. But the convention having then returned to the point whence it started, and having discharged its true mission, which was to establish the republic after having defended it, disappeared from the theatre of the world which it had filled with surprise. A revolutionary power, it ceased as soon as legal order recommenced. Three years of dictatorship had been lost to liberty but not to the revolution.

THE EXECUTIVE DIRECTORY

CHAPTER XII

FROM THE INSTALLATION OF THE DIRECTORY, ON THE 27TH OCTOBER, 1795, TO THE COUP-D'ÉTAT OF THE 18TH FRUCTIDOR, YEAR V. (3RD AUGUST, 1797)

Review of the revolution—Its second character of reorganization; transition from public to private life—The five directors; their labours for the interior—Pacification of La Vendée—Conspiracy of Babeuf; final defeat of the democratic party—Plan of campaign against Austria; conquest of Italy by general Bonaparte; treaty of Campo-Formio; the French republic is acknowledged, with its acquisitions, and its connection with the Dutch, Lombard, and Ligurian republics, which prolonged its system in Europe— Royalist elections in the year V.; they alter the position of the republic—New contest between the counter-revolutionary party in the councils, in the club of Clichy, in the salons, and the conventional party, in the directory, the club of *Salm*, and the army—Coup d'état of the 18th Fructidor; the Vendémiaire party again defeated.

The French revolution, which had destroyed the old government, and thoroughly overturned the old society, had two wholly distinct objects; that of a free constitution, and that of a more perfect state of civilization. The six years we have just gone over were the search for government by each of the classes which composed the French nation. The privileged classes wished to establish their régime against the court and the bourgeoisie, by preserving the social orders and the states-general; the bourgeoisie sought to establish its régime against the privileged classes and the multitude, by the constitution of 1791; and the multitude wished to establish its régime against all the others, by the constitution of 1793. Not one of these governments could become consolidated, because they were all exclusive. But during their attempts, each class, in power for a time, destroyed of the higher classes all that was intolerant or calculated to oppose the progress of the new civilization.

When the directory succeeded the convention, the struggle between the classes was greatly weakened. The higher ranks of each formed a party which still contended for the possession and for the form of government; but the mass of the nation which had been so profoundly agitated from 1789 to 1795, longed to become settled again, and to arrange itself according to the new order of things. This period witnessed the end of the movement for liberty, and the beginning of the movement towards civilization. The revolution now took its second character, its character of order, foundation, repose, after the agitation, the immense toil, and system of complete demolition of its early years.

This second period was remarkable, inasmuch as it seemed a kind of abandonment of liberty. The different parties being no longer able to possess it in an exclusive and durable manner, became discouraged, and fell back from public into private life. This second period divided itself into two epochs: it was liberal under the directory and at the commencement of the Consulate, and military at the close of the Consulate and under the empire. The revolution daily grew more materialized; after having made a nation of sectaries, it made a nation of working men, and then it made a nation of soldiers.

Many illusions were already destroyed; men had passed through so many different states, had lived so much in so few years, that all ideas were confounded and all creeds shaken. The reign of the middle class and that of the multitude had passed away like a rapid phantasmagoria. They were far from that France of the 14th of July, with its deep conviction, its high morality, its assembly exercising the all-powerful sway of liberty and of reason, its popular magistracies, its citizen-guard, its brilliant, peaceable, and animated exterior, wearing the impress of order and independence. They were far from the more sombre and more tempestuous France of the 10th of August, when a single class held the government and society, and had introduced therein its language, manners, and costume, the agitation of its fears, the fanaticism of its ideas, the distrust of its position. Then private life entirely gave place to public life; the republic presented, in turn, the aspect of an assembly and of a camp; the rich were subject to the poor; the creed of democracy combined with the gloomy and ragged administration of the people. At each of these periods men had been strongly attached to some idea: first, to liberty and constitutional monarchy; afterwards, to equality, fraternity, and the republic. But at the beginning of the directory, there was belief in nothing; in the great shipwreck of parties, all had been lost, both the virtue of the bourgeoisie and the virtue of the people.

Men arose from this furious turmoil weakened and wounded, and each, remembering his political existence with terror, plunged wildly into the pleasures and relations of private life which had so long been suspended. Balls, banquets, debauchery, splendid carriages, became more fashionable than ever; this was the reaction of the ancient régime. The reign of the sans-culottes brought back the dominion of the rich; the clubs, the return of the salons. For the rest, it was scarcely possible but that the first symptom of the resumption of modern civilization should be thus irregular. The directorial manners were the product of another society, which had to appear again before the new state of society could regulate its relations, and constitute its own manners. In this transition, luxury would give rise to labour, stock-jobbing to commerce; salons bring parties together who could not approximate except in private life; in a word, civilization would again usher in liberty.

The situation of the republic was discouraging at the installation of the directory. There existed no element of order or administration. There was no money in the public treasury; couriers were often delayed for want of the small sum necessary to enable them to set out. In the interior, anarchy and uneasiness were general; paper currency, in the last stage of discredit, destroyed confidence and commerce; the dearth became protracted, every one refusing to part with his commodities, for it amounted to giving them away; the arsenals were exhausted or almost empty. Without, the armies were destitute of baggage-wagons, horses, and supplies; the soldiers were in want of clothes, and the generals were often unable to liquidate their pay of eight francs a month in specie, an indispensable supplement, small as it was, to their pay in assignats; and lastly, the troops, discontented and undisciplined, on account of their necessities, were again beaten, and on the defensive.

Things were at this state of crisis after the fall of the committee of public safety. This committee had foreseen the dearth, and prepared for it, both in the army and in the interior, by the requisitions and the *maximum*. No one had dared to exempt himself from this financial system, which rendered the wealthy and commercial classes tributary to the soldiers and the multitude, and at that time provisions had not been withheld from the market. But since violence and confiscation had ceased, the people, the convention, and the armies were at the mercy of the landed proprietors and speculators, and terrible scarcity existed, a reaction against the *maximum*. The system of the convention had consisted, in political economy, in the consumption of an immense capital, represented by the assignats. This assembly had been a rich government, which had ruined itself in defending the revolution. Nearly half the French territory, consisting of domains of the crown, ecclesiastical property, or the estates of the emigrant nobility, had been sold, and the produce applied to the support of the people, who did little labour, and to the external defence of the republic by the armies. More than eight milliards of assignats had been issued before the 9th Thermidor, and since that period thirty thousand millions had been added to that sum, already so enormous. Such a system could not be continued; it was necessary to begin the work again, and return to real money.

The men deputed to remedy this great disorganization were, for the most part, of ordinary talent; but they set to work with zeal, courage, and good sense. "When the directors," said M. Bailleul,[7] "entered the Luxembourg, there was not an article of furniture. In a small room, at a little broken table, one leg of which was half eaten away with age, on which they placed some letter-paper and a calumet standish, which they had fortunately brought from the committee of public safety, seated on four straw-bottom chairs, opposite a few logs of dimly-burning wood, the whole borrowed from Dupont, the porter; who would believe that it was in such a condition that the members of the new government, after having investigated all the difficulties, nay, all the horror of their position, resolved that they

[7] *Examen Critique des Considérations de Madame de Staël, sur la Révolution Française,* by M. J. Ch. Bailleul, vol. ii., pp. 275, 281.

would face all obstacles, and that they would either perish or rescue France from the abyss into which she had fallen? On a sheet of writing-paper they drew up the act by which they ventured to declare themselves constituted; an act which they immediately despatched to the legislative chambers."

The directors then proceeded to divide their labours, taking as their guide the grounds which had induced the constitutional party to select them. Rewbell, possessed of great energy, a lawyer versed in government and diplomacy, had assigned to him the departments of law, finance, and foreign affairs. His skill and commanding character soon made him the moving spirit of the directory in all civil matters. Barras had no special knowledge; his mind was mediocre, his resources few, his habits indolent. In an hour of danger, his resolution qualified him to execute sudden measures, like those of Thermidor or Vendémiaire. But being, on ordinary occasions, only adapted for the surveillance of parties, the intrigues of which he was better acquainted with than any one else, the police department was allotted to him. He was well suited for the task, being supple and insinuating, without partiality for any political sect, and having revolutionary connexions by his past life, while his birth gave him access to the aristocracy. Barras took on himself the representation of the directory, and established a sort of republican regency at the Luxembourg. The pure and moderate La Réveillère, whose gentleness tempered with courage, whose sincere attachment for the republic and legal measures, had procured him a post in the directory, with the general consent of the assembly and public opinion, had assigned to him the moral department, embracing education, the arts, sciences, manufactures, etc. Letourneur, an ex-artillery officer, member of the committee of public safety at the latter period of the convention, had been appointed to the war department. But when Carnot was chosen, on the refusal of Sieyès, he assumed the direction of military operations, and left to his colleague Letourneur the navy and the colonies. His high talents and resolute character gave him the upper hand in the direction. Letourneur attached himself to him, as La Réveillère to Rewbell, and Barras was between the two. At this period, the directors turned their attention with the greatest concord to the improvement and welfare of the state.

The directors frankly followed the route traced out for them by the constitution. After having established authority in the centre of the republic, they organized it in the departments, and established, as well as they could, a correspondence of design between local administrations and their own. Placed between the two exclusive and dissatisfied parties of Prairial and Vendémiaire, they endeavoured, by a decided line of conduct, to subject them to an order of things, holding a place midway between their extreme pretensions. They sought to revive the enthusiasm and order of the first years of the revolution. "You, whom we summon to share our labours," they wrote to their agents, "you who have, with us, to promote the progress of the republican constitution, your first virtue, your first feeling, should be that decided resolution, that patriotic faith, which has also produced its enthusiasts and its miracles. All will be achieved when, by your care, that sincere love of liberty which sanctified the dawn of the revolution, again animates the heart of every Frenchman. The banners of liberty floating on every house, and the republican device written on every door, doubtless form an interesting sight. Obtain more; hasten the day when the sacred name of the republic shall be graven voluntarily on every heart."

In a short time, the wise and firm proceedings of the new government restored confidence, labour, and plenty. The circulation of provisions was secured, and at the end of a month the directory was relieved from the obligation to provide Paris with supplies, which it effected for itself. The immense activity created by the revolution began to be directed towards industry and agriculture. A part of the population quitted the clubs and public places for workshops and fields; and then the benefit of a revolution, which, having destroyed corporations, divided property, abolished privileges, increased fourfold the means of civilization, and was destined to produce prodigious good to France, began to be felt. The directory encouraged this movement in the direction of labour by salutary institutions. It re-established public exhibitions of the produce of industry, and improved the system of education decreed under the convention. The national institute, primary, central, and normal schools, formed a complete system of republican institutions. La Réveillère, the director intrusted with the moral department of the government, then sought to establish, under the name of *Theophilanthropie*, the deistical religion which the committee of public safety had vainly endeavoured to establish by the *Fête à l'Etre Suprême*. He provided temples, hymns, forms, and a kind of liturgy, for the new religion; but such a faith could only be individual, could not long continue public. The *theophilanthropists*, whose religion was opposed to the political opinions and the unbelief of the revolutionists, were much ridiculed. Thus, in the passage from public institutions to individual faith, all that had been liberty became civilization, and what had been religion became opinion. Deists remained, but *theophilanthropists* were no longer to be met with.

The directory, pressed for money, and shackled by the disastrous state of the finances, had recourse to measures somewhat extraordinary. It had sold or pledged the most valuable articles of the Wardrobe, in order to meet the greatest urgencies. National property was still left; but it sold badly, and for assignats. The directory proposed a compulsory loan, which was decreed by the councils. This was a relic of the revolutionary measures with regard to the rich; but, having been irresolutely adopted, and executed without due authority, it did not succeed. The directory then endeavoured to revive paper money; it proposed the issue of *mandats territoriaux*, which were to be substituted for the assignats then in circulation, at the rate of thirty for one, and to take the place of money. The councils decreed the issue of *mandats territoriaux* to the amount of two thousand four hundred millions. They had the advantage of being exchangeable at once and upon presentation, for the national domains which represented them. Their sale was very extensive, and in this way was completed the revolutionary mission of the assignats, of which they were the second period. They procured the directory a momentary resource; but they also lost their credit, and led insensibly to bankruptcy, which was the transition from paper to specie.

The military situation of the republic was not a brilliant one; at the close of the convention there had been an abatement of victories. The equivocal position and weakness of the central authority, as much as the scarcity, had relaxed the discipline of the troops. The generals, too, disappointed that they had distinguished their command by so few victories, and were not spurred on by an energetic government, became inclined to insubordination. The convention had deputed Pichegru and Jourdan, one at the head of the army of the Rhine, the other with that of the Sambre-et-Meuse, to surround and capture Mayence, in order that they might occupy the whole line of the Rhine. Pichegru made this project completely fail; although possessing the entire confidence of the republic, and enjoying the greatest military fame of the day, he formed counter-revolutionary schemes with the prince of Condé; but they were unable to agree. Pichegru urged the emigrant prince to enter France with his troops, by Switzerland or the Rhine, promising to remain inactive, the only thing in his power to do in favour of such an attempt. The prince required as a preliminary, that Pichegru should hoist the white flag in his army, which was, to a man, republican. This hesitation, no doubt, injured the projects of the reactionists, who were preparing the conspiracy of Vendémiaire. But Pichegru wishing, one way or the other, to serve his new allies and to betray his country, allowed himself to be defeated at Heidelberg, compromised the army of Jourdan, evacuated Mannheim, raised the siege of Mayence with considerable loss, and exposed that frontier to the enemy.

The directory found the Rhine open towards Mayence, the war of La Vendée rekindled; the coasts of France and Holland threatened with a descent from England; lastly, the army of Italy destitute of everything, and merely maintaining the defensive under Schérer and Kellermann. Carnot prepared a new plan of campaign, which was to carry the armies of the republic to the very heart of the hostile states. Bonaparte, appointed general of the interior after the events of Vendémiaire, was placed at the head of the army of Italy; Jourdan retained the command of the army of the Sambre-et- Meuse, and Moreau had that of the army of the Rhine, in place of Pichegru. The latter, whose treason was suspected by the directory, though not proved, was offered the embassy to Sweden, which he refused, and retired to Arbois, his native place. The three great armies, placed under the orders of Bonaparte, Jourdan, and Moreau, were to attack the Austrian monarchy by Italy and Germany, combine at the entrance of the Tyrol and march upon Vienna, in echelon. The generals prepared to execute this vast movement, the success of which would make the republic mistress of the headquarters of the coalition on the continent.

The directory gave to general Hoche the command of the coast, and deputed him to conclude the Vendéan war. Hoche changed the system of warfare adopted by his predecessors. La Vendée was disposed to submit. Its previous victories had not led to the success of its cause; defeat and ill-fortune had exposed it to plunder and conflagration. The insurgents, irreparably injured by the disaster of Savenay, by the loss of their principal leader, and their best soldiers, by the devastating system of the infernal columns, now desired nothing more than to live on good terms with the republic. The war now depended only on a few chiefs, upon Charette, Stofflet, etc. Hoche saw that it was necessary to wean the masses from these men by concessions, and then to crush them. He skilfully separated the royalist cause from the cause of religion, and employed the priests against the generals, by showing great indulgence to the catholic religion. He had the country scoured by four powerful columns, took their cattle from the inhabitants, and only restored them in return for their arms. He left no repose to the armed party, defeated Charette in several encounters, pursued him from one retreat to another, and at last made him prisoner. Stofflet wished to raise the Vendéan standard again on his territory; but it was given up to the republicans. These two chiefs, who had witnessed the beginning of the insurrection, were present at its close. They died courageously; Stofflet at Angers, Charette at Nantes, after having displayed character and talents worthy of a larger theatre. Hoche likewise tranquillized Brittany. Morbihan was occupied by numerous bands of Chouans, who formed a formidable association, the principal leader of which was George Cadoudal. Without entering on a campaign, they were mastering the country. Hoche directed all his force and activity against them, and before long had destroyed or exhausted them. Most of their leaders quitted their arms, and took refuge in England. The directory, on learning these fortunate pacifications, formally announced to both councils, on the 28th Messidor (June, 1796), that this civil war was definitively terminated.

In this manner the winter of the year IV. passed away. But the directory could hardly fail to be attacked by the two parties, whose sway was prevented by its existence, the democrats and the royalists. The former constituted an inflexible and enterprising sect. For them, the 9th Thermidor was an era of pain and oppression: they desired to establish absolute equality, in spite of the state of society, and democratic liberty, in spite of civilization. This sect had been so vanquished as effectually to prevent its return to power. On the 9th Thermidor it had been driven from the government; on the 2nd Prairial, from society; and it had lost both power and insurrections. But though disorganized and proscribed, it was far from having disappeared. After the unfortunate attempt of the royalists in Vendémiaire, it arose through their abasement.

The democrats re-established their club at the Panthéon, which the directory tolerated for some time. They had for their chief, "Gracchus" Babeuf, who styled himself the "Tribune of the people." He was a daring man, of an exalted imagination, an extraordinary fanaticism of democracy, and with great influence over his party. In his journal, he prepared the reign of general happiness. The society at the Panthéon daily became more numerous, and more alarming to the directory who at first endeavoured to restrain it. But the sittings were soon protracted to an advanced hour of the night; the democrats repaired thither in arms, and proposed marching against the directory and the councils. The directory determined to oppose them openly. On the 8th Ventôse, year IV. (February, 1796), it closed the society of the Panthéon, and on the 9th, by a message informed the legislative body that it had done so.

The democrats, deprived of their place of meeting, had recourse to another plan. They seduced the police force, which was chiefly composed of deposed revolutionists; and in concert with it, they were to destroy the constitution of the year III. The directory, informed of this new manoeuvre, disbanded the police force, causing it to be disarmed by other troops on whom it could rely. The conspirators, taken by surprise a second time, determined on a project of attack and insurrection: they formed an insurrectionary committee of public safety, which communicated by secondary agents with the lower orders of the twelve communes of Paris. The members of this principal committee were Babeuf, the chief of the conspiracy, ex-conventionalists, such as Vadier, Amar, Choudieu, Ricord, the representative Drouet, the former generals of the decemviral committee, Rossignol, Parrein, Fyon, Lami. Many cashiered officers, patriots of the departments, and the old Jacobin mass, composed the army of this faction. The chiefs often assembled in a place they called the Temple of Reason; here they sang lamentations on the death of Robespierre, and deplored the slavery of the people. They opened a negotiation with the troops of the camp of Grenelle, admitted among them a captain of that camp, named Grisel, whom they supposed their own, and concerted every measure for the attack.

Their plan was to establish common happiness; and for that purpose, to make a distribution of property, and to cause the government of true, pure, and absolute democrats to prevail; to create a convention composed of sixty-eight members of the Mountain, the remnant of the numbers proscribed since the reaction of Thermidor, and to join with these a democrat for each department; lastly, to start from the different quarters in which they had distributed themselves, and march at the same time against the directory and against the councils. On the night of the insurrection, they were to fix up two placards; one, containing the words, "The Constitution of 1793! liberty! equality! common happiness!" the other, containing the following declaration, "Those who usurp the sovereignty, ought to be put to death by free men." All was ready; the proclamations printed, the day appointed, when they were betrayed by Grisel, as generally happens in conspiracies.

On the 21st Floréal (May), the eve of the day fixed for the attack, the conspirators were seized at their regular place of meeting. In Babeuf's house were found a plan of the plot and all the documents connected with it. The directory apprised the councils of it by a message, and announced it to the people by proclamation. This strange attempt, savouring so strongly of fanaticism, and which could only be a repetition of the insurrection of Prairial, without its means and its hopes of success, excited the greatest terror. The public mind was still terrified with the recent domination of the Jacobins.

Babeuf, like a daring conspirator, prisoner as he was, proposed terms of peace to the directory:—

"Would you consider it beneath you, citizen directors," he wrote to them, "to treat with me, as power with power? You have seen what vast confidence centres in me; you have seen that my party may well balance equally in the scale your own; you have seen its immense ramifications. I am convinced you have trembled at the sight." He concluded by saying: "I see but one wise mode of proceeding; declare there has been no serious conspiracy. Five men, by showing themselves great and generous may now save the country. I will answer for it, that the patriots will defend you with their lives; the patriots do not hate you; they only hated your unpopular measures. For my part, I will give you a guarantee as extensive as is my perpetual franchise." The directors, instead of this reconciliation, published

Babeuf's letter, and sent the conspirators before the high court of Vendôme.

Their partisans made one more attempt. On the 13th Fructidor (August), about eleven at night, they marched, to the number of six or seven hundred, armed with sabres and pistols, against the directory, whom they found defended by its guard. They then repaired to the camp of Grenelle, which they hoped to gain over by means of a correspondence which they had established with it. The troops had retired to rest when the conspirators arrived. To the sentinel's cry of *"Qui vive?"* they replied: *"Vive la république! Vive la constitution de '93!"* The sentinels gave the alarm through the camp. The conspirators, relying on the assistance of a battalion from Gard, which had been disbanded, advanced towards the tent of Malo, the commander-in-chief, who gave orders to sound to arms, and commanded his half-dressed dragoons to mount. The conspirators, surprised at this reception, feebly defended themselves: they were cut down by the dragoons or put to flight, leaving many dead and prisoners on the field of battle. This ill-fated expedition was almost the last of the party: with each defeat it lost its force, its chiefs, and acquired the secret conviction that its reign was over. The Grenelle enterprise proved most fatal to it; besides the numbers slain in the fight, many were condemned to death by the military commissions, which were to it what the revolutionary tribunals had been to its foes. The commission of the camp of Grenelle, in five sittings, condemned one-and-thirty conspirators to death, thirty to transportation, and twenty-five to imprisonment.

Shortly afterwards the high court of Vendôme tried Babeuf and his accomplices, among whom were Amar, Vadier, and Darthé, formerly secretary to Joseph Lebon. They none of them belied themselves; they spoke as men who feared neither to avow their object, nor to die for their cause. At the beginning and the end of each sitting, they sang the *Marseillaise*. This old song of victory, and their firm demeanour, struck the public mind with astonishment, and seemed to render them still more formidable. Their wives accompanied them to the trial, Babeuf, at the close of his defence, turned to them, and said, *"they should accompany them even to Calvary, because the cause of their punishment would not bring them to shame."* The high court condemned Babeuf and Darthé to death: as they heard their sentence they both stabbed themselves with a poignard. Babeuf was the last leader of the old commune and the committee of public safety, which had separated previous to Thermidor, and which afterwards united again. This party decreased daily. Its dispersal and isolation more especially date from this period. Under the reaction, it still formed a compact mass; under Babeuf, it maintained the position of a formidable association. From that time democrates existed, but the party was broken up.

In the interim between the Grenelle enterprise and Babeuf's condemnation, the royalists also formed their conspiracy. The projects of the democrats produced a movement of opinion, contrary to that which had been manifested after Vendémiaire, and the counter-revolutionists in their turn became emboldened. The secret chiefs of this party hoped to find auxiliaries in the troops of the camp of Grenelle, who had repelled the Babeuf faction. This party, impatient and unskilful, unable to employ the whole of the sectionaries, as in Vendémiaire, or the mass of the councils, as on the 18th Fructidor, made use of three men without either name or influence: the abbé Brothier, the ex-counsellor of parliament, Lavilheurnois, and a sort of adventurer, named Dunan. They applied at once, in all simplicity, to Malo for the camp of Grenelle, in order by its means to restore the ancient régime. Malo delivered them up to the directory, who transferred them to the civil tribunals, not having been able, as he wished, to have them tried by military commissioners. They were treated with much consideration by judges of their party, elected under the influence of Vendémiaire, and the sentence pronounced against them was only a short imprisonment. At this period, a contest arose between all the authorities appointed by the sections, and the directory supported by the army; each taking its strength and judges wherever its party prevailed; the result was, that the electoral power placing itself at the disposition of the counter-revolution, the directory was compelled to introduce the army in the state; which afterwards gave rise to serious inconvenience.

The directory, triumphant over the two dissentient parties, also triumphed over Europe. The new campaign opened under the most favourable auspices. Bonaparte, on arriving at Nice, signalised his command by one of the most daring of invasions. Hitherto his army had hovered idly on the side of the Alps; it was destitute of everything, and scarcely amounted to thirty thousand men; but it was well provided with courage and patriotism; and, by their means, Bonaparte then commenced that world-astonishment by which he carried all before him for twenty years. He broke up the cantonments, and entered the valley of Savona, in order to march into Italy between the Alps and the Apennines. There were before him ninety thousand troops of the coalition, commanded in the centre by Argentau, by Colle on the left, and Beaulieu on the right. This immense army was dispersed in a few days by prodigies of genius and courage. Bonaparte overthrew the centre at Montenotte, and entered Piedmont; at Millesimo he entirely separated the Sardinian from the Austrian army. They hastened to defend Turin and Milan, the capitals of their domination. Before pursuing the Austrians, the republican general threw himself on the left, to cut off the Sardinian army. The fate of Piedmont was decided at Mondovi, and the terrified court of Turin hastened to submit. At Cherasco an armistice was concluded, which was soon afterwards followed by a treaty of peace, signed at Paris, on the 18th of May, 1796, between the republic and the king of Sardinia, who ceded Savoy and the counties of Nice and Tenda. The occupation of Alessandria, which opened the Lombard country; the demolition of the fortresses of Susa, and of Brunette, on the borders of France; the abandonment of the territory of Nice, and of Savoy, and the rendering available the other army of the Alps, under Kellermann, was the reward of a fortnight's campaign, and six victories.

War being over with Piedmont, Bonaparte marched against the Austrian army, to which he left no repose. He passed the Po at Piacenza, and the Adda at Lodi. The latter victory opened the gates of Milan, and secured him the possession of Lombardy. General Beaulieu was driven into the defiles of Tyrol by the republican army, which invested Mantua, and appeared on the mountains of the empire. General Wurmser came to replace Beaulieu, and a new army was sent to join the wrecks of the conquered one. Wurmser advanced to relieve Mantua, and once more make Italy the field of battle; but he was overpowered, like his predecessor, by Bonaparte, who, after having raised the blockade of Mantua, in order to oppose this new enemy, renewed it with increased vigour, and resumed his positions in Tyrol. The plan of invasion was executed with much union and success. While the army of Italy threatened Austria by Tyrol, the two armies of the Meuse and Rhine entered Germany; Moreau, supported by Jourdan on his left, was ready to join Bonaparte on his right. The two armies had passed the Rhine at Neuwied and Strasburg, and had advanced on a front, drawn up in echelons to the distance of sixty leagues, driving back the enemy, who, while retreating before them, strove to impede their march and break their line. They had almost attained the aim of their enterprise; Moreau had entered Ulm and Augsburg, crossed the Leek, and his advanced guard was on the extreme of the defiles of Tyrol, when Jourdan, from a misunderstanding, passed beyond the line, was attacked by the archduke Charles, and completely routed. Moreau, exposed on his left wing, was reduced to the necessity of retracing his steps, and he then effected his memorable retreat. The fault of Jourdan was a capital one: it prevented the success of this vast plan of campaign, and gave respite to the Austrian government.

The cabinet of Vienna, which had lost Belgium in this war, and which felt the importance of preserving Italy, defended it with the greatest obstinacy. Wurmser, after a new defeat, was obliged to throw himself into Mantua with the wreck of his army. General Alvinzy, at the head of fifty thousand Hungarians, now came to try his fortune, but was not more successful than Beaulieu or Wurmser. New victories were added to the wonders already achieved by the army of Italy, and secured the conquest of that country. Mantua capitulated; the republican troops, masters of Italy, took the route to Vienna across the mountains. Bonaparte had before him prince Charles, the last hope of Austria. He soon passed through the defiles of Tyrol, and entered the plains of Germany. In the meantime, the army of the Rhine under Moreau, and that of the Meuse under Hoche, successfully resumed the plan of the preceding campaign; and the cabinet of Vienna, in a state of alarm, concluded the truce of Leoben. It had exhausted all its force, and tried all its generals, while the French republic was in the full vigour of conquest.

The army of Italy accomplished in Europe the work of the French revolution. This wonderful campaign was owing to the union of a general of genius, and an intelligent army. Bonaparte had for lieutenants generals capable of commanding themselves, who knew how to take upon themselves the responsibility of a movement of a battle, and an army of citizens all possessing cultivated minds, deep feeling, strong emulation of all that is great; passionately attached to a revolution which aggrandized their country, preserved their independence under discipline, and which afforded an opportunity to every soldier of becoming a general. There is nothing which a leader of genius might not accomplish with such men. He must have regretted, at this recollection of his earlier years, that he ever centred in himself all liberty and intelligence, that he ever created mechanical armies and generals only fit to obey. Bonaparte began the third epoch of the war. The campaign of 1792 had been made on the old system, with dispersed corps, acting separately without abandoning their fixed line. The committee of public safety concentrated the corps, made them operate no longer merely on what was before them, but at a distance; it hastened their movement, and directed them towards a common end. Bonaparte did for each battle what the committee had done for each campaign. He brought all these corps on the determinate point, and destroyed several armies with a single one by the rapidity of his measures. He disposed of whole masses of troops at his pleasure, moved them here or there, brought them forward, or kept them out of sight, had them wholly at his disposition, when, where, and how he pleased, whether to occupy a position or to gain a battle. His diplomacy was as masterly as his military science.

All the Italian governments, except Venice and Genoa, had adhered to the coalition, but the people were in favour of the French republic. Bonaparte relied on the latter. He abolished Piedmont, which he could not conquer; transformed the Milanese, hitherto dependent on Austria, into the *Cisalpine Republic*; he weakened Tuscany and the petty princes of Parma and Modena by contributions, without dispossessing them; the pope, who had signed a truce on Bonaparte's first success against Beaulieu, and who did not hesitate to infringe it on the arrival of Wurmser, bought peace by yielding Romagna, Bologna, and Ferrara, which were joined to the Cisalpine republic; lastly, the aristocracy of Venice and Genoa having favoured the coalition, and raised an insurrection in the rear of the army, their government was changed, and Bonaparte made it democratic, in order to oppose the power of the people to that of the nobility. In this way the revolution penetrated into Italy.

Austria, by the preliminaries of Leoben, ceded Belgium to France, and recognised the Lombard republic. All the allied powers had laid down their arms, and even England asked to treat. France, peaceable and free at home, had on her borders attained her natural limits, and was surrounded with rising republics, such as Holland, Lombardy, and Liguria, which guarded her sides and extended her system in Europe. The coalition was little disposed to assail anew a revolution, all the governments of which were victorious; that of anarchy after the 10th of August, of the dictatorship after the 31st of May, and of legal authority under the directory; a revolution, which, at every new hostility, advanced a step further upon European territory. In 1792, it had only extended to Belgium; in 1794, it had reached Holland and the Rhine; in 1796, had reached Italy, and entered Germany. If it continued its progress, the coalition had reason to fear that it would carry its conquests further. Everything seemed prepared for general peace.

But the situation of the directory was materially changed by the elections of the year V. (May, 1797). These elections, by introducing, in a legal way, the royalist party into the legislature and government, brought again into question what the conflict of Vendémiaire had decided. Up to this period, a good understanding had existed between the directory and the councils. Composed of conventionalists, united by a common interest, and the necessity of establishing the republic, after having been blown about by the winds of all parties, they had manifested much good-will in their intercourse, and much union in their measures. The councils had yielded to the various demands of the directory; and, with the exception of a few slight modifications, they had approved its projects concerning the finance and the administration, its conduct with regard to the conspiracies, the armies, and

Europe. The anti-conventional minority had formed an opposition in the councils; but this opposition, while waiting the reinforcement of a new third, had but cautiously contended against the policy of the directory. At its head were Barbé-Marbois, Pastoret, Vaublanc, Dumas, Portalis, Siméon, Tronçon-Ducoudray, Dupont de Nemours, most of them members of the Right in the legislative assembly, and some of them avowed royalists. Their position soon became less equivocal and more aggressive, by the addition of those members elected in the year V.

The royalists formed a formidable and active confederation, having its leaders, agents, budgets, and journals. They excluded republicans from the elections, influenced the masses, who always follow the most energetic party, and whose banner they momentarily assume. They would not even admit patriots of the first epoch, and only elected decided counter- revolutionists or equivocal constitutionalists. The republican party was then placed in the government and in the army; the royalist party in the electoral assemblies and the councils.

On the 1st Prairial, year V. (20th May), the two councils opened their sittings. From the beginning they manifested the spirit which actuated them. Pichegru, whom the royalists transferred on to the new field of battle of the counter-revolution, was enthusiastically elected president of the council *des jeunes*. Barbé-Marbois had given him, with the same eagerness, the presidentship of the elder council. The legislative body proceeded to appoint a director to replace Letourneur, who, on the 30th Floréal, had been fixed on by ballot as the retiring member. Their choice fell on Barthélemy, the ambassador to Switzerland, whose moderate views and attachment to peace suited the councils and Europe, but who was scarcely adapted for the government of the republic, owing to his absence from France during all the revolution.

These first hostilities against the directory and the conventional party were followed by more actual attacks. Its administration and policy were now attacked without scruple. The directory had done all it had been able to do by a legal government in a situation still revolutionary. It was blamed for continuing the war and for the disorder of the financial department. The legislative majority skilfully turned its attention to the public wants; it supported the entire liberty of the press, which allowed journalists to attack the directory, and to prepare the way for another system; it supported peace because it would lead to the disarming of the republic, and lastly, it supported economy.

These demands were in one sense useful and national. France was weary, and felt the need of all these things in order to complete its social restoration; accordingly, the nation half adopted the views of the royalists, but from entirely different motives. It saw with rather more anxiety the measures adopted by the councils relative to priests and emigrants. A pacification was desired; but the nation did not wish that the conquered foes of the revolution should return triumphant. The councils passed the laws with regard to them with great precipitation. They justly abolished the sentence of transportation or imprisonment against priests for matters of religion or incivism; but they wished to restore the ancient prerogatives of their form of worship; to render Catholicism, already re-established, outwardly manifest by the use of bells, and to exempt priests from the oath of public functionaries. Camille Jordan, a young Lyonnais deputy, full of eloquence and courage, but professing unreasonable opinions, was the principal panegyrist of the clergy in the younger council. The speech which he delivered on this subject excited great surprise and violent opposition. The little enthusiasm that remained was still entirely patriotic, and all were astonished at witnessing the revival of another enthusiasm, that of religion: the last century and the revolution had made men entirely unaccustomed to it, and prevented them from understanding it. This was the moment when the old party revived its creed, introduced its language, and mingled them with the creed and language of the reform party, which had hitherto prevailed alone. The result was, as is usual with all that is unexpected, an unfavourable and ridiculous impression against Camille Jordan, who was nicknamed *Jordan-Carillon, Jordan-les-Cloches*. The attempt of the protectors of the clergy did not, however, succeed; and the council of five hundred did not venture as yet to pass a decree for the use of bells, or to make the priests independent. After some hesitation, the moderate party joined the directorial party, and supported the civic oath with cries of "Vive la République!"

Meantime, hostilities continued against the directory, especially in the council of five hundred, which was more zealous and impatient than that of the ancients. All this greatly emboldened the royalist faction in the interior. The counter-revolutionary reprisals against the *patriots*, and those who had acquired national property, were renewed. Emigrant and dissentient priests returned in crowds, and being unable to endure anything savouring of the revolution, they did not conceal their projects for its overthrow. The directorial authority, threatened in the centre, and disowned in the departments, became wholly powerless.

But the necessity of defence, the anxiety of all men who were devoted to the directory, and especially to the revolution, gave courage and support to the government. The aggressive progress of the councils brought their attachment to the republic into suspicion; and the mass, which had at first supported, now forsook them. The constitutionalists of 1791, and the directorial party formed an alliance. The club of *Salm*, established under the auspices of this alliance, was opposed to the club of *Clichy*, which for a long time had been the rendezvous of the most influential members of the councils. The directory, while it had recourse to opinion, did not neglect its principal force—the support of the troops. It brought near Paris several regiments of the army of the Sambre-et-Meuse, commanded by Hoche. The constitutional radius of six myriametres (twelve leagues), which the troops could not legally pass, was violated: and the councils denounced this violation to the directory, which feigned an ignorance, wholly disbelieved, and made very weak excuses.

The two parties were watching each other. One had its posts at the directory, at the club of *Salm*, and in the army, the other, in the councils, at *Clichy*, and in the *salons* of the royalists. The mass were spectators. Each of the two parties was disposed to act in a revolutionary manner towards the other. An intermediate constitutional and conciliatory party tried to prevent the struggle, and to bring about an union, which was altogether impossible. Carnot was at its head: a few members of the younger council, directed by Thibaudeau, and a tolerably large number of the Ancients, seconded his projects of moderation. Carnot, who, at that period, was the director of the constitution, with Barthélemy, who was the director of the legislature, formed a minority in the government. Carnot, very austere in his conduct and very obstinate in his views, could not agree either with Barras or with the imperious Rewbell. To this opposition of character was then added difference of system. Barras and Rewbell, supported by La Réveillère, were not at all averse to a coup-d'état against the councils, while Carnot wished strictly to follow the law. This great citizen, at each epoch of the revolution, had perfectly seen the mode of government which suited it, and his opinion immediately became a fixed idea. Under the committee of public safety, the dictatorship was his fixed system, and under the directory, legal government. Recognising no difference of situation, he found himself placed in an equivocal position; he wished for peace in a moment of war; and for law, in a moment of coups- d'état.

The councils, somewhat alarmed at the preparations of the directory, seemed to make the dismissal of a few ministers, in whom they placed no confidence, the price of reconciliation. These were, Merlin de Douai, the minister of justice; Delacroix, minister of foreign affairs; and Ramel, minister of finance. On the other hand they desired to retain Pétiet as minister of war, Bénésech as minister of the interior, and Cochon de Lapparent as minister of police. The legislative body, in default of directorial power, wished to make sure of the ministry. Far from falling in with this wish, which would have introduced the enemy into the government, Rewbell, La Réveillère and Barras dismissed the ministers protected by the councils, and retained the others. Bénésech was replaced by François de Neufchâteau, Pétiet by Hoche, and soon afterwards by Schérer; Cochon de Lapparent, by Lenoir-Laroche; and Lenoir-Laroche, who had too little decision, by Sotin. Talleyrand, likewise, formed part of this ministry. He had been struck off the list of emigrants, from the close of the conventional session, as a revolutionist of 1791; and his great sagacity, which always placed him with the party having the greatest hope of victory, made him, at this period, a directorial republican. He held the portfolio of Delacroix, and he contributed very much, by his counsels and his daring, to the events of Fructidor.

War now appeared more and more inevitable. The directory did not wish for a reconciliation, which, at the best, would only have postponed its downfall and that of the republic to the elections of the year VI. It caused threatening addresses against the councils to be sent from the armies. Bonaparte had watched with an anxious eye the events which were preparing in Paris. Though intimate with Carnot, and corresponding directly with him, he had sent Lavalette, his aid-de-camp, to furnish him with an account of the divisions in the government, and the intrigues and conspiracies with which it was beset. Bonaparte had promised the directory the support of his army, in case of actual danger. He sent Augereau to Paris with addresses from his troops. "Tremble, royalists!" said the soldiers. "From the Adige to the Seine is but a step. Tremble! your iniquities are numbered; and their recompense is at the end of our bayonets." —"We have observed with indignation," said the staff, "the intrigues of royalty threatening liberty. By the manes of the heroes slain for our country, we have sworn implacable war against royalty and royalists. Such are our sentiments; they are yours, and those of all patriots. Let the royalists show themselves, and their days are numbered." The councils protested, but in vain, against these deliberations of the army. General Richepanse, who commanded the troops arrived from the army of the Sambre-et-Meuse, stationed them at Versailles, Meudon, and Vincennes.

The councils had been assailants in Prairial, but as the success of their cause might be put off to the year VI., when it might take place without risk or combat, they kept on the defensive after Thermidor (July, 1797). They, however, then made every preparation for the contest: they gave orders that the *constitutional circles* should be closed, with a view to getting rid of the club of *Salm*; they also increased the powers of the commission of inspectors of the hall, which became the government of the legislative body, and of which the two royalist conspirators, Willot and Pichegru, formed part. The guard of the councils, which was under the control of the directory, was placed under the immediate orders of the inspectors of the hall. At last, on the 17th Fructidor, the legislative body thought of procuring the assistance of the militia of Vendémiaire, and it decreed, on the motion of Pichegru, the formation of the national guard. On the following day, the 18th, this measure was to be executed, and the councils were by a decree to order the troops to remove to a distance. They had reached a point that rendered a new victory necessary to decide the great struggle of the revolution and the ancient system. The impetuous general, Willot, wished them to take the initiative, to decree the impeachment of the three directors, Barras, Rewbell, and La Réveillère; to cause the other two to join the legislative body; if the government refused to obey, to sound the tocsin, and march with the old sectionaries against the directory; to place Pichegru at the head of this *legal insurrection*, and to execute all these measures promptly, boldly, and at mid-day. Pichegru is said to have hesitated; and the opinion of the undecided prevailing, the tardy course of legal preparations was adopted.

It was not, however, the same with the directory. Barras, Rewbell, and La Réveillère determined instantly to attack Carnot, Barthélemy, and the legislative majority. The morning of the 18th was fixed on for the execution of this coup-d'état. During the night, the troops encamped in the neighbourhood of Paris, entered the city under the command of Augereau. It was the design of the directorial triumvirate to occupy the Tuileries with troops before the assembling of the legislative body, in order to avoid a violent expulsion; to convoke the councils in the neighbourhood of the Luxembourg, after having arrested their principal leaders, and by a legislative measure to accomplish a coup-d'état begun by force. It was in agreement with the minority of the councils, and relied on the approbation of the mass. The troops reached the Hôtel de Ville at one in the morning, spread themselves over the quays, the bridges, and the Champs Élysées, and before long, twelve thousand men and forty pieces of cannon surrounded the Tuileries. At four o'clock the alarm-shot was fired, and Augereau presented himself at the gate of the Pont-Tournant.

The guard of the legislative body was under arms. The inspectors of the hall, apprised the night before of the movement in preparation, had repaired to the national palace (the Tuileries), to defend the entrance. Ramel, commander of the legislative guard, was devoted to the councils, and he had stationed his eight hundred grenadiers in the different avenues of the garden, shut in by gates. But Pichegru, Willot, and Ramel, could not resist the directory with this small and uncertain force. Augereau had no need even to force the passage of the Pont-Tournant: as soon as he came before the grenadiers, he cried out, "Are you republicans?" The latter lowered their arms and replied, "Vive Augereau! Vive le directoire!" and joined him. Augereau traversed the garden, entered the hall of the councils, arrested Pichegru, Willot, Ramel, and all the inspectors of the hall, and had them conveyed to the Temple. The members of the councils, convoked in haste by the inspectors, repaired in crowds to their place of sitting; but they were arrested or refused admittance by the armed force. Augereau announced to them that the directory, urged by the necessity of defending the republic from the conspirators among them, had assigned the Odéon and the School of Medicine for the place of their sittings. The greater part of the deputies present exclaimed against military violence and the dictatorial usurpation, but they were obliged to yield.

At six in the morning this expedition was terminated. The people of Paris, on awaking, found the troops still under arms, and the walls placarded with proclamations announcing the discovery of a formidable conspiracy. The people were exhorted to observe order and confidence. The directory had printed a letter of general Moreau, in which he announced in detail the plots of his predecessor Pichegru with the emigrants, and another letter from the prince de Condé to Imbert Colomès, a member of the Ancients. The entire population remained quiet; they were mere spectators of an event brought about without the interference of parties, and by the assistance of the army only. They displayed neither approbation nor regret.

The directory felt the necessity of legalizing, and more especially of terminating, this extraordinary act. As soon as the members of the five hundred, and of the ancients, were assembled at the Odéon and the School of Medicine in sufficient numbers to debate, they determined to sit permanently. A message from the directory announced the motive which had actuated all its measures. "Citizens, legislators," ran the message, "if the directory had delayed another day, the republic would have been given up to its enemies. The very place of your sittings was the rendezvous of the conspirators: from thence they yesterday distributed their plans and orders for the delivery of arms; from thence they corresponded last night with their accomplices; lastly, from thence, or in the neighbourhood, they again endeavoured to raise clandestine and seditious assemblies, which the police at this moment are employed in dispersing. We should have compromised the public welfare, and that of its faithful representatives, had we suffered them to remain confounded with the foes of the country in the den of conspiracy."

The younger council appointed a commission, composed of Sieyès, Poulain-Granpré, Villers, Chazal, and Boulay de la Meurthe, deputed to present a law of *public safety*. The law was a measure of ostracism; only transportation was substituted for the scaffold in this second revolutionary and dictatorial period.

The members of the five hundred sentenced to transportation were: Aubry, J. J. Aimé, Bayard, Blain, Boissy d'Anglas, Borne, Bourdon de l'Oise, Cadroy, Couchery, Delahaye, Delarue, Doumère, Dumolard, Duplantier, Gibert Desmolières, Henri La Rivière, Imbert-Colomès, Camille Jordan, Jourdan (des Bouches-du-Rhône) Gall, La Carrière, Lemarchand-Gomicourt, Lemérer, Mersan, Madier, Maillard, Noailles, André, Mac-Cartin, Pavie, Pastoret, Pichegru, Polissard, Praire-Montaud, Quatremère-Quincy, Saladin, Siméon, Vauvilliers, Vienot-Vaublanc, Villaret-Joyeuse, Willot. In the council of ancients: Barbé-Marbois, Dumas, Ferraud-Vaillant, Lafond-Ladebat, Laumont, Muraire, Murinais, Paradis, Portalis, Rovère, Tronçon-Ducoudray. In the directory: Carnot and Barthélemy. They also condemned the abbé Brottier, Lavilleheurnois, Dunan, the ex-minister of police, Cochon, the ex-agent of the police Dossonville, generals Miranda and Morgan; the journalist, Suard; the ex-conventionalist, Mailhe; and the commandant, Ramel. A few of the proscribed succeeded in evading the decree of exile; Carnot was among the number. Most of them were transported to Cayenne; but a great many did not leave the Isle of Ré.

The directory greatly extended this act of ostracism. The authors of thirty-five journals were included in the sentence of transportation. It wished to strike at once all the avenues of the republic in the councils, in the press, in the electoral assemblies, the departments, in a word, wherever they had introduced themselves. The elections of forty-eight departments were annulled, the laws in favour of priests and emigrants were revoked, and soon afterwards the disappearance of all who had swayed in the departments since the 9th Thermidor raised the spirits of the cast- down republican party. The coup-d'état of Fructidor was not purely central; like the victory of Vendémiaire; it ruined the royalist party, which had only been repulsed by the preceding defeat. But, by again replacing the legal government by the dictatorship, it rendered necessary another revolution, which shall be recounted later.

We may say, that on the 18th Fructidor of the year V. it was necessary that the directory should triumph over the counterrevolution by decimating the councils; or that the councils should triumph over the republic by overthrowing the directory. The question thus stated, it remains to inquire, 1st, if the directory could have conquered by any other means than a coup-d'état; 2ndly, whether it misused its victory?

The government had not the power of dissolving the councils. At the termination of a revolution, whose object was to establish the extreme right, they were unable to invest a secondary authority with the control of the sovereignty of the people, and in certain cases to make the legislature subordinate to the directory. This concession of an experimental policy not existing, what means remained to the directory of driving the enemy from the heart of the state? No longer able to defend the revolution by virtue of the law, it had no resource but the dictatorship; but in having recourse to that, it broke the conditions of its existence; and while saving the revolution, it soon fell itself.

As for its victory, it sullied it with violence, by endeavouring to make it too complete. The sentence of transportation was extended to too many victims; the petty passions of men mingled with the defence of the cause, and the directory did not manifest that reluctance to arbitrary measures which is the only justification of coups-d'état. To attain its object, it should have exiled the leading conspirators only; but it rarely happens that a party does not abuse the dictatorship; and that, possessing the power, it believes not in the dangers of indulgence. The defeat of the 18th Fructidor was the fourth of the royalist party; two took place in order to dispossess it of power, those of the 14th of July and 10th of August; two to prevent its resuming it; those of the 13th Vendémiaire and 18th Fructidor. This repetition of powerless attempts and protracted reverses did not a little contribute to the submission of this party under the consulate and the empire.

CHAPTER XIII

FROM THE 18TH FRUCTIDOR, IN THE YEAR V. (4TH OF SEPTEMBER, 1797), TO THE 18TH BRUMAIRE, IN THE YEAR VIII. (9TH OF NOVEMBER, 1799)

By the 18th Fructidor the directory returns, with slight mitigation, to the revolutionary government—General peace, except with England—Return of Bonaparte to Paris—Expedition into Egypt—Democratic elections for the year VI.—The directory annuls them on the 22nd Floréal—Second coalition; Russia, Austria, and England attack the republic through Italy, Switzerland, and Holland; general defeats—Democratic elections for the year VII.; on the 30th Prairial the councils get the upper hand, and disorganize the old directory—Two parties in the new directory, and in the councils: the moderate republican party under Sieyès, Roger-Ducos, and the ancients; the extreme republican party under Moulins, Golier, the Five Hundred, and the Society of the Manège—Various projects—Victories of Masséna, in Switzerland; of Brune, in Holland—Bonaparte returns from Egypt; comes to an understanding with Sieyès and his party—The 18th and 19th Brumaire—End of the directorial system.

The chief result of the 18th Fructidor was a return, with slight mitigation, to the revolutionary government. The two ancient privileged classes were again excluded from society; the dissentient priests were again banished. The Chouans, and former fugitives, who occupied the field of battle in the departments, abandoned it to the old republicans: those who had formed part of the military household of the Bourbons, the superior officers of the crown, the members of the parliaments, commanders of the order of the Holy Ghost and Saint Louis, the knights of Malta, all those who had protested against the abolition of nobility, and who had preserved its titles, were to quit the territory of the republic. The ci- devant nobles, or those ennobled, could only enjoy the rights of citizens, after a term of seven years, and after having gone through a sort of apprenticeship as Frenchmen. This party, by desiring sway, restored the dictatorship.

At this period the directory attained its maximum of power; for some time it had no enemies in arms. Delivered from all internal opposition, it imposed the continental peace on Austria by the treaty of Campo-Formio, and on the empire by the congress of Rastadt. The treaty of Campo-Formio was more advantageous to the cabinet of Vienna than the preliminaries of Leoben. Its Belgian and Lombard states were paid for by a part of the Venetian states. This old republic was divided; France retained the Ionian Isles, and gave the city of Venice and the provinces of Istria and Dalmatia to Austria. In this the directory committed a great fault, and was guilty of an attempt against liberty. In the fanaticism of a system, we may desire to set a country free, but we should never give it away. By arbitrarily distributing the territory of a small state, the directory set the bad example of this traffic in nations since but too much followed. Besides, Austrian dominion would, sooner or later, extend in Italy, through this imprudent cession of Venice.

The coalition of 1792 and 1793 was dissolved; England was the only remaining belligerent power. The cabinet of London was not at all disposed to cede to France, which it had attacked in the hope of weakening it, Belgium, Luxembourg, the left bank of the Rhine, Porentruy, Nice, Savoy, the protectorate of Genoa, Milan, and Holland. But finding it necessary to appease the English opposition, and reorganize its means of attack, it made propositions of peace; it sent Lord Malmesbury as plenipotentiary, first to Paris, then to Lille. But the offers of Pitt not being sincere, the directory did not allow itself to be deceived by his diplomatic stratagems. The negotiations were twice broken off, and war continued between the two powers. While England negotiated at Lille, she was preparing at Saint Petersburg the triple alliance, or second coalition.

The directory, on its side, without finances, without any party in the interior, having no support but the army, and no eminence save that derived from the continuation of its victories, was not in a condition to consent to a general peace. It had increased the public discontent by the establishment of certain taxes and the reduction of the debt to a consolidated third, payable in specie only, which had ruined the fundholders. It became necessary to maintain itself by war. The immense body of soldiers could not be disbanded without danger. Besides, being deprived of its power, and being placed at the mercy of Europe, the directory had attempted a thing never done without creating a shock, except in times of great tranquillity, of great ease, abundance, and employment. The directory was driven by its position to the invasion of Switzerland and the expedition into Egypt.

Bonaparte had then returned to Paris. The conqueror of Italy and the pacificator of the continent, was received with enthusiasm, constrained on the part of the directory, but deeply felt by the people. Honours were accorded him, never yet obtained by any general of the republic. A patriotic altar was prepared in the Luxembourg, and he passed under an arch of standards won in Italy, on his way to the triumphal ceremony in his honour. He was harangued by Barras, president of the directory, who, after congratulating him on his victories, invited him "to crown so noble a life by a conquest which the great country owed to its insulted dignity." This was the conquest of England. Everything seemed in preparation for a descent, while the invasion of Egypt was really the enterprise in view.

Such an expedition suited both Bonaparte and the directory. The independent conduct of that general in Italy, his ambition, which, from time to time, burst through his studied simplicity, rendered his presence dangerous. He, on his side, feared, by his inactivity, to compromise the already high opinion entertained of his talents: for men always require from those whom they make great, more than they are able to perform. Thus, while the directory saw in the expedition to Egypt the means of keeping a formidable general at a distance, and a prospect of attacking the English by India, Bonaparte saw in it a gigantic conception, an employment suited to his taste, and a new means of astonishing mankind. He sailed from Toulon on the 30th Floréal, in the year VI. (19th May, 1798), with a fleet of four hundred sail, and a portion of the army of Italy; he steered for Malta; of which he made himself master, and from thence to Egypt.

The directory, who violated the neutrality of the Ottoman Porte in order to attack the English, had already violated that of Switzerland, in order to expel the emigrants from its territory. French opinions had already penetrated into Geneva and the Pays de Vaud; but the policy of the Swiss confederation was counter-revolutionary, from the influence of the aristocracy of Berne. They had driven from the cantons all the Swiss who had shown themselves partisans of the French republic. Berne was the headquarters of the emigrants, and it was there that all the plots against the revolution were formed. The directory complained, but did not receive satisfaction. The Vaudois, placed by old treaties under the protection of France, invoked her help against the tyranny of Berne. This appeal of the Vaudois, its own grievances, its desire to extend the directorial republican system to Switzerland, much more than the temptation of seizing the little amount of treasure in Berne, a reproach brought against it by some, determined the directory. Some conferences took place, which led to no result, and war began. The Swiss defended themselves with much courage and obstinacy, and hoped to resuscitate the times of their ancestors, but they succumbed. Geneva was united to France, and Switzerland exchanged its ancient constitution for that of the year III. From that time two parties existed in the confederation, one of which was for France and the revolution, the other for the counter-revolution and Austria. Switzerland ceased to be a common barrier, and became the high road of Europe.

This revolution had been followed by that of Rome. General Duphot was killed at Rome in a riot; and in punishment of this assassination, which the pontifical government had not interfered to prevent, Rome was changed into a republic. All this combined to complete the system of the directory, and make it preponderant in Europe; it was now at the head of the Helvetian, Batavian, Ligurian, Cisalpine, and Roman republics, all constructed on the same model. But while the directory extended its influence abroad, it was again menaced by internal parties.

The elections of Floréal in the year VI. (May, 1798) were by no means favourable to the directory; the returns were quite at variance with those of the year V. Since the 18th Fructidor, the withdrawal of the counter- revolutionists had restored all the influence of the exclusive republican party, which had reestablished the clubs under the name of *Constitutional Circles*. This party dominated in the electoral assemblies, which, most unusually, had to nominate four hundred and thirty-seven deputies: two hundred and ninety-eight for the council of five hundred; a hundred and thirty-nine for that of the ancients. When the elections drew near, the directory exclaimed loudly against the *anarchists*. But its proclamations having been unable to prevent democratic returns, it decided upon annulling them in virtue of a law, by which the councils, after the 18th Fructidor, had granted it the *power of judging* the operations of the electoral assemblies. It invited the legislative body, by a message, to appoint a commission of five members for that purpose. On the 22nd Floréal, the elections were for the most part annulled. At this period the directorial party struck a blow at the extreme republicans, as nine months before it had aimed at the royalists.

The directory wished to maintain the political balance, which had been the characteristic of its first two years; but its position was much changed. Since its last coup-d'état, it could no longer be an impartial government, because it was no longer a constitutional government. With these pretensions of isolation, it dissatisfied every one. Yet it lived on in this way till the elections of the year VII. It displayed much activity, but an activity of a narrow and shuffling nature. Merlin de Douai and Treilhard, who had replaced Carnot and Barthélemy, were two political lawyers. Rewbell had in the highest degree the courage, without having the enlarged views of a statesman. Laréveillère was too much occupied with the sect of the Theophilanthropists for a government leader. As to Barras, he continued his dissipated life and his directorial regency; his palace was the rendezvous of gamesters, women of gallantry, and stock-jobbers of every kind. The administration of the directors betrayed their character, but more especially their position; to the embarrassments of which was added war with all Europe.

While the republican plenipotentiaries were yet negotiating for peace with the empire at Rastadt, the second coalition began the campaign. The treaty of Campo-Formio had only been for Austria a suspension of arms. England had no difficulty in gaining her to a new coalition; with the exception of Spain and Prussia, most of the European powers formed part of it. The subsidies of the British cabinet, and the attraction of the West, decided Russia; the Porte and the states of Barbary acceded to it, because of the invasion of Egypt; the empire, in order to recover the left bank of the Rhine, and the petty princes of Italy, that they might destroy the new republics. At Rastadt they were discussing the treaty relative to the empire, the concession of the left bank of the Rhine, the navigation of that river, and the demolition of some fortresses on the right bank, when the Russians entered Germany, and the Austrian army began to move. The French plenipotentiaries, taken by surprise, received orders to leave in four and twenty hours; they obeyed immediately, and set out, after having obtained safe conduct from the generals of the enemy. At a short distance from Rastadt they were stopped by some Austrian hussars, who, having satisfied themselves as to their names and titles, assassinated them: Bonnier and Roberjot were killed, Jean de Bry was left for dead. This unheard-of violation of the right of nations, this premeditated assassination of three men invested with a sacred character, excited general horror. The legislative body declared war, and declared it with indignation against the governments on whom the guilt of this enormity fell.

Hostilities had already commenced in Italy and on the Rhine. The directory, apprised of the march of the Russian troops, and suspecting the intentions of

Austria, caused the councils to pass a law for recruiting. The military conscription placed two hundred thousand young men at the disposal of the republic. This law, which was attended with incalculable consequences, was the result of a more regular order of things. Levies *en masse* had been the revolutionary service of the country; the conscription became the legal service.

The most impatient of the powers, those which formed the advanced guard of the coalition, had already commenced the attack. The king of Naples had advanced on Rome, and the king of Sardinia had raised troops and threatened the Ligurian republic. As they had not sufficient power to sustain the shock of the French armies, they were easily conquered and dispossessed. General Championnet entered Naples after a sanguinary victory. The lazaroni defended the interior of the town for three days; but they yielded, and the Parthenopian republic was proclaimed. General Joubert occupied Turin; and the whole of Italy was in the hands of the French, when the new campaign began.

The coalition was superior to the republic in effective force and in preparations. It attacked it by the three great openings of Italy, Switzerland, and Holland. A strong Austrian army debouched in the duchy of Mantua; it defeated Scherer twice on the Adige, and was soon joined by the whimsical and hitherto victorious Suvorov. Moreau replaced Scherer, and, like him, was beaten; he retreated towards Genoa, in order to keep the barrier of the Apennines and to join the army of Naples, commanded by Macdonald, which was overpowered at the Trebia. The Austro-Russians then directed their chief forces upon Switzerland. A few Russian corps joined the archduke Charles, who had defeated Jourdan on the Upper Rhine, and was preparing to pass over the Helvetian barrier. At the same time the duke of York disembarked in Holland with forty thousand Anglo-Russians. The small republics which protected France were invaded, and a few more victories would have enabled the confederates to penetrate even to the scene of the revolution.

In the midst of these military disasters and the discontent of parties, the elections of Floréal in the year VII. (May, 1799) took place; they were republican, like those of the preceding year. The directory was no longer strong enough to contend with public misfortunes and the rancour of parties. The retirement of Rewbell, who was replaced by Sieyès, caused it to lose the only man able to face the storm, and brought into its bosom the most avowed antagonist of this compromised and worn-out government. The moderate party and the extreme republicans united in demanding from the directory an account of the internal and external situation of the republic. The councils sat permanently. Barras abandoned his colleagues. The fury of the councils was directed solely against Treilhard, Merlin, and La Réveillère, the last supports of the old directory. They deposed Treilhard, because an interval of a year had not elapsed between his legislative and his directorial functions, as the constitution required. The ex-minister of justice, Gohier, was immediately chosen to replace him.

The orators of the councils then warmly attacked Merlin and La Réveillère, whom they could not dismiss from the directory. The threatened directors sent a justificatory message to the councils, and proposed peace. On the 30th Prairial, the republican Bertrand (du Calvados) ascended the tribune, and after examining the offers of the directors, exclaimed: "You have proposed union; and I propose that you reflect if you yourselves can still preserve your functions. If you love the republic you will not hesitate to decide. You are incapable of doing good; you will never have the confidence of your colleagues, that of the people, or that of the representatives, without which you cannot cause the laws to be executed. I know that, thanks to the constitution, there already exists in the directory a majority which enjoys the confidence of the people, and that of the national representation. Why do you hesitate to introduce unanimity of desires and principles between the two first authorities of the republic? You have not even the confidence of those vile flatterers, who have dug your political tomb. Finish your career by an act of devotion, which good republican hearts will be able to appreciate."

Merlin and La Réveillère, deprived of the support of the government by the retirement of Rewbell, the dismissal of Treilhard, and the desertion of Barras, urged by the councils and by patriotic motives, yielded to circumstances, and resigned the directorial authority. This victory, gained by the republican and moderate parties combined, turned to the profit of both. The former introduced general Moulins into the directory; the latter, Roger Ducos. The 30th Prairial (18th June), which witnessed the breaking up of the old government of the year III., was an act of reprisal on the part of the councils against the directory for the 18th Fructidor and the 22nd Floréal. At this period the two great powers of the state had each in turn violated the constitution: the directory by decimating the legislature; the legislature by expelling the directory. This form of government, which every party complained of, could not have a protracted existence.

Sieyès, after the success of the 30th Prairial, laboured to destroy what yet remained of the government of the year III., in order to establish the legal system on another plan. He was whimsical and systematic; but he had the faculty of judging surely of situations. He re-entered upon the scene of the revolution of a singular epoch, with the intention of strengthening it by a definitive constitution. After having co-operated in the principal changes of 1789, by his motion of the 17 of June, which transformed the states-general into a national assembly, and by his plan of internal organization, which substituted departments for provinces, he had remained passive and silent during the subsequent interval. He waited till the period of public defence should again give place to institutions. Appointed, under the directory, to the embassy at Berlin, the neutrality of Prussia was attributed to his efforts. On his return, he accepted the office of director, hitherto refused by him, because Rewbell was leaving the government, and he thought that parties were sufficiently weary to undertake a definitive pacification, and the establishment of liberty. With this object, he placed his reliance on Roger-Ducos in the directory, on the council of ancients in the legislature, and without, on the mass of moderate men and the middle-class, who, after desiring laws, merely as a novelty, now desired repose as a novelty. This party sought for a strong and secure government, which should have no past, no enmities, and which thenceforward might satisfy all opinions and interests. As all that had been dene, from the 14th of July till the 9th Thermidor, by the people, in connexion with a part of the government, had been done since the 13th Vendémiaire by the soldiers, Sieyès was in want of a general. He cast his eyes upon Joubert, who was put at the head of the army of Italy, in order that he might gain by his victories, and by the deliverance of Italy, a great political importance.

The constitution of the year III. was, however, still supported by the two directors, Gohier and Moulins, the council of five hundred, and without, by the party of the *Manège*. The decided republicans had formed a club that held its sittings in that hall where had sat the first of our assemblies. The new club, formed from the remains of that of Salm, before the 18th Fructidor; of that of the Panthéon, at the beginning of the directory; and of the old society of the Jacobins, enthusiastically professed republican principles, but not the democratic opinions of the inferior class. Each of these parties also had a share in the ministry which had been renewed at the same time as the directory. Cambacérès had the department of justice; Quinette, the home department; Reinhard, who had been temporarily placed in office during the ministerial interregnum of Talleyrand, was minister of foreign affairs; Robert Lindet was minister of finance, Bourdon (of Vatry) of the navy, Bernadotte of war, Bourguignon, soon afterwards replaced by Fouché (of Nantes), of police.

This time Barras remained neutral between the two divisions of the legislature, of the directory and of the ministry. Seeing that matters were coming to a more considerable change than that of the 30th Prairial, he, an ex-noble, thought that the decline of the republic would lead to the restoration of the Bourbons, and he treated with the Pretender Louis XVIII. It seems that, in negotiating the restoration of the monarchy by his agent, David Monnier, he was not forgetful of himself. Barras espoused nothing from conviction, and always sided with the party which had the greatest chance of victory. A democratic member of the Mountain on the 31st of May; a reactionary member of the Mountain on the 9th Thermidor; a revolutionary director against the royalists on the 18th Fructidor; extreme republican director against his old colleagues on the 30th Prairial; he now became a royalist director against the government of the year III.

The faction disconcerted by the 18th Fructidor and the peace of the Continent, had also gained courage. The military successes of the new coalition, the law of compulsory loans and that of hostages, which had compelled every emigrant family to give guarantees to government, had made the royalists of the south and west again take up arms. They reappeared in bands, which daily became more formidable, and revived the petty but disastrous warfare of the Chouans. They awaited the arrival of the Russians, and looked forward to the speedy restoration of the monarchy. This was a moment of fresh competition with every party. Each aspired to the inheritance of the dying constitution, as they had done at the close of the convention. In France, people are warned by a kind of political odour that a government is dying, and all parties rush to be in at the death.

Fortunately for the republic, the war changed its aspect on the two principal frontiers of the Upper and Lower Rhine. The allies, after having acquired Italy, wished to enter France by Switzerland and Holland; but generals Masséna and Brune arrested their hitherto victorious progress. Masséna advanced against Korsakov and Suvorov. During twelve days of great combinations and consecutive victories, hastening in turns from Constance to Zurich, he repelled the efforts of the Russians, forced them to retreat, and disorganized the coalition. Brune also defeated the duke of York in Holland, obliged him to re-embark, and to renounce his attempted invasion. The army of Italy alone had been less fortunate. It had lost its general, Joubert, killed at the battle of Novi, while leading a charge on the Austro-Russians. But this frontier, which was at a distance from the centre of action, despite the defeat of Novi, was not crossed, and Championnet ably defended it. It was soon to be repassed by the republican troops, who, after each resumption of arms, having been for a moment beaten, soon regained their superiority and recommenced their victories. Europe, by giving additional exercise to the military power, by its repeated attacks, rendered it each time more triumphant.

But at home nothing was changed. Divisions, discontent, and anxiety were the same as before. The struggle between the moderate republicans and the extreme republicans had become more determined. Sieyès pursued his projects against the latter. In the Champ-de-Mars, on the 10th of August, he assailed the Jacobins. Lucien Bonaparte, who had much influence in the council of five hundred, from his character, his talents, and the military importance of the conqueror of Italy and of Egypt, drew in that assembly a fearful picture of the reign of terror, and said that France was threatened with its return. About the same time, Sieyès caused Bernadotte to be dismissed, and Fouché, in concert with him, closed the meetings of the Manège. The multitude, to whom it is only necessary to present the phantom of the past to inspire it with fear, sided with the moderate party, dreading the return of the reign of terror; and the extreme republicans failed in their endeavour to declare *la patrie en danger*, as they had done at the close of the legislative assembly. But Sieyès, after having lost Joubert, sought for a general who could enter into his designs, and who would protect the republic, without becoming its oppressor. Hoche had been dead more than a year. Moreau had given rise to suspicion by his equivocal conduct to the directory before the 18th Fructidor, and by the sudden denunciation of his old friend Pichegru, whose treason he had kept secret for a whole year; Masséna was not a political general; Bernadotte and Jourdan were devoted to the party of the Manège; Sieyès was compelled to postpone his scheme for want of a suitable agent.

Bonaparte had learned in the east, from his brother Lucien and a few other friends, the state of affairs in France, and the decline of the directorial government. His expedition had been brilliant, but without results. After having defeated the Mamelukes, and ruined their power in Upper and Lower Egypt, he had advanced into Syria; but the failure of the siege of Acre had compelled him to return to his first conquest. There, after defeating an Ottoman army on the coast of Aboukir, so fatal to the French fleet the preceding year, he decided on leaving that land of exile and fame, in order to turn the new crisis in France to his own elevation. He left general Kléber to command the army of the east, and crossed the Mediterranean, then covered with English ships, in a frigate. He disembarked at Fréjus, on the 7th Vendémiaire, year VIII. (9th October, 1799), nineteen days after the battle of Berghen, gained by Brune over the Anglo-Russians under the duke of York, and fourteen days after that of Zurich, gained by Masséna over the Austro-Russians under

Korsakov and Suvorov. He traversed France, from the shore of the Mediterranean to Paris, in triumph. His expedition, almost fabulous, had struck the public mind with surprise, and had still more increased the great renown he had acquired by the conquest of Italy. These two enterprises had raised him above all the other generals of the republic. The distance of the theatre upon which he had fought enabled him to begin his career of independence and authority. A victorious general, an acknowledged and obeyed negotiator, a creator of republics, he had treated all interests with skill, all creeds with moderation. Preparing afar off his ambitious destiny, he had not made himself subservient to any system, and had managed all parties so as to work his elevation with their assent. He had entertained this idea of usurpation since his victories in Italy. On the 18th Fructidor, had the directory been conquered by the councils, he purposed marching against the latter with his army and seizing the protectorate of the republic. After the 18th Fructidor; finding the directory too powerful, and the inactivity of the continent too dangerous for him, he accepted the expedition to Egypt, that he might not fall, and might not be forgotten. At the news of the disorganization of the directory, on the 30th Prairial, he repaired with haste to the scene of events.

His arrival excited the enthusiasm of the moderate masses of the nation. He received general congratulations, and every party contended for his favour. Generals, directors, deputies, and even the republicans of the Manège, waited on and tried to sound him. Fêtes and banquets were given in his honour. His manners were grave, simple, cool, and observing; he had already a tone of condescending familiarity and involuntary habits of command. Notwithstanding his want of earnestness and openness, he had an air of self-possession, and it was easy to read in him an after-thought of conspiracy. Without uttering his design, he allowed it to be guessed; because a thing must always be expected in order to be accomplished. He could not seek supporters in the republicans of the Manège, as they neither wished for a coup-d'état nor for a dictator; and Sieyès feared that he was too ambitious to fall in with his constitutional views. Hence Sieyès hesitated to open his mind to Bonaparte, but, urged by their mutual friends, they at length met and concerted together. On the 15th Brumaire, they determined on their plan of attack on the constitution of the year III, Sieyès undertook to prepare the councils by the *commissions of inspectors,* who placed unlimited confidence in him. Bonaparte was to gain the generals and the different corps of troops stationed in Paris, who displayed much enthusiasm for him and much attachment to his person. They agreed to convoke an extraordinary meeting of the moderate members of the councils, to describe the public danger to the Ancients, and by urging the ascendancy of Jacobinism to demand the removal of the legislative body to Saint-Cloud, and the appointment of general Bonaparte to the command of the armed force, as the only man able to save the country; and then, by means of the new military power, to obtain the dismissal of the directory, and the temporary dissolution of the legislative body. The enterprise was fixed for the morning of the 18th Brumaire (9th November).

During these three days, the secret was faithfully kept, Barras, Moulins, and Gohier, who formed the majority of the directory, of which Gohier was then president, might have frustrated the coup-d'état of the conspirators by forestalling them, as on the 18th Fructidor. But they gave them credit for hopes only, and not for any decided projects. On the morning of the 18th, the members of the ancients were convoked in an unusual way by the *inspectors;* they repaired to the Tuileries, and the debate was opened about seven in the morning under the presidentship of Lemercier. Cornudet, Lebrun, and Fargues, the three most influential conspirators in the council, drew a most alarming picture of the state of public affairs; protesting that the Jacobins were flocking in crowds to Paris from all the departments; that they wished to re-establish the revolutionary government, and that a reign of terror would once more desolate the republic, if the council had not the courage and wisdom to prevent its return. Another conspirator, Régnier de la Meurthe, required of the ancients already moved, that in virtue of the right conferred on them by the constitution, they should transfer the legislative body to Saint Cloud, and depute Bonaparte, nominated by them to the command of the 17th military division, to superintend the removal. Whether all the members of the council were accomplices of this manoeuvre, or whether they were terrified by so hasty convocation, and by speeches so alarming, they instantly granted what the conspirators required.

Bonaparte awaited with impatience the result of this deliberation, at his house in the Rue Chantereine; he was surrounded by generals, by Lefèvre, the commander of the guard of the directory, and by three regiments of cavalry which he was about to review. The decree of the council of ancients was passed about eight, and brought to him at half-past eight by a state messenger. He received the congratulations of all around him; the officers drew their swords as a sign of fidelity. He put himself at their head, and they marched to the Tuileries; he appeared at the bar of the ancients, took the oath of fidelity, and appointed as his lieutenant, Lefèvre, chief of the directorial guard.

This was, however, only a beginning of success. Bonaparte was at the head of the armed force; but the executive power of the directory and the legislative power of the councils still existed. In the struggle which would infallibly ensue, it was not certain that the great and hitherto victorious force of the revolution would not triumph. Sieyès and Roger Ducos went from the Luxembourg to the legislative and military camp of the Tuileries, and gave in their resignation. Barras, Moulins, and Gohier, apprised on their side, but a little too late, of what was going on, wished to employ their power and make themselves sure of their guard; but the latter, having received from Bonaparte information of the decree of the ancients, refused to obey them. Barras, discouraged, sent in his resignation, and departed for his estate of Gros-Bois. The directory was, in fact, dissolved; and there was one antagonist less in the struggle. The five hundred and Bonaparte alone remained opposed.

The decree of the council of ancients and the proclamations of Bonaparte were placarded on the walls of Paris. The agitation which accompanies extraordinary events prevailed in that great city. The republicans, and not without reason, felt serious alarm for the fate of liberty. But when they showed alarm respecting the intentions of Bonaparte, in whom they beheld a Caesar, or a Cromwell, they were answered in the general's own words: *"Bad parts, worn out parts, unworthy a man of sense, even if they were not so of a good man. It would be sacrilege to attack representative government in this age of intelligence and freedom. He would be but a fool who, with lightness of heart, could wish to cause the loss of the stakes of the republic against royalty after having supported them with some glory and peril.*" Yet the importance he gave himself in his proclamations was ominous. He reproached the directory with the situation of France in a most extraordinary way. "What have you done," said he, "with that France which I left so flourishing in your hands? I left you peace, I find you at war; I left you victories, I find nothing but reverses; I left you the millions of Italy, I find nothing but plundering laws and misery. What have you done with the hundred thousand Frenchmen whom I knew, my companions in glory? They are dead! This state of things cannot last; in less than three years it would lead us to despotism." This was the first time for ten years that a man had ventured to refer everything to himself; and to demand an account of the republic, as of his own property. It is a painful surprise to see a new comer of the revolution introduce himself thus into the inheritance, so laboriously acquired, of an entire people.

On the 19th Brumaire the members of the councils repaired to Saint Cloud; Sieyès and Roger Ducos accompanied Bonaparte to this new field of battle; they went thither with the intention of supporting the designs of the conspirators; Sieyès, who understood the tactics of revolution, wished to make sure of events by provisionally arresting the leaders, and only admitting the moderate party into the councils; but Bonaparte refused to accede to this. He was no party man; having hitherto acted and conquered with regiments only, he thought he could direct legislative councils like an army, by the word of command. The gallery of Mars had been prepared for the ancients, the Orangery for the five hundred. A considerable armed force surrounded the seat of the legislature, as the multitude, on the 2nd of June, had surrounded the convention. The republicans, assembled in groups in the grounds, waited the opening of the sittings; they were agitated with a generous indignation against the military brutalism that threatened them, and communicated to each other their projects of resistance. The young general, followed by a few grenadiers, passed through the courts and apartments, and prematurely yielding to his character, he said, like the twentieth king of a dynasty: "*I will have no more factions: there must be an end to this; I absolutely will not have any more of it,*" About two o'clock in the afternoon, the councils assembled in their respective halls, to the sound of instruments which played the *Marseillaise*.

As soon as the business of the sitting commenced, Emile Gaudin, one of the conspirators, ascended the tribune of the five hundred. He proposed a vote of thanks to the council of ancients for the measures it had taken, and to request it to expound the means of saving the republic. This motion was the signal for a violent tumult; cries arose against Gaudin from every part of the hall. The republican deputies surrounded the tribune and the bureau, at which Lucien Bonaparte presided. The conspirators Cabanis, Boulay (de la Meurthe), Chazal, Gaudin, etc., turned pale on their seats. After a long scene of agitation, during which no one could obtain a hearing, calm was restored for a few moments, and Delbred proposed that the oath made to the constitution of the year III. should be renewed. As no one opposed this motion, which at such a juncture was of vital importance, the oath was taken with an enthusiasm and unanimity which was dangerous to the conspiracy.

Bonaparte, learning what had passed in the five hundred, and in the greatest danger of desertion and defeat, presented himself at the council of ancients. All would have been lost for him, had the latter, in favour of the conspiracy, been carried away by the enthusiasm of the younger council. "Representatives of the people," said he, "you are in no ordinary situation; you stand on a volcano. Yesterday, when you summoned me to inform me of the decree for your removal, and charged me with its execution, I was tranquil. I immediately assembled my comrades; we flew to your aid! Well, now I am overwhelmed with calumnies! They talk of Caesar, Cromwell, and military government! Had I wished to oppress the liberty of my country, I should not have attended to the orders which you gave me; I should not have had any occasion to receive this authority from your hands. Representatives of the people! I swear to you that the country has not a more zealous defender than I am; but its safety rests with you alone! There is no longer a government; four of the directors have given in their resignation; the fifth (Moulins) has been placed under surveillance for his own security; the council of five hundred is divided; nothing is left but the council of ancients. Let it adopt measures; let it but speak; I am ready to execute. Let us save liberty! let us save equality!" Linglet, a republican, then arose and said: "General, we applaud what you say: swear with us to obey the constitution of the year III., which alone can maintain the republic." All would have been lost for him had this motion met with the same reception which it had found in the five hundred. It surprised the council, and for a moment Bonaparte was disconcerted. But he soon resumed: "The constitution of the year III. has ceased to exist; you violated it on the 18th Fructidor; you violated it on the 22nd Floréal; you violated it on the 30th Prairial. The constitution is invoked by all factions, and violated by all; it cannot be a means of safety for us, because it no longer obtains respect from any one; the constitution being violated, we must have another compact, new guarantees." The council applauded these reproaches of Bonaparte, and rose in sign of approbation.

Bonaparte, deceived by his easy success with the ancients, imagined that his presence alone would suffice to appease the stormy council of the five hundred. He hastened thither at the head of a few grenadiers, whom he left at the door, but within the hall, and he advanced alone, hat in hand. At the sight of the bayonets, the assembly arose with a sudden movement. The legislators, conceiving his entrance to be a signal for military violence, uttered all at once the cry of "Outlaw him! Down with the dictator!" Several members rushed to meet him, and the republican, Bigonet, seizing him by the arm, exclaimed, "Rash man! what are you doing? Retire; you are violating the sanctuary of the laws." Bonaparte, pale and agitated, receded, and was carried off by the grenadiers who had escorted him there.

His disappearance did not put a stop to the agitation of the council. All the members spoke at once, all proposed measures of public safety and defence. Lucien Bonaparte was the object of general reproach; he attempted to justify his brother, but with timidity. After a long struggle, he succeeded in reaching the tribune, and urged the assembly to judge his brother with less severity. He protested that he had no design against their liberty; and recalled his services. But several voices immediately exclaimed: "He has lost all their merit; down with the dictator! down with the tyrants!" The tumult now became more violent than ever; and all demanded the outlawry of general Bonaparte. "What," said Lucien, "do you wish me to pronounce the outlawry of my brother?" "Yes! yes! outlawry! it is the reward of tyrants!" In the midst of the confusion, a motion was made and put to the vote that the council should sit permanently; that it should instantly repair to its palace at Paris; that the troops assembled at Saint Cloud should form a part of the guard of the legislative body; that the command of them should be given to general Bernadotte. Lucien, astounded by these propositions, and by the outlawry, which he thought had been adopted with the rest, left the president's chair, and ascending the tribune, said, in the greatest agitation: "Since I cannot be heard in this assembly, I put off the symbols of the popular magistracy with a deep sense of insulted dignity." And he took off his cap, robe, and scarf.

Bonaparte, meantime, on leaving the council of the five hundred, had found some difficulty in regaining his composure. Unaccustomed to scenes of popular tumult, he had been greatly agitated. His officers came around him; and Sieyès, having more revolutionary experience, besought him not to lose time, and to employ force. General Lefèvre immediately gave an order for carrying off Lucien from the council. A detachment entered the hall, advanced to the chair which Lucien now occupied again, placed him in their ranks, and returned with him to the troops. As soon as Lucien came out, he mounted a horse by his brother's side, and although divested of his legal character, harangued the troops as president. In concert with Bonaparte, he invented the story, so often repeated since, that poignards had been drawn on the general in the council of five hundred, and exclaimed: "Citizen soldiers, the president of the council of five hundred declares to you that the large majority of that council is at this moment kept in fear by the daggers of a few representatives, who surround the tribune, threaten their colleagues with death, and occasion the most terrible deliberations. General, and you, soldiers and citizens, you will only recognise as legislators of France those who follow me. As for those who remain in the Orangery, let force expel them. Those brigands are no longer representatives of the people, but representatives of the poignard." After this violent appeal, addressed to the troops by a conspirator president, who, as usual, calumniated those he wished to proscribe, Bonaparte spoke: "Soldiers," said he, "I have led you to victory; may I rely on you?" — "Yes! yes! Vive le Général!" — "Soldiers, there were reasons for expecting that the council of five hundred would save the country; on the contrary, it is given up to intestine quarrels; agitators seek to excite it against me. Soldiers, may I rely on you?" "Yes! yes! Vive Bonaparte." "Well, then, I will bring them to their senses!" And he instantly gave orders to the officers surrounding him to clear the hall of the five hundred.

The council, after Lucien's departure, had been a prey to great anxiety and indecision. A few members proposed that they should leave the place in a body, and go to Paris to seek protection amidst the people. Others wished the national representatives not to forsake their post, but to brave the outrages of force. In the meantime, a troop of grenadiers entered the hall by degrees, and the officer in command informed the council that they should disperse. The deputy Prudhon reminded the officer and his soldiers of the respect due to the representatives of the people; general Jourdan also represented to them the enormity of such a measure. For a moment the troops hesitated; but a reinforcement now arrived in close column. General Leclerc exclaimed: "In the name of general Bonaparte, the legislative body is dissolved; let all good citizens retire. Grenadiers, forward!" Cries of indignation arose from every side; but these were drowned by the drums. The grenadiers advanced slowly across the whole width of the Orangery, and presenting bayonets. In this way they drove the legislators before them, who continued shouting, "Vive la république!" as they left the place. At half-past five, on the 19th Brumaire of the year VIII. (10th November, 1799) there was no longer a representation.

Thus this violation of the law, this coup-d'état against liberty was accomplished. Force began to sway. The 18th of Brumaire was the 31st of May of the army against the representation, except that it was not directed against a party, but against the popular power. But it is just to distinguish the 18th Brumaire from its consequences. It might then be supposed that the army was only an auxiliary of the revolution as it had been on the 13th Vendémiaire and the 18th Fructidor, and that this indispensable change would not turn to the advantage of a man—a single man, who would soon change France into a regiment, and cause nothing to be heard of in a world hitherto agitated by so great a moral commotion, save the tread of his army, and the voice of his will.

THE CONSULATE

CHAPTER XIV

FROM THE 18TH BRUMAIRE (9TH OF NOVEMBER, 1799) TO THE 2ND OF DECEMBER, 1804

Hopes entertained by the various parties, after the 18th Brumaire—Provisional government—Constitution of Sieyès; distorted into the consular constitution of the year VIII.—Formation of the government; pacific designs of Bonaparte—Campaign of Italy; victory of Marengo— General peace: on the continent, by the treaty of Lunéville with England; by the treaty of Amiens—Fusion of parties; internal prosperity of France —Ambitious system of the First Consul; re-establishes the clergy in the state, by the Concordat of 1802; he creates a military order of knighthood, by means of the Legion of Honour; he completes this order of things by the consulate for life—Resumption of hostilities with England— Conspiracy of Georges and Pichegru—The war and royalist attempts form a pretext for the erection of the empire—Napoleon Bonaparte appointed hereditary emperor; is crowned by the pope on the 2nd of December, 1804, in the church of Notre Dame—Successive abandonment of the revolution— Progress of absolute power during the four years of the consulate.

The 18th Brumaire had immense popularity. People did not perceive in this event the elevation of a single man above the councils of the nation; they did not see in it the end of the great movement of the 14th of July, which had commenced the national existence.

The 18th Brumaire assumed an aspect of hope and restoration. Although the nation was much exhausted, and little capable of supporting a sovereignty oppressive to it, and which had even become the object of its ridicule, since the lower class had exercised it, yet it considered despotism so improbable, that no one seemed to it to be in a condition to reduce it to a state of subjection. All felt the need of being restored by a skilful hand, and Bonaparte, as a great man and a victorious general, seemed suited for the task.

On this account almost every one, except the directorial republicans, declared in favour of the events of that day. Violation of the laws and coups-d'état had occurred so frequently during the revolution, that people had become accustomed no longer to judge them by their legality, but by their consequences. From the party of Sieyès down to the royalists of 1788, every one congratulated himself on the 18th Brumaire, and attributed to himself the future political advantages of this change. The moderate constitutionalists believed that definitive liberty would be established; the royalists fed themselves with hope by inappropriately comparing this epoch of our revolution with the epoch of 1660 in the English revolution, with the hope that Bonaparte was assuming the part of Monk, and that he would soon restore the monarchy of the Bourbons; the mass, possessing little intelligence, and desirous of repose, relied on the return of order under a powerful protector; the proscribed classes and ambitious men expected from him their amnesty or elevation. During the three months which followed the 18th Brumaire, approbation and expectation were general. A provisional government had been appointed, composed of three consuls, Bonaparte, Sieyès, and Roger Ducos, with two legislative commissioners, entrusted to prepare the constitution and a definitive order of things.

The consuls and the two commissioners were installed on the 21st Brumaire. This provisional government abolished the law respecting hostages and compulsory loans; it permitted the return of the priests proscribed since the 18th Fructidor; it released from prison and sent out of the republic the emigrants who had been shipwrecked on the coast of Calais, and who for four years were captives in France, and were exposed to the heavy punishment of the emigrant army. All these measures were very favourably received. But public opinion revolted at a proscription put in force against the extreme republicans. Thirty-six of them were sentenced to transportation to Guiana, and twenty-one were put under surveillance in the department of Charante-Inférieure, merely by a decree of the consuls on the report of Fouché, minister of police. The public viewed unfavourably all who attacked the government; but at the same time it exclaimed against an act so arbitrary and unjust. The consuls, accordingly, recoiled before their own act; they first commuted transportation into surveillance, and soon withdrew surveillance itself.

It was not long before a rupture broke out between the authors of the 18th Brumaire. During their provisional authority, it did not create much noise, because it took place in the legislative commissions. The new constitution was the cause of it. Sieyès and Bonaparte could not agree on this subject: the former wished to institute France, the latter to govern it as a master.

The constitution of Sieyès, which was distorted in the consular constitution of the year VIII., deserves to be known, were it only in the light of a legislative curiosity. Sieyès distributed France into three political divisions; the commune, the province or department, and the State. Each had its own powers of administration and judicature, arranged in hierarchical order: the first, the municipalities and *tribunaux de paix* and *de premiere instance;* the second, the popular prefectures and courts of appeal; the third, the central government and the court of cassation. To fill the functions of the commune, the department, and the State, there were three budgets of *notability,* the members of which were only candidates nominated by the people.

The executive power was vested in the *proclamateur-électeur*, a superior functionary, perpetual, without responsibility, deputed to represent the nation without, and to form the government in a deliberating state-council and a responsible ministry. The *proclamateur-électeur* selected from the lists of candidates, judges, from the tribunals of peace to the court of cassation; administrators, from the mayors to the ministers. But he was incapable of governing himself; power was directed by the state council, exercised by the ministry.

The legislature departed from the form hitherto established; it ceased to be a deliberative assembly to become a judicial court. Before it, the council of state, in the name of the government, and the *tribunat*, in the name of the people, pleaded their respective projects. Its sentence was law. It would seem that the object of Sieyès was to put a stop to the violent usurpations of party, and while placing the sovereignty in the people, to give it limits in itself: this design appears from the complicated works of his political machine. The primary assemblies, composed of the tenth of the general population, nominated the local *list of communal candidates*; electoral colleges, also nominated by them, selected from the *communal list* the superior list of provincial candidates and from the *provincial list*, the list of national candidates. In all which concerned the government, there was a reciprocal control. The proclamateur-électeur selected his functionaries from among the candidates nominated by the people: and the people could dismiss functionaries, by not keeping them on the lists of candidates, which were renewed, the first every two years, the second every five years, the third every ten years. But the proclamateur-électeur did not interfere in the nomination of tribunes and legislators, whose attributes were purely popular.

Yet, to place a counterpoise in the heart of this authority itself, Sieyès separated the initiative and the discussion of the law, which was invested in the tribunate from its adoption, which belonged to the legislative assembly. But besides these different prerogatives, the legislative body and the tribunate were not elected in the same manner. The tribunate was composed by right of the first hundred members of the *national list*, while the legislative body was chosen directly by the electoral colleges. The tribunes, being necessarily more active, bustling, and popular, were appointed for life, and by a protracted process, to prevent their arriving in a moment of passion, with destructive and angry projects, as had hitherto been the case in most of the assemblies. The same dangers not existing in the other assembly, which had only to judge calmly and disinterestedly of the law, its election was direct, and its authority transient.

Lastly, there existed, as the complement of all the other powers, a conservatory body, incapable of ordering, incapable of acting, intended solely to provide for the regular existence of the state. This body was the constitutional jury, or conservatory senate; it was to be for the political law what the court of cassation was to the civil law. The tribunate, or the council of state, appealed to it when the sentence of the legislative body was not conformable to the constitution. It had also the faculty of calling into its own body any leader of the government who was too ambitious, or a tribune who was too popular, by the "droit d'absorption," and when senators, they were disqualified from filling any other function. In this way it kept a double watch over the safety of the whole republic, by maintaining the fundamental law, and protecting liberty against the ambition of individuals.

Whatever may be thought of this constitution, which seems too finely complicated to be practicable, it must be granted that it is the production of considerable strength of mind, and even great practical information. Sieyès paid too little regard to the passions of men; he made them too reasonable as human beings, and too obedient as machines. He wished by skilful inventions to avoid the abuses of human constitutions, and excluded death, that is to say, despotism, from whatever quarter it might come. But I have very little faith in the efficacy of constitutions; in such moments, I believe only in the strength of parties in their domination, and, from time to time, in their reconciliation. But I must also admit that, if ever a constitution was adapted to a period, it was that of Sieyès for France in the year VIII.

After an experience of ten years, which had only shown exclusive dominations, after the violent transition from the constitutionalists of 1789 to the Girondists, from the Girondists to the Mountain, from the Mountain to the reactionists, from the reactionists to the directory, from the directory to the councils, from the councils to the military force, there could be no repose or public life save in it. People were weary of worn-out constitutions; that of Sieyès was new; exclusive men were no longer wanted, and by elaborate voting it prevented the sudden accession of counter-revolutionists, as at the beginning of the directory, or of ardent democrats, as at the end of this government. It was a constitution of moderate men, suited to terminate a revolution, and to settle a nation. But precisely because it was a constitution of moderate men, precisely because parties had no longer sufficient ardour to demand a law of domination, for that very reason there would necessarily be found a man stronger than the fallen parties and the moderate legislators, who would refuse this law, or, accepting, abuse it, and this was what happened.

Bonaparte took part in the deliberations of the constituent committee; with his instinct of power, he seized upon everything in the ideas of Sieyès which was calculated to serve his projects, and caused the rest to be rejected. Sieyès intended for him the functions of grand elector, with a revenue of six millions of francs, and a guard of three thousand men; the palace of Versailles for a residence, and the entire external representation of the republic. But the actual government was to be invested in a consul for war and a consul for peace, functionaries unthought of by Sieyès in the year III., but adopted by him in the year VIII.; in order, no doubt, to suit the ideas of the times. This insignificant magistracy was far from suiting Bonaparte. "How could you suppose," said he, "that a man of any talent and honour could resign himself to the part of fattening like a hog, on a few millions a year?" From that moment it was not again mentioned; Roger Ducos, and the greater part of the committee, declared in favour of Bonaparte; and Sieyès, who hated discussion, was either unwilling or unable to defend his ideas. He saw that laws, men, and France itself were at the mercy of the man whose elevation he had promoted.

On the 24th of December, 1799 (Nivôse, year VIII.), forty-five days after the 18th Brumaire, was published the constitution of the year VIII.; it was composed of the wrecks of that of Sieyès, now become a constitution of servitude. The government was placed in the hands of the first consul, who was supported by two others, having a deliberative voice. The senate, primarily selected by the consuls, chose the members of the tribunal and legislative body, from the list of the national candidates. The government alone had the initiative in making the laws. Accordingly, there were no more bodies of electors who appointed the candidates of different lists, the tribunes and legislators; no more independent tribunes earnestly pleading the cause of the people before the legislative assembly; no legislative assembly arising directly from the bosom of the nation, and accountable to it alone—in a word, no political nation. Instead of all this, there existed an all-powerful consul, disposing of armies and of power, a general and a dictator; a council of state destined to be the advanced guard of usurpation; and lastly, a senate of eighty members, whose only function was to nullify the people, and to choose tribunes without authority, and legislators who should remain mute. Life passed from the nation to the government. The constitution of Sieyès served as a pretext for a bad order of things. It is worth notice that up to the year VIII. all the constitutions had emanated from the *Contrat-social*, and subsequently, down to 1814, from the constitution of Sieyès.

The new government was immediately installed. Bonaparte was first consul, and he united with him as second and third consuls, Cambacérès, a lawyer, and formerly a member of the Plain in the convention, and Lebrun, formerly a co-adjutor of the chancellor Maupeou. By their means, he hoped to influence the revolutionists and moderate royalists. With the same object, an ex-noble, Talleyrand, and a former member of the Mountain, Fouché, were appointed to the posts of minister of foreign affairs, and minister of police. Sieyès felt much repugnance at employing Fouché; but Bonaparte wished it. "We are forming a new epoch," said he; "we must forget all the ill of the past, and remember only the good." He cared very little under what banner men had hitherto served, provided they now enlisted under his, and summoned thither their old associates in royalism and in revolution.

The two new consuls and the retiring consuls nominated sixty senators, without waiting for the lists of eligibility; the senators appointed a hundred tribunes and three hundred legislators; and the authors of the 18th Brumaire distributed among themselves the functions of the state, as the booty of their victory. It is, however, just to say that the moderate liberal party prevailed in this partition, and that, as long as it preserved any influence, Bonaparte governed in a mild, advantageous, and republican manner. The constitution of the year VIII., submitted to the people for acceptance, was approved by three millions eleven thousand and seven citizens. That of 1793 had obtained one million eight hundred and one thousand nine hundred and eighteen suffrages; and that of the year III. one million fifty-seven thousand three hundred and ninety. The new law satisfied the moderate masses, who sought tranquillity, rather than guarantees; while the code of '93 had only found partisans among the lower class; and that of the year III. had been equally rejected by the royalists and democrats. The constitution of 1791 alone had obtained general approbation; and, without having been subjected to individual acceptance, had been sworn to by all France.

The first consul, in compliance with the wishes of the republic, made offers of peace to England, which it refused. He naturally wished to assume an appearance of moderation, and, previous to treating, to confer on his government the lustre of new victories. The continuance of the war was therefore decided on, and the consuls made a remarkable proclamation, in which they appealed to sentiments new to the nation. Hitherto it had been called to arms in defence of liberty; now they began to excite it in the name of honour: "Frenchmen, you wish for peace. Your government desires it with still more ardour: its foremost hopes, its constant efforts, have been in favour of it. The English ministry rejects it; the English ministry has betrayed the secret of its horrible policy. To rend France, to destroy its navy and ports, to efface it from the map of Europe, or reduce it to the rank of a secondary power, to keep the nations of the continent at variance, in order to seize on the commerce of all, and enrich itself by their spoils: these are the fearful successes for which England scatters its gold, lavishes its promises, and multiplies its intrigues. It is in your power to command peace; but, to command it, money, the sword, and soldiers are necessary; let all, then, hasten to pay the tribute they owe to their common defence. Let our young citizens arise! No longer will they take arms for factions, or for the choice of tyrants, but for the security of all they hold most dear; for the honour of France, and for the sacred interests of humanity."

Holland and Switzerland had been sheltered during the preceding campaign. The first consul assembled all his force on the Rhine and the Alps. He gave Moreau the command of the army of the Rhine, and he himself marched into Italy. He set out on the 16th Floréal, year VIII. (6th of May, 1800) for that brilliant campaign which lasted only forty days. It was important that he should not be long absent from Paris at the beginning of his power, and especially not to leave the war in a state of indecision. Field-marshal Mélas had a hundred and thirty thousand men under arms; he occupied all Italy. The republican army opposed to him only amounted to forty thousand men. He left the field-marshal lieutenant Ott with thirty thousand men before Genoa; and marched against the corps of general Suchet. He entered Nice, prepared to pass the Var, and to enter Provence. It was then that Bonaparte crossed the great Saint Bernard at the head of an army of forty thousand men, descended into Italy in the rear of Mélas, entered Milan on the 16th Prairial (2nd of June), and placed the Austrians between Suchet and himself. Mélas, whose line of operation was broken, quickly fell back upon Nice, and from thence on to Turin; he established his headquarters at Alessandria, and decided on re-opening his communications by a battle. On the 9th of June, the advance guard of the republicans gained a glorious victory at Monte-Bello, the chief honour of which belonged to general Lannes. But it was the plain of Marengo, on the 14th of June (25th Prairial) that decided the fate of Italy; the Austrians were overwhelmed. Unable to force the passage of the Bormida by a victory, they were placed without any opportunity of retreat between the army of Suchet and that of the first consul. On the 15th, they obtained permission to fall behind Mantua, on condition of restoring all the places of Piedmont, Lombardy, and the Legations; and the victory of Marengo thus secured possession of all Italy.

Eighteen days after, Bonaparte returned to Paris. He was received with all the evidence of admiration that such decided victories and prodigious activity could excite; the enthusiasm was universal. There was a spontaneous illumination, and the crowd hurried to the Tuileries to see him. The hope of speedy peace redoubled the public joy. On the 25th Messidor the first consul was present at the anniversary fête of the 14th of July. When the officers presented him the standards taken from the enemy, he said to them: "When you return to your camps, tell your soldiers that the French people, on the 1st Vendemiaire, when we shall celebrate the anniversary of the republic, will expect either the proclamation of peace, or, if the enemy raise insuperable obstacles, further standards as the result of new victories." Peace, however, was delayed for some time.

In the interim between the victory of Marengo and the general pacification, the first consul turned his attention chiefly to settling the people, and to diminishing the number of malcontents, by employing the displaced factions in the state. He was very conciliatory to those parties who renounced their systems, and very lavish of favours to those chiefs who renounced their parties. As it was a time of selfishness and indifference, he had no difficulty in succeeding. The proscribed of the 18th Fructidor were already recalled, with the exception of a few royalist conspirators, such as Pichegru, Willot, etc. Bonaparte soon even employed those of the banished who, like Portalis, Siméon, Barbé-Marbois, had shown themselves more anti-conventionalists than counter-revolutionists. He had also gained over opponents of another description. The late leaders of La Vendée, the famous Bernier, curé of Saint-Lo, who had assisted in the whole insurrection, Châtillon, d'Autichamp and Suzannet had come to an arrangement by the treaty of Mont-Luçon (17th January, 1800). He also addressed himself to the leaders of the Breton bands, Georges Cadoudal, Frotté, Laprévelaye, and Bourmont. The two last alone consented to submit. Frotté was surprised and shot; and Cadoudal defeated at Grand Champ, by General Brune, capitulated. The western war was thus definitively terminated.

But the *Chouans* who had taken refuge in England, and whose only hope was in the death of him who now concentrated the power of the revolution, projected his assassination. A few of them disembarked on the coast of France, and secretly repaired to Paris. As it was not easy to reach the first consul, they decided on a conspiracy truly horrible. On the third Nivôse, at eight in the evening, Bonaparte was to go to the Opera by the Rue Saint-Nicaise. The conspirators placed a barrel of powder on a little truck, which obstructed the carriage way, and one of them, named Saint Regent, was to set fire to it as soon as he received a signal of the first consul's approach. At the appointed time, Bonaparte left the Tuileries, and crossed the Rue Nicaise. His coachman was skilful enough to drive rapidly between the truck and the wall; but the match was already alight, and the carriage had scarcely reached the end of the street when *the infernal machine* exploded, covered the quarter of Saint-Nicaise with ruins, shaking the carriage, and breaking its windows.

The police, taken by surprise, though directed by Fouché, attributed this plot to the democrats, against whom the first consul had a much more decided antipathy than against the *Chouans*. Many of them were imprisoned, and a hundred and thirty were transported by a simple senatus- consultus asked and obtained during the night. At length they discovered the true authors of the conspiracy, some of whom were condemned to death. On this occasion, the consul caused the creation of special military tribunals. The constitutional party separated still further from him, and began its energetic but useless opposition. Lanjuinais, Grégoire, who had courageously resisted the extreme party in the convention, Garat, Lambrechts, Lenoir-Laroche, Cabanis, etc., opposed, in the senate, the illegal proscription of a hundred and thirty democrats; and the tribunes, Isnard, Daunou, Chénier, Benjamin Constant, Bailleul, Chazal, etc., opposed the special courts. But a glorious peace threw into the shade this new encroachment of power.

The Austrians, conquered at Marengo, and defeated in Germany by Moreau, determined on laying down arms; On the 8th of January, 1801, the republic, the cabinet of Vienna, and the empire, concluded the treaty of Lunéville. Austria ratified all the conditions of the treaty of Campo-Formio, and also ceded Tuscany to the young duke of Parma. The empire recognised the independence of the Batavian, Helvetian, Ligurian, and Cisalpine republics. The pacification soon became general, by the treaty of Florence (18th of February 1801,) with the king of Naples, who ceded the isle of Elba and the principality of Piombino, by the treaty of Madrid (29th of September, 1801) with Portugal; by the treaty of Paris (8th of October, 1801) with the emperor of Russia; and, lastly, by the preliminaries (9th of October, 1801) with the Ottoman Porte. The continent, by ceasing hostilities, compelled England to a momentary peace. Pitt, Dundas, and Lord Grenville, who had maintained these sanguinary struggles with France, went out of office when their system ceased to be followed. The opposition replaced them; and, on the 25th of March, 1802, the treaty of Amiens completed the pacification of the world. England consented to all the continental acquisitions of the French republic, recognised the existence of the secondary republics, and restored our colonies.

During the maritime war with England, the French navy had been almost entirely ruined. Three hundred and forty ships had been taken or destroyed, and the greater part of the colonies had fallen into the hands of the English. San Domingo, the most important of them all, after throwing off the yoke of the whites, had continued the American revolution, which having commenced in the English colonies, was to end in those of Spain, and change the colonies of the new world into independent states. The blacks of San Domingo wished to maintain, with respect to the mother country, the freedom which they had acquired from the colonists, and to defend themselves against the English. They were led by a man of colour, the famous Toussaint-L'Ouverture. France should have consented to this revolution which had been very costly for humanity. The metropolitan government could no longer be restored at San Domingo; and it became necessary to obtain the only real advantages which Europe can now derive from America, by strengthening the commercial ties with our old colony. Instead of this prudent policy, Bonaparte attempted an expedition to reduce the island to subjection. Forty thousand men embarked for this disastrous enterprise. It was impossible for the blacks to resist such an army at first; but after the first victories, it was attacked by the climate, and new insurrections secured the independence of the colony. France experienced the twofold loss of an army and of advantageous commercial connexions.

Bonaparte, whose principal object hitherto had been to promote the fusion of parties, now turned all his attention to the internal prosperity of the republic, and the organization of power. The old privileged classes of the nobility and the clergy had returned into the state without forming particular classes. Dissentient priests, on taking an oath of obedience, might conduct their modes of worship and receive their pensions from government. An act of pardon had been passed in favour of those accused of emigration; there only remained a list of about a thousand names of those who remained faithful to the family and the claims of the pretender. The work of pacification was at an end. Bonaparte, knowing that the surest way of commanding a nation is to promote its happiness, encouraged the development of industry, and favoured external commerce, which had so long been suspended. He united higher views with his political policy, and connected his own glory with the prosperity of France; he travelled through the departments, caused canals and harbours to be dug, bridges to be built, roads to be repaired, monuments to be erected, and means of communication to be multiplied. He especially strove to become the protector and legislator of private interests. The civil, penal, and commercial codes, which he formed, whether at this period, or at a later period, completed, in this respect, the work of the revolution, and regulated the internal existence of the nation, in a manner somewhat more conformable to its real condition. Notwithstanding political despotism, France, during the domination of Bonaparte, had a private legislation superior to that of any European society; for with absolute government, most of them still preserved the civil condition of the middle-ages. General peace, universal toleration, the return of order, the restoration, and the creation of an administrative system, soon changed the appearance of the republic. Attention was turned to the construction of roads and canals. Civilization became developed in an extraordinary manner; and the consulate was, in this respect, the perfected period of the directory, from its commencement to the 18th Fructidor.

It was more especially after the peace Amiens that Bonaparte raised the foundation of his future power. He himself says, in the Memoirs published under his name,[8] "The ideas of Napoleon were fixed, but to realise them he required the assistance of time and circumstances. The organization of the consulate had nothing in contradiction with these; it accustomed the nation to unity, and that was a first step. This step taken, Napoleon was indifferent to the forms and denominations of the different constituted bodies. He was a stranger to the revolution. It was his wisdom to advance from day to day, without deviating from the fixed point, the polar star, which directed Napoleon how to guide the revolution to the port whither he wished to conduct it."

In the beginning of 1802, he was at one and the same time forming three great projects, tending to the same end. He sought to organize religion and to establish the clergy, which as yet had only a religious existence; to create, by means of the Legation of Honour, a permanent military order in the army; and to secure his own power, first for his life, and then to render it hereditary. Bonaparte was installed at the Tuileries, where he gradually resumed the customs and ceremonies

---

[8] *Mémoires pour servir à l'Histoire de France sous Napoléon, écrits à Sainte Hélène*, vol. i. p. 248.

of the old monarchy. He. already thought of placing intermediate bodies between himself and the people. For some time past he had opened a negotiation with Pope Pius VII., on matters of religious worship. The famous concordat, which created nine archbishoprics, forty-one bishoprics, with the institution of chapters, which established the clergy in the state, and again placed it under the external monarchy of the pope, was signed at Paris on the 16th of July, 1801, and ratified at Rome on the 15th of August, 1801.

Bonaparte, who had destroyed the liberty of the press, created exceptional tribunals, and who had departed more and more from the principles of the revolution, felt that before he went further it was necessary to break entirely with the liberal party of the 18th Brumaire. In Ventôse, year X. (March, 1802), the most energetic of the tribunes were dismissed by a simple operation of the senate. The tribunate was reduced to eighty members, and the legislative body underwent a similar purgation. About a month after, the 15th Germinal (6th of April, 1802), Bonaparte, no longer apprehensive of opposition, submitted the concordat to these assemblies, whose obedience he had thus secured, for their acceptance. They adopted it by a great majority. The Sunday and four great religious festivals were re-established, and from that time the government ceased to observe the system of decades. This was the first attempt at renouncing the republican calendar. Bonaparte hoped to gain the sacerdotal party, always most disposed to passive obedience, and thus deprive the royalist of the clergy, and the coalition of the pope.

The concordat was inaugurated with great pomp in the cathedral of Nôtre-Dame. The senate, the legislative body, the tribunate, and the leading functionaries were present at this new ceremony. The first consul repaired thither in the carriages of the old court, with the etiquette and attendants of the old monarchy; salvos of artillery announced this return of privilege, and this essay at royalty. A pontifical mass was performed by Caprara, the cardinal-legate, and the people were addressed by proclamation in a language to which they had long been unaccustomed. "Reason and the example of ages," ran the proclamation, "command us to have recourse to the sovereign pontiff to effect unison of opinion and reconciliation of hearts. The head of the church has weighed in his wisdom and for the interest of the church, propositions dictated by the interest of the state."

In the evening there was an illumination, and a concert in the gardens of the Tuileries. The soldiery reluctantly attended at the inauguration ceremony, and expressed their dissatisfaction aloud. On returning to the palace, Bonaparte questioned general Delmas on the subject. *"What did you think of the ceremony? "* said he. *"A fine mummery"* was the reply. *"Nothing was wanting but a million of men slain, in destroying what you re-establish. "*

A month after, on the 25th Floréal, year X. (15th of May, 1802), he presented the project of a law respecting *the creation of a legion of honour*. This legion was to be composed of fifteen cohorts, dignitaries for life, disposed in hierarchical order, having a centre, an organization, and revenues. The first consul was the chief of the legion. Each cohort was composed of seven grand officers, twenty commanders, thirty officers, and three hundred and fifty legionaries. Bonaparte's object was to originate a new nobility. He thus appealed to the ill- suppressed sentiment of inequality. While discussing this projected law in the council of state, he did not scruple to announce his aristocratic design. Berlier, counsellor of state, having disapproved an institution so opposed to the spirit of the republic, said that: "Distinctions were the playthings of a monarchy." "I defy you," replied the first consul, "to show me a republic, ancient or modern, in which distinctions did not exist; you call them toys; well, it is by toys that men are led. I would not say as much to a tribune; but in a council of wise men and statesmen we may speak plainly. I do not believe that the French love *liberty and equality*. The French have not been changed by ten years of revolution; they have but one sentiment—*honour*. That sentiment, then, must be nourished; they must have distinctions. See how the people prostrate themselves before the ribbons and stars of foreigners; they have been surprised by them; and they do not fail to wear them. All has been destroyed; the question is, how to restore all. There is a government, there are authorities; but the rest of the nation, what is it? Grains of sand. Among us we have the old privileged classes, organized in principles and interests, and knowing well what they want. I can count our enemies. But we, ourselves, are dispersed, without system, union, or contact. As long as I am here, I will answer for the republic; but we must provide for the future. Do you think the republic is definitively established? If so, you are greatly deceived. It is in our power to make it so; but we have not done it; and we shall not do it if we do not hurl some masses of granite on the soil of France."[9] By these words Bonaparte announced a system of government opposed to that which the revolution sought to establish, and which the change in society demanded.

Yet, notwithstanding the docility of the council of state, the purgation undergone by the tribunal and the legislative body, these three bodies vigorously opposed a law which revived inequality. In the council of state, the legion of honour only had fourteen votes against ten; in the tribunal, thirty-eight against fifty-six; in the legislative body, a hundred and sixty-six against a hundred and ten. Public opinion manifested a still greater repugnance for this new order of knighthood. Those first invested seemed almost ashamed of it, and received it with a sort of contempt. But Bonaparte pursued his counterrevolutionary course, without troubling himself about a dissatisfaction no longer capable of resistance.

He wished to confirm his power by the establishment of privilege, and to confirm privilege by the duration of his power. On the motion of Chabot de l'Allier, the tribunal resolved: "That the first consul, general Bonaparte, should receive a signal mark of national gratitude." In pursuance of this resolution, on the 6th of May, 1802, an organic senatus- consultus appointed Bonaparte consul for an additional period of ten years.

But Bonaparte did not consider the prolongation of the consulate sufficient; and two months after, on the 2nd of August, the senate, on the decision of the tribunate and the legislative body, and with the consent of the people, consulted by means of the public registers, passed the following decree:

---

[9] This passage is extracted from M. Thibaudeau's *Mémoires* of the Consulate. There are in these *Mémoires*, which are extremely curious, some political conversations of Bonaparte, details concerning his internal government and the principal sittings of the council of state, which throw much light upon this epoch.

"I. The French people nominate, and the senate proclaim Napoleon Bonaparte first consul for life.

"II. A statue of Peace, holding in one hand a laurel of victory, and in the other, the decree of the senate, shall attest to posterity the gratitude of the nation.

"III. The senate will convey to the first consul the expression of the confidence, love, and admiration of the French people."

This revolution was complete by adapting to the consulship for life, by a simple senatus-consultus, the constitution, already sufficiently despotic, of the temporary consulship. "Senators," said Cornudet, on presenting the new law, "we must for ever close the public path to the Gracchi. The wishes of the citizens, with respect to the political laws they obey, are expressed by the general prosperity; the guarantee of social rights absolutely places the dogma of the exercise of the sovereignty of the people in the senate, which is the bond of the nation. This is the only social doctrine." The senate admitted this new social doctrine, took possession of the sovereignty, and held it as a deposit till a favourable moment arrived for transferring it to Bonaparte.

The constitution of the 16th Thermidor, year X. (4th of August, 1802,) excluded the people from the state. The public and administrative functions became fixed, like those of the government. The first consul could increase the number of electors who were elected for life. The senate had the right of changing institutions, suspending the functions of the jury, of placing the departments out of the constitution, of annulling the sentences of the tribunals, of dissolving the legislative body, and the tribunate. The council of state was reinforced; the tribunate, already reduced by dismissals, was still sufficiently formidable to require to be reduced to fifty members.

Such, in the course of two years, was the terrible progress of privilege and absolute power. Towards the close of 1802, everything was in the hands of the consul for life, who had a class devoted to him in the clergy; a military order in the legion of honour; an administrative body in the council of state; a machinery for decrees in the legislative assembly; a machinery for the constitution in the senate. Not daring, as yet, to destroy the tribunate, in which assembly there arose, from time to time, a few words of freedom and opposition, he deprived it of its most courageous and eloquent members, that he might hear his will declared with docility in all the assemblies of the nation.

This interior policy of usurpation was extended beyond the country. On the 26th of August, Bonaparte united the island of Elba, and on the 11th of September, 1802, Piedmont, to the French territory. On the 9th of October he took possession of the states of Parma, left vacant by the death of the duke; and lastly, on the 21st of October, he marched into Switzerland an army of thirty thousand men, to support a federative act, which regulated the constitution of each canton, and which had caused disturbances. He thus furnished a pretext for a rupture with England, which had not sincerely subscribed to the peace. The British cabinet had only felt the necessity of a momentary suspension of hostilities; and, a short time after the treaty of Amiens, it arranged a third coalition, as it had done after the treaty of

Campo-Formio, and at the time of the congress of Rastadt. The interest and situation of England were alone of a nature to bring about a rupture, which was hastened by the union of states effected by Bonaparte, and the influence which he retained over the neighbouring republics, called to complete independence by the recent treaties. Bonaparte, on his part, eager for the glory gained on the field of battle, wishing to aggrandize France by conquests, and to complete his own elevation by victories, could not rest satisfied with repose; he had rejected liberty, and war became a necessity.

The two cabinets exchanged for some time very bitter diplomatic notes. At length, Lord Whitworth, the English ambassador, left Paris on the 25th Floréal, year XI. (13th of May, 1803). Peace was now definitively broken: preparations for war were made on both sides. On the 26th of May, the French troops entered the electorate of Hanover. The German empire, on the point of expiring, raised no obstacle. The emigrant Chouan party, which had taken no steps since the affair of the infernal machine and the continental peace, were encouraged by this return of hostilities. The opportunity seemed favourable, and it formed in London, with the assent of the British cabinet, a conspiracy headed by Pichegru and Georges Cadoudal. The conspirators disembarked secretly on the coast of France, and repaired with the same secrecy to Paris. They communicated with general Moreau, who had been induced by his wife to embrace the royalist party. Just as they were about to execute their project, most of them were arrested by the police, who had discovered the plot, and traced them. Georges Cadoudal was executed, Pichegru was found strangled in prison, and Moreau was sentenced to two years' imprisonment, commuted to exile. This conspiracy, discovered in the middle of February, 1804, rendered the person of the first consul, whose life had been thus threatened, still dearer to the masses of the people; addresses of congratulation were presented by all the bodies of the state, and all the departments of the republic. About this time he sacrificed an illustrious victim. On the 15th of March, the duc d'Enghien was carried off by a squadron of cavalry from the castle of Ettenheim, in the grand-duchy of Baden, a few leagues from the Rhine. The first consul believed, from the reports of the police, that this prince had directed the recent conspiracy. The duc d'Engbien was conveyed hastily to Vincennes, tried in a few hours by a military commission, and shot in the trenches of the château. This crime was not an act of policy, or usurpation; but a deed of violence and wrath. The royalists might have thought on the 18th Brumaire that the first consul was studying the part of general Monk; but for four years he had destroyed that hope. He had no longer any necessity for breaking with them in so outrageous a manner, nor for reassuring, as it has been suggested, the Jacobins, who no longer existed. Those who remained devoted to the republic, dreaded at this time despotism far more than a counter-revolution. There is every reason to think that Bonaparte, who thought little of human life, or of the rights of nations, having already formed the habit of an expeditious and hasty policy, imagined the prince to be one of the conspirators, and sought, by a terrible example, to put an end to conspiracies, the only peril that threatened his power at that period.

The war with Britain and the conspiracy of Georges Cadoudal and Pichegru, were the stepping-stones by which Bonaparte ascended from the consulate to the empire. On the 6th Germinal, year XII. (27th March, 1804), the senate, on receiving intelligence of the plot, sent a deputation to the first consul. The president, François de Neufchâteau, expressed himself in these terms: "Citizen first consul, you are founding a new era, but you ought to perpetuate it: splendour is nothing without duration. We do not doubt but this great idea has had a share of your attention; for your creative genius embraces all and forgets nothing. But do not delay: you are urged on by the times, by events, by conspirators, and by ambitious men; and in another direction, by the anxiety which agitates the French people. It is in your power to enchain time, master events, disarm the ambitious, and tranquillize the whole of France by giving it institutions which will cement your edifice, and prolong for our children what you have done for their fathers. Citizen first consul, be assured that the senate here speaks to you in the name of all citizens."

On the 5th Floréal, year XII. (25th of April, 1804), Bonaparte replied to the senate from Saint-Cloud, as follows: "Your address has occupied my thoughts incessantly; it has been the subject of my constant meditation. You consider, that the supreme magistracy should be hereditary, in order to protect the people from the plots of our enemies, and the agitation which arises from rival ambitions. You also think that several of our institutions ought to be perfected, to secure the permanent triumph of equality and public liberty, and to offer the nation and government the twofold guarantee which they require. The more I consider these great objects, the more deeply do I feel that in such novel and important circumstances, the councils of your wisdom and experience are necessary to enable me to come to a conclusion. I invite you, then, to communicate to me your ideas on the subject." The senate, in its turn, replied on the 14th Floréal (3rd of May): "The senate considers that the interests of the French people will be greatly promoted by confiding the government of the republic to *Napoleon Bonaparte*, as hereditary emperor." By this preconcerted scene was ushered in the establishment of the empire.

The tribune Curée opened the debate in the tribunate by a motion on the subject. He dwelt on the same motives as the senators had done. His proposition was carried with enthusiasm. Carnot alone had the courage to oppose the empire: "I am far," said he, "from wishing to weaken the praises bestowed on the first consul; but whatever services a citizen may have done to his country, there are bounds which honour, as well as reason, imposes on national gratitude. If this citizen has restored public liberty, if he has secured the safety of his country, is it a reward to offer him the sacrifice of that liberty; and would it not be destroying his own work to make his country his private patrimony? When once the proposition of holding the consulate for life was presented for the votes of the people, it was easy to see that an after-thought existed. A crowd of institutions evidently monarchical followed in succession; but now the object of so many preliminary measures is disclosed in a positive manner; we are called to declare our sentiments on a formal motion to restore the monarchical system, and to confer imperial and hereditary dignity on the first consul.

"Has liberty, then, only been shown to man that he might never enjoy it? No, I cannot consent to consider this good, so universally preferred to all others, without which all others are as nothing, as a mere illusion. My heart tells me that liberty is attainable; that its regime is easier and more stable than any arbitrary government. I voted against the consulate for life; I now vote against the restoration of the monarchy; as I conceive my quality as tribune compels me to do."

But he was the only one who thought thus; and his colleagues rivalled each other in their opposition to the opinion of the only man who alone among them remained free. In the speeches of that period, we may see the prodigious change that had taken place in ideas and language. The revolution had returned to the political principles of the ancient regime; the same enthusiasm and fanaticism existed; but it was the enthusiasm of flattery, the fanaticism of servitude. The French rushed into the empire as they had rushed into the revolution; in the age of reason they referred everything to the enfranchisement of nations; now they talked of nothing but the greatness of a man, and of the age of Bonaparte; and they now fought to make kings, as they had formerly fought to create republics.

The tribunate, the legislative body, and the senate, voted the empire, which was proclaimed at Saint-Cloud on the 28th Floréal, year XII. (18th of May, 1804). On the same day, a senatus-consultum modified the constitution, which was adapted to the new order of things. The empire required its appendages; and French princes, high dignitaries, marshals, chamberlains, and pages were given to it. All publicity was destroyed. The liberty of the press had already been subjected to censorship; only one tribune remained, and that became mute. The sittings of the tribunate were secret, like those of the council of state; and from that day, for a space of ten years, France was governed with closed doors. Joseph and Louis Bonaparte were recognised as French princes. Bethier, Murat, Moncey, Jourdan, Masséna, Augereau, Bernadotte, Soult, Brune, Lannes, Mortier, Ney, Davoust, Bessières, Kellermann, Lefèvre, Pérignon, Sérurier, were named marshals of the empire. The departments sent up addresses, and the clergy compared Napoleon to a new Moses, a new Mattathias, a new Cyrus. They saw in his elevation "the finger of God," and said "that submission was due to him as dominating over all; to his ministers as sent by him, because such was the order of Providence." Pope ·Pius VII. came to Paris to consecrate the new dynasty. The coronation took place on Sunday, the 2nd of December, in the church of Notre-Dame.

Preparations had been making for this ceremony for some time, and it was regulated according to ancient customs. The emperor repaired to the metropolitan church with the empress Josephine, in a coach surmounted by a crown, drawn by eight white horses, and escorted by his guard. The pope, cardinals, archbishops, bishops, and all the great bodies of the state were awaiting him in the cathedral, which had been magnificently decorated for this extraordinary ceremony. He was addressed in an oration at the door; and then, clothed with the imperial mantle, the crown on his head, and the sceptre in his hand, he ascended a throne placed at the end of the church. The high almoner, a cardinal, and a bishop, came and conducted him to the foot of the altar for consecration. The pope poured the threefold unction on his head and hands, and delivered the following prayer:—"O Almighty God, who didst establish Hazael to govern Syria, and Jehu king of Israel, by revealing unto them thy purpose by the mouth of the prophet Elias; who didst also shed the holy unction of kings on the head of Saul and of David, by the ministry of thy prophet Samuel, vouchsafe to pour, by my hands, the treasures of thy grace and blessing on thy servant Napoleon, who, notwithstanding our own unworthiness, we this day consecrate emperor in thy name."

The pope led him solemnly back to the throne; and after he had sworn on the Testament the oath prescribed by the new constitution, the chief herald-at-arms cried in a loud voice—"*The most glorious and most august emperor of the French is crowned and enthroned! Long live the emperor!* " The church instantly resounded with the cry, salvoes of artillery were fired, and the pope intoned the Te Deum. For several days there was a succession of fêtes; but these fêtes *by command*, these fêtes of absolute power, did not breathe the frank, lively, popular, and unanimous joy of the first federation of the 14th of July; and, exhausted as the people were, they did not welcome the beginning of despotism as they had welcomed that of liberty.

The consulate was the last period of the existence of the republic. The revolution was coming to man's estate. During the first period of the consular government, Bonaparte had gained the proscribed classes by recalling them, he found a people still agitated by every passion, and he restored them to tranquillity by labour, and to prosperity by restoring order. Finally he compelled Europe, conquered for the third time, to acknowledge his elevation. Till the treaty of Amiens, he revived in the republic victory, concord, and prosperity, without sacrificing liberty. He might then, had he wished, have made himself the representative of that great age, which sought for that noble system of human dignity the consecration of far-extended equality, wise liberty, and more developed civilization. The nation was in the hands of the great man or the despot; it rested with him to preserve it free or to enslave it. He preferred the realization of his selfish projects, and preferred himself to all humanity. Brought up in tents, coming late into the revolution, he only understood its material and interested side; he had no faith in the moral wants which had given rise to it, nor in the creeds which had agitated it, and which, sooner or later, would return and destroy him. He saw an insurrection approaching its end, an exhausted people at his mercy, and a crown on the ground within his reach.

THE EMPIRE

CHAPTER XV

FROM THE ESTABLISHMENT OF THE EMPIRE, 1804-1814

Character of the empire—Change of the republics created by the directory into kingdoms—Third coalition; capture of Vienna; victories of Ulm and Austerlitz; peace of Pressburg; erection of the two kingdoms of Bavaria and Wurtemberg against Austria—Confederation of the Rhine—Joseph Napoleon appointed king of Naples; Louis Napoleon, king of Holland—Fourth coalition; battle of Jena; capture of Berlin; victories of Eylau and Friedland; peace of Tilsit; the Prussian monarchy is reduced by one half; the kingdoms of Saxony and Westphalia are instituted against it; that of Westphalia given to Jerome Napoleon—The grand empire rises with its secondary kingdoms, its confederation of the Rhine, its Swiss mediation, its great fiefs; it is modelled on that of Charlemagne—Blockade of the continent—Napoleon employs the cessation of commerce to reduce England, as he had employed arms to subdue the continent—Invasion of Spain and Portugal; Joseph Napoleon appointed to the throne of Spain; Murat replaces him on the throne of Naples—New order of events: national insurrection of the peninsula; religious contest with the pope—Commercial opposition of Holland—Fifth coalition—Victory of Wagram; peace of Vienna; marriage of Napoleon with the archduchess Marie Louise—Failure of the attempt at resistance; the pope is dethroned; Holland is again united to the empire, and the war in Spain prosecuted with vigour—Russia renounces the continental system; campaign of 1812; capture of Moscow; disastrous retreat—Reaction against the power of Napoleon; campaign of 1813; general defection—Coalition of all Europe; exhaustion of France; marvellous campaign of 1814—The allied powers at Paris; abdication at Fontainbleau; character of Napoleon; his part in the French revolution—Conclusion.

After the establishment of the empire, power became more arbitrary, and society reconstructed itself on an aristocratic principle. The great movement of recomposition, which had commenced on the 9th Thermidor went on increasing. The convention had abolished classes; the directory defeated parties; the consulate gained over men; and the empire corrupted them by distinctions and privileges. This second period was the opposite of the first. Under the one, we saw the government of the committees exercised by men elected every three months, without guards, honours, or representation, living on a few francs a day, working eighteen hours together on common wooden tables; under the other, the government of the empire, with all its paraphernalia of administration, it chamberlains, gentlemen, praetorian guard, hereditary rights, its immense civil list, and dazzling ostentation. The national activity was exclusively directed to labour and war. All material interests, all ambitious passions, were hierarchically arranged under one leader, who, after having sacrificed liberty by establishing absolute power, destroyed equality by introducing nobility.

The directory had erected all the surrounding states into republics; Napoleon wished to constitute them on the model of the empire. He began with Italy. The council of state of the Cisalpine republic determined on restoring hereditary monarchy in favour of Napoleon. Its vice-president, M. Melzi, came to Paris to communicate to him this decision. On the 26th Ventôse, year XIII. (17th of March, 1805), he was received with great solemnity at the Tuileries. Napoleon was on his throne, surrounded by his court, and all the splendour of sovereign power, in the display of which he delighted. M. Melzi offered him the crown, in the name of his fellow-citizens. "Sire," said he, in conclusion, "deign to gratify the wishes of the assembly over which I have the honour to preside. Interpreter of the sentiments which animate every Italian heart, it brings you their sincere homage. It will inform them with joy that by accepting, you have strengthened the ties which attach you to the preservation, defence, and prosperity of the Italian nation. Yes, sire, you wished the existence of the Italian republic, and it existed. Desire the Italian monarchy to be happy, and it will be so."

The emperor went to take possession of this kingdom; and, on the 26th of May, 1805, he received at Milan the iron crown of the Lombards. He appointed his adopted son, prince Eugene de Beauharnais, viceroy of Italy, and repaired to Genoa, which also renounced its sovereignty. On the 4th of June, 1805, its territory was united to the empire, and formed the three departments of Genoa, Montenotte, and the Apennines. The small republic of Lucca was included in this monarchical revolution. At the request of its gonfalonier, it was given in appanage to the prince of Piombino and his princess, a sister of Napoleon. The latter, after this royal progress, recrossed the Alps, and returned to the capital of his empire; he soon after departed for the camp at Boulogne, where a great maritime expedition against England was preparing.

This project of descent which the directory had entertained after the peace of Campo-Formio, and the first consul, after the peace of Lunéville, had been resumed with much ardour since the new rupture. At the commencement of 1805, a flotilla of two thousand small vessels, manned by sixteen thousand sailors, carrying an army of one hundred and sixty thousand men, nine thousand horses, and a numerous artillery, had assembled in the ports of Boulogne, Etaples, Wimereux,

Ambleteuse. and Calais. The emperor was hastening by his presence the execution of this project, when he learned that England, to avoid the descent with which it was threatened, had prevailed on Austria to come to a rupture with France, and that all the forces of the Austrian monarchy were in motion. Ninety thousand men, under the archduke Ferdinand and general Mack, had crossed the Jura, seized on Munich, and driven out the elector of Bavaria, the ally of France; thirty thousand, under the archduke John, occupied the Tyrol, and the archduke Charles, with one hundred thousand men, was advancing on the Adige. Two Russian armies were preparing to join the Austrians. Pitt had made the greatest efforts to organize this third coalition. The establishment of the kingdom of Italy, the annexation of Genoa and Piedmont to France, the open influence of the emperor over Holland and Switzerland, had again aroused Europe, which now dreaded the ambition of Napoleon as much as it had formerly feared the principles of the revolution. The treaty of alliance between the British ministry and the Russian cabinet had been signed on the 11th of April, 1805, and Austria had acceded to it on the 9th of August.

Napoleon left Boulogne, returned hastily to Paris, repaired to the senate on the 23rd of September, obtained a levy of eighty thousand men, and set out the next day to begin the campaign. He passed the Rhine on the 1st of October, and entered Bavaria on the 6th, with an army of a hundred and sixty thousand men. Masséna held back Prince Charles in Italy, and the emperor carried on the war in Germany at full speed. In a few days he passed the Danube, entered Munich, gained the victory of Wertingen, and forced general Mack to lay down his arms at Ulm. This capitulation disorganized the Austrian army. Napoleon pursued the course of his victories, entered Vienna on the 13th of November, and then marched into Moravia to meet the Russians, round whom the defeated troops had rallied.

On the 2nd of December, 1805, the anniversary of the coronation, the two armies met in the plains of Austerlitz. The enemy amounted to ninety-five thousand men, the French to eighty thousand. On both sides the artillery was formidable. The battle began at sunrise; these enormous masses began to move; the Russian infantry could not stand against the impetuosity of our troops and the manoeuvres of their general. The enemy's left was first cut off; the Russian imperial guard came up to re-establish the communication, and was entirely overwhelmed. The centre experienced the same fate, and at one o'clock in the afternoon the most decisive victory had completed this wonderful campaign. The following day the emperor congratulated the army in a proclamation on the field of battle itself: "Soldiers," said he, "I am satisfied with you. You have adorned your eagles with immortal glory. An army of a hundred thousand men, commanded by the emperors of Russia and Austria, in less than four days has been cut to pieces or dispersed; those who escaped your steel have been drowned in the lakes. Forty flags, the standards of the Russian imperial guard, a hundred and twenty pieces of cannon, twenty generals, more than thirty thousand prisoners, are the result of this ever memorable day. This infantry, so vaunted and so superior in numbers, could not resist your shock, and henceforth you have no more rivals to fear. Thus, in two months, this third coalition has been defeated and dissolved." A truce was concluded with Austria; and the Russians, who might have been cut to pieces, obtained permission to retire by fixed stages.

The peace of Pressburg followed the victories of Ulm and Austerlitz; it was signed on the 26th of December. The house of Austria, which had lost its external possessions, Holland and the Milanese, was now assailed in Germany itself. It gave up the provinces of Dalmatia and Albania to the kingdom of Italy; the territory of the Tyrol, the town of Augsburg, the principality of Eichstett, a part of the territory of Passau, and all its possessions in Swabia, Brisgau, and Ortenau to the electorates of Bavaria and Wurtemberg, which were transformed into kingdoms. The grand duchy of Baden also profited by its spoils. The treaty of Pressburg completed the humiliation of Austria, commenced by the treaty of Campo-Formio, and continued by that of Lunéville. The emperor, on his return to Paris, crowned with so much glory, became the object of such general and wild admiration, that he was himself carried away by the public enthusiasm and intoxicated at his fortune. The different bodies of the state contended among themselves in obedience and flatteries. He received the title of Great, and the senate passed a decree dedicating to him a triumphal monument.

Napoleon became more confirmed in the principle he had espoused. The victory of Marengo and the peace of Lunéville had sanctioned the consulate; the victory of Austerlitz and peace of Pressburg consecrated the empire. The last vestiges of the revolution were abandoned. On the 1st of January, 1806, the Gregorian calendar definitively replaced the republican calendar, after an existence of fourteen years. The Panthéon was again devoted to purposes of worship, and soon even the tribunate ceased to exist. But the emperor aimed especially at extending his dominion over the continent. Ferdinand, king of Naples, having, during the last war, violated the treaty of peace with France, had his states invaded; and Joseph Bonaparte on the 30th of March was declared king of the Two Sicilies. Soon after (June 5th, 1806), Holland was converted into a kingdom, and received as monarch Louis Bonaparte, another brother of the emperor. None of the republics created by the convention, or the directory, now existed. Napoleon, in nominating secondary kings, restored the military hierarchical system, and the titles of the middle ages. He erected Dalmatia, Istria, Friuli, Cadore, Belluno, Conegliano, Treviso, Feltra, Bassano, Vicenza, Padua, and Rovigo into duchies, great fiefs of the empire. Marshal Berthier was invested with the principality of Neufchâtel, the minister Talleyrand with that of Benevento. Prince Borghese and his wife with that of Guastalla, Murat with the grand-duchy of Berg and Clèves. Napoleon, not venturing to destroy the Swiss republic, styled himself its mediator, and completed the organization of his military empire by placing under his dependence the ancient Germanic body. On the 12th of July, 1806, fourteen princes of the south and west of Germany united themselves into the confederation of the Rhine, and recognized Napoleon as their protector. On the 1st of August, they signified to the diet of Ratisbon their separation from the Germanic body. The empire of Germany ceased to exist, and Francis II. abdicated the title by proclamation. By a convention signed at Vienna, on the 15th of December, Prussia exchanged the territories of Anspach, Clèves, and Neufchâtel for the electorate of Hanover. Napoleon had all the west under his power. Absolute master of France and Italy, as emperor and king, he was also master of Spain, by the dependence of that court; of Naples and Holland, by his two brothers; of Switzerland, by the act of mediation; and in Germany he had at his disposal the kings of Bavaria and Wurtemberg, and the confederation of the Rhine against Austria and Prussia. After the peace of Amiens, by supporting liberty he might have made himself the protector of France and the moderator of Europe; but having sought glory in domination, and made conquest the object of his life, he condemned himself to a long struggle, which would inevitably terminate in the dependence of the continent or in his own downfall.

This encroaching progress gave rise to the fourth coalition. Prussia, neutral since the peace of Basle, had, in the last campaign, been on the point of joining the Austro-Russian coalition. The rapidity of the emperor's victories had alone restrained her; but now, alarmed at the aggrandizement of the empire, and encouraged by the fine condition of her troops, she leagued with Russia to drive the French from Germany. The cabinet of Berlin required that the French troops should recross the Rhine, or war would be the consequence. At the same time, it sought to form in the north of Germany a league against the confederation of the south. The emperor, who was in the plenitude of his prosperity and of national enthusiasm, far from submitting to the *ultimatum* of Prussia, immediately marched against her.

The campaign opened early in October. Napoleon, as usual, overwhelmed the coalition by the promptitude of his marches and the vigour of his measures. On the 14th of October, he destroyed at Jena the military monarchy of Prussia, by a decisive victory; on the 16th, fourteen thousand Prussians threw down their arms at Erfurth; on the 25th, the French army entered Berlin, and the close of 1806 was employed in taking the Prussian fortresses and marching into Poland against the Russian army. The campaign in Poland was less rapid, but as brilliant as that of Prussia. Russia, for the third time, measured its strength with France. Conquered at Zurich and Austerlitz, it was also defeated at Eylau and Friedland. After these memorable battles, the emperor Alexander entered into a negotiation, and concluded at Tilsit, on the 21st of June, 1807, an armistice which was followed by a definitive treaty on the 7th of July.

The peace of Tilsit extended the French domination on the continent. Prussia was reduced to half its extent. In the south of Germany, Napoleon had instituted the two kingdoms of Bavaria and Wurtemberg against Austria; further to the north, he created the two feudatory kingdoms of Saxony and Westphalia against Prussia. That of Saxony, composed of the electorate of that name, and Prussian Poland, called the grand-duchy of Warsaw, was given to the king of Saxony; that of Westphalia comprehended the states of Hesse-Cassel, Brunswick, Fulde, Paderborn, and the greatest part of Hanover, and was given to Jerome Napoleon. The emperor Alexander, acceding to all these arrangements, evacuated Moldavia and Wallachia. Russia, however, though conquered, was the only power unencroached upon. Napoleon followed more than ever in the footsteps of Charlemagne; at his coronation, he had had the crown, sword, and sceptre, of the Frank king carried before him. A pope had crossed the Alps to consecrate his dynasty, and he modelled his states on the vast empire of that conqueror. The revolution sought the establishment of ancient liberty; Napoleon restored the military hierarchy of the middle ages. The former had made citizens, the latter made vassals. The one had changed Europe into republics, the other transformed it into fiefs. Great and powerful as he was, coming immediately after a shock which had exhausted the world by its violence, he was enabled to arrange it for a time according to his pleasure. The *grand empire* rose internally by its system of administration, which replaced the government of assemblies; its special courts, its lyceums, in which military education was substituted for the republican education of the central schools; its hereditary nobility, which in 1808 completed the establishment of inequality; its civil discipline, which rendered all France like an army obedient to the word of command; and externally by its secondary kingdoms, its confederate states, its great fiefs, and its supreme chief. Napoleon, no longer meeting resistance anywhere, could command from one end of the continent to the other.

At this period all the emperor's attention was directed to England, the only power that could secure itself from his attacks. Pitt had been dead a year, but the British cabinet followed with much ardour and pertinacity his plans with respect to France. After having vainly formed a third and a fourth coalition, it did not lay down arms. It was a war to the death. Great Britain had declared France in a state of blockade, and furnished the emperor with the means of cutting off its continental intercourse by a similar measure. The continental blockade, which began in 1807, was the second period of Bonaparte's system. In order to attain universal and uncontested supremacy, he made use of arms against the continent, and the cessation of commerce against England. But in forbidding to the continental states all communication with England, he was preparing new difficulties for himself, and soon added to the animosity of opinion excited by his despotism, and the hatred of states produced by his conquering domination, the exasperation of private interests and commercial suffering occasioned by the blockade.

Yet all the powers seemed united in the same design. England was placed under the ban of continental Europe, at the peace. Russia and Denmark in the Northern Seas; France, Spain, and Holland, in the Mediterranean and the ocean, were obliged to declare against it. This period was the height of the imperial sway. Napoleon employed all his activity and all his genius in creating maritime resources capable of counter-balancing the forces of England, which had then eleven hundred ships of war of every class. He caused ports to be constructed, coasts to be fortified, ships to be built and prepared, everything for combating in a few years upon this new battle-field. But before that moment arrived, he wished to secure the Spanish peninsula, and to found his dynasty there, for the purpose of introducing a firmer and more favourable policy. The expedition of Portugal in 1807, and the invasion of Spain in 1808, began for him and for Europe a new order of events.

Portugal had for some time been a complete English colony. The emperor, in concert with the Bourbons of Madrid, decided by the treaty of Fontainebleau, of the 27th of October, 1807, that the house of Braganza had ceased to reign. A French army, under the command of Junot, entered Portugal. The prince-regent embarked for Brazil, and the French took possession of Lisbon on the 30th of November, 1807. This invasion was only an approach towards Spain. The royal family were in a state of the greatest anarchy. The favourite, Godoy, was execrated by the people, and Ferdinand, prince of the Asturias, conspired against the authority of his father's favourite. Though the emperor had not much to fear from such a government, he had taken alarm at a clumsy armament prepared by Godoy during the Prussian war. No doubt, at this time he formed the project of putting one of his brothers on the throne of Spain; he thought he could easily overturn a divided family, an expiring monarchy, and obtain the consent of a people whom he would restore to civilization. Under the pretext of the maritime war and the blockade, his troops entered the peninsula, occupied the coasts and principal places, and encamped near Madrid. It was then suggested to the royal family to retire to Mexico, after the example of the house of Braganza. But the people rose against this departure; Godoy, the object of public hatred, was in great risk of losing his life, and the prince of the Asturias was proclaimed king, under the title of Ferdinand VII. The emperor took advantage of this court revolution to bring about his own. The French entered Madrid, and he himself proceeded to Bayonne, whither he summoned the Spanish princes. Ferdinand restored the crown to his father, who in his turn resigned it in favour of Napoleon; the latter had it decreed on his brother Joseph by a supreme junta, by the council of Castille, and the municipality of Madrid. Ferdinand was sent to the Château de Valençay, and Charles VI. fixed his residence at Compiègne. Napoleon called his brother-in-law, Murat, grand-duke of Berg, to the throne of Naples, in the place of Joseph.

At this period began the first opposition to the domination of the emperor and the continental system. The reaction manifested itself in three countries hitherto allies of France, and it brought on the fifth coalition. The court of Rome was dissatisfied; the peninsula was wounded in its national pride by having imposed upon it a foreign king; in its usages, by the suppression of convents, of the Inquisition, and of the grandees; Holland suffered in its commerce from the blockade, and Austria supported impatiently its losses and subordinate condition. England, watching for an opportunity to revive the struggle on the continent, excited the resistance of Rome, the peninsula, and the cabinet of Vienna. The pope had been cold towards France since 1805; he had hoped that his pontifical complaisance in reference to Napoleon's coronation would have been recompensed by the restoration to the ecclesiastical domain of those provinces which the directory had annexed to the Cisalpine republic. Deceived in this expectation, he joined the European counter-revolutionary opposition, and from 1807 to 1808 the Roman States became the rendezvous of English emissaries. After some warm remonstrances, the emperor ordered general Miollis to occupy Rome; the pope threatened him with excommunication; and Napoleon seized on the legations of Ancona, Urbino, Macerata, and Camerino, which became part of the Italian kingdom. The legate left Paris on the 3rd of April, 1808, and the religious struggle for temporal interests commenced with the head of the church, whom Napoleon should either not have recognised, or not have despoiled.

The war with the peninsula was still more serious. The Spaniards recognised Ferdinand VII. as king, in a provincial junta, held at Seville, on the 27th of May,

1808, and they took arms in all the provinces which were not occupied by French troops. The Portuguese also rose at Oporto, on the 16th of June. These two insurrections were at first attended with the happiest results; in a short time they made rapid progress. General Dupont laid down arms at Baylen in the province of Cordova, and this first reverse of the French arms excited the liveliest hope and enthusiasm among the Spaniards. Joseph Napoleon left Madrid, where Ferdinand VII. was proclaimed; and about the same time, Junot, not having troops enough to keep Portugal, consented, by the convention of Cintra, to evacuate it with all the honours of war. The English general, Wellington, took possession of this kingdom with twenty-five thousand men. While the pope was declaring against Napoleon, while the Spanish insurgents were entering Madrid, while the English were again setting foot on the continent, the king of Sweden avowed himself an enemy of the European imperial league, and Austria was making considerable armaments and preparing for a new struggle.

Fortunately for Napoleon, Russia remained faithful to the alliance and engagements of Tilsit. The emperor Alexander had at that time a fit of enthusiasm and affection for this powerful and extraordinary mortal. Napoleon wishing to be sure of the north, before he conveyed all his forces to the peninsula, had an interview with Alexander at Erfurt, on the 27th September, 1808. The two masters of the north and west guaranteed to each other the repose and submission of Europe. Napoleon marched into Spain, and Alexander undertook Sweden. The presence of the emperor soon changed the fortune of the war in the peninsula. He brought with him eighty thousand veteran soldiers, just come from Germany. Several victories made him master of most of the Spanish provinces. He made his entry into Madrid, and presented himself to the inhabitants of the peninsula, not as a master, but as a liberator. "I have abolished," he said to them, "the tribunal of the Inquisition, against which the age and Europe protested. Priests should direct the conscience, but ought not to exercise any external or corporal jurisdiction over the citizens. I have suppressed feudal rights; and every one may set up inns, ovens, mills, fisheries, and give free impulse to his industry. The selfishness, wealth, and prosperity of a few did more injury to your agriculture than the heats of the extreme summer. As there is but one God, one system of justice only should exist in a state. All private tribunals were usurped and opposed to the rights of the nation. I have suppressed them. The present generation may change its opinion; too many passions have been brought into play; but your grandchildren will bless me as your regenerator; they will rank among their memorable days those in which I appeared among you, and from those days will Spain date its prosperity."

Such was indeed the part of Napoleon in the peninsula, which could only be restored to a better state of things, and to liberty, by the revival of civilization. The establishment of independence cannot be effected all at once, any more than anything else; and when a country is ignorant, poor, and backward, covered with convents, and governed by monks, its social condition must be reconstructed before liberty can be thought of. Napoleon, the oppressor of civilized nations, was a real regenerator for the peninsula. But the two parties of civil liberty and religious servitude, that of the cortes and that of the monks, though with far different aims, came to an understanding for their common defence. The one was at the head of the upper and the middle classes, the other of the populace; and they vied with each other in exciting the Spaniards to enthusiasm with the sentiments of independence or religious fanaticism. The following is the catechism used by the priests: "Tell me, my child, who you are? A Spaniard by the grace of God.—Who is the enemy of our happiness? The emperor of the French.—How many natures has he? Two: human and diabolical.—How many emperors of the French are there? One true one, in three deceptive persons.—What are their names, Napoleon, Murat, and Manuel Godoy.—Which of the three is the most wicked? They are all three equally so.—Whence is Napoleon derived? From sin.—Murat? From Napoleon. —And Godoy? The junction of the two.—What is the ruling spirit of the first? Pride and despotism.—Of the second? Rapine and cruelty.—Of the third? Cupidity, treason, and ignorance.—Who are the French? Former Christians become heretics.—Is it a sin to kill a Frenchman? No, father; heaven is gained by killing one of these dogs of heretics.—What punishment does the Spaniard deserve who has failed in his duty? The death and infamy of a traitor.—What will deliver us from our enemies? Confidence in ourselves and in arms."

Napoleon had engaged in a long and dangerous enterprise, in which his whole system of war was at fault. Victory, here, did not consist in the defeat of an army and the possession of a capital, but in the entire occupation of the territory, and, what was still more difficult, the submission of the public mind. Napoleon, however, was preparing to subdue this people with his irresistible activity and inflexible determination, when the fifth coalition called him again to Germany.

Austria had turned to advantage his absence, and that of his troops. It made a powerful effort, and raised five hundred and fifty thousand men, comprising the Landwehr, and took the field in the spring of 1809. The Tyrol rose, and king Jerome was driven from his capital by the Westphalians; Italy wavered; and Prussia only waited till Napoleon met with a reverse, to take arms; but the emperor was still at the height of his power and prosperity. He hastened from Madrid in the beginning of February, and directed the members of the confederation to keep their contingents in readiness. On the 12th of April he left Paris, passed the Rhine, plunged into Germany, gained the victories of Eckmühl and Essling, occupied Vienna a second time on the 15th of May, and overthrew this new coalition by the battle of Wagram, after a campaign of four months. While he was pursuing the Austrian armies, the English landed on the island of Walcheren, and appeared before Antwerp; but a levy of national guards sufficed to frustrate the expedition of the Scheldt. The peace of Vienna, of the 11th of October, 1809, deprived the house of Austria of several more provinces, and compelled it again to adopt the continental system.

This period was remarkable for the new character of the struggle. It began the reaction of Europe against the empire, and announced the alliance of dynasties, people, nations, the priesthood, and commerce. All whose interests were injured made an attempt at resistance, which at first was destined to fail. Napoleon, since the peace of Amiens, had entered on a career that must necessarily terminate in the possession or hostility of all Europe. Carried away by his character and position, he had created against the people a system of administration of unparalleled benefit to power; against Europe, a system of secondary monarchies and grand fiefs, which facilitated his plans of conquest; and, lastly, against England, the blockade which suspended its commerce, and that of the continent. Nothing impeded him in the realization of those immense but insensate designs. Portugal opened a communication with the English: he invaded it. The royal family of Spain, by its quarrels and vacillations, compromised the extremities of the empire: he compelled it to abdicate, that he might reduce the peninsula to a bolder and less wavering policy. The pope kept up relations with the enemy: his patrimony was diminished. He threatened excommunication: the French entered Rome. He realized his threat by a bull: he was dethroned as a temporal sovereign in 1809. Finally, after the battle of Wagram, and the peace of Vienna, Holland became a depot for English merchandise, on account of its commercial wants, and the emperor dispossessed his brother Louis of that kingdom, which, on the 1st of July, 1810, became incorporated with the empire. He shrank from no invasion, because he would not endure opposition or hesitation from any quarter. All were compelled to submit, allies as well as enemies, the chief of the church as well as kings, brothers as well as strangers; but, though conquered this time, all who had joined this new league only waited an opportunity to rise again.

Meantime, after the peace of Vienna, Napoleon still added to the extent and power of the empire. Sweden having undergone an internal revolution, and the king, Gustavus Adolphus IV., having been forced to abdicate, admitted the continental system. Bernadotte, prince of Ponte-Corvo, was elected by the states-general hereditary prince of Sweden, and king Charles XIII. adopted him for his son. The blockade was observed throughout Europe; and the empire, augmented by the Roman States, the Illyrian provinces, Valais, Holland, and the Hanse Towns, had a hundred and thirty departments, and extended from Hamburg and Dantzic to Trieste and Corfu. Napoleon, who seemed to follow a rash but inflexible policy, deviated from his course about this time by a second marriage. He divorced Josephine that he might give an heir to the empire, and married, on the 1st of April, 1810, Marie-Louise, arch-duchess of Austria. This was a decided error. He quitted his position and his post as a parvenu and revolutionary monarch, opposing in Europe the ancient courts as the republic had opposed the ancient governments. He placed himself in a false situation with respect to Austria, which he ought either to have crushed after the victory of Wagram, or to have reinstated in its possessions after his marriage with the arch-duchess. Solid alliances only repose on real interests, and Napoleon could not remove from the cabinet of Vienna the desire or power of renewing hostilities. This marriage also changed the character of his empire, and separated it still further from popular interests; he sought out old families to give lustre to his court, and did all he could to amalgamate together the old and the new nobility as he mingled old and new dynasties. Austerlitz had established the plebeian empire; after Wagram was established the noble empire. The birth, on the 20th of March, 1811, of a son, who received the title of King of Rome, seemed to consolidate the power of Napoleon by securing to him a successor.

The war in Spain was prosecuted with vigour during the years 1810 and 1811. The territory of the peninsula was defended inch by inch, and its was necessary to take several towns by storm. Suchet, Soult, Mortier, Ney, and Sebastiani made themselves masters of several provinces; and the Spanish junta, unable to keep their post at Seville, retired to Cadiz, which the French army began to blockade. The new expedition into Portugal was less fortune. Masséna, who directed it, at first obliged Wellington to retreat, and took Oporto and Olivença; but the English general having entrenched himself in the strong position of Torres-Vedras, Masséna, unable to force it, was compelled to evacuate the country.

While the war was proceeding in the peninsula with advantage, but without any decided success, a new campaign was preparing in the north. Russia perceived the empire of Napoleon approaching its territories. Shut up in its own limits, it remained without influence or acquisitions; suffering from the blockade, without gaining any advantage by the war. This cabinet, moreover, endured with impatience a supremacy to which it itself aspired, and which it had pursued slowly but without interruption since the reign of Peter the Great. About the close of 1810, it increased its armies, renewed its commercial relations with Great Britain, and did not seem indisposed to a rupture. The year 1811 was spent in negotiations which led to nothing, and preparations for war were made on both sides. The emperor, whose armies were before Cadiz, and who relied on the co-operation of the West and North against Russia, made with ardour preparations for an enterprise which was intended to reduce the only power as yet untouched, and to carry his victorious eagles even to Moscow. He obtained the assistance of Prussia and Austria, which engaged by the treaties of the 24th of February and the 14th of March, 1812, to furnish auxiliary bodies; one of twenty, and the other of thirty thousand men. All the unemployed forces of France were immediately on foot. A senatus-consultus divided the national guard into three bodies for the home service, and appropriated a hundred of the first line regiments (nearly a hundred thousand men) for active military service. On the 9th of March, Napoleon left Paris on this vast expedition. During several months he fixed his court at Dresden, where the emperor of Austria, the king of Prussia, and all the sovereigns of Germany, came to bow before his high fortune. On the 22nd of June, war was declared against Russia.

In this campaign, Napoleon was guided by the maxims he had always found successful. He had terminated all the wars he had undertaken by the rapid defeat of the enemy, the occupation of his capital, and concluded the peace by parcelling out his territory. His project was to reduce Russia by creating the kingdom of Poland, as he had reduced Austria by forming the kingdoms of Bavaria and Wurtemberg, after Austerlitz; and Prussia, by organizing those of Saxony and Westphalia, after Jena. With this object, he had stipulated with the Austrian cabinet by the treaty of the 14th of March, to exchange Gallicia for the Illyrian provinces. The establishment of the kingdom of Poland was proclaimed by the diet of Warsaw, but in an incomplete manner, and Napoleon, who, according to his custom, wished to finish all in one campaign, advanced at once into the heart of Russia, instead of prudently organizing the Polish barrier against it. His army amounted to about five hundred thousand men. He passed the Niemen on the 24th of June, took Vilna, and Vitepsk, defeated the Russians at Astrowno, Polotsk, Mohilev, Smolensk, at the Moskva, and on the 14th of September, made his entry into Moscow.

The Russian cabinet relied for its defence not only upon its troops, but on its vast territory and on its climate. As the conquered armies retreated before ours, they burnt all the towns, devastated the provinces, and thus prepared great difficulties for the foe in the event of reverses or retreat. According to this plan of defence, Moscow was burnt by its governor Rostopchin, as Smolensk, Dorigoboui, Viasma, Gjhat, Mojaisk, and a great number of other towns and villages had already been. The emperor ought to have seen that this war would not terminate as the others had done; yet, conqueror of the foe, and master of his capital, he conceived hopes of peace which the Russians skilfully encouraged. Winter was approaching, and Napoleon prolonged his stay at Moscow for six weeks. He delayed his movements on account of the deceptive negotiations of the Russians, and did not decide on a retreat till the 19th of October. This retreat was disastrous, and began the downfall of the empire. Napoleon could not have been defeated by the hand of man, for what general could have triumphed over this incomparable chief? what army could have conquered the French army? But his reverses were to take place in the remote limits of Europe; in the frozen regions which were to end his conquering domination. He lost, with the close of this campaign, not by a defeat, but by cold and famine, in the midst of Russian snows and solitude, his old army, and the *prestige* of his fortune.

The retreat was effected with some order as far as the Berezina, where it became one vast rout. After the passage of this river, Napoleon, who had hitherto accompanied his army, started in a sledge for Paris, in great haste, a conspiracy having broken out there during his absence. General Mallet, with a few others, had conceived the design of overthrowing this colossus of power. His enterprise was daring; and as it was grounded on a false report of Napoleon's death, it was necessary to deceive too many for success to be probable. Besides, the empire was still firmly established, and it was not a plot, but a slow and general defection which could destroy it. Mallet's plot failed, and its leaders were executed. The emperor, on his return, found the nation astounded at so unusual a disaster. But the different bodies of the state still manifested implicit obedience. He reached Paris on the 18th of December, obtained a levy of three hundred thousand men, inspired a spirit of sacrifice, re-equipped in a short time, with his wonderful activity, a new army, and took the field again on the 15th of April, 1813.

But since the retreat of Moscow, Napoleon had entered on a new series of events. It was in 1812 that the decline of the empire manifested itself. The weariness of his domination became general. All those by whose consent he had risen, took part against him. The priests had conspired in secret since his rupture with the pope. Eight state prisons had been created in an official manner against the dissentients of his party. The national masses were as tired of conquest as they had formerly been of factions. They had expected from him consideration for private interests, the promotion of commerce; respect for men; and they were oppressed by conscriptions, taxes, the blockade, provost courts, and duties which were the inevitable consequences of this conquering system. He had no longer for adversaries the few who remained faithful to the political object of the revolution, and whom he styled *idéologues*, but all who, without definite ideas, wished for the material advantages of better civilization. Without, whole nations groaned beneath the military yoke, and the fallen dynasties aspired to rise again. The whole world was ill at ease; and one check served to bring about a general rising. "I triumphed," says Napoleon himself, speaking of the preceding campaigns, "in the midst of constantly reviving perils. I constantly required as much address as voice. Had I not conquered at Austerlitz, all Prussia would have been upon me; had I not triumphed at Jena, Austria and Spain would have attacked my rear; had I not fought at Wagram, which action was not a decided victory, I had reason to fear that Russia would forsake, Prussia rise against me, and the English were before Antwerp."[10] Such was his condition; the further he advanced in his career, the greater need he had to conquer more and more decisively. Accordingly, as soon as he was defeated, the kings he had subdued, the kings he had made, the allies he had aggrandized, the states he had incorporated with the empire, the senators who had so flattered him, and even his comrades in arms, successively forsook him. The field of battle extended to Moscow in 1812, drew back to Dresden in 1813, and to Paris in 1814: so rapid was the reverse of fortune.

The cabinet of Berlin began the defections. On the 1st of March, 1813, it joined Russia and England, which were forming the sixth coalition. Sweden acceded to it soon after; yet the emperor, whom the confederate powers thought prostrated by the last disaster, opened the campaign with new victories. The battle of Lützen, won by conscripts, on the 2nd of May, the occupation of Dresden, the victory of Bautzen, and the war carried to the Elbe, astonished the coalition. Austria, which, since 1810, had been on a footing of peace, was resuming arms, and already meditating a change of alliance. She now offered to act as mediator between the emperor and the confederates. Her mediation was accepted; an armistice was concluded at Plesswitz, on the 4th of June, and a congress assembled at Prague to negotiate peace. It was impossible to come to terms. Napoleon would not consent to diminished grandeur; Europe would not consent to remain subject to him. The confederate powers, joined by Austria, required that the limits of the empire should be to the Rhine, the Alps, and the Meuse. The negotiators separated without coming to an agreement. Austria joined the coalition, and war, the only means of settling this great contest, was resumed.

The emperor had only two hundred and eighty thousand men against five hundred and twenty thousand; he wished to force the enemy to retire behind the Elbe, and to break up, as usual, this new coalition by the promptitude and vigour of his blows. Victory seemed, at first, to second him. At Dresden, he defeated the combined forces; but the defeats of his lieutenants deranged his plans. Macdonald was conquered in Silesia; Ney, near Berlin; Vandamme, at Kulm. Unable to obstruct the enemy, pouring on him from all parts, Napoleon thought of retreating. The princes of the confederation of the Rhine chose this moment to desert the cause of the empire. A vast engagement having taken place at Leipzic between the two armies, the Saxons and Wurtembergers passed over to the enemy on the

---

[10] *Mémorial de Saint Hélène,* tome ii. p. 221.

field of battle. This defection to the strength of the allied powers, who had learned a more compact and skilful mode of warfare, obliged Napoleon to retreat, after a struggle of three days. The army advanced with much confusion towards the Rhine, where the Bavarians, who had also deserted, attempted to prevent its passage. But it overwhelmed them at Hanau, and re-entered the territory of the empire on the 30th of October, 1813. The close of this campaign was as disastrous as that of the preceding one. France was threatened in its own limits, as it had been in 1799; but the enthusiasm of independence no longer existed, and the man who deprived it of its rights found it, at this great crisis, incapable of sustaining him or defending itself. The servitude of nations is, sooner or later, ever avenged.

Napoleon returned to Paris on the 9th of November, 1813. He obtained from the senate a levy of three hundred thousand men, and made with great ardour preparations for a new campaign. He convoked the legislative body to associate it in the common defence; he communicated to it the documents relative to the negotiations of Prague, and asked for another and last effort in order to secure a glorious peace, the general wish of France. But the legislative body, hitherto silently obedient, chose this period to resist Napoleon.

It shared the common exhaustion, and without desiring it, was under the influence of the royalist party, which had been secretly agitating ever since the decline of the empire had revived its hopes. A commission, composed of MM. Lainé, Raynouard, Gallois, Flaugergues, Maine de Biran, drew up a very hostile report, censuring the course adopted by the government, and demanding that all conquests should be given up, and liberty restored. This wish, so just at any other time, could then only favour the invasion of the foe. Though the confederate powers seemed to make the evacuation of Europe the condition of peace, they were disposed to push victory to extremity. Napoleon, irritated by this unexpected and harassing opposition, suddenly dismissed the legislative body. This commencement of resistance announced internal defections. After passing from Russia to Germany, they were about to extend from Germany and Italy to France. But now, as before, all depended on the issue of the war, which the winter had not interrupted. Napoleon placed all his hopes on it; and started from Paris on the 25th of January, for this immortal campaign.

The empire was invaded in all directions. The Austrians entered Italy; the English, having made themselves masters of the peninsula during the last two years, had passed the Bidassoa, under general Wellington, and appeared on the Pyrenees. Three armies pressed on France to the east and north. The great allied army, amounting to a hundred and fifty thousand men, under Schwartzenberg, advanced by Switzerland; the army of Silesia, of a hundred and thirty thousand, under Blücher, by Frankfort; and that of the north, of a hundred thousand men, under Bernadotte, had seized on Holland and entered Belgium. The enemies, in their turn, neglected the fortified places, and, taking a lesson from the conqueror, advanced on the capital. When Napoleon left Paris, the two armies of Schwartzenberg and Blücher were on the point of effecting a junction in Champaigne. Deprived of the support of the people, who were only lookers on, Napoleon was left alone against the whole world with a handful of veterans and his genius, which had lost nothing of its daring and vigour. At this moment, he stands out nobly, no longer an oppressor; no longer a conqueror; defending, inch by inch, with new victories, the soil of his country, and at the same time, his empire and renown.

He marched into Champaigne against the two great hostile armies. General Maison was charged to intercept Bernadotte in Belgium; Augereau, the Austrians, at Lyons; Soult, the English, on the Spanish frontier. Prince Eugene was to defend Italy; and the empire, though penetrated in the very centre, still stretched its vast arms into the depths of Germany by its garrisons beyond the Rhine. Napoleon did not despair of driving these swarms of foes from the territory of France by means of a powerful military reaction, and again planting his standards in the countries of the enemy. He placed himself skilfully between Blücher, who was descending the Marne, and Schwartzenberg, who descended the Seine; he hastened from one of these armies to the other, and defeated them alternately; Blücher was overpowered at Champ-Aubert, Montmirail, Château-Thierry, and Vauchamps; and when his army was destroyed, Napoleon returned to the Seine, defeated the Austrians at Montereau, and drove them before him. His combinations were so strong, his activity so great, his measures so sure, that he seemed on the point of entirely disorganizing these two formidable armies, and with them annihilating the coalition.

But if he conquered wherever he came, the foe triumphed wherever he was not. The English had entered Bordeaux, where a party had declared for the Bourbon family; the Austrians occupied Lyons; the Belgian army had joined the remnant of that of Blücher, which re-appeared on Napoleon's rear. Defection now entered his own family, and Murat had just followed, in Italy, the example of Bernadotte, by joining the coalition. The grand officers of the empire still served him, but languidly, and he only found ardour and fidelity in his subaltern generals and indefatigable soldiers. Napoleon had again marched on Blücher, who had escaped from him thrice: on the left of the Marne, by a sudden frost, which hardened the muddy ways amongst which the Prussians had involved themselves, and were in danger of perishing; on the Aisne, through the defection of Soissons, which opened a passage to them, at a moment when they had no other way of escape; and Laon, by the fault of the duke of Ragusa, who prevented a decisive battle, by suffering himself to be surprised by night. After so many fatalities, which frustrated the surest plans, Napoleon, ill sustained by his generals, surrounded by the coalition, conceived the bold design of transporting himself to Saint-Dizier and closing on the enemy the egress from France. This daring march so full of genius, startled for a moment the confederate generals, from whom it cut off all retreat; but, excited by secret encouragements, without being anxious for their rear, they advanced on Paris.

This great city, the only capital of Europe which had not been the theatre of war, suddenly saw all the troops of Europe enter its plains, and was on the point of undergoing the common humiliation. It was left to itself. The empress, appointed regent a few months before, had just left it to repair to Blois. Napoleon was at a distance. There was not that despair and that movement of liberty which drive a people to resistance; war was no longer made on nations, but on governments, and the emperor had centred all the public interest in himself, and placed all his means of defence in mechanical troops. The exhaustion was great; a feeling of pride, of very just pride, alone made the approach of the stranger painful, and oppressed every Frenchman's heart at seeing his native land trodden by armies so long vanquished. But this sentiment was not sufficiently strong to raise the masses of the population against the enemy; and the measures of the royalist party, at the head of which the prince of Benevento placed himself, called the allied troops to the capital. An action took place, however, on the 30th of March, under the walls of Paris; but on the 31st, the gates were opened to the confederate forces, who entered in pursuance of a capitulation. The senate consummated the great imperial defection by forsaking its old master; it was influenced by M. de Talleyrand, who for some time had been out of favour with Napoleon. This voluntary actor in every crisis of power had just declared against him. With no attachment to party, of a profound political indifference, he foresaw from a distance with wonderful sagacity the fall of a government; withdrew from it opportunely; and when the precise moment for assailing it had arrived, joined in the attack with all his talents, his influence, his name, and his authority, which he had taken care to preserve. In favour of the revolution, under the constituent assembly; of the directory, on the 18th Fructidor; for the consulate, on the 18th Brumaire; for the empire, in 1804, he was for the restoration of the royal family, in 1814; he seemed grand master of the ceremonies for the party in power, and for the last thirty years it was he who had dismissed and installed the successive governments. The senate, influenced by him, appointed a provisional government, and declared Napoleon deposed from his throne, the hereditary rights of his family abolished, the people and army freed from their oath of fidelity. It proclaimed him *tyrant* whose despotism it had facilitated by its adulation. Meantime, Napoleon, urged by those about him to succour the capital, had abandoned his march on Saint-Dizier, and hastened to Paris at the head of fifty thousand men, in the hope of preventing the entry of the enemy. On his arrival (1st of April), he heard of the capitulation of the preceding day, and fell back on Fontainebleau, where he learned the defection of the senate, and his deposition. Then finding that all gave way around him in his ill fortune, the people, the senate, generals and courtiers, he decided on abdicating in favour of his son. He sent the duke of Vicenza, the prince of the Moskva, and the duke of Tarento, as plenipotentiaries to the confederates; on their way, they were to take with them the duke of Ragusa, who covered Fontainebleau with a corps.

Napoleon, with his fifty thousand men, and strong military position, could yet oblige the coalition to admit the claim of his son. But the duke of Ragusa forsook his post, treated with the enemy, and left Fontainebleau exposed. Napoleon was then obliged to submit to the conditions of the allied powers; their pretensions increased with their power. At Prague, they ceded to him the empire, with the Alps and the Rhine for limits; after the invasion of France, they offered him at Châtillon the possessions of the old monarchy only; later, they refused to treat with him except in favour of his son; but now, determined on destroying all that remained of the revolution with respect to Europe, its conquest and dynasty, they compelled Napoleon to abdicate absolutely. On the 11th of April, 1814, he renounced for himself and children the thrones of France and Italy, and received the little island of Elba in exchange for his vast sovereignty, the limits of which had extended from

Cadiz to the Baltic Sea. On the 20th, after an affecting farewell to his old soldiers, he departed for his new principality.

Thus fell this man, who alone, for fourteen years, had filled the world. His enterprising and organising genius, his power of life and will, his love of glory, and the immense disposable force which the revolution placed in his hands, have made him the most gigantic being of modern times. That which would have rendered the destiny of another extraordinary, scarcely counts in his. Rising from an obscure to the highest rank; from a simple artillery officer becoming the chief of the greatest of nations, he dared to conceive the idea of universal monarchy, and for a moment realized it. After having obtained the empire by his victories, he wished to subdue Europe by means of France, and reduce England by means of Europe, and he established the military system against the continent, the blockade against Great Britain. This design succeeded for some years; from Lisbon to Moscow he subjected people and potentates to his word of command as general, and to the vast sequestration which he prescribed. But in this way he failed in discharging his restorative mission of the 18th Brumaire. By exercising on his own account the power he had received, by attacking the liberty of the people by despotic institutions, the independence of states by war, he excited against himself the opinions and interests of the human race; he provoked universal hostility. The nation forsook him, and after having been long victorious, after having planted his standard in every capital, after having during ten years augmented his power, and gained a kingdom with every battle, a single reverse combined the world against him, proving by his fall how impossible in our days is despotism.

Yet Napoleon, amidst all the disastrous results of his system, gave a prodigious impulse to the continent; his armies carried with them the ideas and customs of the more advanced civilization of France. European societies were shaken on their old foundations; nations were mingled by frequent intercourse; bridges thrown across boundary rivers; high roads made over the Alps, Apennines, and Pyrenees, brought territories nearer to each other; and Napoleon effected for the material condition of states what the revolution had done for the minds of men. The blockade completed the impulse of conquest; it improved continental industry, enabling it to take the place of that of England, and replaced colonial commerce by the produce of manufactures. Thus Napoleon, by agitating nations, contributed to their civilization. His despotism rendered him counter-revolutionary with respect to France; but his spirit of conquest made him a regenerator with respect to Europe, of which many nations, in torpor till he came, will live henceforth with the life he gave them. But in this Napoleon obeyed the dictates of his nature. The child of war—war was his tendency, his pleasure: domination his object; he wanted to master the world, and circumstances placed it in his hand, in order that he might make use of it.

Napoleon has presented in France what Cromwell presented for a moment in England; the government of the army, which always establishes itself when a revolution is contended against; it then gradually changes, and from being civil, as it was at first, becomes military. In Great Britain, internal war not being complicated with foreign war, on account of the geographical situation of the country, which isolated it from other states, as soon as the enemies of reform were vanquished, the army passed from the field of battle to the government. Its intervention being premature, Cromwell, its general, found parties still in the fury of their passions, in all the fanaticism of their opinions, and he directed against them alone his military administration. The French revolution taking place on the continent saw the nations disposed for liberty, and sovereigns leagued from a fear of the liberation of their people. It had not only internal enemies, but also foreign enemies to contend with; and while its armies were repelling Europe, parties were overthrowing each other in the assemblies. The military intervention came later; Napoleon, finding factions defeated and opinions almost forsaken, obtained obedience easily from the nation, and turned the military government against Europe.

This difference of position materially influenced the conduct and character of these two extraordinary men. Napoleon, disposing of immense force and of uncontested power, gave himself up in security to the vast designs and the part of a conqueror; while Cromwell, deprived of the assent which a worn out people could give, and, incessantly attacked by factions, was reduced to neutralise them one by the other, and keep himself to the end the military dictator of parties. The one employed his genius in undertaking; the other in resisting. Accordingly, the former had the frankness and decision of power; the other, the craft and hypocrisy of opposed ambition. This situation would destroy their sway.

All dictatorships are transient; and however strong or great, it is impossible for any one long to subject parties or long to retain kingdoms. It is this that, sooner or later, would have led to the fall of Cromwell (had he lived longer,) by internal conspiracies; and that brought on the downfall of Napoleon, by the raising of Europe. Such is the fate of all powers which, arising from liberty, do not continue to abide with her. In 1814, the empire had just been destroyed; the revolutionary parties had ceased to exist since the 18th Brumaire. All the governments of this political period had been exhausted. The senate recalled the old royal family. Already unpopular on account of its past servility, it ruined- itself in public opinion by publishing a constitution, tolerably liberal, but which placed on the same footing the pensions of senators and the guarantees of the nation. The Count d'Artois, who had been the first to leave France, was the first to return, in the character of lieutenant- general of the kingdom. He signed, on the 23rd of April, the convention of Paris, which reduced the French territory to its limits of the 1st of January, 1792, and by which Belgium, Savoy, Nice, and Geneva, and immense military stores, ceased to belong to us. Louis XVIII. landed at Calais on the 24th of April, and entered Paris with solemnity on the 3rd of May, 1814, after having, on the 2nd, made the Declaration of Saint Omer, which fixed the principles of the representative government, and which was followed on the 2nd of June by the promulgation of the charter.

At this epoch, a new series of events begins. The year 1814 was the term of the great movement of the preceding five and twenty years. The revolution had been political, as directed against the absolute power of the court and the privileged classes, and military, because Europe had attacked it. The reaction which arose at that time only destroyed the empire and brought about the coalition in Europe, and the representative system in France; such was to be its first period. Later, it opposed the revolution, and produced the holy alliance against the people, and the government of a party against the charter. This retrograde movement necessarily had its course and limits. France can only be ruled in a durable manner by satisfying the twofold need which made it undertake the revolution. It requires real political liberty in the government; and in society, the material prosperity produced by the continually progressing development of civilization.

Lector House believes that a society develops through a two-fold approach of continuous learning and adaptation, which is derived from the study of classic literary works spread across the historic timeline of literature records. Therefore, we aim at reviving, repairing and redeveloping all those inaccessible or damaged but historically as well as culturally important literature across subjects so that the future generations may have an opportunity to study and learn from past works to embark upon a journey of creating a better future.

This book is a result of an effort made by Lector House towards making a contribution to the preservation and repair of original ancient works which might hold historical significance to the approach of continuous learning across subjects.

HAPPY READING & LEARNING!

LECTOR HOUSE LLP
E-MAIL: lectorpublishing@gmail.com